The Evangelical Rhetoric of Ramon Llull

The Evangelical Rhetoric of Ramon Llull

*Lay Learning and Piety
in the Christian West around 1300*

Mark D. Johnston

New York   Oxford
Oxford University Press
1996

Oxford University Press

Oxford   New York
Athens   Auckland   Bangkok
Calcutta   Cape Town   Dar es Salaam   Delhi
Florence   Hong Kong   Istanbul   Karachi
Kuala Lumpur   Madras   Madrid   Melbourne
Mexico City   Nairobi   Paris   Singapore
Taipei   Tokyo   Toronto

and associated companies in
Berlin   Ibadan

Copyright © 1996 by Mark D. Johnston

Published by Oxford University Press, Inc.
198 Madison Avenue, New York, New York 10016

Oxford is a registered trademark of Oxford University Press, Inc.

Library of Congress Cataloging-in-Publication Data
Johnston, Mark D. (Mark David), 1952–
The evangelical rhetoric of Ramon Llull : lay learning and piety
in the Christian West around 1300 / Mark D. Johnston.
p. cm.   Includes bibliographical references and index.
ISBN 0-19-509005-5
1. Llull, Ramon, d. 1316.
2. Rhetoric, Medieval.
3. Spiritual life—Christianity—History of doctrines—Middle Ages, 600–1500.
I. Title.   B765.L84J63   1995
189'.4—dc20   94-44362

1 3 5 7 9 8 6 4 2

Printed in the United States of America
on acid-free paper

illi quae vere "gratia" nominatur

Acknowledgments

While studying in Barcelona as a graduate student during the fall of 1976, I had the good fortune to discuss my plans for a doctoral dissertation on Ramon Llull with the late Jordi Rubió i Balaguer, one of the most distinguished and beloved scholars of Catalan literature in this century. I explained to him that I was interested broadly in medieval literary and linguistic theory and wished to explore Llull's contribution to this field, but that I certainly did not consider myself to be a Lullist exclusively. He repeated my statement quietly to himself, perhaps wondering what kind of "Lullist" I meant, and then laughed softly. Modern usage, I now realize, applies the term "Lullist" both to fervent disciples and to scholars of Ramon Llull's work. I have often wished that Dr. Rubió had lived long enough to see the results of my efforts, but his response then suggested that he probably foresaw them anyway.

The doctoral dissertation that I eventually completed at Johns Hopkins in 1977, "The Semblance of Significance: Language and Exemplarism in the *Art* of Ramon Llull," proved to be merely the manifesto for a far vaster program of scholarly study. Almost twenty years later I am still exploring Ramon Llull's contributions to the medieval trivium of grammar, rhetoric, and logic. *The Spiritual Logic of Ramon Llull,* published by Clarendon Press in 1987, surveys his logical doctrines. Various articles examine aspects of his linguistic and literary ideas: "*Affatus:* Natural Science as Moral Theology," *Estudios Lulianos* 30 (1990): 3–30, 139–59; "Ramon Llull's Language of Contemplation and Action," *Forum for Modern Language Studies* 27 (1991): 100–112; and "Exemplary Reading in Ramon Llull's *Libre de meravelles,*" *Forum for Modern Language Studies* 28 (1992): 235–50. Chapters 2 and 3 below also deal broadly with elements of Llull's linguistic theories. Most of this book is devoted, as its title indicates, to detailed examination of Ramon Llull's theories of eloquence. Two previously published essays offer provisional assessments of this topic: "The Natural Rhetoric of Ramon Llull," in *Proceedings of the Illinois Medieval Association,* vol. 3, edited by David Wagner et al. (DeKalb: Northern

Illinois University, 1986), 174–92; and "Sermon Theory as Devotional Literature: The Rhetoric of Ramon Llull," in *De ore domini: Preacher and Word in the Middle Ages,* edited by Thomas L. Amos, Eugene A. Green, and Beverly M. Kienzle, Studies in Medieval Culture, no. 27 (Kalamazoo, Mich.: Medieval Institute, 1989), 119–46. These researches on Ramon Llull's proposals for the medieval arts of language have allowed me to explore with felicitous results many other aspects of medieval and Renaissance culture. Despite the range of these other investigations, I fear that I have definitely become what I denied to Dr. Rubió, namely, a Lullist. Now that I have fulfilled, at least provisionally, my original plan to study the Lullian arts of language, I look forward to writing a new series of studies on Llull's role in the academic and ecclesiastical institutions of his era.

None of my researches to date would ever have reached fruition were it not for the assistance provided by Carol Ruyle and her staff in the Interlibrary Loan Office of Milner Library at Illinois State University. Their efforts make it possible for faculty at a struggling public college to pursue advanced research on difficult topics such as Ramon Llull. Stan Gutzman, the humanities librarian at Milner Library, has also provided patient assistance with my reference queries and sympathetic responses to my requests for unusual acquisitions in medieval studies. Early stages of my research for this book benefited from the excellent facilities at the Main Library of the University of Iowa, the Folger Shakespeare Library, the Library of Congress, and the Newberry Library in Chicago.

Ramon Llull remains an esoteric and little-understood figure in European intellectual history. Specialists in medieval studies often know little more than his name or his eccentric reputation. Even in Spain Llull is best known from apocryphal pious legends. For English-speaking audiences, scholarly knowledge of Ramon Llull would remain very limited indeed if Oxford University Press had not published the only book-length critical and historical studies of Llull to appear in English during the past fifty years. To Cynthia Read and the staff at the Oxford University Press offices in New York I am very grateful for their acceptance and careful production of this new volume. Two wonderfully unselfish colleagues, Phyllis Roberts and SunHee Kim Gertz, performed the onerous favor of reading the original, very lengthy manuscript. Their detailed recommendations greatly assisted my attempt to make this study as appealing as possible to a wider range of readers in the world of medieval studies.

Since Llull is such a difficult figure to understand, I appreciate deeply the interest that my work has elicited in recent years from other scholars. Colleagues at the University of Iowa, St. Bonaventure University, and the University of Texas at Austin have kindly invited me to speak on Llull at their campuses. The organizers of sessions at the annual International Congress on Medieval Studies in Kalamazoo have frequently provided me with a forum to discuss my research in progress. I owe particular thanks to Larry Simon for repeatedly including me in panels on the history of the Crown of Aragon. Various members of the International Society for the History of Rhetoric—especially Martin Camargo, Jerry Murphy, Emil Polak, and John Ward—have provided valuable guidance for my studies on the medieval arts of language. The enthusiasm of Robert D. F. Pring-Mill, one of the most eminent modern scholars of Llull's work, remains as gratifying now as when he read my first study on Llull. Finally, many friends from diverse areas of medieval studies—among them Tom Amos, John Bollweg, Tom Burman, Paul Gehl, George Greenia, Valerie Lagorio, Richard Newhauser, and Donna Rogers—have made working on Ramon Llull much more fun than I ever imagined it would be. And when it isn't, my wife, a very postmodern medievalist, is always ready to say, "Look, maybe this would sell better as a screenplay."

Note on References and Quotations

Because one of this study's main purposes is to demonstrate relationships between Ramon Llull's views of eloquence and those of his contemporaries, it cites a large number of classical and medieval authorities. All of these citations appear parenthetically in the text, in order to reduce the number of notes that offer only brief references. The author or title cited should be clear from the text itself. The editions used appear in the Works Cited at the end of this study. References include short titles (usually abbreviated) only to distinguish between several works by one author. When all the citations for an author refer to the same work, no title appears. The numbers and letters used in the references indicate textual divisions (such as book, chapter, and paragraph) or pages (for texts without divisions) from the editions given in the Works Cited. Wherever possible, I cite the textual divisions most commonly used in modern editions of well-known texts. However, for the sake of clarity, these references use only Arabic numerals. Roman page numbers or Greek and Roman letters of textual divisions remain as given in the edition cited. Some references include the abbreviations "prol.," "intro.," and so forth, where necessary to identify portions of a work. Notes giving exact page references accompany all long quotations set off from the body of the text.

All citations of modern critical and scholarly studies appear in the notes. These give only the author's surname, a short title of the material cited, and specific pages (where relevant). Some references include the author's first initials with the surname in order to distinguish between authors with the same surname. Full citations for all secondary studies appear in the Works Cited.

I have translated all quotations into English, with any problematic terms from Ramon Llull's original Latin or Old Catalan texts provided in italics within parentheses. All the works of Llull cited in this study are readily available in modern printed editions. Repeating long quotations from these works in their original language seems unnecessary for the purposes of this study, since few readers will know Old Catalan, Llull's Latin style is largely unremarkable, and his peculiar terminology receives extensive analysis in the study itself. However, to avoid confusion, common medieval Latin terms and the titles of medieval works remain untranslated. Unless otherwise indicated, all translations are my own.

The following abbreviations appear in the parenthetical citations and the notes without further explanation:

1a.10,1	Thomas Aquinas, *Summa theologiae*, first part, question 10, article 1 (and so forth for all other parts, questions, and articles of the *Summa*)
"Arbre elemental"	Ramon Llull, *Arbre de sciència*, "Arbre elemental" (and so forth for each "Arbre" of the text)
DC	Augustine, *De doctrina christiana*
ed. Mainz	Ramon Llull, *Opera omnia*
NEORL	Ramon Llull, *Nova edició de les obres de Ramon Llull*
ORL	Ramon Llull, *Obres originals*
PL	J.-P. Migne, *Patrologia Latina*
RLOL	Ramon Llull, *Opera Latina*
SD	Vincent of Beauvais, *Spectrum doctrinale*

Complete bibliographical information for these works appears in the Works Cited.

Contents

The Evangelical Rhetoric of Ramon Llull

Introduction

Literacy and Popular Culture in the Late Middle Ages

The spread of literacy beyond the great convents and the major schools was one of the most consequential changes in European culture around 1300.[1] This development affected the Crown of Aragon no less than other regions of the medieval West.[2] Two examples from diverse circumstances aptly illustrate its effects there. In the fall of 1292, King James II of Aragon sent brief letters to Ricard de Passanet, a "knight," and to Roger de Vilaragut, the "portulan master for Sicily," ordering them to return certain books, designated only as *Librus romancii* and *Thesaurus*, which they had borrowed from the king.[3] Other records indicate that James was indeed an active collector and lender of books. In 1354 Vicar-General Francesc Ruffach issued a compilation of synodal statutes for the diocese of Barcelona. These rules included the provision, already in force, that all parish priests, whether engaged in the care of souls or not, must own a copy of the guide to pastoral care prepared for them by John of Alexandria.[4] These documents indicate situations—book lending among the aristocracy and widespread literacy among parish clergy—that would have been rare, if not impossible, a few centuries earlier. To be sure, illiterate nobles and priests certainly continued to function happily around 1300, but it is clear that by then a significant population of lay and clerical readers existed outside the cloisters and classrooms of Aragon. For example, records regarding private book ownership in Majorca for the period from 1258 to 1400 show 170 Christian owners of some 751 books.[5] Of those books, 336 (45 percent) were the property of clergy from various ranks and orders. Another 164 (22 percent) belonged to nonprofessional laypeople ranging from artisans and town dwellers to merchants and nobles. Some 250 books (33 percent) belonged to notaries, jurists, and doctors. Majorca during this era possessed no major schools. Moreover, only a portion of the clergy were cloistered. Consequently, the vast majority of the owners represented in these statistics were individuals who used books to exercise a profession, pursue knowledge, seek

3

recreation, or practice devotion, but did so apart from major religious houses or any university.

Scholarly attention to these lower and middle classes of medieval readers has surged lately, but continues to struggle with some well-known practical and method-ological obstacles. Practically, we possess little documentation regarding the development of learning or piety outside the biggest universities and cloistered communities. Parish priests, artisans, local grammar masters, merchants, and even bishops and great nobles have left us frustratingly scant records of their spiritual and intellectual readings. Methodologically, the multifarious literary, religious, or learned activities of these diverse lay and clerical audiences remains undifferentiated within a vast realm of "popular culture."[6] The cultural contributions of religious confraternities, lesser aristocratic courts, professional guilds, parish priests, and even local grammar schools await study in most parts of Europe. Scholarship on the vernacular languages has provided the most detailed investigations of that activity in most cases. As a result, Dante, Juan Manuel, Boccaccio, Christine de Pizan, and Chaucer enjoy formidable bellelettristic reputations. Thanks to this esteem, most general histories of medieval Europe continue to cite these authors alongside Scholastic philosophers and theologians as the major "cultural figures" or even "intellectuals" of their era, without differentiating very sharply their respective spheres of activity. Attempts to distinguish vernacular authors from university masters as "weak" from "strong" intellectuals merely compound the confusion, by introducing an implicit value judgment.[7] Similarly, broad models of cultural exchange organized around simple axes of "vertical" or "horizontal" transmission require considerable refinement.[8] Studies devoted to the "influence" of Scholastic learning on vernacular literature (or vice versa) too easily treat this cultural interaction as a quasi-metaphysical relationship. Even so, many of these commonly accepted notions about medieval literary culture already suggest useful points of departure for further inquiry. For example, accounts of this activity readily show how the citation of vernacular texts in other vernacular texts promotes the formation of some class of "popular" or "national" literature. Similarly, the appearance of "original" literary devices, philosophical doctrines, or theological convictions in vernacular texts easily defines the development of "lay learning" or "popular piety." Any scholar interested in these developments from late medieval culture cannot fail to notice the work of the Majorcan lay evangelist and reformer Ramon Llull (1232–1316). Llull exemplifies, perhaps better than any other figure from his era, the capacity for innovation and dissemination that popular learning and spirituality had achieved in Western Europe around 1300.

Ramon Llull: Lay Evangelist and Reformer

The career of Ramon Llull poses some paradoxical problems for modern historians. Llull was extraordinarily active: he traveled constantly through Aragon, France, and Italy; frequently entreated popes, secular rulers, and powerful laypeople to support his evangelical projects; often visited universities and religious houses to present his ideas; and made missionary journeys to North Africa and the eastern Mediterranean. Nonetheless, the extant documentation concerning his life is so limited that we do not even know the exact dates of his birth and death. This lack of biographical detail contrasts with Llull's own prolific written production: he composed nearly three hundred works of philosophy and theology in Latin, Arabic, and his native Catalan. Yet this voluminous oeuvre fails to illuminate many circumstances of Llull's career: it includes far fewer autobiographical references than we might expect, typically presents every idea through his own idiosyncratic system of argument, and rarely cites any authorities but his own writings. As a result, many details of Llull's life story will probably remain unknown forever. The following sketch of his career focuses on four aspects that seem most relevant to the development of his philosophical and theological learning: his early training, his years of private study, his relationship to the schools, and his contacts with other learned laypeople. Readers seeking more extensive analyses of his career may consult the excellent detailed accounts available in recent scholarship.[9]

Ramon Llull's social and economic background is perhaps the least remarkable aspect of his career. He was born on the island of Majorca, probably in 1232, only a few years after King James I of Aragon conquered it from the Muslims. The scion of a prosperous family from the Catalan-Aragonese merchant class, Llull presumably received the kind of privileged upbringing appropriate to his rank. Our chief source of knowledge about Llull's life is a hagiographic *Vita* composed from his recollections by friends at Paris in 1311, but it says very little about his youth or his early adult years. Other documents indicate that he married Blanca Picany in 1257, and that the couple had two children. The *Vita* claims that Llull became seneschal for the king of Majorca and indulged in many worldly delights (par. 2). The life of a courtier undoubtedly offered many material pleasures, but did not lack opportunities for intellectual or spiritual development.[10] The *Vita* specifically describes Llull as an assiduous cultivator of troubadour love lyrics. This representation is perhaps only a hagiographic fiction designed to contrast his original sinful pursuit of secular letters with his subsequent pious dedication to sacred learning. Nonetheless, Llull does recognize the cultivation of popular poetry as an established, though morally reprehensible, art in his later writings. His voluminous production of Catalan prose also demonstrates his undeniably expert command of the vernacular as a literary medium.[11] Moreover, the perfection of vernacular literacy, especially for use in composing courtly verse, was certainly consistent with the training in "literature and nurture" commonly given to well-born youths in this era.[12] Llull recommends education in the vernacular and Latin for laypeople throughout his works, usually mentioning some traditional scheme like the seven liberal arts.[13] A century later, education in grammar, logic, and "all other knowledge well and honorably necessary to our condition" is the preparation that a leading citizen of Barcelona expects for his son.[14] Llull perhaps received a similar education, as well as training in courtly virtues and skills.[15] Ultimately, however, this phase of his career probably contributed least to the spiritual and intellectual doctrines expounded in his copious later writings.

The second phase of Ramon Llull's career began sometime after he reached age thirty, perhaps around 1263, when he underwent a profound religious awakening, which his *Vita* calls a "conversion to penitence."[16] This text tells how he saw repeated visions of Christ crucified, the first of which came to him one night as he composed a love poem. These visions spurred such remorse of conscience concerning the Savior's sacrifice that Llull resolved to abandon the world and serve God instead (par. 4–5). He pledged himself to evangelize the Muslims, by undertaking his own missions among them, writing a single great book of irrefutable apologetic arguments, and campaigning for the establishment of schools to train missionaries in the Oriental languages. After making some pilgrimages, he decided to seek education at Paris, since he possessed "no knowledge and only a little grammar," according to the *Vita* (par. 5). This "grammar" presumably means aptitude in Latin, and hence some modern scholars have questioned whether Llull ever really learned that language well, especially since he later employed secretaries and translators to prepare Latin versions of some of his works. Nonetheless, the Latinity of his writings differs little from that displayed in works by other nonacademic laypeople. Family and friends, including the Dominican leader Ramon de Penyafort, persuaded Llull to remain on his native island, instead of going to Paris (par. 10). In the city of Majorca he learned "a little grammar" and studied Arabic intensively. For the latter purpose he purchased a Muslim slave who tutored him for nine years (par. 11). The source of his Latin instruction remains unknown, but grammar teachers were certainly available on the island by this time.[17] However, since their schools typically served juvenile pupils, the most likely recourse for a wealthy adult such as Llull was simply individual instruction. In addition, laypeople interested in more advanced learning were perhaps able to audit classes at the mendicant houses, as Dante did at Santa Maria Novella in Florence. Both the Dominicans and the Franciscans were operating convents on Majorca in Llull's day. The Order of Preachers' recent initiatives in overseas missions would have especially attracted Llull.[18]

During this phase of his career, Llull evidently acquired most of his learning through an eremitic life of study and meditation. By 1276 his dedication to these studies became so intense that his wife sought an administrator for their temporal affairs, arguing that her husband was so absorbed in the "contemplative life" that he neglected their estate.[19] The knowledge that Llull attained through this private study culminated in a special revelation that guided all his later endeavors. The *Vita* recounts how he went to practice contemplation on a nearby mountain, usually identified with Mount Randa, where God revealed to him a plan for his book of apologetic arguments, which became his famed Great Universal Art of Finding Truth (par. 14).[20] Llull built a hermitage on Mount Randa and worked to finish his book at a local abbey, evidently the Cistercian house of La Real. Although the intellectual resources available at the abbey were not extraordinary, it must have offered him some assistance. An inventory from 1386 describes a library of some two hundred volumes, concentrated in theology but also including works on grammar, logic, and other arts.[21] None of these works correspond exactly to the few authorities that Llull cites in his own writings, a discrepancy that has encouraged some scholars to deny a major role for La Real in Llull's education. However, the abbey did possess numerous works—such as Isidore's *Etymologiae,* Peter Lombard's *Sententiae,* and various summae—that easily match the range of Llull's knowledge in the arts, theology, and philosophy. Moreover, it is hazardous to make any judgments based on

Llull's citation of sources, since he regularly refuses to employ arguments based on authority. It is perhaps more revealing that Arab Christian apologetic texts (like the *Contrarietas alfolica*) and twelfth-century contemplative writers (like Richard of St. Victor) do appear among the handful of *auctoritates* whom Llull actually names in his oeuvre.[22] References to these sources neatly suggest the two areas of interest—apologetic and mystical theology—that Llull must have explored most enthusiastically during his years of private study. This dual emphasis is obvious in his first major writing, the *Libre de contemplació en Déu* (an encyclopedic guide to contemplation), and informs the structure of his entire Great Art, which offers a combined system of meditation and argumentation. His training probably did not include the study of the trivium typically acquired by thirteenth-century pupils in elementary "grammar schools" or secondary "arts schools."[23] The final lines of Llull's *Declaratio Raymundi* (a refutation of Scholastic doctrines written at Paris in 1298) invite anyone who reads the treatise to polish its rough manner, and blames its lack of "good style" (*bono dictamine*) on his own lack of grammatical and rhetorical training (*quia sufficiens grammaticus non sum nec rhetoricus*).[24] However, Llull's zeal for controversial debate did lead him to study logic, the art that most directly served his apologetic purposes. His earliest writings include a vernacular verse rendering of Algazel's treatise on logic, which may also have served him as a textbook for the practice of Arabic. In any case, there is no reason to expect that Ramon Llull would have sought or received on his native island a comprehensive training in the arts, theology, or philosophy. As a layman studying privately, he apparently designed his own curriculum, without direction from academic statutes or ecclesiastical rules.

Ramon Llull's years of private study established a foundation for all his subsequent interaction with the schools and other learned laypeople. The inalienable purposes of that interaction were the spiritual and intellectual ideals that he acquired from his early education and then synthesized into his own Great Art. Llull's conviction that God had revealed to him the method of his system understandably fueled his lifelong zeal for promoting its application and dissemination. This zeal eventually led him to adopt a very antagonistic perspective toward the schools. This conflict was probably an inevitable consequence of Llull's "conversion to penitence." His dedication to contemplation and evangelism suited the cloister and public plaza far better than the classroom. The first indications of this antagonism are already apparent in work that Llull did during his early years of study. One of his earliest writings, a rhymed vernacular compendium of Algazel's *Logic*, announces his intent to educate laypeople ignorant of Latin or Arabic (ll. 5–10) and to seek knowledge of God above all else (ll. 1044–79). Llull's first formal encounter with higher academic authorities evidently occurred around 1275, when King James of Majorca summoned him to Montpellier in order to have his writings examined by a friar at the Franciscan theological school there. The *Vita* reports the friar's admiration for the "Catholic prophecy and devotion" displayed in Llull's works (par. 16). The *Vita* adds that he "publicly read" (i.e., taught) his Great Art at Montpellier and composed many other works there. This examination and public reading at Montpellier (which probably conflates several incidents) is the first of various scenes in the *Vita* that depict Llull's approval by clerical authorities. These episodes also specify Llull's prophetic abilities and

public teaching, probably in order to invest him with an authority that he would otherwise lack as a layman. Soon after his visit to Montpellier, Llull began four decades
of virtually constant peregrination around the western Mediterranean world.

His travels included at least four visits to Paris, as well as frequent stays in
Montpellier. The *Vita* (par. 42) reports that a "multitude" of Parisian university students and masters heard him defend the Great Art during his last visit there, from
1309 to 1311. During these years Llull wrote numerous treatises denouncing
Scholastic doctrines that he considered heterodox, and he also solicited various letters of recommendation for his projects from clerical and secular authorities.[25] He
probably sought these documents, like the *Vita* itself, as support for the missionary
proposals that he wished to present at the forthcoming Council of Vienne. The letters
that Llull obtained from King Philippe of France and his university audience simply
testify to his good moral character and edifying intentions. More suggestive comments appear in a letter provided by Francesco Caroccioli, chancellor of the
University of Paris. Caroccioli uses scriptural allusions to compare Llull's writings
with the poor widow's offering (Mark 12:42, and Luke 21:2) and with the humbler
furnishings provided for the Tabernacle by the Israelites (Exodus 25:3–4).[26] Both
analogies were exordial commonplaces copied from Jerome's prologue to the
Vulgate.[27] The reference to the widow especially suggests an equation between Llull
and traditional images of women as simple messengers of divine wisdom, sent to
humble the proud.[28] In short, Chancellor Caroccioli expresses appreciation for Llull's
pious zeal, but regards his work as very modest.[29] Other authorities evidently proffered less flattering assessments. In some works, Llull complains bitterly that his
contemporaries ignore him, and even suggests that they scorn him as a "fool."[30] This
label perhaps implies the designation of *idiota* used by clerics to condemn those
heretics or laypeople whose ideas challenged academic or clerical learning.[31]
However, it also links Llull with many previous "fools for God," "divine jongleurs,"
and *ioculatores Dei* who readily accepted this humble persona.[32]

The public spectacle of the "fool" also suggests the fourth aspect of Ramon
Llull's career that concerns his learning and piety, namely, his fervent commitment
to promoting evangelism and reform among the laity. The *Vita* explicitly states that
he composed many applications of his system "according to the capacity of the
simple" (par. 14), while works from his early *Libre de contemplació* to the *Liber de
novo modo demonstrandi* of 1312 all manifest his zeal for leading the mind from ignorance to knowledge, or conversely, for bringing learning to the unlearned. Llull's
constant efforts to promote his work shows that he regarded this education not simply
as an abstract spiritual or intellectual exercise, but as a pragmatic social or cultural
undertaking. To what extent the pious, learned layman Ramon Llull could claim authority to preach or teach remains one of the most basic and obscure questions from
his entire career.[33] Any preaching or teaching that he did certainly raises two more
specific questions of immediate relevance to this study: what audiences did Llull so-
licit and how did he communicate with them? Llull did not present his appeals
exclusively—or perhaps even very often—to popes, kings, and university masters.
The *Vita* suggests that he also solicited support from educated laypeople and regular
or secular clergy outside the schools. In these groups he found support for various

aspects of his evangelizing and reforming proposals. For example, the *Vita* itself was written by admirers from the Carthusian house of Vauvert at Paris, while colophons from some of Llull's own writings name other religious houses whose hospitality he enjoyed, such as the monastery of San Donnino in Pisa.[34] His chief Parisian disciple was a master of medicine, Thomas Le Myésier. Franciscan secretaries from Catalonia assisted Llull in his last years.[35] Lay audiences in northern Italy appear to have been especially receptive to his solicitations. The *Vita* mentions a tour in 1308 that generated letters of support from the town councils of Pisa and Genoa, as well as financial pledges from "many devout matrons and widows" (par. 42). At Genoa Llull also found at least one ardent lay disciple in the man-of-affairs Percival Spinola.

Llull's success in attracting French and Italian supporters raises an obvious question of communication. When a modern scholar claims that Llull preached to the people of Genoa and Pisa, we cannot avoid asking what language he used.[36] As it happens, none of his writings ever mention him speaking in French, Provençal, Italian, or any *lingua vulgaris* other than Catalan. Still, Llull's commitment to using other vernaculars is obvious from his own study of Arabic and his lifelong insistence on the need to train missionaries in the Oriental languages. Throughout his career he explicitly justified composing works in his native Catalan as a means of promoting popular instruction. His enthusiasm for this recourse was hardly novel, since Church authorities had been recommending vernacular preaching at least since the Council of Tours in 813.[37] In Llull's day, facility in local languages was obligatory for Dominican and Franciscan preachers.[38] Thus, Saint Anthony of Padua earned a chronicler's praise for his command of Italian, while Saint Bonaventure apologized to a Parisian audience for his imperfect ability in French.[39] Nonetheless, neither Llull's writings nor his *Vita* ever refer to this question. However, they do advocate using Latin as a universal language. While this proposal expresses a commonplace Western Christian solution to the punishment of Babel, it may also reflect Llull's own solution to the problem of linguistic diversity.[40] He must have found himself often able to communicate with patrons or disciples only through his simple Latin. This limitation may explain his frequent stays in a university town such as Montpellier or his extended visits to northern Italy, where lay knowledge of Latin was evidently more common. Many Genoese merchants possessed the same basic command of Latin as did Llull.[41] Thus, both he and they illustrate the diffusion of simple Latinity as a kind of koine in the late Middle Ages.[42] At the same time, Llull continued to write in Catalan and Arabic throughout his career.

Ultimately, Ramon Llull's commitment to reaching local audiences through their vernaculars and his insistence on propagating knowledge and devotion through Latin are complementary, rather than contradictory, solutions. Llull's dual use of the vernacular and Latin, like his adoption of a hybrid lay and clerical vocation, both enabled and symbolized the cultural exchange that fostered popular learning and spirituality. His contribution to this exchange continued even after his death, which evidently occurred early in 1316, as he returned to Majorca from his last missionary venture in North Africa. His will mandated that the Carthusian monastery of Vauvert in Paris, his friend Percival Spinola in Genoa, and various religious houses on Majorca all receive copies of his writings.[43]

Purpose and Plan of This Study

This study continues an ongoing investigation of Ramon Llull's role in the development of lay learning and piety during the late Middle Ages. My work thus far has concentrated on several areas that seem especially important for understanding Llull as an evangelist and reformer, namely, his proposals regarding the arts of language. A previous study examined in detail his theories of logical argumentation, which are fundamental to his Great Art as a method for "proving" Catholic beliefs and to his proposals for revising the logical doctrines of the schools. This new study examines the theories of eloquence expounded in his works on rhetoric and preaching. Despite their obvious importance for understanding Llull's enterprise, these remain among the least studied areas of his work. Like all of his doctrines, his theories of eloquence depend fundamentally on the techniques of his Great Art, yet incorporate numerous received ideas. Many of Llull's precepts derive, not surprisingly, from guides to popular preaching. However, his proposals about rhetoric and preaching also include much material adapted from ethical literature and from vernacular arts of eloquence. Llull's synthesis of this material into a broad art of Christian communication exemplifies his larger effort to create a single program for evangelizing unbelievers, reforming Christian society, and promoting spiritual perfection.

The organization of this study aims to make Llull's ideas as comprehensible as possible to readers unfamiliar with his work, but interested generally in medieval intellectual or cultural history, and especially in the arts of eloquence. His proposals concerning rhetoric and preaching generally emphasize three broad areas: beauty, order, and propriety. Llull inevitably explains these according to the metaphysical, epistemological, and dialectical principles of his own Great Art. Hence, in order to make these explanations intelligible, chapter 1 explains how Ramon Llull's Great Universal Art of Finding Truth functions as a system of argumentation and contemplation, provides a model for "retracing the arts to theology," and thus establishes the foundation for his general conception of rhetoric and preaching as arts. Chapters 2 and 3 examine the commonplace metaphysical and epistemological principles that Llull typically invokes in order to explain human communication, including the artful use of language. Chapters 4 through 8 explain in detail Llull's proposals regarding beauty, order, and propriety, showing how they compare or contrast with conventional rhetorical functions of invention, style, disposition, and delivery. Chapter 9 analyzes the ethical doctrines that Llull recommends in order to ensure the union of virtue and eloquence. Chapter 10 reviews several model discourses from his sermon collections, as practical applications of his rhetorical and homiletic theory. The conclusion considers the later medieval reception of Llull's writings on eloquence, and returns to the general question of how his work can improve our understanding of popular learning and spirituality in the late Middle Ages.

The analyses offered throughout this study rely heavily on comparisons between Llull's proposals and doctrines from classical and medieval authorities. Our incomplete knowledge about Llull's education and the peculiar features of his writings make all these comparisons somewhat tentative. I beg in advance the reader's indulgence for the frequent claims about what Llull "suggests," "implies," "echoes," "seems to argue," and so forth. All these references to Llull's intentions are in any case a kind of antonomastic fiction. Indeed, my analyses of his work often conclude that his arguments result more from the internal necessity of his discursive methods than from his conscious will to expression as an "author" in any modern sense.[44] While this perspective may trouble readers accustomed to regarding Llull's writings as the direct manifestation of his intellectual, spiritual, or literary genius, it does in fact respect the function of his Great Art as a system for "finding truth." In short, I offer my conclusions as interpretations of texts ascribed to Ramon Llull, understood in comparison to other extant texts of the thirteenth and fourteenth centuries. My construction of a common sense among these texts is most obvious in my conclusion that Llull's proposals on eloquence attempt to achieve the moral reform of all human communication. The chapters that follow explain how his theories of rhetoric and preaching synthesize a wide range of received psychological, moral, metaphysical, and rhetorical doctrines into a general art of secular and sacred eloquence. However, none of Llull's writings explicitly proposes this utopian ideal of discourse. I offer it nonetheless as a plausible corollary to the "evangelical allegory" (imitation of apostolic Christianity) and "philosophical anagogy" (universal propagation of the Faith) that Llull unambiguously advocates throughout his oeuvre.[45] The Lullian arts of rhetoric and preaching promote the love of God and neighbor that he considered the most beautiful, orderly, and proper communication.

1

Ramon Llull's Art of Arts

Llull's *Vita* tells us how his original vow to serve God involved a vehement desire to compose the "best book in the world against the errors of the infidels." A subsequent inspiration, which the *Vita* attributes to divine revelation, transformed that simple goal into a much more ambitious project, the Great Universal Art of Finding Truth (par. 6, 14). Llull devoted the rest of his career to perfecting the methods of this idiosyncratic symbolico-dialectical system of argument. He recorded the phases of its development in several redactions of the Great Art itself, as well as in scores of other works applying its system to specialized topics of inquiry. A complete account of this massive project remains unwritten. The following summary offers a necessarily simplified explanation, designed chiefly to help my readers understand how the methods of the Great Art inform Llull's accounts of the arts of eloquence.

Ramon Llull's Great Universal Art of Finding Truth synthesizes a vast range of techniques for private meditation, scriptural exegesis, and apologetic argument into a single system for "discovering" how all knowledge and being reveals divine truth.[1] The general method of this system is comparison or analogy. The Great Art is "universal" and "finds truth" only in so far as it is capable of likening anything known to the Divine Word, which Llull regards as the exemplar of all wisdom. The foundations of Llull's Great Art are nine Divine Dignities or attributes, which are the Absolute Principles of all being and knowledge. Nine additional Relative Principles explain the operation of the Absolute Principles at nine levels of existence called Subjects. In addition, nine heuristic questions called Rules help guide inquiry regarding the Principles and Subjects. The most famous feature of the Great Art is its use of nine letters from the alphabet—B, C, D, E, F, G, H, I, and K—to symbolize the Absolute Principles, Relative Principles, Subjects, Rules, and other sets of nine categories devised by Llull in order to treat particular fields of knowledge (see table 1). The letter A usually serves to indicate the coincidence of all the Absolute Principles in the Godhead. This Lullian Alphabet gives the Great Art its apparently symbolic character.

TABLE 1 The Lullian Alphabet

	Absolute Principles	Relative Principles	Subjects	Rules
B	Bonitas	Differentia	Deus	Utrum?
	Goodness	Difference	God	Whether?
C	Magnitudo	Concordantia	Angelus	Quid?
	Greatness	Concord	Angel	What?
D	Duratio[a]	Contrarietas	Coelum	De quo?
	Duration	Contrariety	Heavens	From what?
E	Potestas	Principium	Homo	Quare?
	Power	Beginning	Human	Why?
F	Sapientia	Medium	Imaginatio	Quantum?
	Wisdom	Middle	Imagination	How much?
G	Voluntas	Finis	Sensitiva	Quale?
	Will	End	Senses	What kind?
H	Virtus	Maioritas	Vegetativa	Quando
	Virtue	Superiority	Vegetal power	When?
I	Veritas	Aequalitas	Elementativa	Ubi
	Truth	Equality	Elements	Where?
K	Gloria	Minoritas	Instrumentativa	Quomodo?[b]
	Glory	Inferiority	Skills and arts	How?

[a] Sometimes identified as *Aeternitas* (Eternity) in different versions of the Great Art
[b] Often combined with *Cum Quo*? (With what?)

Llull's Great Art generates knowledge by combining groups of these letters in circular or tabular diagrams (see figures 1, 2, and 3) and then explicating the meaning of those combinations. These groups of two or more letters, Llull assumes, must constitute viable formulations of all possible philosophical and theological propositions, because the Absolute Principles and the other categories that the letters symbolize are indisputably true and necessary. Finding truth through this *ars combinatoria* depends heavily, if not completely, on correct understanding of the terms signified by the letters. This understanding usually involves careful interpretative work, guided by unswerving fidelity to the fundamental tenets of Catholic dogma. Llull's system provided Christians with a method of "quickly finding" spiritual truths that they already possessed, just as the new Scholastic techniques of indexing and alphabetizing provided students and masters with methods of rapidly locating information in texts.[2] The labor of explicating these letter combinations fills thousands of pages in Llull's writings. Some modern scholars have sought a formal logical system in the *ars combinatoria* of Llull's letter symbolism.[3] Others have suggested that the symbolic diagrams of the Great Art serve a sheerly mechanical or mnemonic function. My study of Llull's logical doctrines finds that they owe little to the Aristotelian propositional logic and syllogistics of his Scholastic peers, but instead apply a wide range of analogical, allegorical, comparative, symbolic,

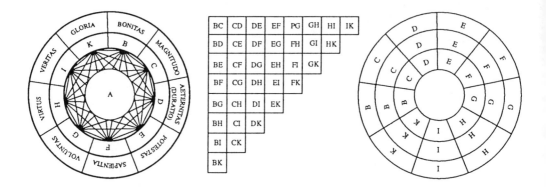

Figure 1. Llull's "Figure A."   Figure 2. A combinatory table.   Figure 3. A combinatory figure
                                                                                (the inner circles revolve).

proportional, and figural arguments, which Llull regards as "necessary reasons."[4] In his hands, these arguments all serve one purpose: to demonstrate the correlation of philosophical or scientific knowledge with Christian doctrine. Llull's Great Art is perhaps the Middle Age's most ambitious attempt at systematizing the Christian Neoplatonic understanding of all creation as *symbola similia et dissimilia* of the Creator.[5]

This general characterization of the method and form of Llull's Great Art must suffice for the immediate purposes of this study, but a few of its more peculiar strategic features also require mention here. First, Llull almost never cites authorities to support his arguments, preferring instead to rely on the ratiocinations that he calls "necessary reasons." In manifestos such as his *Petitio ad Celestinum V papam* and his *Petitio Raymundi in Concilio Generali,* he insists that this mode of argumentation will best convince unbelievers who do not recognize the same authorities as Christians. Llull does cite Scripture in his catechetical and apologetic writings, but usually mentions other classical, Christian, and Arab authors only as representatives of their doctrines or schools. Second, Llull regularly reformulates philosophical or theological doctrines in his own terminology. That is, the vocabulary of the Absolute Principles, Relative Principles, Rules, Subjects, and so forth from his Great Art provides the common, often highly repetitious, idiom for his exposition of every topic. Llull especially favors inventing new terms that use standardized suffixes to indicate metaphysical relationships. For example, his later writings commonly employ the Latin endings *-ivum* (or *-icans*), *-icabile* (or *-icatus*), and *-icare* to name the "innate correlatives" of activity, passivity, and action that he attributes to every phenomenon.[6] In this way, Llull often revises, extends, or simply replaces the sense of conventional terminology.

These peculiar features of Llull's method occur within the context of two broader, less remarkable tactics that he employs: exposition through *distinctiones* and moralization. These practices, which Llull applies to virtually every topic that he treats, constitute his most obvious debt to contemporary theological learning, especially as used in popular preaching. Recent scholarship has demonstrated how the lists of word meanings called *distinctiones* enjoyed a tremendous vogue as intellectual tools from the twelfth century on. Originally compilations of the multiple senses of terms from Scripture created to assist exegesis, these lists evolved during the thirteenth century into massive inventories of anonymous citations drawn from texts of moral and natural science alike. Indexed and alphabetized for ease of consultation, they became especially popular as sermon aids.[7] The use of *distinctiones* in popular preaching and the devotional literature derived from it virtually guaranteed dissemination of this device throughout the Latin and vernacular literature created for lay audiences. The artful or at least exhaustive exposition of *distinctiones* evidently provided a useful method of invention and disposition for a wide range of imaginative and didactic composition.[8] Ramon Llull excels in constructing texts where "one organized system of information, taken as a whole system, is placed in parallel with another, as its equivalent and interpretation."[9] A glance at the table of contents from almost any text by Llull readily reveals the extent of this practice in his work. For example, the introduction to his *Libre de demostracions* simply declares that "the rubrics contained in this book serve as description and as demonstration in this investigation."[10] The exposition of *distinctiones* in Llull's works rarely involves the strict task of explicating the diverse senses of a particular term. Instead, it typically combines with the more basic tactic of division commonly used by Scholastic commentators or preachers and even with the simple strategy of enumeration. Nonetheless, Llull's explications share a fundamental function with distinctional exposition in their struggle to find a common (usually moral or theological) truth in every topic that they expound. Thus, the prologue to the *Libre de contemplació* explains at length how that work's 365 chapters (each consisting of thirty paragraphs) comprise various *distinctiones* and divisions, ranging from the five wounds and the forty days in the wilderness of Jesus to the Ten Commandments and the thirteen apostles. The first *distinctio* cited in the prologue to the *Libre de contemplació* are the two immediate and ultimate intentions (understood in the Lullian sense discussed below) that guide the work's composition. This initial appeal to the moral finality of his enterprise neatly suggests how his reliance on exposition through *distinctiones* supports his pervasive exercise of moral allegory.

Moralization was a common strategy of both academic scriptural exegesis and popular preaching in Llull's era.[11] He would also have found abundant examples of its uses in many Arab authorities, from the Brethren of Purity to Avicenna.[12] The contribution of moralization to medieval Christian culture would be difficult to overestimate: we could aptly liken it to the twentieth-century faith in scientific method. Moralization becomes a distinguishing feature of the vernacular sermons collected as pious readings for literate laypeople, and appears in many other genres of popular devotional literature as well.[13] The practice of moralization—in the broadest sense of "spiritual allegory"—appears in even the simplest types of preaching. The diffusion of this allegorical interpretation is already evident from its use among popular spiritual movements in the eleventh century.[14] Recourse to radical allegoresis often proved necessary for Cathars, Joachimites, and other heterodox groups to justify their special interpretation of Scripture.[15] The flourishing activity of these groups in the Midi and the Crown of Aragon during Llull's lifetime may have created very receptive audiences for programs of popular piety and learning such as the Great Art.[16] Ramon Llull both imitates and fosters a very broad, popular exercise of moral allegory by treating every thing as an opportunity "for knowing and having good moralities."[17] Llull's virtually exclusive reliance on moralization contrasts with the more diverse tactics of contemporary Scholastic exegetes, who often explore questions of natural science in their literal commentaries on Scripture.

Llull's reliance on moralization reflects the very fundamental role of moral theology in his Great Art, which constantly invokes the ethical doctrine that he calls "first and second intentions."[18] These terms indicate the basic obligations of every creature to serve the Creator primarily and all other things secondarily. For Llull, these obligations define the innate "meaning" of any being. His doctrine of the two intentions synthesizes a wide range of commonplaces from Christian ethics.[19] It also has parallels in Arab doctrines known from the Brethren of Purity or later adaptations of their work.[20] Llull's doctrine corresponds especially well to Avicenna's distinction between the two "faces of the soul," which Franciscan authors favor.[21] Whatever its precedents might have been, Llull's extension of this dichotomy from moral theology to metaphysics illustrates well how he exercises moralization as a virtually universal "way of knowing."

The uncertain precedents for Ramon Llull's doctrine of two intentions also illustrate a problem that continues to vex modern study of his work, the identification of "sources" for his ideas and methods. The inspiration for his use of letter symbolism organized in charts has long fascinated researchers. Renaissance devotees of Llull's Great Art already associated it with Jewish cabbalism. This esoteric and orientalizing view continues to intrigue some twentieth-century scholars, although others dismiss the parallels between Llull's Art and the Cabbala as superficial.[22] In any case, the use of diagrams and symbolic notation was commonplace in many branches of medieval Latin and Arabic learning.[23] Llull's zeal for this device, like his contemporary Juan Manuel's enthusiasm for cryptograms and ciphers, is probably a distinguishing feature of semilearned culture.[24] The idiosyncratic quality of many Lullian doctrines has also generated various modern studies that seek to identify specific (sometimes esoteric) Christian or Islamic authorities as principal sources for Llull's ideas. For example, many of his arguments resemble Neoplatonic theories found in John Scotus Eriugena, although it is not clear how Llull would have known his work.[25] Llull's pervasive emphasis on Nature as an expression of divinely established archetypes also suggests theories popularized by the Chartrean Platonists, but his writings have little of the literary artifice or specifically Platonic doctrine found in Bernardus Silvestris's *Cosmographia* or Alan of Lille's *De planctu naturae*. There are also frequent correspondences between Llull's metaphysics or epistemology and the views of twelfth-century Latin authorities. Llull does in fact refer once to Richard of St. Victor, whose contemplative schemes perhaps offer the closest parallels to Llull's own. Of course, Ramon Llull also learned Arabic well enough to read and write learned works in that language. Thus, Llull's earliest writings include an adaptation of Algazel's treatise on logic and he cites several apologetic arguments from Arab Christian authorities.[26] At the same time, Llull's oeuvre includes remarkably few references to contemporary Scholastic authorities or concerns, a characteristic that has prompted some scholars to regard his work as somewhat old-fashioned. However, this feature of Llull's work readily accords with his rejection of contemporary philosophical and theological inquiry as perversions of knowledge (see the further discussion below). Moreover, he often professes his intent to harmonize the basic doctrines acceptable to Christians, Muslims, and Jews alike, an objective that makes his work simultaneously very synthetic and very superficial. Subsequent chapters in this study will show that many of Llull's precepts repeat commonplace doctrines widely available since the twelfth century in *florilegia* and compendia. This is especially noticeable in the case of the universal allegory that underlies the method of his Great Art. Its most basic features are simple axioms of Neoplatonist metaphysics and Christian spiritual psychology, which Llull combines into a kind of natural theology for the lay Church militant.

Reductio artium ad theologiam

Although the original inspiration and ultimate purpose of Llull's Great Art is clearly the conversion of unbelievers to Christianity, he insists as well that it is "general" and "universal," an "art of arts" capable of discovering the truth about any subject, whether considered through evangelism, contemplation, or study. For this reason Étienne Gilson concluded that Llull's Art depends heavily on the unified view of knowledge developed by thirteenth-century Augustinians.[27] While it remains difficult to place a writer as idiosyncratic as Llull in any particular philosophical or theological school, it is nonetheless easy to recognize the affinity of his ideals with the views that Gilson identified as Augustinian. For instance, Llull vigorously defends the broad thesis of *credo ut intelligam,* as developed in Christian theology from Augustine to Anselm: he consistently demands belief as the basis for understanding.[28] More important for Llull's treatment of any branch of learning is his conviction that sacred wisdom excels secular knowledge. His defenses of this ideal often echo patristic and early Scholastic authorities.[29] Like Cassiodorus's *Institutiones* (1.28.4), the Lullian Art defines a comprehensive program for exploiting any field of inquiry according to Augustine's famous principle of "Egyptian gold" (*DC* 2.40.60).[30] Llull's *Proverbis de Ramon* succinctly states that "[a]ll knowledge exists for the sake of theology" and "[p]hilosophy prepares the explanation of theology" (276.4, 20).[31] The opening lines of his *Declaratio Raimundi* present theology as the mistress of philosophy, the mother and mirror through which the human mind knows the Divine Dignities and their effects in this world.[32] Llull's enumerations of the branches of learning very aptly illustrate Hugh of St. Victor's definition of the seven liberal arts as propaedeutic steps toward theology (*De sacr.* 1, prol.). Llull would certainly have found support for this view among the Arab authorities that he probably read.[33] It appears explicitly in the writings of Algazel, whom he studied early in his career.[34] However, unlike these earlier Christian or Islamic authorities, Llull rarely recommends the progress from philosophy to theology as a quest for spiritual repose. His own career developed in exactly the opposite direction: he abandoned his initial contemplative retreat in favor of evangelical action.[35] His program thus contrasts with those of twelfth-century authorities, such as Adelard of Bath's *De eodem et diverso* and Godefroy of St. Victor's *Fons philosophiae,* that emphasize contempt for worldly affairs as an integral premise of the search for moral wisdom through philosophical knowledge.[36] By contrast, Llull invokes the common ideal of the *vita apostolica* in order to advocate the pursuit of wisdom through preaching and the exercise of *contemptus mundi* through poverty.[37] Devotion to the apostolic ideal informs his enterprise far more than modern scholarship has acknowledged.[38]

In Llull's own era, Bonaventure's well-known arguments regarding the *reductio artium ad theologiam* probably constitute the closest analogue to Llull's treatment of the arts and sciences.[39] Indeed, it would not be unfair to see the Great Art as simply a massive amplification of the Seraphic Doctor's little treatise. However, where Bonaventure carefully prescribes the steps that lead from secular learning to sacred wisdom, Llull usually regards this progression as a comprehensive exercise in moral and intellectual reform, a complete personal conversion like the one that he experienced. For example, the prologue to his *Art demostrativa* of 1283 explains:

> If you learn this Art and follow its principles as we have taught, you will know how to find the secrets of nature with divine help; you will also attain knowledge of God, the soul, first principles, virtue and vice, salvation and metaphysics, and truth and falsehood; and you will know how to design *(atrobar)* and make books, and you will know how to determine whether there is error in the ancient sciences, or whether those who discovered them attained true doctrine, or whether they organized them from natural principles *(seyn)*. This Art will provide you with rules and instruction for correcting anything where they have erred through ignorance, and will make their sciences more attractive in those matters where their understanding did not go astray. (3.6.5)[40]

This passage offers a virtually paradigmatic statement of Llull's conviction that all human inquiry should lead to discovery of divine truth. This principle guides his entire enterprise; it is surely incorrect to regard the Great Art as a neutral system of scientific inquiry that happens to include theology.[41] Llull's project is not a kind of medieval scheme for "information processing," capable of transmitting any body of knowledge.[42] For Ramon Llull, knowledge of God is the truest, highest, and best kind of knowledge. The implications of this conviction for Llull's treatment of specific branches of knowledge—including the arts of eloquence—are wide reaching.

First and most broadly, Llull's zeal for retracing the arts to theology conflicts with the academic vocation of his contemporaries in the schools. Not surprisingly, he is sharply critical, even contemptuous, of the Schoolmen. The final lines in the quotation above from the *Art demostrativa* already imply this antagonistic stance. The *Vita* suggests that Llull was disappointed by what he found during his first visit to the University of Paris (par. 19). As Llull's acquaintance with the schools deepened during subsequent visits to Paris, he began to denounce academic study as an outright perversion of knowledge. In his *Declaratio Raymundi* of 1298, the figure of Raymundus evaluates the errors condemned at Paris in 1277.[43] This concern for the circulation of Aristotelian doctrines in the late 1290s seems somewhat misdirected, since acceptance of the philosopher's works in the Paris curriculum was well established by this time.[44] Nonetheless, Raymundus vehemently refutes each doctrine presented by a figure named Socrates, who evidently personifies pagan philosophy.[45] Llull's hostility to the philosophers is patent in his treatment of the twenty-fourth condemned proposition, "That all knowledge is unnecessary except philosophical learning, and only necessary except as custom." Socrates states that philosophy studies real natural truths, while all other disciplines simply help people live well and morally. Raymundus's refutation mixes metaphysics and theology, arguing that God is the first cause of all being and therefore divine truths are the most necessary to know, especially since they help people attain eternal salvation. Recognizing Llull's commitment to defending moral truth against philosophical knowledge makes it hard to accept modern claims that he taught in the schools and easy to understand why he promoted his Great Art as an alternative to academic study.

Second, Llull's insistence on the *reductio artium ad theologiam* as a universal ideal of knowledge tends to discourage interest in particular arts and sciences for their own sake. Llull does share with early and contemporary Scholastic authorities a keen concern for defining the basic principles, rules, maxims, and precepts in each branch of learning.[46] However, where the investigations of the Schoolmen tended to increase conceptual distinctions in a field of inquiry, Llull tries to reduce them. Simply put, Llull always seeks one truth from many; he regards the multiplication of ideas as virtually an evil in itself. He repeatedly denounces as perverse the propagation of varying philosophical doctrines or theological arguments in the schools, seeing it as a sinful multiplication of deviant particulars that defer recognition of the one universal truth. Llull illustrates his view in chapter 86 of the *Libre de Blaquerna,* which offers proposals for reform of the schools. In this scene Pope Blaquerna entrusts one of his cardinals with the task of "endeavoring that the human Intellect be exalted to understand God so that God might be known and loved by all people" (86.1).[47] That is, he will work to help people fulfill better their Lullian first intention. The cardinal and the pope hear a series of reports by scholars from different disciplines; their accounts constitute exempla illustrating the dangerous confusion caused by the proliferation of opinions in the various arts and sciences. Needless to say, Llull adamantly opposes any arguments in favor of a "double truth" that might separate philosophical from theological knowledge, in the manner that Aquinas (1a.1, 1) or other Scholastics argue. The doctrine of a "double truth" is one of the heterodox positions that Llull attacks most stridently in the "anti-Averroist" writings composed during his last visit to Paris from 1309 to 1311. The title of a work such as his *Liber de convenientia fidei et intellectus, quam habent fides et intellectus in subiecto et obiecto* (1309) neatly expresses his opposition to the theory that philosophy and theology concern separate objects of inquiry. However, Llull is not simply opposed to seeking distinct truths. He discourages as well the creation of distinct methods or vocabulary, thereby rejecting a feature that had virtually defined Scholastic learning since the twelfth century.[48] Ramon Llull simply did not share the "new vision of the potential complexity and variety of intellectual exercise"[49] that characterizes the work of so many twelfth- and thirteenth-century Scholastic authorities. His acute concern for the proliferation of opinions especially affected his view of the dialectical methods that his contemporaries cultivated so enthusiastically. His logical writings

regularly treat differences in argumentation or terminology as the result of equivocation, rather than contradiction, a tactic that allows him to assert the similarity, rather
than the difference, of conflicting doctrines.[50]

Finally, Llull's opposition to the diversification of academic inquiry reflects not
only fears about the reception of pagan error but also the traditional moral criticism
of secular learning as vainglory or *curiositas*.[51] Virtually all of Llull's charges against
the schools echo commonplace complaints from the antiacademic satire and invec-
tive of his era.[52] His objections to the sophistications of Scholastic argument recall
the castigations of monastic, especially Carthusian, polemicists, as well as doubts
raised by university masters such as John of Jandun.[53] Llull's criticisms go far beyond
lambasting the moral failings of students or masters, however. He opposes generally
the development of academic philosophy or theology as professional vocations.[54] His
ideal of inquiry is the *sacrum studium* defined so well by Rupert of Deutz in the early
twelfth century and still alive in the monastic spirituality of the thirteenth.[55] Hence,
it is not difficult to regard Llull's advocacy of the *reductio artium ad theologiam* as
an intervention in the debate, still urgent in his day, over the relative merits of classroom and cloister.[56] Mendicant teachers of the mid-thirteenth century continued to
warn their students about the dangers of corrupting theology with too much philosophy.[57] The controversy over university studies was especially acute among Cistercian
authorities of this era.[58] Yet Llull's hostility to the schools is not absolute. He does
not mimic a severe monastic critic like Peter Damian, who dismisses outright all
study of the arts and simply declares that "Christ is my grammar" (*Dominus vobiscum* 1; Ep. 8. 8). Rather, Llull offers his Great Art as a scheme for turning all learning
toward its ultimate object, divine truth.

Llull's Great Art as an Art of Arts

Given Llull's commitment to the ideal of retracing the arts to theology, it is easy to
understand why he regularly advertises the unification of knowledge as a major
benefit of his Great Art. His system is capable of attaining such an ambitiously
comprehensive goal, he claims, because its general principles embrace the particular
principles from all branches of learning. Simply put, the Great Art is an art of arts.
Therefore, all particular branches of knowledge are subsumed—or "implicated," as
he prefers to say—in the Great Universal Art of Finding Truth. Llull usually relies
on three basic tactics for demonstrating this implication: distinctional exposition of
categories from a field of knowledge; moralization of inquiry in that field in order to
reveal its spiritual lessons; and direct application of his own Great Art to another
discipline. Thanks to Llull's reliance on these tactics, his accounts of the arts and sciences typically neglect two topics that Latin and Arab authorities commonly consider
fundamental, namely, the definition of *ars* itself and the organization of the various
arts and sciences. His study of older Islamic philosphers would easily have brought
to his notice works like Alfarabi's popular treatises on the origin and classification
of knowledge. Contemporary encyclopedists like Vincent of Beauvais (*Spec. doct.*

1.9–22) typically begin their compilations by surveying the various concepts of knowledge, philosophy, and art. Llull's disregard for these issues seems especially puzzling, since he calls his own system an "art" and this term appears ubiquitously in his oeuvre. Perhaps Llull considered Scholastic analyses of these questions—such as Aquinas's commentary (chap. 5–6) on the *De trinitate* of Boethius or Giles of Rome's treatise on the differences between rhetoric, ethics, and politics—to be superfluous, if not pernicious, contributions to the diversity of knowledge in the schools.[59] In any case, his disregard for any systematic explanation of the interrelations among the various arts rejects what was arguably one of the most important achievements from the schools of the preceding century.[60] A few examples from Llull's writings illustrate how he instead uses distinctional exposition, moralization, and application of his own system to define a single unitary system for all learning, including the arts of eloquence.

Distinctional exposition and moralization are Llull's two fundamental tactics of argumentation, which he employs both within the system of his own Great Art and in certain texts not based directly on its methods. An excellent example of their use apart from the Great Art is his *Doctrina pueril,* a didactic primer composed around 1282–1283 for his son. This work uses the traditional division of divine and human letters to organize a wide-ranging series of *distinctiones* and other divisions. Its one hundred chapters, divided into ten sections, in effect offer a thirteenth-century, popularized rewriting of Cassiodorus's *Institutiones.* The first nine sections comprise seventy-two chapters that review the elements of Christian dogma: the fourteen articles, the Ten Commandments, the seven sacraments, the seven gifts of the Spirit, the seven blessings, the seven joys of the Virgin, the seven virtues and vices, and the three laws. The tenth section, entitled "On the Seven Arts," devotes twenty-eight chapters to reviewing a wide range of secular learning and moral theology, in the following order: (73) grammar, logic, rhetoric, (74) geometry, arithmetic, music, astronomy, (75) theology, (76) law, (77) natural science, (78) medicine, (79) mechanical arts, (80) princes, (81) clerics, (82) religion, (83) converting the wayward, (84) prayer, (85) the soul, (86) the human body, (87) life, (88) death, (89) hypocrisy and vainglory, (90) temptation, (91) nutrition, (92) movement, (93) customs, (94) the four elements, (95) fate and fortune, (96) the Antichrist, (97) the seven ages of the world, (98) angels, (99) hell, and (100) paradise. This sequence broadly leads from secular learning to sacred truth, using conventional categories from the arts and theology as *distinctiones* to organize moral instruction. It begins with a definition of art (*art*) as "a plan established *(ordonament e establiment)* for knowing the purpose of something about which one desires knowledge" (73.1).[61] The terms "plan established" perhaps recall the emphasis on fixed standards in Isidore's definition: "Art is truly so-called because it consists of the precepts and rules of art" (*Etym.* 1.2.2). The reference to "purpose" may also recall an often-cited Aristotelian maxim: "For art seems to be nothing more than a definite and fixed procedure established by reason, whereby human acts reach their due end through appropriate means" (*Anal. post.* 2.19 100a3–9). Despite its somewhat tautological diction, this idiosyncratic characterization of art is in fact one of the few definitions available from Llull's entire oeuvre.

Chapters 73 and 74 from the *Doctrina pueril* use the traditional scheme of the seven liberal arts as a simple *distinctio*. The preeminence of Llull's own Great Art and his hostility to the schools preclude the elaborate allegorical representations of the seven arts or extended praises of their contribution to human culture, like those found in so many medieval authorities.[62] Although these two chapters unmistakably divide the seven liberal arts into the ancient divisions of trivium and quadrivium, Llull almost never uses these terms.[63] Chapter 79 of the *Doctrina pueril* treats the traditional category of the mechanical arts in a way that clearly illustrates Llull's tendency to moralize the arts and sciences. His exposition says almost nothing about specific mechanical crafts, but instead offers social criticism of parents who fail to teach their children a trade and of artisans who misguidedly aspire to live as wealthy burghers. The political values implicit in these criticisms suggest that chapters 79–81 comprise a redefinition of the traditional "three estates" as mechanicals, princes, and religious. Similar redefinitions appear in other thirteenth-century authorities, such as Jacques de Vitry.[64] Llull uses these three estates as a loose *distinctio* for organizing moral *exempla* about political science.

Where the *Doctrina pueril* relies on distinctional exposition and moralization for retracing all secular knowledge to sacred truth, Llull's *Aplicació de l'art general* of 1300 displays superlatively and exclusively the "application" of his Great Art to all other fields of learning. This correlative application becomes Llull's preeminent method of explaining how his system functions as an art of arts, although distinctional exposition and moralization remain constant features of his work. From the late 1290s on, Llull seeks with increasing zeal to demonstrate the universal applicability of his Great Art. He composes a series of works that attempt to reform all other arts and sciences by basing them on the terms of his own system: these writings all have titles like *Nova geometria*, *Nova logica,* and so forth, where the adjective "new" indicates their reforming purpose. The *Aplicació de l'art general* offers a sort of manifesto for this project, which Llull eventually summarizes in the lengthy section on "Application" from his *Ars generalis ultima* of 1308, which is the last complete version of his entire Art. Similar sections of application also appear in many of Llull's other writings throughout his later years. This extrapolation of the Great Art to all other arts and sciences implies Llull's popularizing and antiacademic attitudes in its attempt to allow facile, virtuous, and correct acquisition of all knowledge. The *Aplicació de l'art general* underscores this function in its use of vernacular verse. A modern editor of the text has complained that this poetic form makes its arguments harder, rather than easier, to grasp.[65] However, the bold strategies of verbal and conceptual association necessary to correlate terms from each field of knowledge with those of Llull's system also contribute to the undeniable obscurity of the *Aplicació*. The doctrine presented in the *Aplicació de l'art general* is even more rudimentary than that offered in the *Doctrina pueril*. It covers seven disciplines: theology, philosophy, law, medicine, logic, rhetoric, and ethics. This selection obviously does not correspond to any scheme of seven liberal or mechanical arts, but may imitate other general classifications of knowledge, like Hugh of St. Victor's (*Didasc.* bk. 2) or Dominicus Gundissalinus's (*De div. philos.* prol.). Of course, where these authorities seek to demonstrate the diverse concerns of each art, Llull seeks to affirm their unitary basis in his own system. He divides his treatment of each art into several "distinctions" that explain how elementary doctrines from the art depend on the Absolute Principles, Rules, and so forth of the Great Art. This explanation consists largely in simply asserting this derivation, while providing little explication of the doctrines indicated by those terms.

For example, the discussion of law cites the commonplace axiom of distributive justice, "rendering unto each his own," and mentions as well the commonplace division between "natural" and "positive" law (ll. 566, 629–30). The rest of the text simply reiterates the need to understand these concepts through the terms of Llull's Great Art. The "distinction" on application of the Lullian Rules to law explains that:

> You will learn how to form questions
> and to give answers for them
> according to the plan *(ordonament)* of law,
> by following the questioning
> that is in this distinction,
> following its plan *(ordonament)*
> of affirming or denying
> as you see us employ it;
> so make the application
> wherever you seek truth *(retràs raó)*
> according to the example given for it
> in this Art truly. (ll. 661–72)[66]

The reference to "this distinction" probably indicates the corresponding section of the complete Lullian Art, since these few lines from the *Aplicació* offer so little instruction on jurisprudence itself. The *Aplicació* evidently assumes a reader already familiar both with the Great Art and with law.[67] At best, Llull's verse treatise simply advertises the promise fulfilled in other works such as the *Nova geometria, Nova logica,* and *Rethorica nova.* The main value of the *Aplicació* seems to be its zealous insistence on the possibility, if not the necessity, of accepting the Lullian Great Art as an art of arts. However, its almost exclusive reliance on the correlation of Llull's vocabulary with terms from other arts and sciences makes it difficult to see whether this application of Llull's system consists of anything more than a kind of wordplay, offered as a semantic filing system or "one-size-fits-all" scheme of *distinctiones.* The Alphabet and the Principles of the Great Art appear to offer a highly schematized application of the techniques of alphabetization and classification that Scholastic authorities were striving to develop, in order to ease the task of quickly finding information in books. Llull's system promises a method for achieving this goal through one book alone.

Ultimately, the *Aplicació* suggests two broad and related consequences of adopting Llull's Great Art as an art of arts. First, the application of Llull's program to any art is fundamentally an exercise in moralization; that is, it seeks above all to establish the moral finality—to "rectify" in Anselmian terms—that branch of knowledge. The preeminence of this objective explains why texts like the *Aplicació* emphasize the terms of Llull's Art, which guarantee attainment of that moral finality, while giving minimal attention to received doctrines. Second, this ultimate objective of moralizing and rectifying an art allows Llull considerable freedom in treating details of knowledge. That is, the end of ensuring that all knowledge leads to God justifies the means of demonstrating how this occurs. Llull relies on the metaphysics and epistemology of resemblance to explain how any correlation that the mind discovers also exists in reality, as chapters 2 and 3 will describe. At the same time, this liberty probably reflects as well a desire to avoid the vanity of striving to grasp subtle *curiositates.* Modern readers nonetheless may find startling the incongruous, unusual, or even absurd doctrines that Llull confects in the process of achieving the *reductio artium ad theologiam* through his Great Art.

The Lullian Arts of Eloquence: Rhetoric and Preaching

The scheme of Llull's Great Art described above provides the context for all his treatment of the arts of language. Although he occasionally cites all three arts of the trivium—grammar, rhetoric, and logic—his attention to each varies tremendously. Logic is the verbal discipline that Llull investigates most thoroughly. My earlier study, *The Spiritual Logic of Ramon Llull,* treats in detail his extensive efforts to develop a new art of demonstration by reforming conventional Scholastic logical doctrines. This study focuses on rhetoric and includes preaching, which are the chief exercises of secular and sacred eloquence that Llull recognizes. It also covers his scant treatment of grammar, which usually appears in connection with the arts of eloquence. In general, Ramon Llull's presentation of the language arts, like the entire project of his Great Art, serves his fundamental evangelizing and reforming goals. Nonetheless, we should recognize that even though rhetoric and preaching are clearly means toward Llull's ultimate ends, they are virtually obligatory means. All his plans for missions among unbelievers and for the moral regeneration of Christian society depend inherently on the effective exercise of verbal communication. The arts of language are surely central to the Lullian Great Art.[68] It is hardly surprising that virtually every page of his oeuvre mentions some problem of signification, communication, interpretation, translation, or persuasion. Indeed, the importance of language for Llull's enterprise perhaps explains why his accounts of communication offer some of his most innovative proposals, like the reduction of all logical fallacies to one, recognition of speech as a sixth sense, or arrangement of discourse by degrees of dignity.[69] To modern readers familiar with more conventional Scholastic arts of language, the results of Llull's efforts can seem bizarrely singular.[70] They scarcely resemble the literary devices that Geoffrey of Vinsauf uses to insinuate his ideals of personal and social reform in the *Poetria nova.*[71] Nonetheless, all of Llull's proposals for the arts of communication are consistent insofar as they offer tactics for fostering the love of God and neighbor.[72] This broad conception ultimately guides his most extended treatments of eloquence.

   The primacy of this objective, along with Llull's constant reliance on exposition through *distinctiones* and moralization, do not favor recognizing rhetoric or preaching as autonomous disciplines. Even though he occasionally cites the scheme of the seven liberal arts, Llull does not maintain the traditional distinction among the trivial arts, which the Schoolman William of Sherwood succinctly rehearses as "grammar, which teaches to speak correctly, and rhetoric, which teaches to speak ornately, and logic, which teaches to speak truly" (*Intro. in log.*). Llull more often deals with artful language in a general way, just as do earlier medieval compendia like the Isidoran *Sententiae* (2.29, 3.13). He does not develop the Aristotelian view, especially championed in the Arab tradition by Alfarabi, of linking poetics, rhetoric, and logic as arts of persuasion.[73] Among Llull's contemporaries, the closest parallel for his view of the language arts is probably Bonaventure's *De reductione*, which assigns to grammar, logic, and rhetoric alike the general tasks of producing fitting, true, and ordered speech (chaps. 17–18). This broad concern for the righteous use of language ultimately leads Llull to treat sacred and secular eloquence as a common discourse of Christian love and truth. The following discussion reviews the chief functions that Llull associates with rhetoric and preaching as arts of eloquence.

The art of rhetoric regularly appears in Llull's abstract enumerations of the seven liberal arts, but he rarely discusses the practical circumstances of its use. His narrative works, so rich in exemplary scenes of social and cultural activity, include few illustrations of either the academic study or the political, judicial, and epideictic exercise of eloquence. Nonetheless, some secular, vernacular context seems implicit from several passages in his writings. For example, the *Libre de contemplació* mentions the long-winded orator (*arengador*) who ruins a lovely speech by making it too long (359.27). The term *arengador* perhaps recalls the *ars arengandi* or art of civil oratory, developed in northern Italy and evidently practiced in Aragon during Llull's era.[74] Chapter 7 discusses the doctrines that he adapts from this art. Llull's works often mention as well the poetry of minstrels and jongleurs, which his *Vita* portrays him practicing when young. Nonetheless, most of his references to the practice of poetry or jongleuresque lyric simply condemn it for the moral license that it fosters. Thus, Llull devotes a complete chapter of the *Libre de contemplació* (chap. 118) to excoriating the evils of minstrels and troubadours. Despite this antipathy, he does not hesitate to posit broad parallels between popular lyric and formal eloquence: in the *Libre de contemplació* he notes that "just as the minstrel has an art and means of making sound with the flute, so it is fitting that one have an art and means for saying rhetorical and orderly words" (359.1).[75] This comparison perhaps echoes the theoretical relationship between music and eloquence suggested by ancient encyclopedists such as Isidore (*Etym.* 3.15.1) and elaborated in contemporary manuals such as John of Garland's *Parisiana poetria de arte prosayca, metrica, et rithmica.*[76] However, Llull's tendency to conflate all practices of verbal ornament more likely reflects his insistence on their common moral finality. Thus, his frequent descriptions of divine jongleurs in the *Libre de contemplació, Libre de Blaquerna,* and *Libre de meravelles* use this traditional image precisely to urge reforming popular entertainment for purposes of moral edification.[77]

Most of Llull's references to rhetoric as a specific art of language concern its academic cultivation as a branch of the trivium. It appears thus in works from throughout his career, such as the *Libre de contemplació* (240.22–24, 359.1) of 1272, the *Ars mystica* (5.9.2.6) of 1309, and the *Liber de quinque principiis* (9.5) of 1312. He typically dedicates a whole paragraph or chapter to rhetoric in his encyclopedic works, such as the *Doctrina pueril*, the *Arbre de sciència*, or the *Ars generalis ultima*. Whether long or short, virtually all Llull's references to rhetoric as a branch of learning emphasize three basic elements: beauty, order, and propriety (observing the appropriate conditions for speaking). This passage from the *Doctrina pueril* is typical:

> Rhetoric is beautiful and orderly speaking through which words are agreeably arranged and one is often favorably heard.
>
> Rhetoric teaches how one should speak and which words one should say first or which last or in the middle; and through rhetoric words that are long seem short.
>
> If you, son, wish to speak rhetorically, give beautiful examples of beautiful things in the beginning of your speech; and let the best material of your speech be last, so that you will leave a desire for listening in the hearts of those that hear you.
>
> Time, place, truth, status, suitable length of time, necessity, and other things similar to these befit rhetoric. So, son, if you wish to speak rhetorically, it behooves you to harmonize all these things with your words, so that you will be pleasing to people and to God. (73.9–12)[78]

This brief characterization nearly exhausts the range of rhetorical devices and strategies that Llull develops in his longer works.[79] Subsequent chapters in this study analyze all these tactics and techniques in detail. Llull's overall conception of rhetoric as the beautiful, orderly, and appropriate exercise of language is clear in the organization of his major treatise on this art, the *Rethorica nova*:

Part 1. Order
        Chap. 1.   In the form, matter, and end of speech
        Chap. 2.   In the beginning, middle, and end of speech
        Chap. 3.   In petitions, accusations, and counsel
Part 2. Beauty
        Chap. 1.   Words (in form, matter, and end)
        Chap. 2.   Principles (truth, courage, affection, humility, continuity)
        Chap. 3.   Comparisons (positive, comparative, superlative; between parts of speech)
        Chap. 4.   Exempla (twenty-four complete exempla)
        Chap. 5.   Ornament (dignities, colors, gesture, apparel)
        Chap. 6.   Statements (conjunctions and disjunctions among parts of speech)
        Chap. 7.   Proverbs (forty-nine proverbs)
Part 3. Knowledge
        Chaps. 1–9.   Lullian Absolute Principles
        Chaps. 10–12. Lullian Relative Principles
        Chaps. 13–21. Lullian Rules
Part 4. Love
        Chaps. 1–10. Ten proverbs and exempla to illustrate loving speech

The first and second sections correspond nominally to the emphases on order, beauty, and propriety already noted from the passage in the *Doctrina pueril*. The third section virtually replicates all three emphases in itself, thanks to its comprehensive distinctional review of rhetorical lore using the Lullian Principles and

Rules. The prologue to the *Rethorica nova* suggests that Llull might have designed it originally as a kind of *ars praedicandi*, but the scope of its examples and precepts extend to virtually all oral communication.[80] The four parts of Llull's treatise obviously owe little to the five Ciceronian divisions of invention, arrangement, style, delivery, and memory, which the school curricula taught. Nor do they manifest any debt to the summaries of Aristotelian rhetoric provided by Arab authorities such as Alfarabi or Averroes, whose works Llull could have read either in Arabic or their medieval Latin translations.[81] Instead, Ramon Llull's conception of his Great Art as an art of arts, his treatment of intellection as a hermeneutic process, and his conviction that all use of language must serve the mind's quest for truth establish a clear, closed context for his treatment of all these traditional divisions. In fact, Llull's Great Art virtually subsumes invention and memory. Its simple Alphabet and *ars combinatoria* replace both the arduous task of finding arguments and the elaborate systems of artificial memory. For this reason Llull rarely referred to invention as a rhetorical operation and never wrote any work on mnemonics.[82] Nonetheless, esteem for the Great Art as a discursive machine and *ars memoriae* readily lead its Renaissance devotees to compose various Lullian treatises on the discovery of knowledge and artificial memory.[83]

Llull's *Rethorica nova* is his work that most obviously strives to define a general art of communication. Although it superficially resembles a manual for training preachers, such as Humbert of Romans's *De eruditione praedicatorum*, its scope corresponds better to a work of moral literature on speech, such as Albertano da Brescia's *De arte loquendi et tacendi*.[84] The *Rethorica nova* begins by declaring that "speech is the medium and instrument through which speakers and listeners come together for one end" (0.1).[85] The art of rhetoric, he explains, teaches orderly, ornamented, and beautiful speech, which pleases the listeners and thus achieves the harmonious union, mutual peace, and amity of speaker and audience. As authority for these claims, Llull cites the classical *sententia* "Speaking well is the basis of friendship," which he attributes to Seneca (0.2).[86] Quotations of ancient authorities are of course very rare in Llull's writings, but Seneca's acknowledged position as *magister moralitatis* for the medievals perhaps justifies its appearance here and illustrates as well Llull's debt to medieval moral literature based on Seneca's writings.[87] Of course, the union that Llull most desires is common belief in the one true Faith, and hence he specifically recommends using his *Rethorica nova* to compose sermons. Nonetheless, his general regard for rhetoric as a means of fostering community in human society is one of the features that most distinguishes his accounts of eloquence from conventional Scholastic doctrines. Instead, this emphasis echoes similar concerns in Albertano's treatise.[88]

Llull's accounts of preaching focus, as we would expect, on techniques for composing sermons. They usually treat the same major concerns of beauty, order, and propriety found in his accounts of rhetoric. Preaching was probably the exercise of artful language that Llull knew best.[89] However, his proposals on this art certainly do not acknowledge the entire range of methods employed by his contemporaries. Instead, his precepts usually reflect the simpler practices of popular preaching, rather than the more sophisticated methods of the university sermon. He often cites the latter only as an example of the style that popular preachers should avoid. Llull's focus on popular preaching undoubtedly reflects his zeal for evangelism and reform in society at large. Indeed, popular preaching occupies a central place in his general conception of human communication: it stands as the most formalized exercise of language in a range of uses that includes less formal applications, from simple conversation and friendly correction to giving counsel and making public addresses. Llull's writings offer numerous scenes illustrating the exercise of popular preaching. The *Libre de Blaquerna* mentions holy men sent out to preach "by examples and customs and through metaphors and similitudes,"[90] that is, to exercise the traditional evangelical ideal of *docere verbo et exemplo*.[91] Another passage from this work tells how a certain monk, eager to evangelize rural audiences who live far from any church, sought out shepherds in the mountains and forests:

> In a meadow near a lovely spring stood a number of shepherds watching their animals. The monk came to that meadow and greeted the shepherds. He said that he was a preacher for shepherds and asked them to lend an ear to the sermon that he wanted to tell them. The monk preached to the shepherds with exempla in order to foster better their devotion. The sermons that the monk delivered were so pleasing to the shepherds that they pondered *(cogitaven)* daily what the monk preached to them. Their pondering led them to love honoring God and praying to our Lady. The monk spent seven days with them in that place. On the eighth day, he took leave of them and went to preach to other shepherds in other locales. (66.22)[92]

The mention of the pleasure that leads to cogitation implies the attention to beauty and order, since Llull usually treats these as the causes of the audience's pleasure. The claim that exempla are particularly appropriate devices to employ with uneducated audiences underscores Llull's ultimate concern for disseminating truth: preachers should strive above all to enlighten and thereby save their listeners. Preachers who ignore this objective, especially by using a style or devices too sophisticated for their audiences, incur his criticism. For example, the *Rethorica nova* tells of

> a certain episcopal officeholder in whose cathedral church there was an archdeacon. The bishop was very learned, but the archdeacon was only somewhat educated. Now where the bishop preached lofty words and subtleties using the art of rhetoric, the archdeacon preached humble words piously and based on love. This power of love was so great that the words of the archdeacon, lovingly proffered, edified the people more than the subtle words of the bishop. (4.5)[93]

The bishop clearly fails to observe propriety in speaking by choosing a style ill-suited to his audience. The beauty and order that Llull considers appropriate for the popular exercise of eloquence are not necessarily the same as the ornaments and devices taught in academic rhetoric or the *ars praedicandi*. Indeed, Llull often denounces grandiloquent or inflated preaching, as in his *Cent noms de Déu* (26.7) and his *Liber de praedicatione* (2.B.2.91.2.1). The *Lectura super artem inventivam* succinctly states that verbal ornament is a secondary, but understanding and love a primary, feature of preaching (3.2.852). Although similar criticism commonly appears in contemporary guides to preaching—such as the *Tabula exemplorum* (no. 246), Étienne de Bourbon's *Tractatus de diversis materiis praedicabilibus* (no. 294), or Humbert of Romans's *De eruditione praedicatorum* (1.7)—Llull's exclusive emphasis on this problem is another indicator of his antiacademic attitudes. The passage cited above from the *Libre de Blaquerna* nonetheless illustrates Llull's insistence that a pleasing discourse will somehow be edifying as well. Beauty, order, and propriety are the foundations that sustain the listeners' pleasure and lead to their enlightenment.

Llull's major work on preaching, the *Liber de praedicatione,* clearly demonstrates his concern for the creation of beautiful, orderly, and appropriate discourse. This treatise consists of three disparate parts: a lengthy review of the Great Art, a brief explanation of nine "conditions" of preaching, and a long collection of 108 model sermons. Chapter 10 analyzes in detail several specimens from this collection. Here we may consider his presentation of the Great Art as a basis for preaching and especially the nine conditions that he specifies as general principles of the *ars praedicandi.* The prologue announces Llull's desire to expound homiletic art according to the Principles and Rules of his Great Art, because "they are general principles for everything. And a book about preaching needs to have general principles and general rules, in order to have great material for finding those things that ought to be said in preaching."[94] As explained above, Llull's applications of his Great Art to other disciplines tend to expound his own system at the expense of details from those disciplines. Hence Abraham Soria Flores, the modern editor of the text, concludes that the *Liber de praedicatione* necessarily displays more dissimilarity than similarity with other *artes praedicandi.*[95] Although scholars might see little resemblance between Llull's text and contemporary aids to preaching, the prologue stresses how well the Lullian Art solves one of the thirteenth-century preacher's most vexing problems, namely, finding material, especially for purposes of exemplification. Through Llull's system,

> the preacher can find, exemplify *(exemplificare)*, and also apply purposefully the secrets of beings (showing the natures of things and the way that good or bad things have to occur) with the Senses, Imagination, and Reason. Listeners will rejoice from this instruction, because people will be able to experience naturally *(experiri naturaliter)* in themselves and in others those things that the preacher who knows this art preaches. Thus the preacher will be able to impress well, movingly *(affectuose)*, and clearly glorious virtues and customs upon the listeners. The listeners will be able to adopt virtues easily, and remove and extirpate vice from themselves, by knowing how virtues increase and decrease; and likewise for vices and sins.[96]

This passage is among Llull's most explicit statements of how the audience's pleasure constitutes persuasion. His claims assume the importance of beauty and order in the selection of material and the organization of the discourse, as chapters 4 through 7 will explain. Here, it is sufficient to recognize that the "secrets of beings" and "natures of things" found through the Great Art are Llull's own Principles. The most striking feature of this passage is the claim that a sermon moves an audience when the preacher selects exempla illustrating those Principles and "impresses" them on the listeners, so that they "naturally experience" those Principles in themselves. Sermon theorists and lay audiences alike tended to consider preaching effective if it moved an audience to remorse, usually accompanied by copious weeping.[97] However, Llull's processes of experience and impression rely heavily on metaphysical and epistemological relationships of resemblance, as explained in chapters 2 and 3.

The discursive techniques that achieve this experience and impression are the subject of the opening section from the second distinction of the *Liber de praedicatione*. Here Llull reviews nine conditions of preaching, which he designates with the letters B through K from his Alphabet. There is, as always in Llull's Great Art, no inherent connection between the meanings of these letters and the combinatory manipulation of the letters themselves. Llull uses these conditions to expound a very miscellaneous group of precepts, similar in scope to the second or third distinction of the *Rethorica nova:*

B. Exposition (four exegetical *distinctiones*)
    1. through prior and posterior being
    2. through degrees
    3. through senses of "living"
    4. through senses of "Church"
C. Division
    1. by hypothetical proposition
    2. by categorical proposition
    3. by dividing a word
    4. by exposition and application of the sermon
    5. by recapitulation
D. Organization
    1. of the prologue with an exemplum
    2. of a suitable place, the status of listeners, and statements
    3. of an opportune time, with brevity and prolixity
    4. of an honorable life
E. Investigation or Application (of elements from Llull's Art)
    1. by combining letters
    2. by mixing Principles
    3. by Rules
    4. by the nine Subjects
    5. by virtues and vices
F. Proof
    1. from believing holy authorities
    2. from understanding (demonstratively or by reduction to the absurd)
G. Comparison (of Subjects from Llull's Art)
    1. between one substance and another
    2. between a substance and an accident
    3. between one accident and another
H. Multiplication
    1. of reasonings through Llull's Art
    2. of understanding with authorities and arguments
    3. of loving
    4. of praise for God and the saints

   I.   Ornament
      1. coloring one noun with a noun or adjective
      2. adorning the Intellect with knowledge rather than belief
      3. adorning the Senses with beautiful sensations
      4. in delivery
   K.   Request or Prayer
      1. after stating the theme and dividing the sermon
      2. teaching listeners how to pray to God
      3. praying to God through contemplation, using Llull's Art
      4. praying to God for happiness in the next life

This section of Llull's treatise offers a virtually paradigmatic example of his reliance on distinctional, moralizing exposition: it explicates the various senses of the term "condition" as applied to preaching. This term recalls the enumerations of similar elements in authorities such as Humbert of Romans. However, Llull's nine conditions include far more than the considerations of character, delivery, and preparation usually treated as conditions by contemporary theorists. Just as in the first three distinctions of the *Rethorica nova,* Llull's precepts cover a very eclectic range of devices concerning beauty and order, while ignoring many other aspects of homiletics. Perhaps for this reason Llull calls these nine conditions "preparations for the sermon, so that the preacher might proceed through them in preaching" (2, intro.).[98] Or his scheme may simply assume a prior knowledge of the *ars praedicandi.* In this case its function would simply be to demonstrate the application of Llull's Great Art to preaching.

    Thus, the *Liber de praedicatione* extends preaching to include the entire scope of argumentation exercised through Llull's Great Art, just as the *Rethorica nova* associates rhetoric with the general use of language to foster human community. The *Liber de praedicatione* frequently reiterates the general inventional utility of his system in the initial sections that review the Great Art.[99] However, subsequent sections from this review progressively assimilate the art of preaching into Llull's own Art, and thus include fewer and fewer references to the preacher. In some instances, a section begins without mentioning at all its relevance to sermon composition.[100] Other sections conclude by simply mentioning alternative discourses, examples, or proofs omitted for the sake of avoiding prolixity.[101] The final sections of the first distinction apply Llull's Rules to his Subjects, the virtues, and the vices. It begins review of the Subjects and virtues with the claim that Llull's method provides the "preacher" with great material regarding these topics, but the treatment of the vices mentions only the Lullian "artist."[102] Within these sections there are virtually no references to the preacher or preaching. Ultimately, the *Liber de praedicatione* demonstrates how superficially Llull applies his Great Art to the *ars praedicandi.* A curious indication of their limited coincidence appears in the final lines of the first distinction: there Llull calls his system an "art of preaching/predicating and solving problems" *(ars praedicandi et solvendi quaestiones)* (1.C.3.9.K.2).[103] This play on the dual sense of the verb *praedicare* in effect employs a *concordantia verbalis* to identify preaching with the combinational predication of terms in Llull's Art.[104] It probably reflects as well a common confusion between preaching and teaching as practical clerical duties.[105]

Conclusion

Ramon Llull offers his Great Art of Finding Truth as an art of arts that will retrace all human knowldege, including the arts of eloquence, to divine wisdom. He attempts to accomplish this ambitious aim by subordinating the usual arts and sciences of the university curriculum to his own Art in a relationship that parallels the traditional service of philosophy to theology. Llull believes that because his own Art is based on divine principles, its application to all the arts and sciences will rectify these and thereby forestall further deviation of secular from sacred truth. This application consists preeminently in the distinctional and moralizing exposition of all *scientia* as *sapientia*, the ingenious and often difficult interpretation of every humanly generated datum of science as a cipher of divinely inspired wisdom. Llull often claims that his system in fact simplifies the quest for truth. Hence, Ramon Sugranyes has aptly described the Great Art as "an ingenious mechanism" for shortening the spiritual labor necessary to know God, by explicating all human knowledge as particular manifestations of the universal *veritas salutifera*.[106]

Viewed in relation to the development of Scholastic philosophy and theology in the thirteenth century, Llull's project appears entirely conventional, and even somewhat antiquated. However, the schools were not the sole or even the immediate context of Llull's enterprise. He sought to promote evangelism and reform throughout Christian society at large, as a realization of the *vita apostolica*. His Great Art perhaps offered its combined scheme of apologetic debate and private meditation as a guide to the "mixed life" of action and contemplation. That a layman could develop such a comprehensive alternative plan for spiritual perfection is certainly one of the most remarkable features of Llull's entire career. The strident anti-Scholastic polemic that accompanies his proposals should remind us that they have as much to do with competing claims of social or cultural authority as they do with philosophy or theology.[107] Llull's Great Art appears almost a sort of lay revolt to seize control of the intellectual and spiritual technology that, as Llull understood it, made the *veritas salutifera* accessible. This challenge to clerical authority, as much as the suspected heterodoxy of his ideas, probably provoked the inquisitorial investigation of Lullists in the later fourteenth century, just as the Lollards' propagation of lay preaching and vernacular theological study eventually provoked the repressive Arundel Constitutions of 1407 in England.[108]

The arts of communication like rhetoric and preaching are fundamental components of that technology. Extending the modern idiom, we can see that Ramon Llull regards them as the preeminent "mass communication media" of his culture. He is certainly not the only writer of his era who finds technical parallels between secular and sacred oratory.[109] His broad conception of these media determines his concern for a few basic aspects that he finds in all their applications: beauty, chiefly in the selection of appropriate exemplary material; order, both in the organization of discourse and in the circumstances of its delivery; and propriety, especially regard for the appropriate time, place, and behavior in speaking. These aspects display little connection with the Ciceronian precepts studied in the schools. Likewise, they display little concern for the questions of formal stylistic devices, the role of imagination and mimesis, or the contribution of rhetoric to syllogistic reasoning that exercise various Arab authorities.[110] They may reflect Llull's youthful training in the lyric art of the troubadours, but his concern for beauty and order as strategies for leading the mind to truth more likely derive from doctrines of devotional literature.[111] Llull's commitment to evangelism and reform explains why the *ars praedicandi* would inspire most of his precepts. However, his descriptions of the preacher's art display only incidental knowledge of the elaborate university sermons of his contemporaries. His conception of preaching is instead eminently popular, and in fact embraces practically any exercise of moral exhortation, controversialist disputation, or catechizing.

Ultimately, Ramon Llull attributes to rhetoric and preaching the same purposes that he ascribes to every other branch of learning, namely, loving, honoring, and serving God. By helping to lead oneself and one's neighbor to God, the orator or preacher exercises *caritas* verbally. Llull's reliance on distinctional and moralizing exposition readily allows him to reorganize received commonplaces or precepts in order to define rhetoric or preaching in this way. He treats both arts as exemplary systems of discursive *rectitudo,* arranging them according to the relationships of similitude, analogy, and homology that he finds among the terms, vocabulary, or categories known to him. In analyzing Llull's exposition of this material, subsequent chapters will show in detail how he revises elementary doctrines of rhetoric and the *ars praedicandi* into new arts of language whose ultimate function is to make the discourse of *caritas* serve evangelism, moral reform, and spiritual perfection alike.

2

Language as Being

The analysis of Llull's Great Art as an art of arts in the previous chapter notes at many points that his system comprises a vast program for interpreting all creatures as signs of the Creator. The Lullian Art is truly a universal guide to *allegoria in rebus* and *allegoria in verbis*. It treats all knowledge and being as a book laid open for human reading. This conception of the universe as text is, of course, an ancient, if not universal, way of making sense of the world.[1] It certainly flourished in the medieval Christian West; indeed, Ramon Llull's work is perhaps the outstanding testimony to its diffusion as a popular "worldview." The easiest way to grasp this perspective is to imagine that it regards the existence of all things, their understanding by the human mind, and their representation in words as somehow homologous. Llull's Great Art especially reinforces such a homology because his system establishes a common metaphysical basis for words, concepts, and things alike.[2] Lullian metaphysics is insistently "superrealist" in both a subjective and an objective sense: it tends to conflate the content of understanding or expression with the actual concept or word itself. Since for Llull that understanding or expression includes the perception of so many spiritual truths, this superrealist metaphysics is already a virtual *allegoria in rebus*. Applied globally to things, concepts, and words, it is in fact a universal allegory, a kind of metaphysics of meaning. Insofar as Llull assumes that this meaning necessarily exists in reality prior to existing in thought or language, he never doubts that the world is always speaking even if no human ears or hearts are listening.

Participated Resemblance

Llull's metaphysics finds the meaning and explains the existence of all things, concepts, and words through relationships of "participated resemblance."[3] That is, he seeks likenesses among beings as manifestations of natures that they share or in

34

which they "participate." Although sometimes identified as a specifically Neoplatonic doctrine, the premises of this metaphysics have appeared throughout Western philosophy from the Pre-Socratics to Descartes. In Llull's era, the axioms of this metaphysics of participated resemblance were commonplaces in the learned culture of Christians, Jews, and Muslims alike. Modern scholars recognize the contribution of this metaphysics of participated resemblance in many guises: M.-D. Chenu regards it as a "symbolist mentality"; Michel Foucault calls it "the prose of the world"; and J. B. Allen sees it as a practice of "assimilation."[4] The diversity of these explanations aptly indicates the constructive role that principles of participated resemblance play in so many fields of cultural endeavor, from the plastic arts to learned inquiry to social ritual. In the thirteenth-century West, the application of these principles underwent a notable reorganization in the schools. The Schoolmen's enthusiastic reception of Aristotelian metaphysics favored its explanation of resemblance as a form acquired through causes *(Metaph.* 10.3, 12.3–5). This view tended to build over, rather than to demolish, traditional Neoplatonic theories of likeness as a shared nature. Consequently, many older axioms concerning the metaphysics of likeness remained authoritative for Saint Thomas and his contemporaries.[5] Ramon Llull would have been unlikely to find any educated person unable to accept the claim that likeness between two beings must involve some real relationship between them. However, claims concerning this "realism" did come to receive much closer scrutiny and clearer differentiation of the relationships involved, especially thanks to the arguments of nominalism. Ramon Llull continues to invoke those relationships as self-evident "necessary reasons" drawn directly from the order of creation and applicable without revision to any field of inquiry. His unwillingness to scrutinize and differentiate these necessary reasons, especially according to Aristotelian metaphysical doctrines, is one significant measure of his alienation from the Schoolmen. In fact, the separation of the metaphysics of participated resemblance into special systems such as Llull's Great Art marks the onset of the slow process through which "the profound kinship of language with the world" dissolved in Western culture.[6] Some appeal to the metaphysics of participated resemblance appears on virtually every page of Ramon Llull's writings. It would be impossible to analyze here the entire range of its contribution to his ontology, epistemology, or semiotics. But for the purposes of understanding his arguments about the arts of eloquence, we will consider the three basic principles of this metaphysics that most directly affect his theories of language: likeness, order, and influence.

Likeness

Likeness is unquestionably the most important of these principles. A representative summary of its role appears in this selection of maxims concerning likeness *(semblança)* from chapter 156 of the *Proverbis de Ramon:*

1. A likeness is the image of something else.
2. Accidental forms are likenesses of substantial forms.

4. Every effect has some likeness to its cause.
5. Every act is the likeness of its power.[7]
7. Every likeness is a creature.
8. Every power naturally delights in its likeness.
10. Where one likeness participates most with another, it resembles it most.
11. Likenesses are either parallel or contrary.
14. One likeness comes from another.
16. All likenesses sustained in a body are from one common likeness.
17. Specific likenesses were cocreated in a common likeness.
18. All influence *(impremsió)* exists through likenesses.
20. The influences that heavenly bodies have here below are their likenesses.[8]

These axioms, which virtually cite tenets from the Neoplatonic authority, the *Liber de causis* (e.g., 115, 211), define the most fundamental relationships in Ramon Llull's Great Art. The whole nature and operation of the Absolute Principles, the Relative Principles, and the Rules of Llull's Art depend on likeness. Since the Principles are also the essential constituents of the Godhead, this metaphysics of participated resemblance is a theological as well as an ontological model, a veritable "ontotheology," to borrow Heidegger's term.[9] Llull's insistence on recognizing real likenesses of the Creator in all creatures places him in a tradition of Christian ontology that reaches from Augustine (e.g., *De Gen. lib. imp.* 16.57)[10] to Hugh of St. Victor (e.g., *Exp. in hier. coel.* 3)[11] and Aquinas (1a.44, 3). Llull often rehearses the argument that this likeness draws creatures to their Creator, a doctrine especially developed among earlier authorities such as Aelred and Anselm, and widely available in popular summaries of their theology such as the *Compendium speculi charitatis* (chap. 1). His views regarding creatures as symbols of the Creator especially parallel doctrines from the Victorines, and their adapation by Saint Bonaventure.[12] Indeed, it is difficult to know whether Llull would understand a metaphysics of participated resemblance apart from this Christian "creationary exemplarism." Nonetheless, he assumes that its axioms are equally acceptable to his Jewish and Muslim contemporaries. These axioms include the postulate that similarity results from some constitutive concord, while dissimilarity results from some constitutive contrariety, among any beings. In other words, "[L]ikeness reveals the inner nature of things."[13] Things necessarily produce other things like themselves: "[T]he things that creatures make, they make like themselves."[14] Conversely, lack of similarity results from a fundamental diversity in nature. The paradigm of this similarity and dissimilarity is the distance that separates humans from God.[15]

Order

In addition to this constitutive likeness, Llull's metaphysics of participated resemblance relies on another principle often considered quintessentially Neoplatonic, if not characteristic of the entire medieval worldview: this is the necessary existence of order or hierarchical gradation among all beings.[16] Aquinas's appeal to it in his five proofs of God's existence is the locus classicus of its apodeictic value in Scholastic philosophy (1a.2, 3). Llull's *Phantasticus* defines order as "the form with which one arranges many things for one purpose" (term. 5),[17] thus implying its fundamental role in the return of the many to the One. The Great Art formalizes this order of the many and the one in its nine Subjects, which range from God to the simple elements. This passage from the *Libre de demostracions* succinctly illustrates the necessary truth of this universal order:

> It is known that some goods are greater and others lesser and that some goods are neither greater nor lesser. Thus the heavens are greater than the sun, the sun than the moon, the moon than a star, rational animals than irrational, irrational animals than plants, plants than stones, substance than accident, the soul than the body, sensation than seeing, seeing than smelling, love than hope, and so forth for other things like these. (2.38.1)[18]

Llull presents this hierarchy as an enormous structure of proportionally homologous levels of existence, through which one traces the degrees of similarity and dissimilarity or concord and contrariety that indicate the relative participation and alienation among beings. By far the most important corollary of this universal order is the teleology that it allows: it defines a relation of subsistent dependence for every being, except God, the highest. According to the *Libre de demostracions,* "[I]t necessarily happens that if a lesser good exists, then a highest good exists" (2.27).[19] The lesser always depends in some way on the higher. Thus, the *Phantasticus* explains that a higher spiritual level of existence "orders" *(ordinat)* a lower corporeal level, as a cause does its effects (term. 5).[20] However, the *Liber de inventione maiore* also adds the important limitation that "between the greatest and the least there is no likeness" (3.9).[21] Hence, the gulf between creature and Creator remains insuperable, except through divine grace. Llull's exhaustive meditations on this problem are undoubtedly one aspect of his system that attracted Nicholas of Cusas's later keen interest in the Great Art.[22]

Influence

Influence is the third basic principle in Ramon Llull's metaphysics of participated resemblance. He uses this term—or synonyms like "transmission," "impression," and "communication"—to name virtually any process through which one being affects another. This process commonly consists of transmitting a likeness from one thing to another, which thus establishes an affinity between them. The following maxims on communicative power *(comunicativa)* in the *Proverbis de Ramon* neatly summarize the basic functions of influence as a principle of metaphysics:

1. Communication is distant *(extrema)* participation.
2. A substance communicating its own nature, communicates itself.

4. When fire lends its warmth to air, fire gives of itself to air.
6. The sun does not communicate its brightness to fire, but rather a likeness of it.
9. The object does not communicate its essence to a power, but its likeness.
12. The Imagination communicates to the powers of the soul what it grasps from the Senses.
13. One power communicates to another its force.
14. Communication exists in creatures by appropriation.
17. From communication results a common nature *(propietat)*.
20. The communication of many goods multiplies goodness *(es molt bona)*. (chap. 174)[23]

The Neoplatonic paradigm of this influence is the Sovereign Good, whose power assures that "every goodness propagates itself" *(bonum diffusivum sui)*, a maxim that Llull cites almost literally in his *Liber de perversione entis removenda* (1.6).[24] This influence manifests itself in the natural "desire" or "appetite" of every thing for other things like itself. "Attraction is the natural inclination that joins natural appetites," declares the *Proverbis de Ramon* (161.1).[25] Everything seeks its like, the *Libre de meravelles explains:* "[I]t is natural that every creature desire its like; and insofar as some things resemble others more, so much more do they desire them" (2.13).[26] The hierarchy of likenesses governs this influence: "The strength of a force is more communicable through a greater than through a lesser principle," according to the *Arbre de sciència* ("Arbre de Jesu Christ" 6.87).[27] The *Libre dels àngels* avers that "[t]he force of a substance more readily influences any faculty when it is closest to the thing that receives the force" (2.5.4.).[28] Things seek most the being that possesses their qualities most fully, which is not necessarily one of them. "Just as nothing creates itself, so it does not attract itself," declares the *Proverbis de Ramon* (161.20).[29]

Signification

"Signification" is a term that Llull often uses to name this orderly transmission of likenesses. To modern eyes, this usage undoubtedly appears to project upon things relationships that arise solely in the mind, if not solely in language. In Llull's work, this projection is as real as the likeness, order, and influence that it organizes. The paradigm of this real signification is the mutual communication that exists among the Divine Dignities of the Great Art. For example, the *Ars generalis ultima* explains that "[s]ignification is an implied principle, for its definition is applicable to all explicit rules and principles. Thus, when Greatness is the principle that produces the good, the concrete Goodness signifies to Greatness that a great good produces great good, and likewise for the others" (10.36).[30] Llull's *Liber de significatione* of 1304 distinctionally surveys a wide range of metaphysical and logico-linguistic relationships, defining them all as types of signification.[31] Not surprisingly, he treats most cognitive functions as exercises in signification as well, as chapter 3 will show. The universal realization of this signification through being, mind, and language alike is evident in these definitions of signification from the *Liber de significatione:*

> General signification is through abstract forms. Thus Goodness signifies the common good, and Greatness the common greatness, and so forth for the others. Likewise genus signifies many species, species signifies many individuals, the whole signifies many parts, and so forth for the others.

> Accidental signification is like heat, which signifies heating, justice acting justly, motion moving, joy being joyful, and so forth for others similar to these. Likewise quantity signifies quantifying, quality qualifying, and number enumerating.

> Causal signification is like the maker, form, matter, and purpose. The maker signifies its effect and the effect its maker relatively. The form signifies matter, action, and perfection. The matter signifies passivity, form, and perfection. (1.2.3, 6–7)[32]

This complete collapse of metaphysical and logico-linguistic relationships is startling at first glance, confirming the modern fear that Scholastic philosophy too often fails to distinguish the structure of mental and extramental phenomena. However, Ramon Llull is neither a Schoolman nor a philosopher. At best, his treatment of all these relationships as varieties of signification acknowledges their function in Scholastic learning as accepted warrants for "implication." Since tracing the connections between all creatures and their Creator is the fundamental objective of the Lullian Art, it is scarcely surprising that he regards all relationships in language, thought, or being as "significant." These relationships are ultimately more important than what they relate, insofar as any word, concept, or thing always leads to another, and finally to God.

Thus Ramon Llull's Great Art of Finding Truth creates a model of universal signification based on the metaphysics of likeness, order, and influence. It is important to recognize that this signification does not simply conflate the realms of language, thought, and being. Llull always maintains that concepts and words are tokens of things or of relationships between things. The function of thought is to understand, and the function of language is to represent, being, rather than to supplant and contest it. In fact, Llull's most basic notions about the ontology of language constitute a fairly unremarkable, popularized version of the "Platonist linguistics" found throughout late antique and early medieval philosophy.[33] The central operative premise of this Platonist linguistics is the direct correlation of words with things, which appears in the general preoccupation for defining the status of words according to *what*, rather than *how*, they signify.[34] What distinguishes Llull's accounts of language is his combination of this basic Platonist perspective with an Anselmian doctrine of *rectitudo*, like that from the *De veritate*. Llull insists that words, concepts, and things all ought to function as homologous vehicles of truth.

The Metaphysics of Language

Llull's explanations of how this universal signification joins being and language develop continuously and copiously throughout his career, as an indispensable part of his Great Art. Although likeness, order, and influence remain the fundamental operative elements in this universal signification, Llull's presentation of them changes considerably over the decades. In order to appreciate how his arguments regarding universal signification support his theories of eloquence, we will consider two representative explanations. The first, from his early *Libre de contemplació*, expresses those elements in virtually paradigmatic form. The second, from his later *Rethorica nova,* offers Llull's most elaborate explanation of how likeness, influence, and order constitute a metaphysical basis for language.

Chapter 359 of the *Libre de contemplació* is one of the most quintessentially Lullian passages. Its title announces that it will explain "how someone adoring and contemplating God learns an art and method of speaking words rhetorically organized."[35] This involves reviewing the entire hierarchy of creation and then explaining how some creatures are nobler or worthier than others, and therefore more beautiful to name in language:

> Humble Lord full of mercy and grace! Just as in the heavens and among plants and in spiritual affairs one ought to seek those things about which one can speak most beautifully, so one ought to seek among animals those about which one can deliver and say the most beautiful words and most beautiful arguments and best deeds; for just as some animals are worth more than others and some are more beautiful than others, so one can say more beautiful and reasoned and pleasing words about some animals than about others.
>
> Since this is so, it is more beautiful to name an apostle than a cardinal and a cardinal than a bishop and a bishop or religious than a cleric, and it is more beautiful to name a burgher than a peasant and a knight than a burgher and a count than a knight and a prince than a knight and a king than a prince and an emperor than a king, and it is more beautiful to name good than evil and an honorable person than a sinner and health than illness and loyalty than falseness and peace than war and so on for the other things similar to these.
>
> Honored Lord! Just as it is more beautiful to name some men than others, so among beasts and birds it is more beautiful to name some than others, just like hawk, and falcon, and horse, and lion, and perch, and salmon, which are better to name than rooster, or vulture, or dog, or ass, or ray, or octopus. Hence, since this is so, whoever wishes to deliver beautiful speeches and make beautiful comparisons should know how to speak beautiful words, for from beautiful words one can compose beautiful writings and speeches; and one should know how to speak and make comparisons about the most beautiful parts of animals, for it is more beautiful to speak about what nature does not hide among rational animals than the dirty places where the expulsive power emits its filth and dirt. (359.19–21)[36]

Llull could easily have found some commonplace dialectical or semiotic principles to support this argument. For example, he could have applied to language the differential value that Boethius sees in the universe at large (*Top. Arist. Interp.* 3.1). Or he could have extrapolated Augustine's famous argument that all signs are to be valued for the things that they denote (*DC* 1.2.2–3.3).[37] However, as it stands, Llull's argument does no more than define a simple and broad verbal aesthetic in which beauty results from what words name rather than from the words themselves. For Ramon Llull, just as for William of Conches, "[B]eauty and dignity are scarcely separable in practice from the cosmological and moral meanings that he wishes to elicit."[38] Unlike William, however, Llull does not theoretically distinguish this beautiful meaning from the philosophical-logical analysis of language. In fact, Llull's remarks in this passage suggest that semiosis functions through the real communication or transmission of identity.[39] That is, his arguments imply a virtually magical connection between the affective power of words and the status of the things that they name. This assumption evidently ignores Augustine's distinction between the delight that language causes in, and through, the Senses *(De ord.* 2.11.34). It renders virtually irrelevant as well the Ciceronian distinction of instruction, delight, and persuasion as separate rhetorical functions *(Orat.* 21.69). Where Augustine distinguishes and ranks these three functions *(DC* 4.12.27), Llull's arguments ultimately imply that beautiful words will necessarily instruct and persuade. If this fails to happen, it is not the fault of language itself, but rather of the human mind, as I will explain in the next chapter.

This passage from the *Libre de contemplació* appeals broadly to likeness, order, and influence in order to organize concepts of worthiness, language, and being as homologous hierarchies. This simple model creates some difficult problems regarding the adequacy of theological discourse. According to Llull, God stands at the summit of both the linguistic and the ontological hierarchies, and thus "no words can be found or formed so well about any creature, as they can when one speaks about the Creator and the Creator's virtues, properties, and works" (359.13).[40] This claim appears merely to rephrase commonplace recommendations about Christian rhetoric. For example, Isidore specifies God and human salvation as the paradigmatic issues to treat in the grand style, as defined in the traditional scheme of three levels of style *(Etym.* 2.17).[41] At the same time, Llull's claim about the eminence of discourse concerning God indicates his preference for a *theologia positiva*. Although his arguments often recall Neoplatonic axioms, he rarely acknowledges the dilemma of divine ineffability described so acutely by Neoplatonic authorities such as the *Liber de causis* (5.57; 21.166) or Pseudo-Dionysius *(De div. nom.* 1). Indeed his *Proverbis de Ramon* avers that "[t]he name of God that one speaks is a likeness of God's name" (1.3).[42]

The latter claim suggests how the simple model of universal signification expressed in the *Libre de contemplació* ignores the critical analysis of theological language that motivated the development of so much Scholastic learning. The eucharistic controversies of the ninth and tenth centuries had already scrutinized the function of similitude in spiritual discourse.[43] For example, Lanfranc of Canterbury, in discussing Augustine's definition of sacraments as "sacred signs" *(De civ. Dei* 10.5), tries to explain how even "the sacraments always bear some likeness of the things of which they are sacraments."[44] For Llull's Scholastic contemporaries, the issue was much more urgent: recognizing the relatively literal, analogical, or metaphorical character of language used about God was fundamental to all theological inquiry, as Aquinas's treatment shows (1a.13). Llull's consideration of these issues in the *Libre de contemplació* sometimes extends as far as Lanfranc's, but rarely addresses the concerns argued by Aquinas. Instead, Llull's views display a preeminently moral, rather than a logico-linguistic or philosophical, emphasis. This focus even guides his handling of logical distinctions themselves. For example, a passage from the *Libre de contemplació* notes that the relationship between words spoken of God and words said about God's creatures parallels that between the shape of an animal in itself and the shape of that animal painted on a wall (359.14). This example implies an analogical view of theological language, although Llull never defines it as such. The example of the animal and its representation in a picture is, in any case, a standard Aristotelian illustration of equivocation *(Cat.* 1 1a3). Aquinas completely rejects equivocation as an explanation for theological language (1a.13, 5). Llull, on the other hand, eventually proposes a "universal fallacy of equivocation" as a means of explaining the divergence between his and his opponents' arguments. Their language, he maintains, wrongly relies on corporeal, sense knowledge in order to speak of matters rightly understood only through spiritual, intellectual knowledge.[45] Simply put, they refuse to admit the truths of faith instilled in the soul and heed only the empirical evidence offered to the Senses. Hence Llull often condemns their refusal to believe as a moral error in which a perverse Will constrains an Intellect that would otherwise accept truth. From this perspective, the function of eloquence is not difficult to define: it plays an almost wholly instrumental role as a means for communicating truth between minds.

During the early decades of his career, Llull appeared content to repeat his traditional, largely Neoplatonic model of universal signification based on the broad principles of likeness, order, and influence. The nature and operation of language within this model is largely unproblematic because it bears the same moral finality as all other creatures. However, in the 1290s Llull began to consider these issues much more closely and audaciously, just as he did many other philosophical and theological questions at this time. These developments perhaps resulted from the evolution of his own Great Art or perhaps from his increased contact with the schools. Whatever the motive, Llull attempts to provide in his *Rethorica nova* of 1301 a much more developed account of how universal signification governs the use of language. He achieves this innovation principally by refining his broad appeals to likeness, order, and influence into a more precise hylemorphic model of the nature of language. Similiarity, hierarchy, and communication are still fundamental principles of this model, but they appear expressed in the Aristotelian terms that Llull's Scholastic contemporaries would more readily recognize. The first distinction of the *Rethorica nova* introduces a comprehensive hylemorphic model of language in order to explain the order that should exist in language. This order, Llull asserts, consists of a form, a matter, and an end; each of these displays an essential and an accidental mode (1.1.0). He cites these basic divisions more or less consistently throughout the rest of the treatise. The distinction between essential and accidental being is, of course, a cardinal Aristotelian doctrine *(Metaph.* 7.4 1030a29–31). Llull's tripartite hylemorphic divisions are rather less conventional: he recognizes three terms—form, matter, and end—rather than the two—form and matter—that Aristotelian doctrine considers constitutive of a complete substance *(Phys.* 1.7 191a9–12). Within the system of Llull's Great Art, these three categories of form, matter, and end perhaps marked a stage in the development of his doctrine of "innate correlatives." However, the *Rethorica nova* nowhere mentions the correlatives, and the hylemorphic model used in this treatise does not display the systematic application achieved in Llull's full theory of the correlatives, as set forth in the *Liber correlativorum innatorum* of 1310.[46]

The hylemorphic scheme used in the *Rethorica nova* perhaps imitates ancient and medieval authorities who refer more broadly to the matter and form of words. For example, Llull's arguments resemble those of Proclus, who distinguishes the form and matter of language in his commentary on Plato's *Cratylus,* and thereby explains words "as *material* or phenomenal images of intelligible reality."[47] Similarly, later poetical preceptists like Geoffrey of Vinsauf (*Poetria nova* l. 1.1762) use the terms "matter" and "form" to name simple distinctions like that between content and structure.[48] Among twelfth-century commentators on rhetoric, William of Champeaux also uses basic metaphysical concepts to explain how "a case is an affair so informed that it tends toward some end" and "any affair with which an orator intends to deal is the orator's matter, which then becomes formed as demonstrative, judicial, or deliberative."[49] William's commentary somewhat loosely applies this metaphysical vocabulary to received Ciceronian doctrine. He uses terms like "form," "matter," and "end" as descriptive language without necessarily assuming a metaphysical function for these categories. Likewise, the anonymous twelfth-century *Summa sophisticorum elenchorum* compares the two dialectical functions of invention and judgment to matter and form, but does not attribute to them any precise metaphysical status: it simply states that "invention is like matter and judgment like form."[50] In similar fashion, Llull's own *Libre de contemplació* compares the addition of unnecessary words in a speech to the matter that complements form, but then corrupts it (359.27). The *Art demostrativa* warns that a preacher who fails to choose perfect material will fail to achieve a perfect form in a sermon, and thus his sermon will be useless to the audience (10.8.2). In all these cases, conventional Aristotelian doctrine serves as a sort of metaphysical analogy or exemplum for characterizing a linguistic or rhetorical relationship. Llull's *Rethorica nova*, in contrast, strives to define and then to apply one consistent hylemorphic model for language. Since contemporary modernist logicians and speculative grammarians likewise apply metaphysical categories exhaustively in their analyses of logico-linguistic elements, it is tempting to imagine that Llull's accounts reproduce their efforts. His results remain, nonetheless, far less systematic than those of the *modistae*. Ultimately, it is easiest to understand the tripartite hylemorphic scheme from the *Rethorica nova* as a kind of *distinctio*. That is, Llull employs the categories of form, matter, and end as three necessarily related terms whose sense he explicates each time that he applies them to some group of three linguistic or rhetorical features. He thus employs them as "metaphysical metaphors," just as some literary authorities use legal or grammatical metaphors.[51] Or rather, his schemes resemble the mystical exegesis of Hildegard of Bingen, who lists sound, goodness, and breath as the three "causes" of speech, and then explicates these components as a metaphor for the Trinity (*Scivias* 2.2.7). The following review identifies the distinctive functions that Llull associates with each of his three terms in his *Rethorica nova*.

The form of words, according to the first distinction, is essential when it comes from a word itself and is accidental when it comes from the addition of another word (1.1.1). Llull offers no example, but this division perhaps corresponds to the syntagmatic conditioning or word association defined in medieval poetics with labels such as *determinatio*. The second distinction of the *Rethorica nova* also attributes the beauty of words to their form, but without distinguishing essential or accidental modes. Instead, it simply posits a correspondence between this formal beauty and the beauty of the things that words name. As examples of words with beautiful forms Llull routinely cites "God," "angel," "man," "goodness," "greatness," "king," "queen," "sun," "lion," "rose," "emerald," and other terms that suggest his own Principles and Subjects.

The matter of words also contributes to their order, according to the first distinction, either essentially and properly or accidentally (1.1.2). Llull explains that essential or proper matter sustains the form of words just as the form of a ship is constructed from beams. His explanation of accidental matter is harder to understand:

> There is another accidental matter in speech, as appears in these words, namely, "queen," "greatness," and "goodness." For these are the accidental matter of this form, namely, "The queen has great goodness." Now this form "The queen has great goodness" gives color and beauty to this other form, namely, "The queen has great beauty," as is clear from the aforesaid. In the same way, these words "queen" and "beauty" are primary and proper matter with respect to these words "queen" and "goodness," which are accidental matter, if each matter is referred to the proper form mentioned for it. (1.1.2)[59]

Llull evidently proposes that the phrase whose form includes accidental material ornaments the phrase whose form includes essential material in the same manner that the words from the essential phrase constitute prime matter with respect to the words from the accidental phrase. The final line suggests that this is virtually a reciprocal relationship, in which case its paradigm is probably the mutual or coessential relationship of the Lullian Principles. The *Ars generalis ultima* offers a similarly reciprocal relationship when it explains that "[t]he rhetorician colors material with beautiful form, and with beautiful material ornaments or colors form" (10.86).[53] Just as it does for form, the second distinction of the *Rethorica nova* explains that words possess beautiful matter by virtue of naming beautiful things. As examples Llull mentions "angel" and "star," which are beautiful by virtue of their incorruptible spiritual matter, and "lady," which is beautiful because it designates *(designat)* sovereignty and judgment (2.1.2). While the beauty of an angel or a star clearly depends on its absolute hierarchy in the order of creation, the beauty of a lady in this example depends on the right exercise of political authority, which insinuates a moral finality that becomes patent in Llull's remarks on end.

The end of words, according to the first distinction of the *Rethorica nova*, exists in two modes, "the first in exposition *(explicando)*, the other in what one intends *(intendit)* by speaking and on account of which one speaks" (1.1.3).[54] These evidently constitute something like immediate and remote purposes, which Llull does not explicitly identify as accidental and essential modes. However, since he subsequently refers to the second mode as the "complement and fulfillment of speech" *(complementum verborumque perfectio)*, it seems likely to be the essential or proper end. Hence, the first mode must function instrumentally as an intermediate end. In this respect the two ends correspond to the Lullian intentions and necessarily involve the fundamental moral finality assumed in that doctrine. Llull's use of the verb "intend" and his emphasis on a speaker's ultimate intention as the "perfection" of speech perhaps associates discursive unity with a speaker's conscious intention. This association is a commonplace of literary criticism from ancient grammarians to Neoplatonic exegetes to Scholastic commentators.[55] The second distinction of the *Rethorica nova* more clearly invokes the Lullian intentions when it explains how words possess a beautiful end because their referents have beautiful ends. For example, "[I]ron is for plowing, for sewing, for cutting, and likewise for all other things that have beauty and comeliness from their ordained end" (2.1.3).[56] The beauty of this end clearly depends on a moralized understanding of each thing's purpose. The *Ars generalis ultima* expresses this moral finality somewhat more abstractly when it explains that Beauty exists more through the Relative Principle of Superiority than through Inferiority, "as is clear in rhetoric, where the rhetorician colors words more with a greater purpose than with a lesser one" (10.37).[57]

The examples of form, matter, and end cited thus far from the *Rethorica nova* all come from its first and second distinctions. Llull introduces them to explain, or better to organize, fairly basic remarks on selection of subject matter, word association, and speaker's motive. Few of the passages cited rely on the hylemorphic relationship between form, matter, and end in order to explain the features of discourse to which he applies them. The third distinction carries this application much further, a development that perhaps testifies to the later composition of this section of the treatise or perhaps simply results from the more detailed exposition demanded by the doctrines treated there. The most notable advance in its application of Llull's hylemorphic model is the explicit specification of a larger "form of beauty" that results from the combination of form, matter, and end. For example, in his explanation of verbal Difference, Concord, and Contrariety, Llull observes how the "form that completes the matter of its subject moves it toward its end, so that from the matter, form, and end results that certain formal beauty *(species)* that adorns speech in difference" (3.10.0).[58] This overall beautiful form perhaps corresponds to something like the general tone of a speech defined by some late antique authorities and often mentioned by later medieval preceptists.[59] Since this overall beautiful form is evidently the final metaphysical constitutent of perfected discourse, it may constitute a kind of comprehensive sensible species of the speaker's intentions for the audience.

One suggestively vague detail regarding the nature of this overall beautiful form appears in several passages where Llull compares it to light. For example, the concluding remarks on Goodness explain that:

> anyone who in these things applies to a good end the matter of goodness for whose sake it exists, makes a good form to come forth from these two. And from these three will result the beautiful form of speech that is the light through which good words will also be beautiful. When this is considered thus, it provides the knowledge that enables one to find the beautiful form of words through which one makes, composes, and arranges beautiful speech. (3.1.2)[60]

Elsewhere in his oeuvre Llull rarely invokes the "light metaphysic" favored by contemporaries such as Grosseteste.[61] Nonetheless, its tenets would certainly suit Llull's brand of Neoplatonic metaphysics, especially with respect to the function of emanation.[62] Advocates of a "light metaphysic" often identify light with the ultimate beauty, perfection, or nobility of a being.[63] Metaphors of light are also common in ancient and medieval authorities on poetics: Horace uses several in the *Ars poetica*

(l. 143), as does Geoffrey of Vinsauf in his *Poetria nova* (ll. 118–19). However, the most immediate inspiration for Llull's comparisons to light are probably the commonplace images of the preacher as a light guiding his audience.[64] Llull generalizes this metaphor of preaching as moral and doctrinal illumination to include both the aesthetic force of beauty and the persuasive force of goodness in the discourse. Thus, his comparison of the discourse's affective force to a shining light suggests that speech communicates beauty or pleasure in the manner that light propagates itself. The larger form of beauty evidently constitutes, as it were, the highest substantial form of a discourse, which propagates, manifests, or communicates the discourse's truth as its essential nature.

A second important, though not surprising, refinement in Llull's application of this hylemorphic model is the explicit recognition of the end as the preeminent constitutive element. For example, the account of how the Principle Goodness informs speech explains that "the goodness of form and matter should come from the end" (3.1.0).[65] The end mentioned here is presumably the speaker's purpose, as explained in the first distinction. The exact hylemorphic relationship between this end and the overall beautiful form is unclear, partly because of Llull's typically weak differentiation between substantial and accidental forms. It is noteworthy that the union of form and matter for a guiding end departs from Llull's usual tendency to establish coessential identity among metaphysical constituents. Insofar as this ultimate end corresponds to the speaker's good intentions, its preeminence underscores the importance of moral finality in Llull's conception of the nature and use of language.

Finally, in many passages from the third distinction, Llull applies this hylemorphic model to elementary grammatical, rhetorical, and moral doctrines without clearly specifying the role of form, matter, or end. For example, the account of the Principle Wisdom explains how anyone wishing to speak wisely "should first choose the matter, arrange it for a proper end, and prepare it according to proper form, so that the speech will be orderly and beautiful." The matter consists of ten conditions regarding the appropriate circumstances for speaking, which Llull considers as fundamental to eloquence as beauty and order. Llull concludes that "when the aforesaid conditions are observed in speech, and the words are—according to the matter, form, and end to which the speaker's intention tends—properly arranged, from such an arrangement a most beautiful form will result" (3.5.0; 3.5.2).[66] The hylemorphic terms introduced in this section seem merely to provide a somewhat abstract way of saying that a judicious match between the circumstances of speaking and the speaker's purpose will produce a pleasing speech.

Ultimately, this application of form, matter, and end in the third distinction of the *Rethorica nova* does not define a very rigorous metaphysical model for language. Instead, Llull somewhat broadly uses the terms "form" to indicate any aspect of compositional disposition, "matter" any subject matter, "end" a speaker's intentions, and "overall beautiful form" the affective force of discourse. Llull's vague and variable applications of these terms probably results from their use as devices of distinctional exposition, which encourages their flexible interpretation, rather than their consistent definition, from one application to another. Despite its somewhat diffuse explication, the application of this hylemorphic model in the third distinction of the *Rethorica nova* does demonstrate Llull's concern for the inherent moral finality of language.

Indeed, the most intriguing aspect of this hylemorphic model is perhaps its attempt to define an "overall beautiful form" that will necessarily impress a speaker's good intentions on listeners' minds. This metaphysical model of affective power in language displays superlatively Llull's quest for discovering the moral finality that should guide all exercise of eloquence.

Conclusion

This review of the *Libre de contemplació* and the *Rethorica nova* offers some idea of how Ramon Llull explains language according to a metaphysics of participated resemblance. This explanation did shift during his career, but its fundamental premises remained the same traditional axioms of likeness, order, and influence. Since these premises are foundations of Llull's entire Great Art, his application of its terms and categories to the metaphysics of language only reinforces the assumption that the same principles of likeness, order, and influence govern both words and things. However, it is essential to recognize that these principles do not function transitively between language and being. Rather, the natures of things virtually always determine the natures of the words that name those things; likewise, the relationship between words virtually always parallels the relationship between the things that those words name. Thus the fundamentally representational and therefore unequal relationship between language and being remains undisturbed by their common ontological basis. Consequently, many of Ramon Llull's claims about rhetoric or preaching concern the effective manipulation of words as tokens of things, that is, as tactics of "right representation." The arts of eloquence described by Llull consist preeminently in strategies for using language to transfer the truths of human and divine things from one mind to another: that is, they seek to guide the transmission of the likenesses of truth in an orderly fashion. The next chapter will analyze the sometimes elaborate schemes that Llull proposed for directing the mind's operation in the process of communication.

3

Language in Mind

Viewed from a modern perspective, the universe of signs that Ramon Llull describes seems naively anthropocentric: he attributes to every entity a value relevant only to human beings. Llull's universe is not only anthropocentric but also intensely logocentric: each entity's value consists chiefly in its contribution to the human soul's experience of truth. That experience is the central concern of all Llull's projects for evangelism, moral reform, and spiritual perfection. Consequently, his writings devote more attention to questions of epistemology and psychology than to almost all other philosophical topics. Both logically and practically, his concern for the soul's experience of truth precedes his interest in the arts of eloquence. Hence, the artful exercise of language is always a means to an end for Llull. Of course, we might say the same for Augustine or Cicero, insofar as they regard eloquence not as an end in itself, but as an instrument for persuading, instructing, and delighting. Llull could probably accept these broad classical objectives of eloquence and even the methods employed to achieve them, but he would understand them strictly according to his own general principles of epistemology and psychology. Like most aspects of Llull's work, his theories of knowledge and mind await comprehensive study. This chapter surveys those ideas most relevant to understanding his accounts of rhetoric and preaching. First it reviews the fundamental doctrines that organize his epistemology and psychology: the division of the soul into three levels, explanation of cognition as participated resemblance, notions of intellection as interpretation, and emphasis on the disparity between speech and thought. Then it analyzes examples from the *Libre de contemplació,* the *Rethorica nova,* the *Liber de praedicatione*, and Llull's proposals regarding speech as a sixth sense, in order to show how those doctrines inform his treatment of language. This analysis helps explain why the arts of eloquence—and all other arts, for that matter—possess so little autonomy in Llull's system. His Great Art assumes a model of thought and language that rigorously subordinates all other arts for investigating or communicating knowledge to the one goal of grasping divine truth.

The Divisions of the Soul

Llull propounds a neatly delineated model of human nature: each person consists of a body and a soul that unite sensitive, imaginative, and rational levels of operation. He always divides the rational faculties into the traditional Augustinian powers of Intellect, Will, and Memory.[1] His *Libre de ànima racional* of 1296 offers the fullest exposition of this plan, but it is remarkably consistent from his first to his last writings. The general basis of Llull's model is obviously Aristotelian doctrine from the *De anima* (bks. 2–3), probably as explicated and revised by Avicenna.[2] Although Llull's model corresponds basically to doctrines taught in the schools, it often diverges from typical Scholastic theories. The most obvious difference is his classification of Imagination as a separate level of soul.[3] No single Latin or Arab authority offers an exact precedent for this classification, but Alfarabi favors a very hierarchical arrangement of the powers of the soul in his summaries of classical doctrines, such as the *Philosophy of Plato and Aristotle* or the *Principles of Ancient Philosophy*.[4] Llull perhaps found a synopsis of Alfarabi's arguments about Imagination in some Arab compendium or merely simplified those arguments to suit his own purposes. Support for his very hierarchical scheme of sensation, imagination, and intellection would be available from various well-known Latin authorities. For example, Augustine distinguishes sensual, spiritual, and intellectual levels of "vision" in his *De Genesi ad litteram* (12.6–24), and describes the intermediary level as the faculty that holds "images or similitudes" of things for the mind to interpret.[5] This function correlates easily with the operations assigned to Imagination in Aristotelian psychology (*De an.* 3.3). Augustine's scheme might have come to Llull's notice from compendia such as Alcher of Clairvaux's *De spiritu et anima* (often attributed to Augustine) or from the writings of the Victorines. Hugh of St. Victor mentions a scheme of intelligence, imagination, and sensation (*Didasc.* 2.5).[6] Thus, Llull's classification of Imagination, like so many of his more unusual proposals, probably synthesizes basic doctrines adapted from traditional Arab and Latin authorities well known in his era. Indeed, Llull's willingness to redefine the mind's powers imitates the practice of earlier writers such as Isaac of Stella, who also reworked received doctrines into new schemes.[7] His treatment of Imagination definitely contrasts with the approach of contemporaries such as Aquinas (1a.78, 4), who usually follow Avicenna in treating the imaginative power as one of the internal senses. The *Libre de contemplació* mentions the internal senses as faculties for the exercise of contemplation (193.5), a focus that recalls the spiritual psychology of patristic or Pre-Scholastic authorities.[8] However, they play surprisingly little role in Llull's later acounts of psychology: scattered references to them do appear in the *Liber de ascensu et descensu intellectus* (5.1.10; 6.4.1) and in the *Metaphysica nova* (2.4.1). Some functions of the internal senses evidently contribute to his theory of speech as a sixth sense, but in general they disappear, perhaps because they unnecessarily complicate Llull's schemes for contemplation and demonstration.[9] Llull prefers instead a neat distinction between successive levels of sensation, imagination, and intellection, because this hierarchy best serves his effort to lead the soul from consideration of creatures to knowledge of the Creator.

Cognition as Participated Resemblance

The basic Aristotelian framework in Ramon Llull's model of human nature has led some modern scholars to regard his psychology as conventionally Scholastic.[10] However, his views are very heterogeneous, combining doctrines drawn not only from the *De anima* but also from traditional Christian spiritual psychology and moral theology. By far the most basic of these non-Aristotelian doctrines is the ancient tenet that "like knows like," which defines a model of cognition based almost exclusively on the metaphysics of participated resemblance, as described in the previous chapter. This tenet is axiomatic for a twelfth-century authority such as Hugh of St. Victor (*Didasc.* 1.1). The subsequent reception of Aristotle's *De anima,* with its explanations of cognition based on the metaphysics of causes, potentiality, actuality, powers, and objects, gradually limited the authority of this simple axiom in Llull's era.[11] Aquinas suggests that the principle of "like knows like" is unscientific when he attributes it to the Pre-Socratics and Plato (1a.84, 1–2). The Aristotelian theories certainly did not prevail everywhere or without modification: the academic debates on the nature and operation of the mind remained urgent throughout Llull's lifetime. Within the context of these debates, his arguments constituted a remarkably earnest effort to intervene from outside the schools on behalf of the older doctrines. Llull probably defended the ancient tenets so zealously because they were central to the traditional spiritual psychology and moral theology that he developed in his plans for contemplation, perfection, and evangelical action.

For Llull, the principle that "like knows like" is necessarily implicated in the view of human nature as a microcosm of the creation.[12] His *Libre de ànima racional* explains this well-known doctrine thus:

> The soul is a substance that participates with more creatures than any other substance, since it is conjoined with the human body; for that body participates with the heavens by receiving their influence and existing with them in the species body; and it participates with the four elements, because it is composed of all four; and it participates with plants, because it exists through the vegetative power; and it participates with the sensitive power because it exists through it; and likewise for the imaginative power. (2.4.8)[13]

The universal participation enabled by the homology of microcosm and macrocosm underlies all Llull's arguments about human cognition. Still, his explanations of their correspondence are rarely as developed as those of ancient authorities such as Boethius (*De musica* 1.1). Instead, Llull emphasizes the material basis of this homology, a feature that lends his model a strongly "naturalistic" tenor.[14] In this respect his arguments often resemble commonplace moralizing appeals to natural laws based on the four elements.[15] However, his emphasis on the intermediate place of humans between God and other creatures especially recalls theological arguments from Bonaventure.[16]

Of course, the most important consequence of this participated resemblance between humans and the universe is that it enables the transmission of likenesses from any other level of creation to the human soul. All knowledge or pleasure results from the common union of the *subjective self* with the *objective other.*[17] The power of this interaction depends on the proximity of the soul to its object in the hierarchy of existence, since "it is a natural law that where things are closer, they are perceived and understood sooner," according to the *Libre de contemplació* (162.7).[18] For Llull it is axiomatic that the mind grasps most readily objects that share its spiritual, intellectual nature; by contrast, it has great trouble in correctly apprehending material, corporeal objects. This axiom creates a fundamental difference between the epistemologies of Llull and a contemporary Schoolman like Aquinas. Where Saint Thomas avers repeatedly that things are known according to the nature of the knower (e.g., 1a.84,1; 84,7; 85,1), the entire *Libre de contemplació* is devoted to showing how the nature of the thing perceived determines the quality of perception. Llull insists that the mind must "seek those sense objects that are most suitable to demonstrating and signifying those intellectual objects about which one wishes to be certain" (169.3).[19]

The role of resemblance extends even to the processes of intellection and methods of reasoning themselves. A remarkable naturalistic analogy from the *Libre de contemplació* (291.1–2) asserts that just as air receives heat from fire because it participates with it, so the mind receives knowledge from significations and syllogisms because it participates with them and receives their likenesses. The paradigmatic metaphor for the soul's capacity to receive likenesses is a mirror. Llull develops this traditional image frequently in his *Libre de contemplació* (e.g., 174.8).[20] His *Art amativa* uses it thus in order to explain sensation:

> The glass placed over a colored subject receives the likeness of the color of the subject. The likeness that it receives is a real accident that is an image of the color of the subject in the glass. So it happens with other things similar to these, just as appears in a mirror, which because of its great translucency receives the likenesses of things from without, and these likenesses are real accidents; and so it happens with the five corporeal senses, such as the eyes, which really receive the images of substances, from the substances and the likenesses that the mirror receives from things without. (2.5.5–6)[21]

The association of the comparison to a mirror with the example of color appearing in a glass suggests illuminationist doctrines, which appear occasionally throughout Llull's writings. However, the most important feature in this passage is Llull's explicit insistence that these likenesses are real accidents of the Senses that receive them. When applied to the arts of eloquence, this realism helps explain how rhetoric and preaching necessarily communicate truth, goodness, or virtue by transmitting real likenesses of them in language. Nonetheless, Llull rarely uses the comparison to a mirror in order to explain how this occurs in the arts of eloquence, even though preceptists like Geoffrey of Vinsauf favor mirror analogies to explain poetic processes.[22]

The principle of cognition through resemblance is virtually inseparable from the program of Llull's Great Art as he originally conceived it, probably because it was already a fundamental tenet in the spiritual psychology that he adapted from other traditional authorities. His subsequent encounters with the schools fostered his attention and opposition to the epistemological and psychological questions debated there. Hence, his *Libre de ànima racional* takes up such controverted issues as the distinction between passive, active, and possible Intellect. Llull's treatment of these issues usually achieves only a superficial accommodation between his more traditional views of cognition as participated resemblance and the new theories based on Aristotelian principles of causation, actuality, and potentiality. In the *Libre de ànima racional* this result is obvious from Llull's constant reference to the objects of cognition as "likenesses" and "impressions" received from extramental substances (2.5.6).[23] A contemporary Schoolman like Aquinas typically prefers to call these "forms" or "species," and only occasionally "likenesses" (e.g., 1a.79, 3). Llull's *Arbre de sciència* comes closer to Scholastic theories when it explains how sensible species participate formally with the species of the object of sensation ("Arbre sensual" 3.3.2). This explanation from participation nonetheless appeals to the influence, transmission, or communication of that species between a sense power and its object. Llull rarely mentions the function of abstraction, which his Scholastic contemporaries consider crucial to defining cognition and intellection.[24] Instead he relies on his Great Art and the metaphysics of participated resemblance. For example, the *Arbre de sciència* explains that the Lullian Principles inform the Intellect with their own interrelationships of genus and species; it is this virtually constitutive participation between the mind and these predicables that allows the logician to consider genera and species in extramental beings ("Arbre humanal" 3.b.2, para. 4). Thanks to this insistence on the pervasive role of resemblance in cognition, Llull's explanations can barely acknowledge the instrumental value of intelligible species as "that by which the Intellect understands," in the words of Aquinas (1a.85, 2). Llull's epistemological arguments inevitably return to the ancient tenet that "like knows like." His later writings, such as the *Liber de ascensu et descensu intellectus* (6.2–3) and the *Liber de modo naturali intelligendi* (dist. 3), continue the assimilation of both Scholastic doctrine and terminology to his arguments and vocabulary. In these works the active and passive Intellect become this faculty's "innate correlatives," while the terms "likeness" and "species" appear interchangeably.

Intellection as Interpretation

The fundamental reason why Ramon Llull insists on regarding the forms involved in cognition and intellection as likenesses is surely the need to ensure the mind's participation in the processes of universal signification. Allegory, not abstraction, is the paradigmatic act of understanding for Llull. Just as every being is a sign, so the likeness that each being offers to the mind is a sign. Chapter 2 has already suggested how Llull's arguments regarding universal signification rely on the long tradition of *allegoria in rebus* developed by late antique and earlier medieval authorities. Perhaps the single best-known authority from this tradition is Augustine's definition of a sign as a "thing that, besides the impression made upon the senses, causes from itself something else to come into knowledge" (*DC* 2.1.1). The following maxims regarding signification *(significació)* from the *Proverbis de Ramon* concisely demonstrate this coincidence of understanding and signifying in Llull's program:

2. The perfection *(compliment)* of created Goodness signifies the perfection of uncreated Goodness.

4. The king's arm signifies the Power of God.
11. The greatest evil signifies the Sovereign Good through contrariety.
12. External operations signify internal operations.
13. Because you have little understanding, lesser things signify greater ones to you.
14. If you had great understanding, greater things would signify lesser ones to you.
15. One signification is an opportunity for another.
16. No Sense signifies such great Greatness as speech *(affatus)*.
18. Imagination does not signify such great Greatness as the Intellect.
19. Truth is signified more through the Intellect than through any other power.
20. No power signifies its object with as much difficulty as the Intellect. (chap. 81).[25]

These aphorisms suggest how Llull broadly considers understanding as a process of tracing and evaluating significations. A charming analogy from the *Libre de contemplació* explains the process thus:

> Just as a fisherman, *Lord,* catches one fish with another fish, so the human Intellect grasps and perceives *(pren e aperceb)* some meanings *(significats)* with others, because it understands some things through others; and just as fishermen often fish without a lure, so the human Intellect by itself, without anything else signified to it, but in the thing itself, understands and perceives many things through the meanings alone of the thing that it understands. (162.18)[26]

The pursuit of knowledge thus consists in the serial decoding of signs. Llull's *Regles introductòries* recommends that "you make metaphors, because knowledge begins there" (1.39).[27] Despite Llull's uncertain use of the term "metaphor" (analyzed in detail in chapter 6), pronouncements like this make it difficult not to recognize that the epistemology presented in Llull's Great Art is profoundly interpretative, hermeneutic, or even exegetical in character. Hence, Joan Tusquets aptly notes that for Llull, "to understand is to relate, to interpret what the thing signifies to us."[28] The preeminent model of this enterprise was undoubtedly the moralization practiced in popular preaching, scriptural exegesis, and ascetic literature, whose legitimacy as a "way of knowing" he would scarcely have doubted.

Indeed, Llull could hardly regard the quest for knowledge otherwise: if things offered their significations directly, if the mind grasped those significations completely, and if language expressed those significations univocally, then error or ignorance could scarcely exist. In fact, the world neither signifies directly, nor does the mind grasp signs correctly, nor do words express them univocally. An immense interpretative labor is necessary to understand the truth offered to humankind in the universe of signs that surround it. Llull's *Libre de contemplació* is his first comprehensive guide for this enterprise. It uses the verb "signify" *(significar)* to embrace a broad range of modes of semantic association, from the suggestive "implication" recommended in the *Rhetorica ad Herennium* (4.53.67) to the "signation" that leads from particulars to universals according to Giles of Rome.[29] Llull's expositions of these modes of association are rarely technical, but instead exploit the whole range of application that terms such as "sign" and "symbol" bear in medieval usage.[30] A paradigmatic example of his usage appears in chapter 357, which proposes the four senses of exegesis as universally applicable modes of knowledge:

> Hence, since tropology occurs through comparisons (like understanding a prince from a mountain), and allegory is when one understands from some event another in this world (like Holy Church from Jerusalem), and anagogy is when one understands from this world the next or from corporeal things spiritual things, then whoever wishes to understand these expositions should know the art and method of this chapter and of the other chapters that speak in the fashion of this chapter. (357.1)[31]

Llull's recommendation of fourfold exegesis illustrates the cultural authority that these divisions had achieved thanks to centuries of ancient, patristic, and Scholastic application.[32] The final line explicitly announces Llull's appropriation of moralization as a general model of cognition. He evidently regards this commonplace practice of popular preaching and spiritual literature as a universal—or at least a universally applicable—strategy for evangelism and reform. He in fact begins this chapter with the disclaimer that his arguments emphasize moralization for the benefit of laypeople who do not know Latin. This practice of moralization applies to any situation that requires elucidation. For example, another section of the *Libre de contemplació* stresses the need to order the Senses and the Intellect in the manner most able to grasp the moral signification available from visions, dreams, comparisons, and apologues (356.30).[33] The application of this practice to objects as diverse as visions and fables underscores how completely Llull seeks to moralize all knowledge, whether obtained through study or in daily life.

The orderly exercise of this universal moralization helps the human soul realize its Lullian "first intention":

> Since, *Lord,* some [cognitive] powers expound these expositions to others when they wish to receive them, one understands how to perceive and know the significations and proofs offered in similes, dreams, visions, words, signs, and other things sensed or understood. But when some powers do not wish to receive from others what these signify, then one fails to understand knowledge of the four expositions. For what they should expound historically they expound morally or what they should expound allegorically or anagogically they expound morally, and likewise for the other expositions. Thus people fail to understand use or enjoyment according to the final purpose for which they are created. (357.12)[34]

The last line of this passage unambiguously invokes the principle of *frui et uti* that Augustine applies to correct knowledge of signs and things (*DC* 1.3.3). Perhaps no passage from Llull's entire oeuvre reveals so clearly how traditional Christian doctrines of moral finality guide his arguments regarding right interpretation and universal signification. The emphasis on cooperation of the powers in this passage also illustrates the debt of Llull's arguments to Anselmian principles of *ordinatio* and *rectitudo*. These principles serve a discriminatory function in Llull's account of intellection. That is, they help guide the mind in its basic task of distinguishing worse from better or false from true meanings. This labor of "right thinking" is in effect the lifelong obligation of every Christian. Chapter 298 of the *Libre de contemplació* describes in detail how this corrective ordering is necessary in order to utilize each external and internal faculty of the soul. Maxims 13 and 14 cited above from chapter 81 of the *Proverbis de Ramon* indicate how difficult this task can often be.

The better or truer meanings of some signs are especially obscure. Llull accepts the ancient arguments that regard this obscurity as a license for allegorical interpretation.[35] Again, Augustine's *De doctrina christiana* (3.5.9–12.19) offers the paradigmatic Christian statement of this principle in its discussion of figural language. Llull typically argues the broad position that the more obscure any sign is, the harder the mind must strive to grasp its meaning. His *Libre de meravelles* expounds this general Augustinian argument in this exchange between its hero Felix and the sage hermit Blaquerna:

> Felix asked Blaquerna why the Prophets had spoken so obscurely about the coming of Christ Jesus. If they had spoken more openly, many people would have believed. [However,] these [people], ignorant of Christ's coming, are going to eternal fire. Blaquerna said that reason and faith are creatures of God, and where the Prophets spoke most obscurely about the coming of Christ Jesus, the human Intellect has an opportunity *(ocasionat és)* to excel in discernment *(exalçar si mateix en subtilitat)* and in seeking the internal or external acts of God. From these acts, where the coming of Christ Jesus is secretly announced, the Intellect understands more. The same follows regarding faith, which can increase by believing the coming of Christ Jesus where the Prophets have spoken most obscurely of it. (chap. 11)[36]

Blaquerna subsequently summarizes this doctrine as a general principle of intellection: "[W]here the likeness is more obscure, the Intellect that comprehends the likeness understands more highly" (chap. 14).[37] In short, the obscurity of a sign corresponds to the loftiness of its truth and the intellectual effort necessary to comprehend it. Thus, the introduction to Llull's *Libre de amic e de amat* claims that the cryptic brevity of its 365 "moral metaphors" will exercise the faculties of the soul in its quest for the divine. This is as close as Ramon Llull comes to advocating the traditional poetic justification for *integumenta* or *involucra*.[38] His limited training and interest in the literary methods of the *auctores* probably explains his superficial grasp of this doctrine, but he might have known similar ideas from troubadour poetics,[39] where this obscurity is also regarded as indicative of a text "rich in sense or ornament."[40] The recourse to metaphor for philosophical speculation by Arab authorities, especially Avicenna, would also encourage Llull's use of figural language.[41] His reliance on metaphors, similitudes, comparisons, allegories, and all other forms of exemplary ornament certainly confirms his appreciation of their value, as chapter 6 will explain.

The Disparity between Speech and Thought

Llull's treatment of all intellection as an interpretative process might seem a boldly postmodern argument, an anticipation of recent theories about the inescapable indeterminacy of meaning.[42] But it may also be regarded as one more illustration of a habitual Scholastic inability to separate the functions of thought and language. It is both obvious and predictable that Llull regards speech and thought as corresponding oral and mental modes of discourse. This ancient assumption is virtually a canon of the "logocentric" tradition in Western philosophy.[43] It appears as axiomatic already in Plato and Aristotle, and continues largely unchallenged in the arguments of Stoic, Middle Platonist, and Neoplatonist authorities.[44] It remains an integral element of the psychological and epistemological models of Western Christian authorities from Augustine to Aquinas.[45] Since Llull's Great Art purports to be a system for finding truth by "discoursing," we might expect him simply to affirm Saint Thomas's view that "speech is the proper operation of reason" (1a.91, 3 ad 3). Allusions to this axiom do in fact appear throughout Llull's works, including the *Rethorica nova* (e.g., 3.16).

Nonetheless, Llull also distinguishes thinking and speaking as radically disparate vehicles of meaning. This division, which is fundamental to both his epistemology and his theories of language, arises from the innate duality of human nature. Of course, the ancient dichotomy of body and soul is axiomatic for Llull. Consequently, he accepts that all cognition and communication must proceed through the powers of sensation, imagination, and intellection that organize the body and soul. For example, his *Petitio* to the Council of Vienne succinctly asserts that "the Intellect makes knowledge first with the Senses and Imagination about corporeal and imaginable things, and then ascends to spiritual objects, such as God, the angels, and the soul, and makes knowledge objectively with and about those things that are neither imaginable nor sensible."[46] This is the normative itinerary of understanding for Llull; as noted already, he rarely appeals to divine illumination as a source of understanding. At the same time, Llull subscribes to the long tradition, best represented by Neoplatonic authorities such as Pseudo-Dionysius (*De eccles. hier.* 1.), that denigrates speech as a material function of the body, alien to the spiritual operations of the soul.[47] Hence, the *Libre de contemplació* (155.4) avers that "understanding exists inside the soul and speech exists outside the soul"; as a result, "understanding is closer to the soul than speech is." Moreover, "understanding is more united to the soul than speech is"; therefore, "understanding is better prepared to demonstrate truth than speech is."[48]

In short, Llull regards language and thought as similar yet different, conjoined yet conflicting. The *Libre de contemplació* (155.3) tries to reconcile their affinities and disparities with the argument that "speech is created in humans to reveal and signify understanding, and therefore speech is a servant subject to understanding."[49] From this alliance of unequal partners arise various difficulties. For example, the sense of hearing cannot in itself grasp language fully. Thus, the *Libre de contemplació* (125.10) explains how in "everything that one hears with corporeal ears, the spiritual ears hear error, because the spiritual ears understand that the corporeal ears do not perfectly hear what they hear. This is because many things resemble truth, which are false, and many things resemble falsehood, which are true."[50] The inherent inadequacies of speech often lead to error. The *Libre de contemplació* (125.16) further explains that "because we are weakened by sin, we say things in our mouths that are not like those that we imagine or think in our hearts; therefore our hearing is almost in vain in our ears."[51] This inadequacy is comparable to the difficulty of understanding numerous foreign languages, which seem like the tongues of animals (125.19).[52] The inadequacy of oral speech for expressing the thoughts of the heart is another Augustinian commonplace (*DC* 1.6.6; *De mag.* 14.46; *De ord.* 2.14.39–19.51). This contempt for speech and hearing also simply particularizes the general scorn for the sense organs as "portals of sin," a traditional figure of moral theology that Llull himself cites in his *Liber de praedicatione* (2.B.2.87.2.2).[53] As consequences of the Fall, all these failings will disappear in paradise. The *Libre de contemplació* (127.3–6) explains how the constraints of time, place, speech, and sounds that restrict human communication in this world do not exist for souls in glory. These claims repeat common views regarding the perfection of the resurrected body, as sketched by Bonaventure (*Brevil.* 7.7–8) and Aquinas (*Summa contra gentiles* 4.86). Reference to these issues in a devotional work such as the *Libre de contemplació* is hardly remarkable, but their appearance also reminds us that moral theology served as a major source of ideas about language for Llull.

One of the most important of these received ideas is the Augustinian correlation of three commonplace dichotomies: material language versus spiritual thought; the letter versus the spirit; and faith versus reason.[54] Pre-Scholastic authorities often invoke this correlation, and Llull too cites it repeatedly. Indeed, he insists so vehemently on the correspondence between material language, the letter, and faith that he seems to reject any useful understanding of the letter through the Senses. This attitude contradicts the long tradition, stretching from Philo to the Victorines and the Schoolmen, of recognizing at least a minimal integrity in literal meaning.[55] Of course, this preference for the spiritual sense over the material letter certainly finds encouragement in the moralization that Llull practices so amply. His esteem for allegorical exegesis recalls the early Scholastic authorities who considered the development of interpretative skills a means of refining intellectual virtues. This perspective appeared at least as early as the ninth century, contributing to the general growth of the literate culture that enabled a project like Llull's in the thirteenth.[56] But by his era, the rise of historical criticism in Scholastic biblical exegesis once again favored interest in the letter of the text. The following passage from the *Libre de contemplació* appears to contrast the older perspective that Llull prefers with newer Scholastic interests:

> Since speech fails, *Lord,* to signify all things, and since the Intellect cannot understand all things, it therefore happens that speech has two meanings: some are literal meanings, the others are spiritual meanings. The literal meanings and expositions are from the Senses, like saying "every man is an animal"; and the spiritual meanings and expositions are of the Intellect, like you, *Lord,* who said "let us make man in our likeness and image." Hence, speech and understanding conflict more in the spiritual than in the literal exposition, because speech is inadequate to signify things of the Intellect as well as of the Senses. (155.20–21)[57]

Llull's first example is a commonplace of Aristotelian logic (*Cat.* 3 1b10–16) while the divine command of Genesis 1.26 is the prooftext of exemplarist theology. It is surely no coincidence that they express natural and divine definitions, respectively, of human existence. Llull may have found them paired thus distinctionally in one of his sources. The two phrases epitomize the irreconcilably disparate levels of truth available to the realms of the Senses and the Intellect. Thus Llull identifies knowledge based on sensation with Scholastic dialectic and truth grasped through understanding with the Christian revelation. He repeatedly argues this correlation in the anti-Averroist writings composed during his last visit to Paris.

Hence, the *Libre de contemplació* (155.12) urges great care in determining the truth in words: the mind must always strive to sort the true from the false meanings in speech, just as one winnows grain from chaff. Language that expresses the mysteries of the Faith, such as "God died" or "Christ was born of a virgin," absolutely requires the Intellect to rectify its absurd literal meaning (155.7–10, 13). The same holds for metaphors such as the "eyes of God" (155.11). Where Aquinas analyzes such expressions as metaphors of divine functions (1a.3, 2 ad 3), Llull takes them as challenges to exercise spiritual apprehension. The *Libre de contemplació* (155.15) suggests that this higher understanding at best achieves a kind of "mediation" (*mijà*) between speech and the Intellect. This interesting term perhaps echoes the views, which Aquinas (1a.13, 2) quotes from John of Damascus, that such expressions provide a "mediate" knowledge of God because they signify God's relationship to something else, or something that follows from God's nature or operations. This lone mention of mediation is as close as Llull's arguments come to recognizing analogy in the fashion of the Schoolmen. The final paragraphs of chapter 155 from the *Libre de contemplació* explain how the Scholastic disciplines of logic and scriptural exegesis—which Llull evidently invokes as paradigmatic human and divine arts of understanding—confront that disparity. In logic, when speech and understanding agree they "engender" syllogistic argument, because "sensual things do not impede the intellectual and the intellectual arrange *(endressen)* the sense"; lack of this agreement and arrangement engenders paralogism. The chief cause of this failure is the corrupted sensual nature of humans (155.22–24).[58] Likewise, in scriptural exegesis, literal exposition involves the Senses and leads to error. Spiritual exposition, on the other hand, involves the Intellect and leads to truth. Reprising the teachings of Paul (Rom. 7–8) and Augustine (*DC* 3.5.9–9.13) on the freedom of the spirit, Llull denounces those people who remain enslaved to their sensual nature and thus understand no more than animals do (155.25–27).

Passages like these from chapter 155 of the *Libre de contemplació* demonstrate the moral imperative of striving to reconcile, however imperfectly, the rift between material language and spiritual thought. Indeed, without some accommodation between language and thought, Llull's own Great Art—not to mention communication in general—would be impossible. One strategy for achieving this accommodation is the rectification and ordering of the errant human Senses or Intellect, as explained above. Llull also tries to facilitate this task by clarifying—and even reorganizing—the structures or operation of the mind itself. For example, question 54 from the *Quaestiones per artem demonstrativam solubiles* explicitly divides mental discourse into two varieties, intellectual and sensual, in order to explain how the mind understands both corporeal and spiritual beings:

> The soul generates intelligible speech in one way, and sensible in another way. It generates intelligible speech when it gathers intelligible images, such as Goodness and the rest. From this it generates the speech through which it attains an intelligible object, such as God, an angel, the soul, Memory, etc. or also the Goodness of God, an

angel, the soul, and so forth for the others. But when it gathers images *(phantasias)* from sensible things (which are likenesses of sensible things), then the soul generates sensible speech, thus attaining sensible things without a Sense.[59]

This passage clearly illustrates Llull's concern to protect the higher mode of spiritual truth attained by the Intellect from the lower mode of material knowledge gathered through the Senses. At the same time, the emphasis on these modes as parallel varieties of discourse displays his persistence in seeking their accommodation. This treatment of the two modes as types of speech may seem an unremarkable elaboration of the commonplace notion of thought as the "language of the mind."[60] The authority of this notion perhaps explains Llull's reliance on it in developing his own theories. For Christian theology, the locus classicus of this theme is Augustine's account (*De trin.* 9.7.12, 15.10.18, 15.15.25) of the *verbum quod intus lucet* (word that shines within). For philosophy and the arts, an equal authority is Boethius's distinction (*In De interp.* 1) between written, oral, and mental *orationes*.[61] Llull probably knew it best from Pre-Scholastic authorities on spiritual psychology.[62] Treatments of this mental discourse also appear in Scholastic accounts of faculty psychology, such as Aquinas's *De differentia verbi divini et humani*.[63] This mental language constitutes the basis for communication between angels, as Llull explains in his *Libre dels àngels* and his *De locutione angelorum*.[64] Llull's analyses of this communication differ little from those offered by a Schoolman such as Aquinas (1a.107). Yet, as Joan Tusquets aptly indicates, this mental language is vital to Llull's larger model of communication: it completes a communicative continuum, in which animals have sound but no sense, angels sense but no sound, and humans both sense and sound.[65] Llull's continued speculation on this scheme eventually leads hims to "discover" (as he says) that speech is a sixth sense, and thus make the parallel between language and thought a constitutive feature of human nature.

The Psychology of Communication and Persuasion

The four topics reviewed thus far—the divisions of the soul, cognition as participated resemblance, intellection as interpretation, and the disparity between speech and thought—constitute the common bases of virtually all Llull's speculation on the operation of language, including the arts of eloquence. For Llull, human language is largely an application of human psychology, thanks to the ineluctable but difficult bond that joins the discourses of voice and mind. This psychology of language defines the processes of communication that Llull often invokes in his rhetorical and preaching precepts, which I will analyze in subsequent chapters. Since his paramount concern is the transmission of Christian truth, the psychology of verbal persuasion and argumentation is especially important to his plans for rhetoric and preaching. As I noted already in chapter 1, Llull's accounts of eloquence usually identify this persuasion and argumentation broadly with the appropriate exercise of beautiful, orderly language. He sometimes explains persuasion simply as the influence of his Principles in language, and thus virtually subsumes eloquence into the metaphysics of participated resemblance. At the same time, Llull strives to show how the artful exercise of language, as he defines it, will induce both voluntary belief and rational assent concerning the highest truth and good. Llull's view perhaps reprises the estimation of rhetoric favored by some thirteenth-century theologians, who regard it as the final art of the trivium in plans that retrace all the arts and sciences to theology.[66] This perspective values rhetoric over logic or dialectic as a means of achieving love or hate of the truth, rather than mere assent, as Bonaventure argues in his *Collationes in Hexaëmeron* (4.18). Nonetheless, Llull never mentions the theories of *affectus* that Alexander of Hales and other thirteenth-century theologians had developed into a "theological poetics" based on appeal to the emotions.[67] Attention to functions that we might regard as explicitly "affective" is very limited in Llull's writings. Ultimately, Ramon Llull's characterization of the persuasive power of language corresponds best to Augustine's emphasis on *caritas* as the necessary basis of Christian eloquence.[68] Indeed, Llull's ideal of propriety in communication is probably the loving union of speaker and audience that he cites in the prologue of his *Rethorica nova*. The remainder of this chapter analyzes the two ways in which Llull applies his basic psychological and epistemological principles to explaining the nature and function of language. The first, illustrated with examples from his *Libre de contemplació, Rethorica nova,* and *Liber de praedicatione,* makes speakers and listeners responsible for rectifying their use of language so that it serves human moral finality. The second, represented in his proposal of speech as a sixth sense, tries to control language by integrating speech into the hierarchy of the soul's sensitive, imaginative, and intellective powers.

Ramon Llull's acute concern for making language serve human moral finality guides most of his arguments about the psychology of language throughout his career. Just as it does for so many other issues, the *Libre de contemplació* establishes the basic psycholinguistic model found in many of his later writings. The lengthy section of this text devoted to orderly use of the Senses and the Intellect (chap. 103–226) includes several chapters dealing exclusively with the relations among speech, hearing, and reason (chap. 125–27, 155, and 210). Although these chapters treat language within a psychological or epistemological context, their ultimate concern is always moral. They teach tactics for the mind to recognize sinful discourse, such as blasphemy, gossip, flattery, praise, reproach, false witness, and similar "vices of the tongue."

Chapter 125 includes several noteworthy references to elementary doctrine regarding the sensation of speech in hearing. For example, Llull explains that sounds result from "things moving and striking and speaking and shouting and sounding" (125.1). Oral language in particular "is engendered and formed in the air by the movement of the tongue and lips of the mouth, and then is heard in the ears, and from the ears comes the understanding in the heart" (125.22).[69] These rudimentary remarks adapt commonplace doctrines that ultimately remit to Aristotle's *De anima* (e.g., 2.12 424a17–18 or 3.2 425b26–6a12), but also circulate in school texts adapted from Boethius's long commentary on the *De interpretatione* (chap. 1). Llull's very limited explanation probably relies entirely on an encyclopedist such as Vincent of Beauvais (*Spec. nat.* 25.50–60). His focus on the ethics of communication rarely leads him to consider the difficulties in sensation of sound analyzed by a Schoolman such as Albertus Magnus.[70] Instead, he concentrates on those functions of hearing that relate to moral rectitude. Thus, he repeatedly relates hearing to the "ears of the soul" (125.8–9, 22; 126.3, 15; 127.8). Augustine's "ears of the heart" (*Conf.* 4.15) and their perception of the inner word are cornerstones in the contemplative structures erected by twelfth-century authorities such as Richard of St. Victor (*Ben. maior* 3.9).

The contemporary *Libre de demostracions* also discusses the preeminence of speech as the object of hearing in animals who produce vocal sounds; this relationship is most worthy in rational animals, that is, humans (1.49). Llull's interest in this anthropocentric view, which probably echoes Aristotle (*De an.* 2.8 420b5–6), evidently derives from his concern for defining the Lullian "first intention" of humans, who are the only creatures with an immediate "ordination" toward the Creator, as Aquinas explains (2a.2ae.2, 3). These basic doctrines later become justifications for Llull's new theory of speech as a sixth sense (discussed below). At no point, however, does Llull argue that this anthropologically distinctive function of speech supports general esteem for language as the foundation of human knowledge, in the manner that Adelard of Bath proposes in his *De eodem et diverso*.[71] Instead, the sense of hearing contributes to knowledge only insofar as it serves the Intellect, according to his *Libre de contemplació* (127.28). This contribution is a commonplace in classical and medieval authorities, such as those compiled by Vincent of Beauvais (*Spec. nat.* 25.50–60), and also reappears later in Llull's arguments for speech as a sixth sense. Of course, all knowledge must serve the human final intention of knowing God.

A full model of how the Senses, Imagination, and Intellect must correctly apprehend language appears in chapters 315–66 of the *Libre de contemplació*. These offer an exhaustive guide to right exercise of all the arts of spiritual eloquence: prayer, meditation, exegesis, and preaching. The final chapters in this series employ letter and number symbolism, a strategy that evidently constitutes the genesis of the alphabetical notation of his Great Art.[72] Chapter 359 presents this complete model of right cognition in the following symbolic scheme:

A: Intellectual Motive Power (i.e., Will)
B: Sense Motive Power (i.e., Appetite)
C: Memory, Intellect, and Will
D: Composite of A and B
E: Vegetative, Sensual, Imaginative, and Rational Powers
F: First Motion, Two Intentions, Truth, Devotion, Conscience, Temperance in Animosity, and Hope

The motive powers of the Intellect and Senses (A and B) obviously correspond to the two kinds of desire distinguished in Aristotelian faculty psychology (*De an.* 3.9 432b5–7). In Llull's arguments these function broadly as "corporeal" and "spiritual" forces in the human moral psychomachy. In other respects, the faculties of the soul (C, D, and E) operate in the conventionally understood manner. The ethical values indicated by F introduce the Lullian first intention as a guarantor of *rectitudo* in this scheme. Exercise of these faculties and virtues occurs in five successive stages that produce true discourse by subordinating material speech to spiritual truth. Each stage, which Llull calls a "figure," combines two or more of the elements symbol-ized by the letters A through F:

Figure One: AC
Figure Two: ACD
Figure Three: ACF
Figure Four: ACFE
Figure Five: ABCDEF

These "figures" arise from their constituent letters like plants from their seeds and roots (359.3).[73] Llull's use of the label "figure" for these simple alphabetic symbols perhaps insinuates the need to grasp them with more sophisticated strategies of figural interpretation.[74] The most important connection in these five stages is the combination of sensitive and intellectual powers in B, although this union creates some difficulties, as will become apparent. Llull explains that the first four stages are "intellectual" in nature, despite the inclusion of the sensual motive power in D. The fifth corresponds to discourse itself. Overall, the five stages define how the in-tellectual powers of the soul are prepared to utilize properly the sensual power in speaking, "for otherwise one would not speak nor say rhetorical or beautifully ordered words" (359.2). The five stages operate as follows.

In the first stage, the intellectual motive power (A) inspires the Memory, Intellect, and Will (C) to remember, understand, and love God. God is always the first and proper object of the Intellect in Llull's Art.[75]

In the second stage, the intellectual motive power (A) and the Memory, Intellect, and Will (C) combine (*ajust*) with the union of the intellectual and sense motive powers (D) in order to "compose from A and B the things that one wishes to say, and to consider the individuals from A and B that might be beautiful and appropri-ate to D." This requires "beautiful, ordered, and true composition" (359.5).[76] That is, the rational soul practices a process of invention, selecting appropriate corporeal and spiritual subject matters for discourse. Of course, this selection serves the realization of *rectitudo*. The best subjects are those that best allow the combination of human sensual and intellectual natures in the contemplative ascent from corporeal to spirit-ual matters. Llull's arguments readily recall Anselm's in his *De veritate:* no meaning is right unless it means what it is right to mean; this rightness does not exist through meaning, but rather right meaning exists thanks to rightness.[77]

In the third stage, the intellectual motive power (A) and the Memory, Intellect, and Will (C) adopt the ethical dispositions (F) necessary to make the sense and intel-lectual motive powers "more orderly and beautiful" in the discourse of the fifth stage. Besides devotion, temperance, awareness, and first intention, these dispositions also require that "what one says be true" (359.6). The ethical dispositions identified by (F) correspond to the major "virtues of speaking," which I describe in chapter 9.

In the fourth stage, the intellectual motive power (A), the Memory, Intellect, and Will (C), and the proper ethical dispositions (F) penetrate the vegetative, sensitive, imaginative, and rational powers (E) so that these behave in an orderly manner in the discourse of the fifth stage (359.7). This comprehensive control of body and soul probably includes the use of proper delivery that Llull's accounts of rhetoric often mention, usually drawing on similar precepts from *artes praedicandi* (see chapter 8).

Finally, in the fifth stage itself, the sense motive power (B) must follow the plan *(ordonament)* that "A, C, D, E, and F have intellectually figured" in the four previous stages, just as a blind person follows one who sees. Otherwise, the sense motive power "would not know nor be able to say beautiful, true, or well-ordered words" (359.8).[78] Beautiful speech exists potentially in the sense motive power by virtue of the plan established in the first four figures, just as forms exist potentially in matter through generation and corruption, according to Aristotelian doctrine (*Phys.* 1.7–9 189b30–192b7). This metaphysical analogy bears causal as well as descriptive value: the speech that exists potentially both is and is like forms that exist potentially. This analogy to Aristotelian metaphysics perhaps foreshadows the tripartite hylemorphic model of the later *Rethorica nova,* as explained in chapter 2. More importantly, this scheme includes a critical antecedent of Llull's later theory of speech as a sixth sense, since it recognizes that the sense motive power controls operation of the vocal cords. This fifth stage mediates the otherwise disparate powers of material speech and spiritual understanding, a function later performed by Llull's sixth sense.

The fact that Llull defines five stages in the production of discourse makes it tempting to seek some correspondence between them and the five Ciceronian parts of rhetoric: invention, arrangement, style, memory, and delivery. However, there seems to be only a remote affinity, if any, between Llull's first two stages and invention, or between the final two stages and delivery.[79] Instead, Chapter 359 of the *Libre de contemplació* offers a plan for contemplation as a model for eloquence, a design that matches the development of Llull's own career from ascetic retreat to evangelical action.[80] His text simply shows how eloquence requires the orderly use of body and soul to communicate truth about God.

The psycholinguistic model presented in the *Libre de contemplació* provides the basis for many of Llull's subsequent proposals regarding the arts of eloquence. For example, the *Rethorica nova* repeats the same fundamental distinction between speech and mind (e.g., 3.15–16, 3.20–21) and even the same rudimentary information on the production of vocal sounds (3.15–16). However, his treatises on rhetoric and preaching also offer several especially striking examples of his concepts of the affective power of speech. The most remarkable appears in the *Rethorica nova*, and relies on a commonplace *distinctio* for the senses of the word *virtus* ("power" and "virtue"). Alan of Lille's *Distinctiones* tell how *virtus* means not simply prudence, temperance, wisdom, or fortitude, but also "the effect of a thing, from whence both plants and stones are said to have great virtues, that is effects."[81] Drawing on this distinction, the *Livre des métiers* (ca. 1340) attributed to Isaac du Pré moralizes: "Our Lord left here below divine virtues in speech, in plants, and in stones. Of all words in the world, the best are those that adore and thank their Creator. The worthiest plants are those by which a Christian lives, and these are wheat. The most precious stone is one that grinds the wheat, because everyone needs it and it serves all."[82] These claims echo Llull's own remarks in the *Rethorica nova* (2.1.3) on the beautiful end of speech. He likewise emphasizes the *virtus* analogically found in plants, stones, and words:

> If God put virtues in plants and stones, far more did God do so in speech, which is
> virtuous with the moral and theological virtues existing in the speaker. And therefore
> when a speaker has virtuous words, whose subject or matter is virtue, it colors their
> form. Thanks to this coloring the form is beautiful. And those hearing this ornate form
> accept the words with delight, and lend favorable ears and heart to listening. (3.7)[83]

This passage explicitly plays on the two senses of *virtus:* plants and stones have natural powers, while people have moral virtues. The phrase "ears and heart" is evidently
a condensed allusion to the traditional distinction between corporeal and spiritual
hearing (the latter employs the "ears of the heart"). Elsewhere in the *Rethorica nova*,
Llull suggests that virtue ornaments speech because likenesses of the speaker's humility, arrogance, continuity, or discontinuity imprint themselves on the listeners'
Senses, Imagination, Intellect, Will, and Memory (2.2.4–5). These likenesses cause
pleasure and displeasure, which suggests a function similar to the "estimative intentions" that Albertus Magnus attributes to imaginings in order to explain their
affective reception in the mind (*De an.* 2.4.7, 3.1.2–3).[84] However, Albertus's suggestion involves the "estimative power," one of the internal senses that Llull scarcely
recognizes, as noted above.[85]

Llull's *Taula general* rehearses this same *distinctio* regarding *virtus,* but explains
the influence differently:

> *Virtus* transmits its likeness externally in order to manifest and multiply itself in that
> likeness, and in order to be able to pass into other substances . . . [this happens] in
> words, just as the sensitive power is moved by virtue of hearing true words to [grasp]
> necessary and lovable objects; in plants, as when a plant with the power of healing
> is able to multiply this power from the contrary power; in stones, as when the magnet
> draws iron to itself. (5.5.14)[86]

This explanation abandons wordplay in favor of metaphysics: words, plants, and
stones have power thanks to the Lullian Principle of *Virtus* infused in them all.[87] The
"necessary and lovable objects" mentioned here would, in conventional Scholastic
doctrine, pertain to the Intellect and Will, rather than to the Senses. By attributing
them to the latter, Llull's argument apparently confuses the functions of the sensitive
appetite (Sensuality) and intellectual appetite (Will), which a Schoolman like
Aquinas keeps strictly separate (1a.80, 2). This confusion suggests that Llull eventually came to abandon his earlier preoccupation with segregating the operation of the
sensitive and intellectual faculties, a step that certainly would facilitate his discovery of speech as a sixth sense that combined oral and mental discourse.

Faith and understanding are the two results of persuasion that most interest Llull
the evangelist. During the latter part of his career, he became increasingly preoccu-
pied with showing how effective proselytizing argumentation can induce both
responses in unbelievers. The *Liber de convenientia fidei et intellectus in obiecto* of
1309 offers his most developed presentation of this issue. The *Liber de praedicatione*
and the *Rethorica nova* also offer advice on how a speaker should fashion beautiful, orderly discourse for the purpose of inducing faith and understanding. For
example, the *Liber de praedicatione* (2.A.8.3) explains how a preacher more readily
"adorns" an audience's Intellect and Will by discussing things that are intelligible,
rather than merely believable, and loveable, rather than hateful.[88] The *Ars generalis*

ultima likewise broadly insists that a speaker must harmonize the Intellect and Will in order to speak effectively (10.98). This ornamentation or harmonization is effective insofar as it best allows each faculty to apprehend its highest object, which is of course God. Llull identifies the pleasure of satisfying each faculty's quest with the adornment of the soul. One reason that Llull typically insists on mutual cooperation and satisfaction of all the soul's faculties is to avoid admitting the possibility of separate truths attained through separate exercise of each faculty.

The *Rethorica nova* relates this satisfaction of the mind's faculties to several well-known elements from classical rhetorical doctrine:

> There is another, third mode of true speech, when four conditions render the speech beautiful. Some true words are proven through necessary arguments, but some by authorities, and some by witnesses. Some gain their force of truth from similitudes and conjectures. And because understanding, which responds to proof by necessary reason, is the proper act of the Intellect, the belief that responds to proof based on authority is the appropriated act of the Intellect. Therefore the Intellect understands more and assents more to the truth of words strengthened with necessary arguments— whence they seem more beautiful to it—than to words based on authority. An exception however are the words of Holy Scripture that rest on divine truth, which is a greater authority than any kind of human insight. (3.8.3)[89]

This conception of techniques for generating belief and understanding broadly parallels Aristotle's basic distinction between the tactics of rhetoric and those of dialectic (*Rhet.* 1.1–2) or perhaps between dialectic and demonstration (*Top.* 1.1 100a25–31). Llull may recognize this as a problem for rhetoric thanks to Alfarabi, whose introduction to that art emphasizes the difference between opinion and certitude.[90] The categories of necessary arguments, authorities, witnesses, and similitudes all correspond nominally to types of proof described in the *Rhetorica ad Herennium* (2.5.8; 2.6.9; 2.18.27–19.30; 2.30.48; 3.45.59–48.61). However, Llull is certainly not interested in defining their specific characteristics, in the manner of a school commentator such as William of Champeaux, who discusses the equivocal use of the terms "argument" and "argumentation" in the *De inventione*.[91] Rather, Llull's contrast between the inadequacy of those devices and the strength of "necessary arguments" suggests that those techniques appear chiefly as examples of the weak methods taught in the schools. The *Liber de praedicatione* (2.A.5) likewise contrasts Llull's handling of the relationship between reason and faith with the methods of Aristotelian logical doctrine. There he declares that faith is "positive" and uses authorities such as Scripture, while reason is either "ostensive" or "reduces to the impossible" and uses arguments *propter quid, quia,* or *per aequiparantiam.* The distinctions of ostensive and reduction to the impossible and of *propter quid* and *quia* are Aristotelian (*An. pr.* 1.7 29a31; *An. post.* 1.2 71b9–12), but argument *per aequiparantiam* is the special "logic of coessentiality" that Llull offers as the supreme mode of demonstration in his later logical works.[92] By aligning those conventionally accepted types of proof with Llull's new mode of proof, the *Liber de praedicatione* establishes a moralizing analogy that authorizes *demonstratio per aequiparantiam* as truly probative. This analogy validates Llull's subsequent claim that one can prove the Trinity, the Incarnation, the Resurrection, and "other things that agree with these in their way" (2.A.1.5).[93] This agreement does not consist of a common basis in the formal rules of valid inference, but rather in common derivation from one Supreme Truth, in the same manner that both faith and reason have a "common object."

These claims regarding faith and understanding from the *Rethorica nova* and the *Liber de praedicatione* treat effective persuasion as a problem of spiritual psychology, of fostering the soul's *rectitudo*.[94] Llull's explanations ignore the basic Aristotelian distinction between demonstrative and dialectical reasoning. They concern instead the fundamental dilemmas of Christian inquiry recognized by contemporaries such as Aquinas: argument from authority such as Scripture is merely probable, but faith believes in the truth of Scripture, which is incontestable (1a.1, 8); faith is a lesser mode of knowledge than reason, although its object is more exalted (1a.12, 13 ad 3; 2a.2ae.4, 8). Like Aquinas, Llull offers a solution based on more careful attention to human psychology. Where Saint Thomas (*De ver.* 14, 1–2) suggests that the Will moves the Intellect to assent to some position adequate for the Will, but not properly adequate to the Intellect, Ramon Llull likewise recognizes that the objects of faith and understanding are differently primary and secondary for the Intellect and the Will. Llull's arguments insist, however, that they are the same objects and that all the mental faculties cooperate in apprehending them. Thus the mind ultimately seeks one object alone, which is the single divine truth. The task of eloquence is to assist that quest by presenting suitably intelligible, desirable, and memorable objects to the mind.[95]

The *Libre de contemplació,* the *Rethorica nova,* and the *Liber de praedicatione* all offer psychological and epistemological explanations of eloquence that rely on the same basic strategy, namely, rectifying the exercise of language by making that exercise serve as closely as possible the moral finality of human existence. Around 1294, Llull attempted to seek this same rectification through a different tactic, the integration of language into human nature itself. The result is his extraordinary proposal to classify speech as a sixth sense, which he calls *affatus*. Some modern scholars have sought ancient or medieval sources for Llull's unusual theory, but these efforts must ignore his own insistence that *affatus* is a new discovery.[96] In fact, careful review of Llull's discussions of language prior to 1294 show that his new theory largely arises through his own revision of received doctrines. *Affatus* especially results from his conflation of Scholastic physiological and psychological doctrines regarding the apprehensive and motive powers.[97] Llull treats these very freely because he rarely includes them in his model of human nature. As Vincent of Beauvais's compilation (*Spec. nat.* 25.104) shows, various authorities associate the production of vocal sounds with the sensitive motive power. Among Llull's Scholastic contemporaries, Robert Grosseteste derives this expressive power from the combined action of the sensual motive power's control of voice and the rational faculty.[98] Llull especially exploits this connection in classifying speech as a sense. At the same time, his explanations of *affatus* still appeal to his preferred epistemological and psychological doctrines: the division of the soul into sensitive, imaginative, and intellective powers; the explanation of cognition through resemblance and of intellection as interpretation; and the distinction between oral and mental language. Llull's attempt to make the operation of *affatus* parallel the functioning of the other five senses creates some especially difficult and confused arguments. The most relevant ones for eloquence are those that concern the moral rectification of language.

That rectification depends on a fundamental difference between *affatus* and the other senses. Where touch, taste, vision, hearing, and smell are all "exteroceptive" (i.e., they apprehend objects outside the mind), Llull's sixth sense is "interoceptive" (i.e., it apprehends objects within the mind). The *Liber de affatu* repeatedly claims that the purpose of *affatus* is to allow one animal to share its "internal conceptions" with another animal (280, 293, 296).[99] Even though many thoughts or desires presumably arise from sensations of the external world at large, Llull's discussions of *affatus* usually mention only their appearance within the soul. The *Liber de affatu* explains that animals possess only imaginative concepts and humans possess both intellective and imaginative concepts (280, 294).[100] All these remarks assume basic Aristotelian doctrine (*De an.* 2.8 420b33, 3.3 427b6–8b17). In short, *affatus* provides both humans and animals with a means of giving expression to all those *affectiones* or *passiones* that arise in the Imagination or Intellect. Llull usually refers to these thoughts or desires as concepts, but the *Liber de affatu* also calls them intelligible species (e.g., 280), forms (e.g., 280, 296), and likenesses (e.g., 280, 296).[101] Although this terminology resembles that employed by Latin and Arab authorities, it is difficult to consider this explanation of how concepts inform speech as "purely formal."[102] Llull's fundamental elemental exemplarism just as readily favors organic analogies for describing the process through which concepts inform speech. For example, his *Liber de ascensu et descensu intellectus* (7.2.3) explains that *affatus* transmutes a concept into speech, just as the vegetative power transmutes food and drink into flesh and blood. These organic analogies not only explain the *specificatio* (i.e., "informing") of language, but also validate references to the physiology of speech elsewhere in Llull's analyses of *affatus*. Once this initial stage of apprehension is complete, language functions through *affatus* in the usual fashion: humans or animals utter speech using the tongue and lips, which thus constitute the organs of *affatus*; other humans or animals perceive it with the ears, the organ of hearing.

Thanks to its interoceptive nature, *affatus* functions chiefly as a means of communication among the powers of the soul. It performs an intrasubjective, rather than an intersubjective function. In this regard, *affatus* extends (and perhaps replaces) the mental language mentioned so often in Llull's earlier writings. In its communication with the higher faculties, *affatus* plays an instrumental role. That is, *affatus* serves as a mediator, conceiving imaginable or intelligible concepts and manifesting them in speech (*Liber de affatu* 294). Indeed, the operation of the Imagination is better manifested through *affatus* than any other sense (*Liber de affatu* 290).[103] The *Liber de praedicatione* (2.B.1.36.1) explains that *affatus* also represents "corporeal delights" to the Imagination, which in turn represents them to the soul; touch likewise "manifests" its sensations to the Imagination (*Liber de affatu* 294). One of the most quintessentially Lullian arguments of the entire *Liber de affatu* explains this function of *affatus* in the following sequence of propositions (289). First, there is greater Concord (the Lullian Relative Principle) between a sense and an intellectual power than between two sense powers, because the intellectual power predominates in the union of body and soul (this Concord is evidently a relationship of necessary dependence). Second, only *affatus* manifests the operations of Memory, which is a faculty of the rational soul that informs the body (this seems to be special pleading, since it is hard to understand how another Sense like touch or taste could "express" memories). Third, if the sensitive power acquires any strength (*virtus*) from the objects of Memory, then it must do so through *affatus*, which means that this strength must be as great or greater than the strength transmitted to the sensitive power through the other Senses (this argument continues the special pleading already noted). Finally, if these conditions did not exist, the sensitive power would receive more strength from the other Senses and from Memory through forgetting than through remembering, which is impossible. This conclusion requires, of course, the somewhat paradoxical identification of forgetting as a lesser "strength" received by the sensitive power from Memory. It is interesting that Llull's argument does not mention the Imagination, but rather attributes to *affatus* the mediation between Senses and mind that one might expect the Imagination to perform. This neglect of Imagination and the insistence on the mediating role of *affatus* demonstrates superlatively Llull's effort to define a necessary place for his sixth sense within the levels that constitute human nature. By defining such a place for *affatus,* he subordinates the exercise of language to the same metaphysical and moral principles that govern all human existence.

The interoceptive function of *affatus* and its classification among the Senses thus allow speech to serve more directly the moral finality of human nature. *Affatus* solves, as it were, the problem of how to make the material language of the body serve the spiritual needs of the soul. Subordinating speech to mind as a Sense that serves the Intellect enables human beings to use language much more effectively for loving one another and God. Consequently, the *Liber de affatu* describes at length the wide range of social virtues that *affatus* promotes.[104] Llull's proposal of *affatus* thus provides a naturalistic version of the ancient view, especially known from Cicero (*De inv.* 1.2.2–3) and Augustine (*De civ. Dei* 7.14), that language is essential to human social organization. Nonetheless, the justification for recognizing *affatus* as a Sense that Llull most frequently cites, and which best defines the purpose of this classification, is quite simple: classifying speech as a Sense gives human beings a natural means of apprehending the divine, by naming God. Llull repeats this claim about *affatus* more than any other; in some texts it is his only explanation of the sixth sense.[105] *Affatus* is perhaps Llull's most daring attempt to achieve a closer community between human and divine natures. Just as his *Liber de modo naturali intelligendi* defines a natural use of the mind to know God, so Llull's writings on *affatus* define a natural use of language for this same purpose.

Conclusion

Ramon Llull's Great Art explains the existence of all things, words, and thoughts according to a metaphysics of participated resemblance in which likeness and difference measure the degrees and limits of mutual interaction. Understanding that interaction requires interpreting things, words, and thoughts alike as signs of one another. Llull's works thus describe cognition generally as a discursive exercise through which the mind understands intepretatively its objects. However, the gulf that separates the spiritual mind and its mental objects of knowledge from the material body and its extramental objects of sensation can severely impede this understanding. Consequently, Ramon Llull's accounts of the psychology of language, as expounded in texts from the *Libre de contemplació* to the *Rethorica nova,* largely concern the procedures that the human soul must follow in order to apprehend spiritual truth in, from, and through material discourse. Communication is not so much a process of exchange for Llull as it is a process of ordering and rectifying. The eristic strategy of Llull's entire Art consists basically in training the soul to exercise the "disposition to allegory" that Augustine (*DC* 3.5.9) deemed necessary in order to escape the slavery of the letter and to achieve the freedom of the spirit. That disposition realizes the Lullian first intention of the soul. Accepting the use of discourse to achieve the Augustinian ideal of "understanding faith" makes all Llull's proposals about the psychology of communication necessarily hermeneutic.[106] Where Augustine correlated the move from faith to understanding with the elucidation of figural from literal meaning,[107] Llull's *Libre de contemplació* extends that strategy to sensation and cognition concerning all creatures, since they all offer knowledge of their Creator. For this reason, Llull's general arguments about the epistemology and psychology of communication apply to contemplation and persuasion alike. Those arguments function as dual strategies for exchanging truth and love between oneself, one's neighbor, and God. The greatest novelty in Llull's arguments regarding the affective or cognitive function of communication is ultimately their attempt to enhance the discursive powers of the mind. His proposal of speech as a sixth sense represents his most radical effort to achieve this goal. Later Renaissance enthusiasts of the Great Art likewise appreciated its promise as a "discourse machine" for universal communication or encyclopedic knowledge. Ramon Llull's Great Art is preeminently a guide for the soul seeking to make sense of the world. His arts of eloquence provide methods for the soul to express its discoveries.

4

Invention

Ramon Llull's zeal for leading the mind to truth causes him to treat most aspects of communication first as epistemological or psychological processes and second as linguistic or rhetorical functions. His Great Universal Art of Finding Truth primarily provides a method of discovering or evaluating ideas rather than of generating discursive arguments. This preeminently heuristic purpose ensures that invention is the division of Ciceronian rhetoric that Llull's Great Art most completely replaces. The *Ars compendiosa inveniendi veritatem,* Llull's first full version of his system (composed between 1274 and 1283), treats invention not as discovery of words or reasonings, but as manipulation of concepts through symbolic letters arranged in charts and tables.[1] The *Art demostrativa* of 1283 even notes the traditional division of dialectic into invention and judgment, but treats these sheerly as cognitive practices (4.2.5.62). Nonetheless, insofar as Llull's system treats mental and oral discourse as homologous, it serves the invention of arguments for discursive presentation. The Great Art not only leads the mind to find absolute truth, it helps the mind to defend that truth. Hence, it should hardly surprise us that Llull invariably offers his own system as a method for generating copious material to expound in secular and sacred eloquence. Occasionally he does recommend inventional devices from the contemporary arts of language, but these come almost exclusively from the *ars praedicandi.* This chapter reviews Llull's application of his Great Art to rhetorical invention, the inventional devices that he borrows from contemporary arts of eloquence, and the body of *materia praedicabilis* that he offers.

Lullian Techniques of Invention

The *Libre de contemplació* defines the fundamental Lullian process of rhetorical invention in its explanations of how the mind recognizes which things are most

beautiful to name (chap. 155, 359). The ultimate purpose of this process is to help
the spiritual faculties rectify their use of material language. Llull insists that right
disposition of the sensitive and intellectual powers (described in chapter 3) ensures
discovery of suitable exempla and arguments (359.10). Of course, this material consists of words whose beauty, propriety, and suitability express the excellences of the
things that they name (359.11). Finding these words fosters the Lullian first intention
of language: the most beautiful words are those that best allow humans to praise,
honor, and serve God (359.15). Once Llull establishes his Great Art as a complete
system, his accounts of rhetoric and preaching typically attempt to identify the invention of suitable or beautiful material with the combination of his own Absolute
Principles, Relative Principles, Rules, and other categories. Thus the *Art demostrativa* of 1283 claims that its letter combinations offer the preacher abundant material
and exempla, as well as guidance in the exposition of Scripture (3.8–9). The Great
Art as a whole serves equally well for finding *(atrobar)* secrets in nature and in books
(3.6). The latter application of the term "finding" aptly suggests how broadly Llull
conceives the process of invention.

Llull's *Aplicació de l'art general* of 1301 is the text that most directly and clearly
proposes his Great Art as an inventional process for use in rhetoric. It treats his
system as a comprehensive model for finding beautiful language, chiefly by identi-
fying verbal concordances between the Lullian Principles or Rules and elements from
the arts of eloquence:

> Rhetoric is speaking
> done with beautiful arrangement;
> and one can attain it
> with this Art, and succeed
> mixing the Principles
> from which issue such beautiful orations,
> that rhetoric results,
> speaking righteous discourse *(paraula dreta)*
>   from them
> embellished with Goodness,
> Greatness, and Power
> and the other Principles,
> when one mixes them,
> just as Greatness is ornamented
> when made Good:
> and likewise the adjectives
> that ornament the nouns,
> when one combines them
> through all the Principles. (ll. 806–23)[2]

This passage alludes to functions of invention, arrangement, and style alike. Llull's
advice virtually treats the inventive selection and stylistic deployment of beautiful
language as coincident functions. The comparative phrase "just as" serves through-

out the *Aplicació* to equate the combinatory mechanics of Llull's Great Art with practices from specific arts, as it does here with the appropriate union of nouns and adjectives. This combinatory technique, and its assumption of verbal beauty based on the referential value of terms, remains fundamental to Llull's accounts of rhetoric throughout his career. In other texts composed after the *Aplicació de l'art general,* the combination of the Principles acquires a more separate role as a mode of verbal beauty in itself, but this process still remains difficult to distinguish from the invention of material in general.

Since the Lullian Subjects encompass the entire hierarchy of being, they ought to provide a copious range of subject matter for invention. In fact, Llull usually limits his enumeration of beautiful creatures to a few representative beings from each level of existence. This passage from the *Rethorica nova* is typical:

> [A] word or term is called beautiful when it has a beautiful form, in the way that all the words listed here are ornamented and rendered beautiful. These are "God," "angel," "man," "goodness," "greatness," "eternity," "power," "king," "queen," "serving-girl," "knight," "lady," and so forth, all of which are beautiful words thanks to their form. Now the same can be said of "sun," "star," "radiance," "lion," "horse," "tree," "rose," "violet," "lily," "flower," "gold," "ruby," and "emerald." For these are all beautiful words and when one speaks about them, they ornament that speech with their loveliness. (2.1.1)[3]

Llull's repeated references to kings and queens certainly illustrate his advice about choosing nobler and more beautiful subjects. However, his constant use of the terms suggested in this passage probably reflects a rather unimaginative reliance on the Lullian Subjects. The great contemporary Florentine preacher Giordano da Pisa also uses frequent exempla involving kings and queens, but within a far wider range of illustrative material.[4]

In any case, the restricted range of Llull's examples leaves little room for discussing the criteria of unity, plausibility, simplicity, consistency, variety, and so forth, advocated by poetic preceptists from Horace to Geoffrey of Vinsauf. At best, Llull's arguments resemble the broad advice on matching words to subject matter that appears in ancient encyclopedists such as Sulpitius Victor (chap. 15) or Fortunatianus (3.8). His writings display no knowledge of the traditional doctrine of the three levels of style and corresponding subject matters, as schematized in the popular device of the *Rota Vergilii.*[5] Augustine (*DC* 4.17.34–28.61) provides indisputable authority for its application to Christian eloquence. Thus, a fourteenth-century devotional writer like Richard Rolle readily applies it to distinctions between divine and human subject matters.[6] Unlike Rolle, however, Llull shows no familiarity with any precepts from literary *auctores.*[7] Unambiguous references to invention in the poetic sense of selecting suitable vocabulary—Vinsauf's "clothing a subject in words" (*Poetria nova* l. 61)—or in the rhetorical sense of developing suitable arguments—Cicero's "devising true or verisimilar things to support a case" (*De inv.* 1.7.9)—are consequently very difficult to identify in Llull's oeuvre. For example, the *Ars generalis ultima* only once refers explicitly to choosing rhetorical language without recourse to Llull's *ars combinatoria:*

The rhetorician ornaments with significative speech by saying "April" and "May," which are prettier words to say than "October" and "November," because they signify flowers and leaves and birdsongs and the renewal of the seasons and growing things. October and November do not. The same can be said of springs, rivers, streams, meadows, trees, shade, and so forth, which are beautiful words to sense and to imagine. (10.86)[8]

Llull's examples of beautiful language recall commonplace elements from descriptions of a *locus amoenus* in medieval poetry.[9] Moreover, this passage offers one of his few allusions to the role of Imagination as the creative faculty of verbal invention, which grammatical authorities like Matthew of Vendome typically cite (3.52).[10] The term "significative speech" *(vox significativa)* nonetheless comes from elementary logical doctrine rather than from the *ars poetriae*. Its appearance here suggests very literally how words affect the Senses and Imagination by virtue of the things that they signify, as Llull argues in his *Libre de contemplació.*[11]

Llull's accounts of preaching also invoke his Great Art as a process of invention, but include as well some references to conventional techniques. For example, the *Ars generalis ultima* declares that the combination of Lullian Principles and Rules are the paradigmatic inventional mode for homiletic discourse. Its account of preaching begins:

Preaching is the form with which the preacher disposes the people to good habits and avoiding bad ones. And especially if that mode of discourse were through the Principles and Rules of this Art, and also through the nine Subjects, so that the Intellect of the preacher and listeners abounds in great material. And such preaching is wonderfully beneficial and easy; just as it is wonderfully systematic, and erected on a great subject. (10.98)[12]

Application of the Great Art to other arts endows them all with this same inventive capacity. Llull's subsequent reference to the preacher's Intellect underscores his conception of invention as a fundamentally cognitive and intellective process:

The preacher should thus proceed in preaching as the Intellect does in discovering those things of which there is knowledge. For the Intellect makes knowledge beyond the Senses from the Senses and Imagination. And it also makes knowledge beyond the Imagination from intelligible things in itself. Thus the preacher should descend to the Senses, giving them sense experiences, and afterward ascend to the Imagination, giving it imaginary experiences. And then the Intellect should also ascend, giving it experiences of intelligible things. And thus one could speak of the Will and the Memory in their way. If, however, one does not do this, the sermon will truly be obscure and confusing, because it is weak in the Memory of the listeners, and is unknown in the Intellect, and in the Will such a sermon or preaching is not likeable. (10.98)[13]

The concluding references to the Intellect and the Will especially implicate Llull's concern for apprehending the proper objects of these faculties, namely, the Supreme Truth and the Supreme Good. The overall process recommended here corresponds to the "descent and ascent of the Intellect," described exhaustively in Llull's treatise of the same name. This exercise consists fundamentally in contemplation of the

hierarchy of being defined by the Lullian Subjects. It aptly insinuates how meditation necessarily precedes speech in Llull's program of evangelism. It does not
explain, however, precisely what kind of experiences the preacher acquires in this
way or how they serve to dispel obscurity and confusion among the audience. In
Llull's other writings this procedure usually serves the attainment of spiritual truths,
stripped of their material distortions, but here it perhaps involves simply the acquisition of natural examples from creatures through the Senses.

The *Liber de praedicatione* of 1305 offers Llull's most extensive and diverse
advice about invention for either preaching or rhetoric. Of course, the fundamental
method that it recommends is the Lullian *ars combinatoria*. This brief passage on
"investigation or application" succinctly defines the inventional utility of Llull's letter
combinations (called "flowers" here):

> The first mode is through flowers, such as through BC and BD etc.
>   And this is so that if the preacher wishes to speak in a sermon about those things
> understood by B, and does not know them, the preacher should recur to some better
> known flower; just as if one knows those things that are understood through C, and
> wishes to speak about B, one should investigate knowledge about B through C; and
> likewise for the others. Let the preacher nonetheless proceed so that in the application
> of one flower to another they remain whole and unchanged by means of affirmation
> or negation; and this so that the preacher explains through one flower what is impli-
> cated in another. (2.A.4.1)[14]

This passage demonstrates superlatively how the "implication" of the many in the
one constitutes the master trope of Lullian discourse. It corresponds broadly to the
expositional techniques of finding "one signified in many" and "many signifying
one" recommended by *artes praedicandi* such as Jean de la Rochelle's *Processus
negociandi themata*.[15] Llull cannot allow the preacher to employ any terms or concepts that simply occur through free association. Consequently, he recommends the
exercise of affirmation and negation, which his logical theories routinely employ to
maintain the mind's proper orientation toward its first intention.[16] In addition, the
Liber de praedicatione recommends that the preacher reduce terms not defined in
Llull's Art to those that are (2.A.4.2). The account of "multiplication" in the *Liber
de praedicatione* asserts, without detailed explanation, that discoursing through
combinations of the Principles, Rules, Subjects, virtues, and vices will increase
understanding, love, and praise for God (2.A.7). This section also suggests "drawing out many authorities for the same purpose, and also to prove through arguments
many arguments and authorities" (2.A.7.1–2).[17] This perhaps alludes to the use of
auctoritates to prove the divisions in a sermon, which Parisian preachers elaborately
develop in their theory, according to Robert of Basevorn (chap. 35). The most basic
device for achieving this confirmation is the citation of "real and verbal concordances." Robert carefully distinguishes the two types of concordance. He explains
that "if the theme established is *walk ye,* one can say that the road is threefold:
straight, level, and clear," and thus develop real concordances based on the nature
of roads. Or, "in the theme *walk ye* it is permitted to take an authority in which is
contained any derivative of this word" and thus develop verbal concordances from
forms of the verb "to walk."[18] As we have seen, Llull's epistemology, metaphysics,

and semiotics of resemblance largely obviate the need to distinguish real and verbal concordances. Perhaps for this reason, he simply mentions the citation of authorities in order to suggest its implication in the general inventional procedures of the Lullian *ars combinatoria.*

Invention through Devices of Amplification and Exposition

The explanations of "investigation" and "multiplication" from the *Liber de praedicatione* suggest why Ramon Llull's Great Art cannot rely solely on the combination of symbolic letters to generate knowledge or discourse. No formal rules of deduction or induction govern manipulation of the Lullian *ars combinatoria.* Instead, Llull consistently claims that these letter combinations "imply" a vast range of meanings, which require discovery through interpretative and amplificational associations. Most of these consist in seeking from his letter combinations the manifestations of commonplace philosophical and theological concepts. These concepts thus serve broadly as topics of argumentation, in the fashion recognized by ancient authorities from Aristotle to Boethius.[19] None of Llull's writings ever refers to them as such, but these lists of concepts—such as the inventory of one hundred forms included in versions of his Art—correspond functionally to the lists of topics best known from Boethius and subsequently developed in Scholastic logic.[20] Within the system of Llull's Great Art, the superlative use of such devices is its set of Rules, which parallels the inventional use of questions practiced in rhetoric from ancient times.[21]

Llull's accounts of rhetoric and preaching also occasionally mention other quasi-topical concepts as inventional devices. For example, the *Ars generalis ultima* (10.86) recommends the concepts of possible and impossible, easy and difficult, useful and unuseful, and frequent and rare. Although many of these recommendations correspond functionally to the precepts concerning *amplificatio* defined by literary authorities such as Geoffrey of Vinsauf (*Poetria nova* ll. 203–689), Llull almost never alludes to the terminology or specific practices of the *artes poetriae.* Instead, his methods more often resemble those of the *artes praedicandi.* Most authorities on preaching give detailed advice regarding the means of "amplifying" or "dilating" the minimal material provided by a scriptural theme into sufficient stuff for a complete sermon. The historical and practical precedents for this procedure lie in the interpretative methods of scriptural exegesis, but the sermon theorists avail themselves of inventional resources from virtually all the arts and sciences.[22] Any real, verbal, or conceptual association can serve as interpretative leaven in the sermon loaf. The often repeated list of eight devices recommended in Richard of Thetford's *Ars dilatandi sermones* indicates the predominantly textual character of the amplificational techniques employed in university sermons: (1) definition, description, or interpretation; (2) division; (3) ratiocination, including syllogism, induction, exemplum, or enthymeme; (4) concordant authorities; (5) etymology; (6) metaphors; (7) the four exegetical senses of Scripture; (8) and assigning cause and effect.[23] Like most features of thirteenth-century preaching, the actual use of those devices displays many variations and adaptations. Scholastic authorities deliberately revise their use for sermons delivered to laypeople. For example, Robert of Basevorn comments (chap. 39) that learned clerics can understand very sophisticated distinctions, such as Aristotelian definitions, that laypeople will not grasp. Popular preaching to lay audiences and the devotional literature derived from it tend to adapt simpler devices of allegory, analogy, and verbal association that more readily serve the wide-ranging exercise of moralization.[24]

The amplificational techniques that Llull recommends as inventional methods rely chiefly on relationships of similitude.[25] His most extensive theoretical account of these is the explanation of "exposition" from the *Liber de praedicatione*. Where the *artes praedicandi* typically recommend a wide range of expositional devices for amplifying scriptural themes, Llull presents only a single device: exposition of the distinction between prior and posterior. However, thanks to his own distinctional methods, he manages to invoke various other principles and relationships too. The result is a somewhat heterogeneous *distinctio* on the terms "prior" and "posterior." The passage begins by simply listing its distinctional members:

> This part is divided into four parts. The first is about being. The second about degrees. The third about living. The fourth about the Church.
>
> Being is analogous, because it is said of substance first, and of accident afterward. And thus the preacher should maintain this mode in a sermon, expounding words as prior and posterior. And the preacher should first apply [it to nouns of] first intentions, then afterward apply it to nouns of second intentions. (2.A.1.1)[26]

The first part on "being" in fact introduces the distinction of prior and posterior applied to the three subsequent terms "degree," "living," and "Church." The brief explanation of being expounds basic doctrine commonly found in encyclopedic reviews of metaphysics, such as Vincent of Beauvais's compendium (*SD* 16.60). These typically begin by explaining the multiple senses of being, especially Aristotle's basic doctrines regarding the analogy of substantial to accidental being and the priority of a substance to its accidents (*Metaph.* 4.2 1003a33–4, 5.11 1019a1–14).[27] Llull's recourse to some Scholastic compendium is evident in his use here of the terms "first intention" and "second intention" in their strictly logical sense. This usage is very rare in his writings, where first and second intentions almost always indicate his basic doctrine of moral finality.[28] Moreover, this passage somewhat incongruously correlates the logical sense of first and second intentions with the metaphysical distinction between "prior" and "posterior." Perhaps Llull's examples collate some of the metaphysical distinctions and logical categories recommended as devices of amplification by authorities on preaching such as Richard of Thetford (chap. 33).

Llull's subsequent application of the distinction between prior and posterior to the term "degree" displays superlatively the correlation of divisions that makes distinctional exposition such a fecund method of discourse:

> Among natural things composed of elements, degree can be considered according to prior and posterior, as in pepper, garlic, and so forth. . . . [I]n pepper . . . there is the

fourth degree of heat, the third of dryness, the second of moisture, and the first of coldness. . . .

But the first is always last, or the posterior is attributed to it. And just as degree in common is said of these degrees analogically, that is, prior and posterior, so being [is said] of substance and accident in its way. Whence just as prior and posterior are regarded in nature, so the preacher should consider expounding [through] prior and posterior in a sermon. (2.A.1.2)[29]

Llull often cites examples concerning the four elements and humors, presumably because they offer natural truths of irrefutable authority. The information that he mentions consists entirely of commonplaces available from encyclopedias. For example, Bartholomeus Anglicus, citing Platearius, notes that pepper is both hot and dry in the fourth degree (17.131). Bartholomeus also describes the desiccating and warming effects of garlic, but without specifying the degrees of those qualities in the vegetable (17.11). Llull perhaps specifies dryness and hotness in the third and fourth degrees because it better serves his hierarchical scheme of prior and posterior distinctions. The observation that the "first is always last" may allude to the Gospel (Matt. 19:30). If so, this allusion suggests that Llull's account of "prior and posterior" draws on some homiletic or devotional exposition of that Scripture passage. The concluding recommendation about considering prior and posterior in a sermon presumably refers to the type of exposition just illustrated, but might also readily lead, as so often occurs in Llull's accounts of rhetoric, to discussion of prior and posterior parts in the preacher's own sermon.

The subsequent exposition of "living" according to the distinction between prior and posterior contrasts the relative importance of corporeal and spiritual life. It argues that food and drink are more important than tools and utensils, living well more important than merely living, living well through the theological virtues more important than living well through the cardinal virtues, and living well through the theological virtue of love more important than through faith or hope. This sequence evidently expands the commonplace Scholastic divisions of moral and natural exempla and perhaps recomposes some existing account of a *distinctio* regarding the terms "prior" and "posterior." The echo of Saint Paul's dictum regarding the supremacy of love over faith and hope (1 Cor. 13:13) suggests that the source was some sermon or meditation on this scriptural passage.

Finally, Llull's exposition of the last term, "Church," applies the distinction between prior and posterior to the four traditional exegetical senses of *ecclesia:*

The literal sense, just as the material church composed of stone and wood is understood from "Church."

Allegory, just as the congregation of the faithful is understood from "Church." And thus the prior or priority is attributed to allegory, and the posterior or posteriority to the letter.

Tropology, just as we understand the law from "Church," that is, the articles of faith and sacraments, that is, the Church militant. And thus tropology is prior, and allegory posterior with respect to tropology.

Anagogy, just as we understand the Church triumphant from "Church," that is eternal glory. (2.A.1.4)[30]

These four senses of *ecclesia* are the standard ones for each level of exegesis, disseminated in catalogues of *distinctiones* such as Alan of Lille's *Distinctiones* or the Pseudo-Rabanus's *Allegoriae*. Although Llull's analysis subjects them to the distinction of prior and posterior, sermon theorists like Guibert of Nogent (25D–6A), Richard of Thetford (chap. 46–49), and Robert of Basevorn (chap. 39) do not emphasize the necessary relationship of precedence among the four exegetical senses. Finally, this account of "exposition" from the *Liber de praedicatione* concludes by mentioning several other topics suitable for distinction as prior and posterior: the Old and New Testaments and four exegetical senses for the verb *equitare* ("to ride a horse"). These repeat the interpretations of "horse" commonly found in manuals of *distinctiones* such as Alan of Lille's.

Llull's four examples of exposition through the distinction of prior and posterior presumably illustrate methods of invention applicable to virtually any concept. Thus the dichotomy of substance and accident, expounded according to priority and posterity in the section on "degree," later serves in the account of comparison (Llull's sixth condition of preaching in the *Liber de praedicatione*) to generate arguments about the Trinity (2.A.6). Nonetheless, Llull's heterogeneous conflation of senses for prior and posterior falls far short of providing a universal *distinctio* to guide exposition. It is not as comprehensive as the seven circumstances—subject (*res*), person, place, deed, time, number, and expression (*vox*)—recommended by Jean de la Rochelle in his *Processus negociandi themata*.[31] Rather, Llull simply illustrates exposition by distinctionally collating a few examples of the many techniques that his own writings apply so exhaustively.

Division of Sermon Themes

The most fundamental inventional device in Scholastic preaching is division of the theme. Division of the theme and development of suitable "concordant authorities" was not only the first task facing the preacher, but also one of the most troublesome. The term "negotiate" in the title of Jean de la Rochelle's treatise on this one aspect, *Processus negociandi themata sermonum,* probably gives a good idea of the verbal wrangling demanded of the preacher. The selection of terms to analyze in a scriptural theme is critical because it defines both the topical and formal structure of the sermon. Robert of Basevorn stresses the need to announce a division clearly and to state the parts of the sermon to follow (chap. 20, 33, 42–43). Llull's *Liber de praedicatione* lists "division" among its nine conditions of preaching and relates it to the division of a scriptural theme. However, his moralizing method and limited knowledge of Scholastic practice produces a *distinctio* that broadly—in fact, irrelevantly—reinterprets the types of division that he mentions. The result is a group of precepts that effectively ignores the meaning of the original term itself:

> The first mode, through a hypothetical proposition, is to conjoin several propositions, and from them to make a sermon; just as we would say thus: *In the beginning was the*

Word; and the Word was with God; and the Word was God. From these three propositions the preacher can make a sermon.

The second mode is to divide a categorical proposition, such as dividing this one: *In the beginning was the Word,* into four parts or terms: *In* is one part, *the beginning* is another, *was* another, and *the Word* another.

The third mode is by division, such as dividing through prior and posterior the parts of a categorical proposition, that is, the terms, and expounding these terms, according to the prior instruction given. (2.A.2.1–3)[32]

This passage clearly identifies the standard Scholastic practice of dividing the sermon's theme, and recommends for this purpose applying the logical distinction between categorical and hypothetical propositions. Robert of Basevorn (chap. 31, 33–34) and other sermon theorists likewise recommend using logical distinctions for this purpose.[33] As often happens in Llull's use of distinctional exposition, mention of one term causes digression to another related term. The conflation of logical and preaching doctrine evidently affects the terminology: where the logician Peter of Spain speaks of subjects and predicates when discussing propositions (1.7, 16), Llull's exposition mentions simply words or terms, as a preaching theorist would do when discussing division of a theme. In any case, the suggestion to treat a scriptural theme as a hypothetical proposition leads immediately to discussion of the construction of these propositions and concludes with the advice to make a sermon in this way, which scarcely recognizes the original function of division. The explanation of how to divide a theme as a categorical proposition more closely matches usual sermon practice. The mention of prior and posterior parts evidently incorporates this dichotomy from the previous section on "exposition." The *Ars generalis ultima* (10.98) also mentions division of the theme, but treats it rather idiosyncratically as an exercise in definition: "[T]he preacher in a sermon should define the branches or parts of the theme or sermon, for through definition the people know the thing defined."[34] This simple characterization of definition best matches the summary explanation of an encyclopedist such as Isidore (2.29.1). However, Llull may be rehearsing advice from a guide to preaching, such as Richard of Thetford's popular treatise (chap. 1), since the sermon theorists often list definition as a technique of amplification.

The idiosyncratic character of Llull's advice on dividing a theme from the *Liber de praedicatione* or the *Ars generalis ultima* makes it difficult to imagine its practical application. However, Llull seems keenly concerned to provide a viable method that subsumes conventional practice into the system of his Great Art. One indicator of his continued attention to this problem is his *Ars abbreviata praedicandi* of 1313. This work seeks to "reduce the ample catalogue of Christian themes to the simple mental structure" of Llull's system.[35] It expounds the homiletic application of a simplified version of his Great Art, and illustrates this use with thirty-two short specimen sermons (none longer than two hundred words) and suggestions regarding twenty further topics. The latter range from the nine Lullian Principles to the seven liberal arts and the Aristotelian categories of form and matter. They offer an abbreviated version of the lists of one hundred forms that commonly appear in full accounts of the Great Art. The specimen sermons are excellent examples of how Llull's Great Art serves the needs of homiletic invention and amplification. Each sermon divides its theme using combinations of four Principles from Llull's Art. The specimen sermons in the *Ars abbreviata praedicandi* comprise very ingenious illustrations of the interpretative facility necessary to find connections between Llull's Principles and a scriptural citation. For example,

> If you wish to make a sermon upon "Holy, Holy, Holy," you can go to the chamber of AEFG. According to its definitions, A is "innocent," since in so far as God is Father, God has the power to engender God the Son. God's Intellect knows that, and God's Will desires that. If not, God would be nothing and unholy. Thus there is one "holy" for God the Father, another for God the Son, and another for God the Holy Spirit. Because God's Power, Intellect, and Will are one thing, the three "holy"s are one God, and not more. And God is innocent, who causes no pride, sloth, or envy. (4.2.A.2)[36]

This example displays a typical feature of Llull's distinctional method: the mutual reinforcement of two interpretative devices. The first is a Trinitarian explication of the theme "Holy, Holy, Holy" (Isa. 6:3), following the usual gloss of this passage and apologetic defense of this interpretation against Jewish expositions.[37] The second is an argument proving the doctrine of the Trinity, which functions as a sort of theological topic. Of course, the terms mentioned here—innocence, Intellect, Will, pride, sloth, and so on—are those that correspond to the letters A, E, F, and G in the Alphabet defined for this text's application of Llull's Art. Thus, the "multiplication" of the sermon through his Art consists in seeking values for those letters that develop the Trinitarian allegory. Or, viewed in another way, the four letters from Llull's Alphabet provide a *distinctio* whose guiding interpretative sense is the topical principle "God is three in one."

Llull's Collections of Exempla

All of the advice about invention reviewed thus far consists of rules for generating ideas or discourse according to some method. Ramon Llull also provides, in addition to these generative techniques, a vast mass of ready-made material. Several passages quoted above suggest how the rhetorician or preacher can find suitable items among this material by using the combinatory mechanics of the Great Art. None of Llull's accounts of the arts of language explain this process in detail. The best-known collection of exempla in Llull's oeuvre, the "Tree of Examples" from the *Arbre de sciència,* briefly asserts their inventional application in its prologue.[38] Llull justifies organizing this collection of exempla with arboreal divisions

> so that we can provide exempla about the natures and qualities of the Trees according to their roots, trunks, branches, and so forth. Also, so that we can have great material for providing exempla, since all things are implicated or implied in the fourteen Trees. Moreover, through the exempla that we provide one has instruction in knowing natural and supernatural secrets, and for preaching and having good morals, solace, and

friendship with people. Moreover, one can acquire the universal habit of under-standing many things pleasing to hear and pleasing to understand.[39]

As usual, Llull appeals to the general relationship of implication in order to explain the inventional utility of his collection. Beyond that, he simply offers this collection of exempla as exemplary discourse: it teaches by example how to find and use ex-empla. The prologue concludes by reiterating that one can find material "according to the natures of the Trees" and that the collection "provides instruction" in this method of invention.[40] The reference to natural and supernatural secrets suggests that this method bears heuristic value as a procedure of learning. At the same time, the reference to "good morals, solace, and friendship with people" promises moral and social edification as well. These somewhat vague suggestions imply a very broad ap-plication for this material, which matches the broad use in human communication that Llull often expects for the arts of eloquence. In effect, the "Tree of Examples" from the *Arbre de sciència* offers an encyclopedic corpus of material for discourse on any topic in any situation.

Conclusion

This last passage from the *Arbre de sciència* illustrates how difficult it is to sepa-rate the exercise of invention in rhetoric and preaching from the larger system of Llull's Great Art of Finding Truth. Indeed, it is equally difficult to separate the heur-istic processes of any art that he treats from the devices of his own system. Nonetheless, the techniques noted in this chapter do allow several broad inferences about Llull's recognition of invention as a separate task in the arts of eloquence. The first and most obvious is that they do not depend directly on the received tra-dition of inventional techniques known from classical doctrine regarding rhetoric and dialectic. Llull instead offers three other tactics or resources of invention: the combinatory mechanics of his own Great Art; the techniques of exposition and am-plification recommended for scriptural exegesis and preaching; and the use of exempla and other illustrative material, probably as developed in contemporary sermon aids. These three modes of invention range between two extremes: indi-vidual terms selected and manipulated through an *ars combinatoria* on the one hand and ready-made exempla arranged in vast encyclopedic collections on the other hand. These two extremes form, as it were, a Neoplatonic hierarchy of discourse stretching from the many exemplary particulars of material creation to the few uni-versal exemplars of the Godhead. Much of Llull's advice regarding methods for using these materials consists in explaining how those few universals—the Principles of his Art—inform and sustain the many particulars—the myriad natural and moral exempla and subjects. He most often refers to this relationship with the broad term "implication." Nonetheless, in so far as Llull's three preferred inven-tional methods all depend historically on earlier precedents, it would be easy to argue that received tradition provides the entire basis for Llull's system. That is, the Great Art is simply a vastly synthetic and popularized scheme of artificial eloquence, which is certainly how many of its Renaissance devotees regarded it. Llull himself clearly regards his system as something more than a better way of finding material for discourse. The apparent dependence of the last two types of inventional strategies on contemporary preaching methods indicates the preeminently evangelical concerns of his project. Consequently, the secular arts of eloquence remain inimical to Llull's contemplative, missionary, and reforming ideals. His complaints about the perversion of knowledge in the schools make it easy to imagine why he would prefer to devise an alternative for the Scholastic arts of language. Llull offers his Great Art as a program for finding truth, not words.

5

Beauty in Language

Achieving beauty in language is the objective that Ramon Llull most often ascribes to the arts of eloquence. This focus seems narrower than the conventional definition of rhetoric as the "art of speaking well," which both vernacular and Latin poetics invariably repeat. It may reflect Llull's preference for a somewhat old-fashioned view of the arts curriculum: twelfth-century authorities who teach ethics through the trivium also tend to identify rhetoric largely as the art of verbal ornament.[1] Yet his attitude also parallels that of the great contemporary preacher Remigio de' Girolami, who usually mentions rhetoric in his learned writings only as an art of verbal orna- ment.[2] At times Llull even seems to exclude completely Christian use of the arts of eloquence, in terms that recall the most severe patristic opponents of pagan learn- ing.[3] Still, he does recognizes in his *Libre de contemplació* (240.22–24) that language is not innately sinful: it expresses truth or falsehood equally well. In this respect, Llull faithfully follows Augustine's recommendation (*DC* 4.2.3) to exploit all the means of eloquence for the ends of Christian instruction. In general, Llull's conception of rhetorical ornament probably parallels most closely the view ex- pressed in Grosseteste's *De artibus liberalibus*, which grants rhetoric the use of ornament for the sake of moving the emotions in moral instruction, but considers appeals to the passions unnecessary to teaching truth.

Ultimately, Llull follows the Augustinian bidding (*De musica* 6.17.56) to seek the beauty that comes from God.[4] As a result, Llull's remarks on beauty treat it vir- tually as a transcendental, like truth or unity in the schemes of some Scholastic authorities.[5] Perhaps for this reason his *Rethorica nova* almost exclusively employs the Latin terms *pulcher* and *pulchritudo*, since in medieval usage these typically indicate the intrinsic beauty of a thing.[6] His accounts of eloquence usually treat beauty as an innate constituent of language, like his own Principles, and therefore capable of manipulation by the Christian speaker who rightly orders the powers of body and soul. Chapters 2 through 4 have analyzed how this process depends fun- damentally on the mind's discovery and understanding of beauty in creatures as a manifestation of the Creator. Anything is beautiful insofar as it leads to love, knowledge, and praise of God. The absolute precedence of this objective requires the ontological and epistemological existence of beauty always to precede its linguistic existence for Llull. His insistence on the real causes and right recognition of beauty in language, rather than any concern for cultivation of the verbal arts, determines his arguments regarding all the devices of ornament that correspond to the rhetorical division of style. This chapter reviews these arguments, considering first those regarding the simplest phonic and semantic elements of verbal ornament (sounds, letters, and words) and then those regarding more complex syntagmatic structures of style (clauses and sentences).

The Arts of Language

Llull's accounts of eloquence include very limited advice regarding the multifarious devices of style commonly taught in the arts of language. As I noted in the introduction, he probably did not receive any formal training in the arts curriculum. Moreover, disdain for the immorality and frivolity of secular literature would certainly discourage his interest in the *ars poetriae* or Ciceronian rhetoric taught in the schools. The nonacademic nature of Llull's education may also explain his disregard even for a general science of language. He ignores the proposals of Arab authorities such as Alfarabi (*De scientiis* chap. 1) and Scholastic contemporaries such as Roger Bacon (*De signis*), who recognize a separate, more general field of linguistic inquiry than the individual arts of the trivium. Llull's own *Doctrina pueril* (73.1) simply declares that one should study grammar because worldwide use of Latin would increase communication among all races.

Llull's proposal regarding Latin suggests that he regards language study sheerly as a means to the ends of Christian evangelism. He repeatedly entreats princes and prelates to establish special centers to teach Oriental languages, like those provided by the mendicant orders for their overseas missionaries.[7] Llull did convince King James II of Majorca to found one center at Miramar.[8] In any case, the ultimate objective of this multilingual education is to reduce the divisions caused by the diversity of languages. As the *Libre de Blaquerna* argues, "[T]hrough the participation of one people with another there will be love and concord and the Holy Roman Faith will be preached in the lands of pagans and infidels" (95.4).[9] The terms "participation" and "concord" apply to preaching in particular and cultural behavior in general the same relationships of resemblance that govern all human existence. This quest for the unity of likeness in diversity reinforces his view of Latin as a universal language. The *Libre de Blaquerna* (chap. 94) explains at length how this utopian scheme will remedy the alienation of all races and religions, concluding that "if there is only one language, people will understand one another, and from this understanding they will love one another and adopt from one another similar customs, which will create concord among them" (94.6).[10] His argument assumes traditional moral lessons about the consequences of Babel rather than philosophical inquiry about the general structure of language.[11] Llull's evangelical justifications for a universal language usefully remind us that his cultivation of the vernacular does not seek the "illustration of the mother tongue" heralded in Dante's *De vulgari eloquentia,* but instead pursues the same popularizing and propaedeutic objectives announced by contemporary French and Italian translators.[12] Ultimately, Llull's interest in reaching every believer and nonbeliever through their own languages reflects a popularized nostalgia for the Adamic language and aspiration to union in the mystic Logos.[13]

In short, the same evangelical and reforming ideals that motivate Llull's adult education in general also determine the scope and emphasis of his views regarding the study of language in particular. Consequently, Ramon Llull's oeuvre includes no work on the arts of language that might help us understand better his conception of the phonic or semantic foundations of verbal beauty.[14] Despite its title, his *Liber de significatione* is a work of metaphysics and epistemology. Even his logical treatises say relatively little about the character of linguistic signs, but instead focus chiefly on problems of dialectical argumentation regarding the demonstration of divine truths. They scarcely mention the "properties of terms," "modes of signification," "consignification" or other logico-linguistic issues that the Schoolmen developed and applied to theological inquiry.[15] A singular indication of Llull's limited and utilitarian interest in grammar appears in his *Ars notatoria.* This early work offers a system for creating *reportationes* of disputations or readings, using the terms and categories of the Great Art. Llull proposes a scheme of stenographic notation that first lists symbols for the traditional eight parts of speech, six persons of the verb, and three main tenses, even before listing the symbols used to indicate the elements of his own Art. This preliminary treatment perhaps reflects traditional esteem for grammar as the origin and foundation of the liberal arts, as Isidore calls it (1.5.1). However, the linguistic doctrine that Llull mentions hardly suffices as instruction in grammar. Its inclusion in symbolic form in the *Ars notatoria* is probably more interesting as a reflection of the mnemonic or graphic aids used in elementary grammatical instruction during Llull's era.[16] His longest account of grammar is two chapters from the *Ars generalis ultima* (10.87–88). This passage simply and summarily explains how the eight parts of speech, case, conjunction, declension, gender, regimen, construction, orthography, and figures of speech all derive from application of his Great Art. That review evidently follows the rubrics of some conventional school text on grammar, such as Alexander of Villadei's *Doctrinale,* but again offers no substantive grammatical doctrine.

Sounds and Syllables

Llull offers throughout his writings isolated references to the vowels, consonants, and syllables that constitute the primary elements of language, according to the classical authorities Donatus (1.2–4) and Priscian (1.2.3–3.11; 2.1.1). The ancient grammarians devote particular attention to these elements because they are fundamental to the *enarratio poetarum* that constitutes such a large part of their enterprise.[17] In the thirteenth century, the vernacular *arts de trobar* offer a similar basis for cultivation of the Provençal lyric.[18] Although Llull uses verse for many of his devotional and didactic works, he never gives any systematic account of sounds or prosody. The *Liber de quinque principiis* (9.5.4) briefly characterizes rhetoric as the composition of "syllables, proportionately syncopated, from which beautiful words are generated and beautiful predicates are colored" in composing complete propositions.[19] This allusion perhaps mistakes metrics as a major concern of rhetoric, but does recognize the role of syllables as primary elements of composition. Llull refers occasionally to this fundamental role of syllables in other writings. For example, the *Rethorica nova* mentions them in several contexts. That treatise's explication of the Rule How? cites the "vowel and consonant sounds" created in vocal speech (3.22). Two other sections of that text use the term "syllable" more precisely to discuss the separation of sounds "conjoined under one accent" (3.10.1; 3.12.1). More advanced considerations of metrics rarely occur in Llull's writings. The *Aplicació de l'art general* includes rather cryptic advice about shortening masculine and lengthening feminine words (ll. 824–27). This perhaps alludes to some account of paronomasia, like the advice on shortening or lengthening the quality of sounds from the *Rhetorica ad Herennium* (4.21.29–22.32). The mention of gender perhaps recalls the vernacular grammarian Ramon Vidal's explanation of "how masculine and feminine words become longer or shorter in each case" of Old Provençal (*Razos* 272–73).[20] Without the context of more extensive explanation, it is impossible to know whether Llull understands the function of these precepts or is simply excerpting received doctrine for purposes of illustration.

Words and Locutions

Priscian (2.3.14) defines the word *(dictio)* as the minimal part of a complete sentence and Llull likewise recognizes its basic contribution to language. His own Great Art, of course, relies on individual terms as the primary elements of its discourse. However, in so far as Llull's *ars combinatoria* is more logical than grammatical, it is not surprising to find that his linguistic metalanguage owes more to the logicians than to the grammarians. For example, the *Rethorica nova* defines language as "significant speech" *(vox significativa)* in its analysis of the Rule What? (3.15). The term *vox significativa* ultimately derives from Aristotle's famous phrase "conventionally significant utterance" *(vox significativa ad placitum* in the Latin version of *De interp.* 2 16a19), and commonly appears in the introductory sections of Scholastic logical authorities such as Peter of Spain (1.3). Nonetheless, Llull's incidental use of this well-known label seems to bear little theoretical import. Another section of the *Rethorica nova* explicitly offers the Latin terms *vocabulum* and *dictio* as alternative ways of saying "word" (2.1.1). Imprecise use of school terminology often occurs in vernacular learned literature, so Llull's indecision on such questions is hardly surprising.[21] In general, Llull's use of grammatical terminology in the *Rethorica nova* is most noteworthy for its inattention to definition of the terms themselves. That is, his explanations either assume prior knowledge of grammatical doctrine or simply use grammatical terms in order to illustrate some larger claim about the metaphysical or epistemological status of language.[22] The applied use of this material in the

Rethorica nova suggests that Llull is probably adapting grammatical doctrine as illustrative data from some encyclopedia or compendium. Moreover, his exclusive reference to so many rudimentary elements also implies that these serve an eristic function in the overall plan of the *Rethorica nova*. That is, Llull cites these elements as basic principles of language, following his usual insistence that any knowledge must preexist in its most general principles.

Many of Llull's comments on the role of individual words in verbal ornament synthesize elementary grammatical, logical, or rhetorical lore for the purpose of demonstrating the general application of his own Great Art. For example, the *Aplicació de l'art general* recommends using the predicables of genus and species to ornament rhetorical discourse (ll. 931–37, 943). This advice is unlikely to come from the treatment of ornament in an *ars poetriae*, but may adapt rules for amplification from the *artes praedicandi*. Eiximenis (3.7.4–6) lists the ten logical categories (but not the predicables like genus and species) as suitable devices for amplifying one's material. Another example of Llull's hybrid theorizing appears in his analysis of the Rule How Much? from the *Rethorica nova*. There he distinguishes between "simple" words like "king" or "queen" and "compound" speech like "The king and queen have great beauty" (3.18). The classification of simple and compound speech remits ultimately to Aristotle's *Categories* (2 1a16–9), but recurs under many guises in the Scholastic Old Logic, Arab authorities, and contemporary arts of language. Given the wide diffusion of such elementary distinctions and the universal scope that Llull claims for his Great Art, this synthesizing confection of precepts perhaps represents again his deliberate effort to provide basic principles for all language arts.

Amid so much broadly rudimentary advice regarding the contribution of individual words to verbal ornament, it is surprising to find Llull offering a very concrete recommendation about usage. His explanation of the Rule Why? in the *Rethorica nova* (3.17) advises a speaker to say "I request" *(requiro)* rather than "I beg" *(rogo)* when soliciting a favor. The verb "request" is more beautiful than "beg" because the former derives from "goodness and generosity." These comments on the impropriety of the verb "to beg" ultimately derived from advice in Seneca's *De beneficiis* (1.1.5), and circulated widely in moral compendia such as the *Moralium dogma philosophorum* (1.B.2.a₁). This reliance on ethical literature is probably not coincidental, since Llull's illustration of this precept offers an implicit moral lesson. As an example of avoiding the verb "to beg," he suggests the case of a knight who asks his king for a horse in order to serve the king better. Variations of this example are common in the *Rethorica nova*, perhaps because they illustrate well Llull's advice regarding the choice of superior subjects to teach superior truths.[23] Indeed, the example of the knight requesting a horse in order to serve his king offers a ready allegory for the way humans should use the creation in order to serve their Creator.

New and Strange Words

Llull often recommends achieving verbal beauty through "new and strange words" and cites this recourse to justify the neologisms used in his Great Art. His vernacular writings must frequently introduce new Latinate terminology in order to translate learned vocabulary from that language, as the prologue to his *Art amativa* explicitly argues. His recourse to neologisms offers some interesting parallels and contrasts with the devices taught in vernacular and Latin poetics. Llull most often explains the use of novel word forms as a technique of verbal ornament. Thus, the *Libre de contemplació* incidentally mentions "new expressions" *(novelles raons)* as one of the most attractive elements in jongleuresque lyrics (118.4, 21). Chapter 359 of this work justifies their use more exactly:

> Just as number is more beautiful and greater and major terms exist before the minor, so words are more beautiful when they speak of a greater number, greater comparisons, greater novelties, and strange things.
>
> Hence, blessed be you, Lord God, because the rational soul cannot fully satisfy itself in this world yet desires its fulfillment. Therefore people delight more in hearing new and strange words, because they have the intention of achieving what they desire better through them than through words that they are accustomed to hear. The soul cannot find fulfillment in or through these. Hence, thanks to the pleasure that the soul has when one hears new reasons and demonstrations, they embellish the speech of one who speaks them. Just as a thing is more substantial when it is said about *esse* than about *bene esse,* so every new strange word comes closer to [satisfying] the desire of the soul that lacks it, than do old words that the soul has used in matters where the soul finds no fulfillment (359.25–26).[24]

Overall, these arguments claim that novelty facilitates the soul's Lullian *intentio* by stimulating its quest for truth. Although the *Libre de contemplació* predates Llull's invention of his Great Art, the repeated use of "greater" in the first lines of this passage strongly suggests an argument based on the Lullian Principles of Greatness and Superiority. In this case, greater novelty correlates with greater beauty in the hierarchy of being, discourse, and knowledge. As an example, Llull apparently cites the numbers of arithmetic and the major and minor premises of logic. These comparisons to elements of learning in other arts perhaps imply that use of novel language serves the quest for secular knowledge, and thence to sacred truths. Thus, Llull's subsequent explanation unambiguously treats this usage as a function of spiritual psychology. The term "comparison" employed here evidently refers to the predication of accidents about a substance, which Llull often recommends as a device for comparing different levels of substance and accident in the hierarchy of being (as explained more fully below). Thus, Llull claims that one deals more directly with substance through being alone *(esse)* than through being qualified in some way *(bene esse).* This Aristotelian commonplace *(An. post.* 2.2 90a32) provides analogical support for his claim that the mind gains greater satisfaction from new words than from familiar ones. New words would thus be more "substantial" and familiar ones more "accidental" with respect to the soul's pursuit of knowledge. Novelty, in short, accelerates the signification that creatures provide of the Creator and helps the soul's pursuit of *rectitudo.*

Given the spiritual implications of this argument, it is unclear whether Llull's comments bear any necessary connection with the advice on using new expressions commonly offered by poetic preceptists from Horace *(Ars poetica* ll. 45–72) to Geoffrey of Vinsauf *(Poetria nova* ll. 251–55, 756–64). Opinions about the role of uncommon usage also exist in the troubadour poetics that Llull might have known as a young courtier.[25] He could even have found advice on the use or abuse of neologisms in ethical literature on speech, such as the maxims of Bartolomeo da San Concordio (11.4). Llull also mentions novel language as a means of attracting an audience's attention. This advice corresponds functionally to rhetorical precepts regarding *captatio benevolentiae* in Cicero (*De inv.* 1.16.23) and the *Rhetorica ad Herennium* (1.6.10). For example, Llull's *Aplicació de l'art general* (ll. 972–83) urges its reader to "amplify your sermon" (*montiplica ton sermó*) with novelties because "when one hears something new said, hearing perceives its beauty."[26] The reference to a sermon suggests that the *ars praedicandi* is the context of Llull's advice. Thus, Robert of Basevorn recommends engaging the audiences's interest with marvelous, terrifying, or interesting exempla (chap. 13, 24).

Ramon Llull's most striking use of neologisms is the creation of separable suffixes to indicate his innate correlatives and the parallelistic repetition of these terms in his argumentations.[27] The epilogue to Llull's *Compendium artis demonstrativae* calls this an "Arabic way of speaking" and "not a usual way of speaking among the Latins."[28] He does not indicate exactly which Arabic morphological features this usage imitates or the precise heuristic or eristic advantage that it offers. He simply refers to it as a way of "declining" *(declinare)* terms according to their "force and strength" *(de vi et virtute)*. Presumably this usage makes Lullian arguments more attractive to Arabic listeners, but Llull's comments imply that it holds benefits for Latin and vernacular audiences as well. The model of universal signification reviewed in chapter 4 already justifies this usage as the most appropriate means of naming the real metaphysical relationships that these suffixes indicate.[29] Moreover, the example of Augustine (*De trin.* 8.10.14, 9.2.2) already authorizes expounding theological arguments with the kind of wordplay involved in Llull's parallel suffixes. Augustine's usage in turn probably adapts Greek precedents that suggested similar arguments to Arab authorities such as Algazel, whom Llull certainly knew.[30] Llull's use of this wordplay for stylistic purposes has equally broad precedents. He may have acquired a taste for similar techniques from the vernacular lyric: some troubadour poets use devices of paronomasia, especially as a means to elucidate moral truths.[31] However, Llull's reliance on Latin endings to create the terminology of his innate correlatives suggests imitation of more learned sources.

As a device of style, Llull's use of parallel suffixes resembles most the more elaborate techniques of homoioptoton *similiter cadens* that contemplative and sermon literature often employ. Elaborate devices of paronomasia abound in the texts of twelfth-century authorities such as John of Fécamp. This author's fondness for verbal manipulation reflects the "traditional monastic preoccupation with written words" promoted by the exercise of silent, meditative reading,[32] which Llull certainly fosters through use of his Great Art. Recourse to figures of repetition likewise pervades the sermons and letters of Saint Bernard, which enjoyed wide circulation as texts for meditation and preaching.[33] Robert of Basevorn (chap. 7) cites Bernard's style as a model for his contemporaries. Llull's use of standardized endings to name the innate correlatives also creates ready-made *concordantiae verbales*, like those used to organize dictionaries of Scripture or collections of *materia praedicabilis*. These resources enabled a contemporary preacher like Servasanto da Faenza to use numerous set phrases and expressions.[34] By the time that Thomas

Waleys wrote his treatise *De modo componendi sermones* in the fourteenth century, many preachers were evidently using rhymed terms in *distinctiones* and habitually consulting rhyme lists to find these terms. Hence, Waleys especially criticizes those who fill their sermons with words ending in *bilis, trilis, osus,* and *bosus,* because these devices occupy the corporeal ears with pleasing sounds while the spiritual ears remain unsatisfied (chap. 7).[35] Robert of Basevorn advises that phrases constructed from words of similar endings not exceed three (add.).[36] It is difficult to ignore the parallel between the examples cited by Waleys and the system of suffixes created in Ramon Llull's terminology of "innate correlatives." He would certainly not be the only layperson to imitate the diction of the preachers.[37]

The artistic appeal of these repetitious wordplays is perhaps difficult for modern readers to appreciate. Yet, insofar as they offer a trick to the eye or ear, they seem to provide an occasion for both aesthetic and intellectual *affectio.* This aural appeal perhaps explains why popular preaching uses so many devices of this sort, from alliteration and rhythmic prose to end-rhyme and full verse.[38] Llull's works probably would not benefit from these patterns, because his prose diction is so turgid, even in his most finished model sermons. He almost never employs those stylistic devices, such as fluid use of diacope, that imitate oral delivery. These techniques do appear in the sermons of twelfth-century authors such as Hildebert, whose works circulated in popular thirteenth-century collections.[39] The style of Hildebert's sermons probably resulted in part from reliance on rote oral memorization, rather than consultation of written texts, and oral dictation, rather than direct composition on paper.[40] By contrast, Llull's works, especially those that apply his Great Art, seem composed by and for meditative reading. Nonetheless, his repetition of neologistic forms must have elicited some aesthetic response from readers of his works. It perhaps prompted the same admiration as the frequent citation of Latin *auctoritates,* which some contemporary preachers used as a conscious means of achieving greater stylistic magnificence or even of insinuating the presence of the Verbum.[41] Thus, the terminology of Llull's innate correlatives constantly invokes the greatness and the authority of their divine exemplar. Or, it possibly evoked respect as a realization of the traditional ideal of *sermo humilis.* However, Llull's writings do not display the kind of simplicity admired, for example, in the sermons of Geoffrey of Babion. Known only as a *magister scholae* from Angers, Geoffrey composed discourses prized enough to pass under the names of Hildebert and Augustine. His knowledge of grammar, the Old Logic, and patristic literature probably did not exceed Llull's, but he applied it in straightforward presentations of moral doctrine, with little allegorical or distinctional flourish.[42] Llull's idiosyncratic nomenclature would be more likely to elicit the kind of judgments rendered on the style of humble macaronic language called *sancta rusticitas*, which later medieval preachers developed.[43] Although some authorities found this semilearned speech charming, it became a constant target of later humanist satires on Scholasticism.[44] Consequently, other authors and translators of vernacular spiritual literature in the later fourteenth century began seeking ways to avoid such devices.[45] By the end of the fifteenth century an early Renaissance devotee of Lullism like Jacques Lefèvre d'Étaples considered Llull's terminology barbarous.[46]

Lullian *Determinatio*

The technique for creating verbal beauty that Llull mentions most often is the appropriate combination of words. His recommendations correspond functionally to the devices of *determinatio* described by grammarians such as Geoffrey of Vinsauf (*Poetria nova* ll. 1761–841).[47] However, Llull's precepts rarely approach the aesthetic or linguistic complexity of advice proffered in the *artes poetriae*. In fact, his interest in the association of terms may simply represent an application of his own *ars combinatoria*. His explanations of this technique certainly do not recommend any special attention to nuances of connotation or contextual meaning. Instead, they typically offer general rules that function virtually without reference to pragmatic considerations of context. For example, the *Rethorica nova* explains that

> this word "queen" has in itself great beauty and decorum, which is its essential form. It also has an accidental form, which results if one adds a word signifying goodness to it. For goodness greatly adorns the loveliness and beauty that this word "queen" signifies, when one says "The queen has great goodness" or "The queen is good." The reason for saying this is obvious, because the beauty that this word "queen" signifies best agrees with goodness. And therefore goodness, the accidental form, adorns and beautifies the beauty of the queen, the essential form. (1.1.1)[48]

The hylemorphic model applied in this passage almost undermines the value of this advice as poetic precept. Llull's advocacy of subsistent substantial and accidental essences tends to weaken his appeals to the distinction between a being's essence and its particular accidents. In fact, the correlation of these essential and accidental forms with Lullian Principles such as Goodness or Greatness suggests that essence and accident simply enjoy the same "coessentiality" as the Principles themselves. Thus, the distinction of essence from accident and its correlation with Lullian Principles actually explain how the terms "queen," "goodness," and "beauty" necessarily belong together, rather than how one might artfully conjoin them. This explanation relies fundamentally on Llull's insistence that language mirrors being but depends as well on a basic ethical norm. That is, "goodness" should adorn the beauty of "queen" because a queen should possess moral virtue as well as physical attractiveness. Llull expresses this ideal in the phrase "best agrees" (*optime . . . concordat*), which implicitly appeals to the Lullian Relative Principle of Concord. As so often happens in Llull's discourse, the terminology of his Great Art formalizes some basic natural truth or moral law.

This generation of rhetorical precept through application of Lullian categories is clear in the transition from this example of Concord to an example of Contrariety. The *Rethorica nova* continues immediately to the following recommendation:

> And this is also manifest to the Senses in its contrary. For if one were to say "The queen who has great beauty has great malice," we see clearly that malice ousts, annihilates, and befouls the first, essential form. Now here is instruction for distinguishing either form of a word, so that one can adorn the beauty of its essential form with the beauty of the accidental form, and avoid the contrary that annihilates it. For no one speaks rhetorically who says "The queen has great beauty and great malice" or "has great goodness and great foolishness." (1.1.1)[49]

Thus Llull's Relative Principles of Concord and Contrariety provide a *distinctio* for expounding verbal ornament. Even though Llull's explanation continues to invoke the distinction of essential from accidental form, its most compelling claim is simply the straightforward assertion that statements attributing defects to a monarch are "not rhetorically said." Again, the hylemorphic model and Lullian terminology of this passage simply serve to express a very ordinary norm of courtly decorum. Similarly, the *Ars generalis ultima* explains that a beautiful adjective can "disornament" a beautiful subject, giving the example "The queen is dishonest," while arguing that "dishonest" is a more beautiful word than "malice" (10.86). This advice directly recalls the simple cautions found in contemporary manuals of courtesy such as the *Tesoretto* of Brunetto Latini (16.171–230). This kind of pragmatic advice—which Llull perhaps knew well from his own experience—may comprise the basis for much of his doctrine concerning public eloquence. The function of his explanation is evidently to provide a universally valid theoretical foundation for those practical precepts.

The *Rethorica nova* also includes several passages on word combination that abandon metaphysical distinctions altogether. Instead, they directly rely on apprehending things, people, and their relationships through the words that name them. For example, Llull illustrates the various degrees of comparison with sentences such as "The queen and the handmaid are beautiful" or "The queen and the serving girl are very lovely." These statements, he observes, are not beautiful because it is improper (*indecens*) to compare a queen to a handmaid or a serving girl (2.3.1).[50] The impropriety of these sentences arises directly from the social disparity of the personages named in them. Although Llull does not say so, this same criterion apparently applies to these "comparisons" using nouns and verbs: "The queen sings better than the lady-in-waiting" or "The queen and the lady-in-waiting perform a very beautiful song" (2.3.2).[51] It seems unlikely that these explanations adapt any particular precepts from the arts of language. They do not invoke any definite categories for the proper match of words to subject matter, in the manner of the *Rota Vergilii* or other schemes of poetic decorum. Nor do they cite any precise rules for relating persons of different offices or ranks, in the manner that the *Rationes dictandi* (chap. 5) prescribes for composing salutations in letters. At best they reflect a general pragmatic concern for respecting social status in a courtly setting. Thus, another section of the *Rethorica nova* explains how words like "queen" and "maid" are equal in number of syllables but unequal in dignity because "queen" possesses the Lullian Relative Principle of Superiority (3.12.1).

Some of Llull's claims regarding fitting word combination also simply serve to demonstrate the application of his Great Art. Thus, he applies his Relative Principles of Difference, Concord, and Contrariety to the gender of nouns, arguing that

> there is greater agreement between masculine and masculine than between masculine
> and feminine, between feminine and feminine than between feminine and masculine
> or neuter, and between neuter and neuter than between neuter and feminine. Hence
> one should say "The king is handsome," "The queen is beautiful," "The king has a
> beautiful palace." And so universally in speech involving these genders or the genera
> of any other differences, wherever one finds greater concord and agreement, there will
> be greater beauty in the conjunction of words. Thus between "king" and "good" there

is greater agreement, because they are of one gender, than between "king" and "goodness," which are of different genders. (3.10.2)[52]

The intimation of a naturalistic basis for gender appears already in Priscian (4.1.1) and ultimately appeals to ancient conceptions of the natural origin of words.[53] Nonetheless, Llull's suggestion that gender admits degrees arises sheerly from application of his Relative Principles. Their general scope evidently attracts another sense of the Latin term *genus* in the phrase "genera of any other differences," which refers to the logical predicables of genus and difference rather than to the grammatical notion of gender. The last lines apparently try to explain the solecism of combining two nouns as a failure to observe agreement in gender.[54] Such an explanation could hardly come from Donatus *(Ars gram.* 3.3) or any medieval grammatical authority. Ultimately, Llull's arguments simply affirm that agreement in gender is beautiful because it respects the Lullian Relative Principles of Difference, Concord, and Contrariety.

Finally, other passages from the *Rethorica nova* do discuss word combination using vocabulary more clearly based on received doctrine regarding the language arts, although the exact doctrine expounded in these passages can be difficult to grasp. For example, the analysis of the Principle of Truth in the third distinction identifies four principles of true speech: expression (*vox*), tense (*tempus*), verb (*verbum*), and noun (*nomen*). Llull refers to expression as the subject (*subiectum*) of speech, as though speech were an accident of expression. This claim in fact involves a somewhat controverted issue: Vincent of Beauvais (*SD* 2.2) rejects the view suggested by Llull, although the speculative grammarian Boethius of Dacia (quest. 6) does call expression the subject of the modes of signifying. Llull adds that a verb is the necessary part of speech for indicating tense, while a noun is also necessary "because without it the speech is unable to be called beautiful" (3.8.1).[55] This reference to the verb's function as indicator of tense in a sentence recalls the basic doctrine specified by Priscian (8.1.1). However, Llull's subsequent comment on the noun shifts somewhat abruptly from recognizable details of grammatical theory to his general concern for beautiful discourse.[56] Nonetheless, this leap from particular elements of correct speech to the general goal of lovely speech exemplifies Llull's whole process in expounding the arts of language: he subordinates right usage to right eloquence as he conceives it.

Lullian *Constructio* and Composition

In addition to offering advice on word combination that corresponds functionally to contemporary theories of *determinatio,* Ramon Llull also mentions aspects of composition that correspond to grammatical theory on sentence construction and rhetorical doctrine on style. The standard classical grammatical authority on sentence construction is Priscian (bks. 17–18), who deals chiefly with questions of agreement and government. The Scholastic speculative grammarians or *modistae* developed very complex and sometimes highly artificial explanations of agreement and government as functions of word order.[57] Since modistic doctrines are far more sophisticated than any described by Ramon Llull, it is not surprising that his works offer virtually no discernible allusions to them. His remarks on word order parallel in function the precepts of classical rhetorical authorities who treat word order as a function of compositional style. Their treatments rely heavily on the figures of speech or thought, which appear as elements of composition even in summary treatments such as Isidore's (*Etym.* 2.20). The definitions of the figures of speech underwent continuous reclassification and elaboration during the Middle Ages and Renaissance, especially in order to meet the stricter limitations of word order in the modern vernacular languages.[58] However, Ramon Llull never mentions any figures except simile and metaphor, which he regards preeminently as devices of exemplification, as I will explain in chapter 6. Consequently, his precepts on composition scarcely resemble ancient or medieval doctrines on either sentence construction or style. Instead, Llull's recommendations on these issues virtually always seek to promote the homology between the orders of language and being.

Llull's suggestions regarding beautiful construction and composition include an even more eclectic range of grammatical, logical, and rhetorical lore than his advice on beautiful combination of words. Thus, his *Aplicació de l'art general* (l. 835) applies the phrase "beautiful style" (*bel estil*) to various devices of composition and ornament that it mentions, although its cryptic diction obscures their exact functions. Llull's references to stylistic techniques in other works are not much clearer. For example, the *Rethorica nova* explains that

> [c]ompound speech is like this: "The king and queen have great beauty." One calls it compound speech (*compositio verborum*) when many clauses are conjoined and words multiplied. For example, if one said "The king who is good and handsome, goes to the church to pray to God, where he finds the queen who is good and beautiful, who also entreats the Lord." (3.18)[59]

These two examples of "compound speech" perhaps illustrate the "multiplication of words" mentioned here, and thus offer Llull's version of the *amplificatio* prescribed by authorities on poetics. Llull's first example is as simple as the statement "This woman is beautiful," which Geoffrey of Vinsauf (*Documentum* 2.2.3) uses to illustrate discourse that needs ornamentation. The tactics that Llull typically proposes, however, bear little resemblance to those from the *artes poetriae*. The complete lack of specific parallels between Llull's precepts and school doctrines reinforces the inference that either his own literary education or his spiritual ideals must have excluded any study of the language arts.

Llull's unfamiliarity with stylistic techniques from poetics or rhetoric probably encouraged his adaptation of logical doctrines to describe methods of beautiful composition. Thus, the *Aplicació de l'art general* (ll. 931–37, 943) recommends the union of antecedent and consequent as an ornament. Although the inspiration for such advice could be the listing of logical consequence as a figure of thought in the *Rhetorica ad Herennium* (4.54.67), Llull is more likely to have known such usage from the *artes praedicandi*. Richard of Thetford (chap. 37) recommends using syllogisms, inductions, or enthymemes, while Eiximenis (3.7.4–6) adds antecedents and consequents, oppositions, the ten categories, and logical topics. Guides to preaching are evidently the inspiration for the advice to "embellish sermons" with definitions, which appears in the *Aplicació* (ll. 910–15 and 919–31). Although this precept may ultimately remit to the technique of *definitio* that *artes poetriae* draw from the *Rhetorica ad Herennium* (4.25.35), it more likely reflects the counsel of a sermon theorist such as Richard of Thetford (chap. 33). As in Llull's treatment of other elementary doctrines from the language arts, his somewhat vague recommendations about definition may represent a deliberate effort to synthesize the elementary devices that he considers common to grammar, logic, and rhetoric. Llull's appreciation of the general application of definitions is apparent from its role as a basic heuristic device of his Great Art in the contemporary *Taula general* and *Art amativa*.[60] Overall, his occasional references to logical relationships do not provide a comprehensive plan for either construction or composition. Rather, recourse to these relationships makes discourse beautiful because it fosters the mind's grasp of truth.

Beautiful Style as Moralization

Ramon Llull's *Rethorica nova* includes several recommendations for achieving beautiful language by using word order to represent moral truth. The beauty attained through these techniques is clearly the spiritual pulchritude of virtue. Some of Llull's suggestions probably adapt advice from moral or courtesy literature. For example, the second distinction of his treatise describes a method for recasting *(reducere)* potentially offensive statements in more polite forms. The general injunction against coarse or obscene speech *(scurrilitas)* appears in virtually all genres of medieval ethical and courtesy literature on speech.[61] Aristotle censures it in his *Nicomachean Ethics* (4.8), one of the *loci classici* of later literature on verbal morals. Similar prohibitions occur in works as diverse as Humbert of Romans's account of the *officium praedicandi* (7.49–50), Middle English adaptations of the courtesy primer *Stans puer ad mensam,*[62] and Giles of Rome's mirror for princes, *De regimine principum* (2.2.10). Llull himself offers similar advice in his list of maxims concerning courtliness from the *Proverbis de Ramon* (chap. 244). However, the advice offered in the *Rethorica nova* involves more exalted concerns than simply avoiding obscenity. Llull explains that the statement "The queen who is beautiful is not good" is foul speech *(turpia verba)*. One should instead say "It is a serious matter that the beautiful queen of great nobility and exalted excellence, since she is the wife of a king, should be defiled by the stain of any sin, because through the stain of sin all beauty is befouled" (2.5.5).[63] The contrast between the beauty of virtues and the stain of sin is a commonplace topic of contemporary moral theology (as in Aquinas 3a.87, 3 ad 3). The paraphrase suggested here evidently achieves the same purpose as the judiciously discrete exhortation that Eiximenis (3.6) recommends for preachers. Llull adds that the beauty of the revised phrase results from the good intentions *(bonum desiderium)* of the speaker and thus defines this use of paraphrase as a strategy of verbal *rectitudo*. It achieves the love of neighbor and God illustrated in all the exempla from the fourth distinction of the *Rethorica nova*.

Several passages from Llull's rhetorical treatise also recommend stylistic techniques that attempt to manifest the moral finality of language through the composition of discourse itself. Most of these recommendations involve arranging words within a sentence according to the relative dignity of the things that they name. This necessarily generates some highly artificial syntagmatic schemes. This strategy corresponds functionally to the traditional figure of *gradatio* recommended in the *Rhetorica ad Herennium* (4.25.34). However, the application that Llull advocates would generate very awkward, if not impossible, sentence structures. The classical authorities do, of course, allow altering natural word order for the sake of prose rhythm: the *Rhetorica ad Herennium* (4.32.44) justifies use of hyperbaton solely on these grounds, while Quintilian (8.6.62) admits as reasons both sentence structure and ornamental effect. However, some of Llull's proposals exceed even the limits of hyperbaton. These more extreme recommendations must relax ordinary expectations of government or modification and simply treat complete sentences as "syntactic emblems" of moral values. Perhaps the closest parallel to these devices of composition are the strategies of interpretation used in scriptural exegesis. For example, Llull's proposals recall Fulgentius's exposition of word order in Virgil's *Aeneid*[64] or Hugh of St.-Cher's interpretation of why the phrase "kingdom of priests" from Exodus (19.6) appears as "royal priesthood" in 1 Peter (2.9).[65] Monastic practices of meditative reading offered a well-developed precedent for seeking higher truths in the *ordo locutionis* of divinely inspired Scripture.[66] Use of grammatical metaphors remained popular for centuries, as Erasmus reveals in his account of a friar who likened the relationships between letters, syllables, and nouns or adjectives to the composition of the Holy Trinity.[67] However, Llull seeks to extend this same quest from the interpretation of sacred revelation to the composition of profane discourse. His precepts about the relative position of words within a sentence readily illustrate the presumed medieval propensity to regard any written text as a verbal icon.[68] It is probably not coincidental that Llull's proposals apply to natural language the arbitrary syntax displayed by the combination of terms through his own Great Art.

For example, the second distinction of the *Rethorica nova* offers this advice regarding the composition of beautiful "comparisons":

> Someone who says "The queen is beautiful" speaks beautifully by putting a substantive before an adjective in this speech. This is because a substantive has greater essence and nobility *(dignitatem)* than an adjective predicated of it, which would lack a place to exisit without it. And so it happens that one who puts an adjective before a substantive in speech—as when one says "Beautiful is the queen"—utters foul and disordered speech. This is called foul because it does not maintain the proper nobility of the substantive. Similarly, if one says "More lovely is the queen than the lady-in-waiting" and "The beauty is exceedingly greater in the lady-in-waiting than in the queen." Rather, one should say "The queen is more beautiful than the lady-in-waiting," or "The queen and the lady-in-waiting have very great beauty." (2.3.3)[69]

Although Llull concludes this section with the claim that these comparisons are useful for speaking "rhetorically," the justification that he offers relies largely on elementary grammatical doctrine. Priscian (2.5.22–28) classifies both substantives and adjectives as subspecies of the noun, which signifies substance and quality. The ancient grammarian does not actually use the terms "substantive" and "adjective" to indicate major subdivisions of a noun. Medieval school authorities like Alexander of Villadei and Geoffrey of Vinsauf use other terms as well. Hence, Llull's usage probably imitates some other source, such as the *arts de trobar* that commonly emphasize the role of substantives and adjectives (as in Ramon Vidal's *Razos de trobar* ll. 96–133). It may also derive from an *ars praedicandi* such as Robert of Basevorn's (chap. 34), which discusses how to analyze the collocation of nouns and adjectives in order to "declare the parts" of a sermon theme. All these authorities accept the same basic doctrine regarding the adjective, namely, that it signifies only quality or quantity, and must refer to some subject already understood.[70] Llull refers to this conception by saying that the adjective "would lack a place to exist" without a substantive. Considered thus, the substantive that signifies substance possesses "greater essence and nobility" than the adjective that only signifies quality or quantity. The modistic grammarian Thomas of Erfurt (10.19) formalizes the distinction to which Llull appeals by stating that the substantive noun signifies through the mode of determinate essence, while the adjective signifies through the mode of adherence to another being. Llull never uses the terminology of the *modi significandi* and hence simply attributes a "greater essence and nobility" directly to the substantive. Of course, none of this requires the application to composition that Llull advocates. His proposal to place all substantives before adjectives at best inaccurately forces vernacular word order onto Latin syntax and at worst rejects outright the stylistic techniques taught in the schools. Llull's scheme completely subordinates the material conditions of language to the representation of spiritual virtues.

The third distinction of the *Rethorica nova* offers two similarly drastic proposals. Llull's analysis of language according to his Relative Principles of Superiority, Equality, and Inferiority recommends arranging words in a sentence according to their length in syllables. That is, those with fewest syllables belong at the beginning, those with equal syllables in the middle, and those with most syllables at the end (3.12.1). Applied literally, this proposal is only feasible in sentences where each word has a different length in syllables. Even if restricted to sentences where it could logically function, this scheme would greatly impede the use of the cursus or any of the other medieval techniques of rhythmic prose.[71] The same problem arises from Llull's advice regarding the Relative Principles of Beginning, Middle, and End. It invokes a naturalistic understanding of grammatical gender in order to propose the following scheme of syntagmatic order:

> Since moreover some words are of masculine gender, some feminine, and some neuter, the speaker should prudently and carefully arrange these, in order to place words of masculine gender first. Those of neuter gender should be placed in the middle, but those that are of feminine gender in the end. Words of neuter gender should be placed in the middle because they share in nature with words of either gender—namely, masculine and feminine—or because by avoiding either they are a middle between either gender. Hence one ought to say "Good is the king and good the queen," and not "Good is the queen and good the king." And likewise one ought to say "The king has a beautiful gold apple (*pomum*, neuter) that he gives to the queen." But if one were to say "One beautiful gold apple holds the king, which he gives to the queen," it would not be beautifully nor well said according to rhetoric. (3.11.2)[72]

Llull's two explanations of neuter words recall the definition of epicene nouns as "usually signifying animals of either nature" in Priscian (5.1.1)[73] and the definition of neuter words as signifying "lack of either gender" that Thomas of Erfurt rejects (16.27).[74] Llull's argument completely ignores the conventional Scholastic grammatical distinction between gender in reality *(secundum rem)* and gender in language *(secundum vocem),* which Vincent of Beauvais explains *(SD* 2.48). Instead, his attempt to organize words by their natural gender demonstrates unambiguously his superrealist understanding of all logico-linguistic features. It illustrates once again how thoroughly willing he is to moralize the exercise of language at every level. Llull strove to fulfill his objectives by exploiting as completely as possible the literary resources that he possessed. Where the twelfth-century monastic hagiographer Walter Daniel, trained in the language arts, employs extravagant hyperbole as a rhetorical device for expressing higher truths,[75] the thirteenth-century layman Ramon Llull, competent only in reading and writing the language, manipulates word order as a linguistic icon for the same end.

Conclusion

Beauty is the aspect of eloquence that Ramon Llull mentions most often in his remarks on the arts of language, yet his detailed explanations of that beauty are very limited. They ignore almost completely the rules of prosody and varieties of tropes or figures that comprise so much of medieval poetic and rhetorical doctrine. Llull occasionally alludes to these technical interests, but his allusions generally serve as illustrations that simply assume a wider prior knowledge, either as implicit attempts to define the basic principles of eloquence, or as demonstrations of the application of the Great Art to the arts of language. This limited interest in the techniques of discursive embellishment probably reflects Llull's limited experience with their treatment in a school arts curriculum. Yet, this circumstance cannot completely explain why his writings ignore the issues argued so fervently by contemporary Scholastic grammarians, rhetoricians, and logicians. Llull's focus reflects as well his intellectual formation through private contemplation and his subsequent devotion to the active promotion of evangelism and reform. It combines the mystical pursuit of truth from traditional monastic theology with contemporary calls for renewal of the *vita apostolica* throughout society. His willingness to moralize word order itself certainly indicates his profoundly thorough assimilation of the diction cultivated in contemplative and homiletic discourse. Llull's attention to word order displays an equally astonishing literalism, though his interpretations are perhaps no less unusual than those of the English Dominican Richard Helmyslay, who was prosecuted in 1380 for publicly teaching that the Church's mandate of annual confession applied only to hermaphrodites, because the Fourth Lateran Council's decree referred to Christians "of both sexes" *(omnis utriusque sexus).*[76]

In any case, Llull's support for missionary language schools shows that he is not oblivious to the practical use of language, nor does he regard it strictly as a transparent medium of communication. Rather, his concern for language always strives to ascend from the disorder of literal words to the order of spiritual truth. The results of his zeal are obvious in those precepts that moralize word order as virtual syntactic emblems of ethical or social values. This focus on the moral finality of language is implicit in nearly all the stylistic precepts that Llull offers. Each technique recommended necessarily involves imposing beauty on language by establishing a strict correspondence between words and things. In the *Rethorica nova,* the tripartite hylemorphic model especially assists the definition of *intentio* by providing a set of universal constituent features for all words. Ultimately, even his recourse to extravagant neologisms is thus not a symptom of ecstatic rapture, as one modern scholar suggested,[77] but instead places his work in a broader medieval tradition of mystical "uglossias" or imaginary languages that attempt to escape the material limits of the human condition.[78]

6

Beauty through Resemblance

The limited techniques of verbal ornament reviewed in chapter 5 do not indicate that Ramon Llull possessed a very wide or profound knowledge of poetical and rhetorical doctrine regarding style. Despite its narrow theoretical foundation, his work does display a broad practical familiarity with certain very popular techniques of verbal ornament. He especially recommends a wide range of devices that we would call symbols, personifications, metaphors, comparisons, similes, proverbs, analogies, exempla, and fables. Taken together, these devices comprise a discourse of resemblance that virtually defines verbal ornament for Llull. His preference results from the preeminently hermeneutic function of his own Great Art: the devices of likeness that Llull favors are all means to interpret signs. His reliance on these techniques of likening reinforces the conviction that language obeys the same metaphysics of participated resemblance found in all being and thought. Llull displays his broad appreciation of these techniques terminologically in his interchangeable use of labels such as exemplum, similitude, metaphor, comparison, or even proverb to name any sort of figural or illustrative discourse.[1] Such flexible terminology is hardly peculiar to Llull among vernacular authors: his Castilian contemporary Juan Manuel regards proverbs and exempla as functionally equivalent;[2] a century later the great preacher Vicent Ferrer uses the terms *exemple, miracle, semblança,* and even *rahó* more or less interchangeably.[3] This loose usage renders difficult a distinction between exempla regarded as "any kind of brief narrative used to illustrate or confirm the preacher's message" and similitudes regarded as comparisons lacking specific or historical detail.[4] In fact, Llull's alternating terms probably reflect the functional equivalence of these devices in popular preaching. For example, Robert of Basevorn recommends a wide range of methods as equally suitable means of beginning a sermon (chap. 31). Likewise, Llull's own *Liber de praedicatione* (2.A.3.1) virtually identifies the introduction of a sermon with proverbs and exempla. Even so, the "discourse of resemblance" functions so broadly in Llull's oeuvre that his general application of these techniques is unlikely to reflect the practices of any single language art. As I explained in chapter 3, the chief importance of these techniques lies in their contribution to the exercise of cognition through interpretation. They all help the mind achieve its Lullian *intentio* of knowing, serving, and honoring God. For Llull, this function ultimately constitutes their beauty as devices of ornament in oral or mental discourse. This chapter reviews the major categories that Llull recognizes in his accounts of eloquence, beginning with the simplest (metaphors and proverbs) and advancing to the most complex (exempla, histories, and fictions).

Metaphor

I noted in chapter 3 how Llull employs the term "signification" very broadly. Consequently, his precepts concerning verbal ornament scarcely acknowledge the distinction between "proper" or "improper" signification that usually underlies the definition of metaphor in contemporary logical or grammatical doctrine. For Scholastic authorities, metaphor heads the list of improper types of signification. Ockham the logician (3–4.3) considers careful study of its use essential to understanding the intentions of sacred as well as secular authors. Aquinas the theologian defines metaphor as comparison between two things by virtue of common effects or accidents, and distinguishes this from analogy, defined as a new way of signifying some thing's *ratio propria*.[5] Llull rarely considers these literary or metaphysical questions. He does not specifically apply the term "metaphor" to a word used in a different sense for stylistic purposes. Moreover, he hardly considers the metaphysical status of that sense, despite presenting a hylemorphic model of essential and accidental meaning in the *Rethorica nova*. Instead, Llull most often regards metaphor simply as another broad label for exemplary discourse. Thus, the prologue of the "Divine Tree" in the *Arbre de sciència* announces that it will speak "metaphorically" about God. This term evidently refers to the whole range of similes, comparisons, and exempla that this section of the text employs.

Llull's most detailed analysis of metaphor appears in an unlikely context, his *Liber de principiis medicinae* (probably composed in 1274–1278). This review of the rudiments of medical learning substitutes the term "metaphor" for the term "sign" traditionally used to name symptoms of disease or health. Hence, Llull's text jointly reviews metaphor, pulse, and urine. The latter two are the "common signs of bodily dispositions" listed in encyclopedias such as Vincent's *Speculum doctrinale* (13.158–75). Llull's text attributes to these bodily metaphors the same broadly cognitive functions that he recognizes for all signs:

> We treat of metaphor in this Art so that it will be a system for exalting the Intellect in this Art and in other arts. . . . Especially since metaphor is the bond and connection of operation among the three faculties of the soul, which are set up to remember, understand, and love one purpose, and because of the great exertion that the Intellect makes when one listener understands another. (1.5)[6]

The last line evidently alludes to the exaltation of understanding that Llull attributes to all figural language, as I explained in chapter 3. This broad cognitive function allows Llull to combine the term "metaphorically" with diverse verbs in this treatise: he describes how one thing metaphorically "signifies," "reveals," "demonstrates," and even "seeks" another. The text summarizes this wide function in the succinct definition "metaphor signifies one thing through another" (10.36.1).[7] Llull's phrasing suggests a relationship between things, rather than the discursive technique of "transferring a word from one thing to another, according to some likeness," which medieval authorities repeat from the *Rhetorica ad Herennium* (4.34.45). Thus, Geoffrey of Vinsauf (*Poetria nova* ll. 765–918) analyzes closely the clever recognition of likenesses among things, which constitutes the means of achieving this transference. Llull focuses instead on the things likened, that is, the end sought through exercise of this recognition. This is the purpose mentioned in the passage above from the *Liber de principiis medicinae*. Consequently, the metaphors analyzed in this text include revelations and significations of theological or philosophical truths that lie far beyond the scope of medicine.[8] The text explicitly offers some of these as analogies between health of body and spirit. Thus it moralizes the art of medicine according to the basic *distinctio* of "care of body and soul" widely developed in medieval moral and spiritual literature.[9] Indeed, the entire *Liber de principiis medicinae* may constitute an attempt to bring medicine within the universal moral finality recognized in Llull's Great Art. His peculiar redefinition of bodily signs as metaphors thus indicates exactly the point of intersection between medicine and the Great Art, by rectifying the feature of medical lore most amenable to his moralizing concerns.

Proverbs

The proverb is the genre of exemplary discourse whose nomenclature shows the least variation in Llull's writings: only occasionally does he apply the term "proverb" to discourse that is not a maxim, dictum, or sententia of some sort. Llull cultivates this minor genre assiduously, chiefly in collections. The largest of these, his *Proverbis de Ramon* of 1296, offers one hundred chapters on topics from divine, natural, and moral science, with each chapter listing twenty proverbs. Use of proverbs is a nearly ubiquitous stylistic device in all the medieval poetic and rhetorical arts.[10] Collections of proverbs are a well-represented genre in medieval literature.[11] Most compendia of proverbs from the Middle Ages offer moral adages exclusively, but Llull provides several encyclopedic collections that effectively restate the entire range of his theological and philosophical knowledge in sententious form. In practice, he thus imitates those popular preachers who created their own proverbs or sententiae as needed to embellish their discourses.[12]

Llull's writings use proverbs freely as devices of introduction and exemplification in all types of discourse. Indeed, the prologue to the *Proverbis de Ramon* claims that its maxims are useful in preaching and disputation alike.[13] The *Rethorica nova* treats proverbs more strictly as devices of introduction. The second distinction on beautiful language includes a brief collection of forty-nine proverbs, which it introduces with this sententious definition: "A proverb is a brief statement containing a great idea" (2.7.0). This characterization recalls Isidore's description of the aphorism (*Etym.* 4.10.1), as well as many others from the arts of language. Llull then explains that "the proverb is an introduction to the speaker's words, conferring courage and wisdom," which are virtues that adorn a discourse. The brief preface to his *Mil proverbis* likewise recommends using its maxims as "an exemplum at the beginning of one's words."[14] This exordial use of proverbs, maxims, and other *auctoritates* is common to all the medieval arts of speaking, from the *ars poetriae* (e.g., Vinsauf's *Poetria nova* ll. 126–54) to the *ars praedicandi* (e.g., Basevorn's *Forma praedicandi* chap. 31). The *artes dictaminis* especially urge using proverbs in the salutation or *captatio benevolentiae* of a letter. As a result, many collections of proverbs circulated as ancillary aids to dictaminist treatises, as in the Baumgartenberg *Formularius de modo prosandi* (6.1) or Bernold of Kaisersheim's *Summula dictaminis* (P. 2).[15] The *ars arengandi* in turn imitates this dictaminist practice.[16]

This widespread use of proverbs perhaps encouraged Llull to regard them as a fundamental device for ornament.[17] This fundamental status is implicit in the recommendation from his *Rethorica nova* (2.7.0) to use proverbs "according to the needs of the matter, form, and end of the speech," that is, according to the three hylemorphic principles inherent in every element of language. The *Rethorica nova* illustrates using introductory maxims by paraphrasing the idea *(sententia)* expressed in the first proverb from its list of forty-nine. Llull explains that "from this sort of exposition of a proverb, which is appropriate *(conveniens)* to it, one can investigate expositions appropriate *(congruentes)* to all the other proverbs by considering a similar sort of exposition" (2.7.1.).[18] Insofar as this exposition simply paraphrases the proverb, it corresponds best to the vernacular paraphrase of a Latin sermon theme that popular preachers necessarily provided for their unlearned audiences. Llull may in fact have used Latin proverbs like Scripture passages, a practice apparently common in popular preaching.[19] Although this brief practical example from the *Rethorica nova* does not clarify very fully his use of introductory proverbs, he cites this chapter as a model elsewhere in the same treatise (4.0) and in his *Ars generalis ultima* (10.86). Only a handful of Llull's proverbs from the *Rethorica nova* have the ring of *auctoritas antiquorum* (e.g., nos. 5 and 19). In general, the diction of Llull's maxims is thoroughly ordinary. Most are evidently his own compositions, either extracted or adapted from his other writings, rather than from standard medieval collections. Some paraphrase his favorite theological or moral axioms: for example, the thirty-ninth rehearses the Anselmian dictum *credo ut intelligam*. None are aphoristic allusions to famous fables or exempla, as occasionally happens in the development of popular sayings.[20] Thirteen deal specifically with communication—nos. 3, 6, 8, 13, 14, 18, 22, 23, 24, 34, 38, and 40—while the rest deal with a wide range of moral concerns. Whatever their source or topic, Llull's proverbs are not simply ornaments of style. Like any device of exemplary discourse, they must help lead the mind to knowledge by stimulating it to grasp ever more exalted truths. Insofar as proverbs constitute a likeness of that truth, they contribute to the vast Lullian discourse of resemblance.

Comparisons and Contrasts

Ramon Llull's Great Art depends preeminently on methods for recognizing similarity or dissimilarity among things, words, and ideas. Exposition of these relationships among the terms conjoined with the Lullian *ars combinàtoria* occurs through a simple dialectic of affirmation and negation, which thus plays a basic role in his proposals for the reform of Scholastic logic.[21] Mental or oral discourse enacts these affirmative and negative processes chiefly through techniques of comparison and contrast. Llull typically applies the labels "comparison" and "contrariety" to almost any apposition and opposition among the terms of mental or oral discourse, always explicated referentially as tokens of real beings. These comparisons and contrasts create correlations and distinctions between specific things or their qualities. Hence, they function more or less as analogies and antitheses, although Llull never employs these terms. In any case, his frequent introduction of these devices as techniques of verbal ornament underscores his belief in the extent to which discursive beauty consists in assisting the mind's quest for truth.

Llull's attention to the heuristic exercise of comparison and contrast perhaps results from a focus on logic during his early education. The comparisons and contrasts that Llull offers regarding things and their qualities usually rely on Aristotle's distinction between essential and accidental predication (*An. post.* 1.19 81b23–29). The medieval Latin text of Algazel's *Logic,* which Llull studied during his early years of training, regularly refers to this relationship of predication as a kind of "comparison." Llull repeats this usage throughout his career.[22] This logical sense, with its basis in fundamental metaphysical distinctions, probably justifies its use as a device of probative argument for Llull. He finds it especially useful for defining steps in the contemplative ascent or descent of the hierarchy of being, which involves comparing diverse levels of substantial and accidental existence. Thus, the *Libre de contemplació* uses the term "comparison" to name analogical arguments based on relationships of substantial or accidental predication. For example, chapter 216 argues that a disputant guides an adversary's understanding of a problem better through "proper, natural, substantial comparisons" than through "improper, accidental, unnatural comparisons or likenesses or examples" (216. 8).[23] The alternative terms indicated in the latter phrase neatly reveal Llull's tendency to equate this metaphysical and logical comparison with other discursive techniques of likening. More importantly, the fundamental premise of this advice is that paying attention to the substantial features of beings best assists the mind in its effort to rise through the hierarchy of existence to God. Llull does recognize that these comparisons pose particular problems regarding the adequacy of theological language. Thus the *Libre de contemplació* advises against comparing the Trinity to corporeal beings because "then the perspicacity of the soul weakens and becomes dull concerning divine generation and procession, on account of the obstacle that exists in imagining corporeal generation and procession" in God (215.17).[24] However, as I noted in chapter 2, Llull rarely abandons the *via positiva* for the *via negativa* of theological knowledge. In the *Libre de contemplació* and throughout his career he treats this issue as a problem for spiritual psychology, of making the soul as receptive as possible to the higher truths that it should seek. The metaphysical and epistemological conditions of that reception, which preoccupy Llull's Scholastic contemporaries, scarcely arise in his arguments.

Consequently, the *Rethorica nova* readily presents the comparison of substantial and accidental natures as a basic technique of discursive ornament. The second distinction presents comparison as the third of eight ways to beautify speech. The chapter devoted to comparison (2.3) distinctionally expounds at least three different devices: using positive, comparative, and superlative degrees of adjectives; combining parts of speech; and rearranging the order of nouns and adjectives. Llull's explanation of the first device constitutes in itself a kind of "grammatical metaphor." It applies the three degrees of adjectives referentially to

> speech having a beautiful form, end, and matter. For it is beautiful to say "The rose and violet are beautiful flowers" [i.e., with the positive degree of adjective], "The rose is a more beautiful flower than the violet" [i.e., with the comparative degree] or "The rose is the most beautiful of flowers and so is more beautiful than the almond flower" [i.e., the superlative degree]. Likewise if one were to say "Gold and iron have a good end." The end of iron is more beneficial than the end of gold, since greater good is done with iron than with gold, even though gold is more precious than iron. (2.3.1)[25]

The three degrees of comparison appear throughout Llull's writings as a kind of topical inference warrant of hierarchy.[26] The *Ars generalis ultima* simply states that the comparative form of an adjective is more beautiful than the positive, and the superlative more than the comparative, according to the Lullian Relative Principles of Superiority and Inferiority (10.86). Comparison through degrees of adjectives is a well-known stylistic device, but the overtly moralizing focus of Llull's precept especially implies an adaptation of preaching doctrine. Richard of Thetford lists this kind of comparison in his *Ars dilatandi sermones* as the fifth mode of amplifying sermons, Jean de la Rochelle notes it as a mode of dividing the theme in his *Processus negociandi themata,*[27] and Robert of Basevorn mentions it as a means of both division and amplification in his *Forma praedicandi* (chap. 34, 39). Moreover, comparison of relative beauty among flowers (especially in contrast to their relative nobility or longevity) is a commonplace of sermon and devotional literature, catalogued amply in the collections of *distinctiones.*[28] The example of gold and iron again shows how Llull's comparisons ultimately function as referential devices in which words stand as tokens of things. They allow in discourse the same comparative collocation of terms or beings that Llull's *ars combinatoria* accomplishes with symbolic letters.

The *Liber de praedicatione* (2.A.6) also lists comparison as one of its nine conditions of preaching. Here Llull offers easily comprehensible analogies for specific Catholic doctrines. Consequently, this passage provides one of his clearest explanations of the use of figurative language in theological discourse. His analogies consist of seven natural (as opposed to moral) exempla drawn from the nine Subjects of his Great Art. They illustrate combinations of substance with substance, substance with accident, and accident with accident, a scheme that Llull often recommends.[29] The first comparison cites as scriptural authority *(auctoritatem)* the first verse of Genesis— "In the beginning God created the heavens and the earth"—and uses it to prove the Incarnation by comparing created and uncreated beginnings.

This commonplace argument appears in Bonaventure *(Brevil.* 4.1.2) and in Aquinas (3a.3, 8) too. Llull might have known it especially as an argument against the purportedly Averroist doctrine of an eternal world. He also recommends expounding this comparison by citing his Principles and Rules, perhaps in order to assert the value of his methods for proving a doctrine otherwise based only on authority. Next, Llull reviews several comparisons in order to explain their suitability for use in arguments about the Trinity:

> if a preacher wishes to prove the Trinity through comparison to the soul, there are three faculties in the soul and these three are one soul, just as in God three Persons are one God, one substance. . . . And this comparison is anagogical because it is internal, natural, and exalted as much as it can be.
>
> But the comparison made between the Trinity and the sun is not superior, since the sun is one substance and its light is an accident and its heat exists as a secondary effect. So this comparison is allegorical and is posterior; for this reason it is not proportionate to the Trinity.
>
> Say that an apple has three things, namely, flavor, odor, and color. However there are various other accidents, such as quantity, relation, etc., and these are not one substance, because they are accidents. Hence this comparison does not fit the Trinity. (2.A.6)[30]

Llull's explanation employs the distinctions between priority and posteriority and between the four senses of exegesis, already introduced in this section of the *Liber de praedicatione* as devices of exposition. The specifically "anagogical" character of the first comparison is difficult to see, although the second is more obviously "allegorical" in a general sense. It is interesting that Llull disapproves of comparing the Trinity to an apple, since this would be the kind of humble example especially suitable for use in sermons to lay audiences. In any case, all of Llull's claims about the relationship of substance to accident in the Godhead express the same fundamental trinitarian dogma expounded by Scholastic authorities such as Aquinas (e.g., 1a.28, 2; 77, 5; 77, 6; or 39, 1).

The *Liber de praedicatione* next offers three more comparisons concerning the Trinity. These rely largely on the more idiosyncratic methods of Llull's Great Art. The first rejects assigning to the three Persons the respective qualities of power, wisdom, and goodness because these, like Llull's Principle of Goodness, pertain to each Person "coessentially." A marginal notation in one manuscript of the treatise indicates that this view is "contrary to the theologians."[31] Llull's claim indeed ignores the distinctions regarding the appropriation of essential attributes that Bonaventure *(Brevil.* 1.6) and Aquinas (1a.39, 7) introduce. The next comparison suggests imagining the syllogism as an eternal, infinite, substantial being. One could then rightly liken the syllogism to the Trinity, since the Son comes from the Father as the minor from the major premise, and the Holy Spirit from the Father and Son as the conclusion from the premises. Another marginal manuscript notation marks this argument "contrary to the logicians,"[32] probably because the minor premise does not literally "come from" the major premise, as Peter of Spain (4.2) clearly explains. Nonetheless, "logical metaphors" like this figure prominently in Llull's moralization of conventional logical doctrine concerning the syllogism.[33] Similar allegories appear in compendia of basic Catholic dogma such as Guibert of Tournai's *Rudimentum doctrinae*.[34] Finally, Llull suggests that the three innate correlatives of a simple, immaterial fire (if such a thing were to exist) would correspond to the three Persons of the Trinity, since they are one in substance, nature, and essence. The latter claim involves conventional assumptions that Aquinas explains in detail (1a.29, 1–2), but the comparison to innate correlatives obviously relies on purely Lullian theories. This review of comparisons from the *Liber de praedicatione* constitutes one of Llull's most precise inquiries into the questions of adequate theological language that so often occupy his contemporaries in the schools. His rejection of certain comparisons because they foster inaccurate understanding of the Godhead shows his emphasis on these devices as heuristic, rather than simply ornamental, techniques of discourse. Nonetheless, his uncertain use of terms (e.g., "anagogical") and sweeping correlations (e.g., the Trinity as syllogism) make it difficult for his arguments to achieve the precision found in Aquinas's comments on similar analogies (1a.4, 3; 32, 1; 45, 7). The aspirations and shortcomings in Llull's explanation of comparisons from the *Liber de praedicatione* demarcate well the level of lay learning that his work attains.

Comparisons between substances and accidents offer fruitful opportunities for adorning one's discourse with *allegoria per similia*. Some of the examples already cited, like the comparison of the Trinity to an apple, function equally well if understood contrastively as *allegoria per contraria*. Llull occasionally recognizes this use of counteranalogies as a separate device of verbal embellishment or exposition. Nothing in his works suggests any connection between his precepts and the *allegoria per contrarium* defined by the *Rhetorica ad Herennium* (4.34.46) or the exegesis *per contrarium* recommended by Augustine (*DC* 3.25.36). Instead, Llull creates contrary examples that appeal directly to real beings or their qualities. Thus, his *Rethorica nova* (3.10.3) argues that "'good' and 'evil' are contrary through contrary ends," while "'white' and 'black' are contrary because they differ most in the genus of color. And likewise 'fire' and 'water' because they have contrary qualities." Moreover, "the contrarity of 'good' and 'evil' seems greater than of 'white' and 'black,' and of 'heat' and 'cold' than of 'black' and 'cold,' since blackness and coldness are not properly contrary but rather disparate."[35] These last comments evidently allude to basic Aristotelian logical doctrine (*Cat.* 10–11), although this is not necessary to understanding the simple contrariety suggested by Llull.[36] The *Rethorica nova* further explains that

> "goodness" is called a beautiful word, because goodness is contrary to badness. And likewise truth, which is opposed to falsehood, and generosity, which stands against avarice through contrary opposition. Now the contrariety in these—or any other opposition—is the matter of these words through which beauty inheres in these words. (2.1.2)[37]

The last line of this passage underscores the idiosyncratic divergence of Llull's hylemorphic model of language from Aristotelian metaphysical doctrine. Aristotle posits that contrariety must be a form (*Metaph.* 10.4 1055a33–b17) while matter is contrary to nothing (*Metaph.* 12.10 1075a25–33). Llull's explanation chiefly serves to claim a real basis for discursive examples of contrary characteristics in beings, and thus to establish their opposition as a kind of axiom of nature. The *Rethorica nova* later invokes this contrariety as a natural truth and applies it to moral instruction in its analysis of the Relative Principle of Contrariety:

> Contrariety of this kind occurs in speech so that it will be directed toward the good end of true speech through justice. We can explain this in an example as well. For we see that a preacher reviles and destroys lust more by commending and urging the chastity contrary to it, than by justice. And likewise the preacher denounces misdeed and injustice more through justice than through chastity. And likewise fire is more contrary to water through heat (which is a proper quality of fire) than through dryness (which is proper to earth and not to fire). (3.10.4)[38]

Condemning vice and urging virtue by contrasting them is a basic concern of all *artes praedicandi* from Guibert of Nogent (26CD) to Eiximenis (3.5). The somewhat abrupt appeal to the example of fire and water creates an analogy between *naturalia* and *moralia,* as recommended elsewhere in the *Rethorica nova* (3.1.1). Llull's writings often cite the distinction between natural and moral subject matter, which collections of *materia praedicabilis* frequently use to organize their material. Llull's correlation of the two areas in this precept implicitly argues that the moral contrariety between virtue and vice is as intrinsic as the natural contrariety between fire and water. In any case, he ultimately explains the rhetorical value of this procedure with a simple appeal to homology, namely, contrariety among the things described in discourse will match the contrariety or antagonism in the speaker's purpose. Simply put, someone who wants to criticize something must use adverse language. This justification apparently underlies Llull's further suggestion that when "contrariety ought to exist between the speaker and audience—just as between a lawyer and an opponent—the speaker should consider these contrarieties. This is because the greater the contrariety among words, the more beautiful will be speech about that matter" (3.10.4).[39] The *Aplicació de l'art general* (ll. 837–40) alludes to this same function, mentioning as well that this use of contrarieties constitutes verbal ornament. This treatment of antagonistic language as ornament demonstrates again how Llull tends to identify discursive beauty with any device that contributes to edifying the audience.

Finally, Llull does occasionally describe ways of using counterexamples that depend more on the verbal effects created than on direct reference to things and their qualities. For example, the *Ars generalis ultima* explains that

> [j]ust as the rhetorician praises friends with beautiful words directed toward a good purpose, so the rhetorician vituperates and scorns enemies with beautiful words diverted and changed from their purpose. Thus one says to a dishonest cleric "If I were a cleric, I would use lovely and honest language." And this is clear from the definition of the purpose of concordance and contrariety. (10.86)[40]

It is tempting to regard this brief passage as one of Llull's very few allusions to the classical view of praise and blame as the purposes of poetry. His identification of the rhetorician's discourse as beautiful words used for either purpose certainly underscores his tendency to identify verbal ornament with the persuasive power of language. However, the contrariety described in this passage seems more like a kind of irony: words normally used to describe good behavior are applied to bad behavior. Llull apparently equates that descriptive function with an ordinary, referential use of words. The example that he offers suggests that he is adapting advice about moral correction from some guide to clerical conduct. His characterization of this adversarial relationship clearly esteems the speaker's virtue in suffering tribulations as much as any skill in persuading a hostile listener. Humbert of Romans (4.18; 6.29) treats the latter problem at length. Llull's explanation especially recalls warnings about antagonistic criticism of an audience's faults, as in the preaching manual of Géraud du Pescher (chap. 5). More self-interested advice about caution in criticizing peers or superiors also typically appears in courtesy manuals, such as the *Ensenhament* (ll. 56–89) of Amaneo Des-Escás, and in ethical florilegia, such as the *De verborum copia* (chap. 1). This passage thus indicates again the debt of Llull's theories on eloquence to moral literature on speech and to pragmatic norms of courtly conduct.

Similitudes

Llull's comments on using comparison or contrast to create analogies or antitheses constitute his most rigorous precepts regarding the vast range of figural devices that he recognizes. These also include many less formal types of similes, extended allegories, personifications, or even paradoxes and enigmas. Llull variously labels all these devices metaphors, similitudes, comparisons, or even exempla. The Catalan text of the *Libre de meravelles* repeatedly uses the term "similitude" *(semblança)* to name these recourses (although it tends to restrict the label *exemplis* to full-fledged exempla and extended personifications). Thus, the term "similitude" introduces the following story, which the hermit sage Blaquerna uses to instruct Felix, the itinerant hero of Llull's "spiritual romance":

> Under a beautiful tree, near a spring, were a philosopher and a shepherd. The philosopher spoke to the shepherd words of philosophy, which the shepherd did not understand. While the shepherd marvelled at the words that the philosopher had spoken to him, wolves came upon the sheep of the shepherd and devoured a great part of the sheep. (1.7)[41]

Blaquerna does not explicate this allegory, which evidently concerns those shepherds of the Christian flock who neglect their pastoral duties in order to ponder philosophical puzzles. Eventually Felix learns to recognize the lesson in these allegories, and perfects a technique of expounding one similitude with another. As I explained in chapter 3, one likeness always leads to another in the discourse of resemblance, and thus obscurity leads to eventual illumination.

Llull also uses the term "comparison," though somewhat less frequently, as a name for this kind of figural speech. For example, the *Libre de Blaquerna* tells how a deacon at Rome, having just sung the Gospel lesson for a great feast day, ponders the "comparison" offered in Christ's warning that "[i]t would be a better thing to enter into paradise with one eye and one foot, than into hell with two eyes and two feet" (92.1).[42] The circumstances of this comparison, which condenses Mark 9:42–72 or Matthew 18:8–9, offers an especially interesting illustration of how Llull's Scriptural learning, like that of most laypeople, probably depended largely on the cycle of liturgical readings. After hearing this "comparison," the deacon asks Pope Blaquerna to appoint him to go around the world making similar comparisons to people everywhere. The pope, however, assigns a cardinal to oversee a great corps of "officials for comparisons," who will perform precisely this task. This cardinal prepares a book of comparisons for his "disciples" to use as a resource of *materia praedicabilis* in their work as "criers" (92.1).[43] Rather than a great collection of exempla, this book is instead probably a list of simple spiritual allegories, proverbs or extended metaphors, like those provided to parish priests or mendicant preachers.[44] For example, the cardinal counsels a king seeking restoration to his stolen throne that "it is better to be dispossessed and just and patient, than to be unjust, greedy, and proud" (92.1).[45] Similarly, one of the criers asks passerbys in a plaza "What is worth more—a beautiful woman who displays her lustful desires or an ugly woman who maintains a chaste appearance?" (92.5).[46] The mission of these criers using simple comparisons corresponds to the kind of moral exhortation that Church legislation usually allowed laypeople to exercise as preaching.[47] This episode from the *Libre de Blaquerna* not only indicates the debt of Llull's ideas to contemporary practices of popular preaching, but also his recognition of how these practices depend on a corresponding literature, in this case the great book of comparisons prepared by the cardinal.

One of the best known writings from Llull's entire oeuvre, the *Libre de amic e de amat,* consists entirely of 365 similar comparisons, offered as short passages for daily meditation. Llull's text presents these under the rubric of "moral metaphors."[48] The devotional function of these comparisons or metaphors clearly determines their moral character, but this spiritual value is not really distinct from their cognitive value as figurative language. Ultimately, they all share the value suggested by Llull's *Art demostrativa,* which recommends that the exercise of solving questions use "metaphors and similitudes so that love and justice will exist between the respondent and the questioner; for this reason before responding to a question it is suitable to offer some metaphor from the figure of the elements that suits the conclusion, so that it will be a common principle for both disputants" (3.10.3).[49] As always in Lullian argument, the right moral disposition always leads disputants to true conclusions. The literal or figural likeness that joins all these similitudes, comparisons, and metaphors accumulates a kind of "thick resemblance" whose depth promotes spiritual insight.[50]

Exempla

Although Ramon Llull's flexible terminology makes it difficult for us to distinguish between his richly varied techniques of likening, the illustrative anecdotes that we commonly call exempla surely constitute the single most developed device of resemblance from his entire oeuvre. The exemplum was, arguably, the most important narrative invention of the Middle Ages, and a major contribution to the development of vernacular literature.[51] Ancient authorities like the *Rhetorica ad Herennium* (4.49.62) usually treat it as one among many figures of thought, and almost as a subtype of comparison.[52] Later medieval poetic authorities like Vinsauf (*Poetria nova* ll. 1255–57) or John of Garland (1.147–51, 6.358–61) continue to recommend it as an ornament. The exemplum achieved its importance as a narrative device through its dissemination in the popular sermon, which employed it almost as a defining feature.[53] Thirteenth-century sermon theorists axiomatically assert that exempla are the most suitable devices for instructing popular audiences composed of *rudes* and *simplices*.[54] Use of exempla became so pervasive so quickly that the chronicler Géraud de Frachet, writing only a few decades after Saint Dominic, already attributed to him the accomplished and consistent manipulation of exempla.[55] Whether this was true or not, Géraud's association of the little genre with the saint's authority readily demonstrates the thirteenth-century acceptance of exempla as the defining device of popular preaching.

The intense cultivation of exempla fostered the compilation of scores of vernacular and Latin collections as aids to preaching, an enterprise that evidently reached its peak during Ramon Llull's own day.[56] Thus, although modern literary histories sometimes treat him as the progenitor of exemplary literature in Catalan, in fact collections in his native tongue appeared well before, and continued to appear for decades after, his lifetime.[57] Among the most impressive thirteenth- and fourteenth-century texts in Catalan are the *Libre d'exemples de Sants Pares* (a translation of the *De vitis patrum*), vernacular versions of the famous *Somme le Roi* (or *Somme Lorens*), and the massive digest *Recull de eximplis e miracles, gestes e faules e altres ligendes ordenades per A-B-C*.[58] Llull's ability to create and collate so many exempla is itself proof of the tremendous diffusion that the genre must have attained by 1300.

In fact, the widespread cultivation of the exemplum in Llull's day raises the question of why he considered it necessary to produce so much new material at all. By the end of the thirteenth century, the mendicant preachers already possessed numerous manuals and compendia. These usually employ Latin in order to ensure their maximum utility to preachers throughout Europe, while vernacular redactions typically serve more limited audiences, such as the devout laypersons or religious literate only in their native language. Consequently, it is easier to see the value of Llull's Catalan works for lay readers than it is to imagine the appeal of his Latin collections for clerics. His frequent presentation of material according to the hierarchy of nine Subjects from his Great Art or through its *ars combinatoria* largely explains this divergent relevance. Where lay readers might find Llull's system a helpful aid to devotion, clerical readers might see it as cumbersome packaging. Moreover, Llull's zeal for promoting the *vita apostolica* and his concern for the efficacy of evangelical discourse typically restrict the range of exempla that he offers. He rarely includes the terrifying, sensational, marvelous, or frivolous anecdotes that so many contempory compendia provide. Any discourse generated through Llull's Great Art must maintain the first intention of knowing, loving, and honoring God. Consequently, he prefers to create a moralized Book of Nature to accompany the Scriptures, which Saint Francis once deemed the only book necessary for his friars.[59] Llull perhaps seeks to recover the chaste wisdom of those early Franciscans by equipping new "jongleurs of God" with arguments drawn from natural truth alone, rather than from authority, following his conviction that understanding is a mode of knowledge superior to mere belief. Thus, he offers his *Libre de contemplació* as a program for these new divine troubadours (118.21). His *Libre de Blaquerna* (88.7) describes in detail how these holy minstrels use edifying *exempla* for evangelism and moral reform. Pope Blaquerna sends out a corps of "recounters" who "take the office of relating to people exempla and good words so that they would often remember the Son of God" and who wander "through towns and cities and castles and before officials, to whom they told good exempla."[60] These episodes from *Blaquerna* do not offer a practical model for disseminating Llull's teachings so much as they advocate the moralization of secular entertainment and rectification of popular preaching.[61] The power attributed to their discourse ultimately depends on the moral and metaphysical likenesses of virtue that inform their exemplary speech and behavior, according to the processes that I described above in chapters 2 and 3.

Thanks to this broad view of the use of exempla, Llull rarely alludes to any specific Scholastic doctrines regarding their rhetorical or dialectical function. The *Libre de demostracions* (4.20.3) simply claims that use of exempla and comparisons renders any demonstration more probable. This observation perhaps alludes to the Aristotelian view of exempla as devices of probable, rather than certain, proof, which a Schoolman like Peter of Spain (5.3) typically cites. The *Libre de Blaquerna* (66.4, 22) illustrates the usual preference for preaching to laypeople such as shepherds with exempla, but also claims that this works best because these rustics accept "probable necessary reasons" more readily than arguments from authority.[62] Passages like this imply that Llull's necessary reasons may ultimately coincide with exemplary discourse, thereby effacing all conventional dialectical distinctions between probable and demonstrative proof. More often, however, Llull simply recognizes for exempla the same function that all human words and deeds bear, namely, promoting love of God and neighbor. His own use of exemplary material superlatively fulfills Saint Vicent Ferrer's advice to preachers: "[A]s far as you are able, insist with exempla, so that any sinner having that sin [exemplified], seems moved, as if you were preaching to that person alone."[63] Llull treats exempla as general means to the end of demonstrating Christian truth, just as do other compilers of *materia praedicabilis* like Odo of Cheriton.[64]

Llull's broad esteem for exempla leads him to use them in many ways, without recommending any one in particular. He even seems to avoid some commonplace uses. For example, he does not typically use exempla to close a sermon, in the manner of many preachers from Stephen Langton to Giordano da Pisa.[65] Servasanto da Faenza habitually concludes sermons on the saints with a reference to some miracle or other important achievement of the saint.[66] Nor does Llull employ the sorts of exempla or scriptural events developed as dramatic dialogues that become common in later medieval moral preaching.[67] On the other hand, Llull does cast many of his apologetic and philosophical works in the form of a dialogue and his spiritual romances often dramatize philosophical or theological lessons. Moreover, much of his work—especially those in which personifications debate—display the conflux of courtly and clerical allegory that Zink finds in much vernacular sermon literature.[68] This feature aptly reflects Llull's regular association with both courtly patrons and university adversaries. Finally, many scenes from his narrative writings do illustrate the use of exemplary discourse in everyday communication. For example, in the *Libre de Blaquerna* (1.17), the hero's parents debate domestic problems with many "good arguments and lovely exempla."[69] This conjunction of these two devices probably indicates Llull's esteem for them as probative strategies that mutually reinforce one another. This favorable portrayal of laypeople reasoning through exempla also constitutes a noteworthy appropriation of the more condescending clerical argument that laypeople must rely on exempla in order to understand difficult issues. Ultimately, Llull's enthusiasm for using exempla coincides with his general role as a popularizer and mediator between lay and clerical culture.

Histories and Fictions

The exemplary material that Ramon Llull offers as ornament for eloquence includes few historical anecdotes and far less imaginative fiction than we might expect. For example, the 182 sermons collected in his *Summa sermonum* (which occupy 470 pages in their modern printed edition) offer only three dozen references to groups such as Averroists, Jews, and Saracens, along with some fifty references to more specific persons or places.[70] His model sermons and collections of *materia praedicabilis* thus tend to be very anonymous, a characteristic that perhaps corresponds to his broad understanding of the term exemplum itself. The absence of local color is harder to explain. Where Federico Visconti, archbishop of Pisa, sprinkles his sermons with references to political affairs and events of the 1270s,[71] Llull almost never appeals to his own personal experience. Perhaps he hesitates to invoke his own authority, just as he refuses to cite learned *auctoritates*. Nonetheless, since the exempla collections of Llull's era typically offer huge quantities of material without attribution, the lack of local color in his work is perhaps not surprising.[72] Finally, a very large proportion of the exempla in his writings simply describe doctrine from the medieval natural sciences or employ stereotypical characters who personify the virtues and vices of Christian moral theology.

The small proportion of patently imaginary stories or tales that Llull recommends may reflect his disdain for secular literature. Even though he treats exempla as devices of verbal ornament, he always regards them preeminently as instruments for promoting his spiritual goals of contemplation, evangelism, and moral reform. Consequently, he almost never recognizes their secular use for recreation or entertainment, as in the literature of *fabliaux, novelle, romans,* and tales.[73] Thus, when the introduction to the "Tree of Examples" from the *Arbre de sciència* promises "many things pleasant to understand and pleasant to hear,"[74] this pleasure is surely the delight of the mind that finds God, as described in the *Libre de contemplació*. When he recommends stories about great deeds, these are from the Bible and hagiography. For example, the *Rethorica nova* observes that words recited for a fitting purpose are beautiful, like the "words of the Gospel, all the Sacred Scriptures, and the stories of those glorious people who, although they have left this world, nonetheless live on in memory. And therefore they are recited to us continuously, so that we will imitate their example" (3.3).[75] The context makes it unlikely that these stories are heroic tales sung by jongleurs, but the emphasis on memory suggests that these sacred stories do fulfill the same function of perpetutation as secular epic.[76] Nonetheless, Llull almost never includes stories about particular saints, probably because these would have had scant appeal or authority for the non-Christian audiences whom he hoped to evangelize.[77]

Still, Llull evidently recognizes in histories some value for spiritual edification. For example, the *Libre de meravelles* (chap. 57) tells how a certain king acquires a beautifully illuminated encyclopedia of science and history, which he uses for meditation on God. Even so, Llull uses historical anecdotes so infrequently in his own writings that they are scarcely noticeable among the vast number of exempla drawn from natural science, philosophy, and moral theology. A possible explanation for this imbalance appears in the prologue (par. 16) to the *Libre de Sancta Maria* of 1290.[78] The personifications Lady Praise, Lady Prayer, and Lady Intention discuss the lack of concern for the common welfare in Christian society. When Lady Praise cites the example of the ancient Romans, Lady Prayer dismisses it in favor of the example of the contemporary Tartars. L. Badia suggests that this preference reflects Llull's zeal for missionary action: the empire of the Caesars is long gone, while these Asian invaders, along with Muslims and Jews, demand the attention of modern Christians.[79]

Among the few historical exempla that Llull does offer are two well-known stories about Trajan and Alexander, which appear in the *Rethorica nova* (1.3.1; 3.2.5).[80] The former readily illustrates Llull's adaptation of received material. His analysis of the Principle of Greatness offers the widely repeated story of how Emperor Trajan was stopped on his way into battle by a woman seeking justice for the murder of her son. This story appears in John the Deacon's ninth-century *Sancti Gregorii Magni vita* (2.44) and Dante also uses it (*Purgatorio* 10.73–96).[81] The Florentine poet evidently adapted it from the *Fiore di filosofi*, which in turn followed the version of Vincent of Beauvais in his *Speculum historiale* (10.46.385). Vincent tells how Trajan promised justice to the woman upon his return from war. The woman asked what would happen if Trajan failed to return and he replied that his successor would attend to the matter. But the woman objected that it was not the duty of his successor, but of Trajan himself, to redress the wrong committed under his rule. So Trajan dismounted and immediately investigated the affair. Llull's version ascribes the event to a "certain Roman emperor" and then explains how this "king" allows the woman to imprison his own son until the king returns from war.[82] The substitution of "king" for "emperor" results from the same process of free adaptation that places his campaign in India. No other version includes this erroneous geographical information, which pertains more obviously to the adventures of Alexander the Great. In fact, a summary of the story about Alexander's liberal gift of a city to one of his soldiers, recounted more fully elsewhere in the *Rethorica nova* (1.3.1), appears immediately after this story of the "Roman emperor." The alterations in the story do not result from Llull's ineptitude as a storyteller, but instead from the freedom of adaptation typically enjoyed by all contemporary writers who drew on a common stock of received material.[83] Ultimately, it was this same freedom that allowed Llull the moralizer to reinterpret any creature as a sign of the Creator.

Llull's most obvious borrowings from contemporary genres of fictional or imaginative literature are fables. He includes three animal fables as exempla in the *Rethorica nova* (2.4.11–13) and specifically identifies the story of the council of the beasts as coming "from the stories of the ancients" (2.4.12).[84] In fact, these all derive from the Oriental collection translated into Castilian as *Calila e Dimna* and widely disseminated thereafter.[85] In Llull's own era, Raymond of Béziers translated the vernacular *Calila e Dimna* into Latin in 1313.[86] Llull adapts extensive material from it in the *Libre de bèsties* that forms part of his *Libre de meravelles* (chap. 37–43). Nonetheless, apart from the obvious didactic function of these adaptations, there is little in Llull's work that explains his views of their poetic value, rhetorical force, or moral authority. His willingness to use fables evidently constitutes his response to the question of whether Christian instruction should use fictional material, an issue that his contemporaries in the schools commonly debate.[87] Since the poetics and rhetoric of the schools hold little interest for Llull, he never discusses this issue in detail. One passage from the *Arbre de sciència* ("Arbre questional" 5.5.j.184) perhaps alludes to it, however. In response to the question whether rhetoric is "as beautiful through humble and pious words as through true ones," Llull responds that the ultimate objective of rhetoric is truth, and therefore "it often happens that rhetoric moves people to piety and love with false words."[88] The sense of the phrase "false words" here is certainly vague: it could indicate flagrantly preposterous fictions or simply invented exempla. The exempla collections of Llull's era do not reveal much concern for a firm distinction between true and false discourse. Still, preceptists such as Géraud du Pescher (chap. 5) do occasionally denounce the use of patently fantastic or incredible stories. At least one authority proscribes fables and Scholastic sophistications alike as unedifying to popular audiences.[89] Llull sometimes includes unusual geographical lore, like the Mandevillean wonders described in his *Libre de Blaquerna* (chap. 88), but he invariably moralizes these details in order to expound a particular ethical lesson. Thus Llull, like so many other sermon theorists and compilers of *materia praedicabilis,* basically fulfills Augustine's charge to exploit pagan learning as Egyptian gold (*DC* 2.40.60). Étienne de Bourbon expresses the common attitude when he praises the universal utility of the material collected in his *Tractatus de diversis materiis praedicabilibus* (prol.). Similarly, Robert of Basevorn allows the use of virtually any kind of exemplary material, arguing that the preacher's intention determines its effect (chap. 24). The florilegist Bartolomeo da San Concordio simply states that "the knowledge of stories aids in understanding Scripture" (11.11.1).[90] Ultimately, the best index of Llull's attitude is the well-circumscribed and overtly moralized use of fables and other fictions that appears in his own work.

Conclusion

Metaphors, proverbs, similitudes, comparisons, analogies, and exempla constitute the preeminent devices of verbal ornament in both Ramon Llull's own writings and his precepts on eloquence. This discourse of resemblance provides him with a rich and diverse range of techniques for constructing philosophical or theological arguments (not to mention narrative plots) through the interweaving of successive verbal, conceptual, or dramatic likenesses. Llull's works constitute exceptional testimony to the diffusion of moralization, glossing, and allegory as strategies of popular litera-ture, learning, and piety in the later thirteenth century. At the same time, his zeal for using these methods to communicate Christian truth also recalls contemporary reformers' appeals for plain-speaking evangelism and their criticisms of extravagant allegorizing.[91]

The widespread exercise of these strategies might justify the conclusion that there is nothing distinctive or novel in Llull's practice of them. Similarly, the apparent lack of any precise or profound explanation of their functions might cast doubt on claims that this discourse of resemblance necessarily involves exemplary relationships at the epistemological or metaphysical level as well. Nonetheless, recognizing the broadly discursive, cognitive, and metaphysical import of Llull's metaphors, similitudes, or exempla is essential to understanding his claims regarding the necessary, natural, and true force of his methods. Modern readers undoubtedly find it hard to recognize in the discourse of his Great Art the same rigor developed in the logical systems of his Scholastic contemporaries. However, the strength of Llull's arguments from likeness is their approximation to Supreme Truth. The truth—as created and as known—always already exists for Llull. The function of discourse is to communicate that truth by matching it as closely as possible. Llull rejects the verbal arts cultivated in the schools precisely because they seem to degrade language by diverting it from truth. His allegories, similitudes, comparisons, and exempla adorn language by guiding the soul to divine wisdom.

7

Order

After beauty, order is the aspect of discourse most often mentioned in Ramon Llull's precepts on eloquence. His accounts of rhetoric invariably relate order closely to beauty, an association already commonplace in late antique encyclopedists such as Fortunatianus and Cassiodorus.[1] Although this regular mention of order and its close association with beauty certainly implies the importance of order for eloquence, Llull nonetheless devotes far less attention to order than he does to beauty. His specific suggestions regarding arrangement rarely exceed the recommendations cited above regarding the correct placement of words at the beginning, middle, or end of one's discourse. At the same time, the comments that he does offer extend the definition of order far beyond the concern for disposition taught in Ciceronian rhetoric *(De inv.* 1.7.9; *Rhet. ad Her.* 1.2.3). Llull's conception of order typically includes not only the arrangement of words in discourse but also propriety in speaking, which he treats as cognate linguistic and ethical modes of orderliness. This broad view of order and its invariable association with beauty define an aesthetics that serves the natural theology of Llull's Great Art. Every creature signifies the Creator according to the beauty (or better, dignity) of its place in the order of creation. Llull in effect treats speech (and even individual words) as one of those creatures. This association of beauty and order may reflect the traditional Boethian definition of beauty as "right proportion" or "order," a formula that often appears in Scholastic authorities such as Aquinas (1a.5, 4 ad 1).[2] Analyses of the beautiful by early Schoolmen especially arise in the context of arguments regarding moral finality, as in William of Auvergne's *De bono et malo.*[3] Llull's joint attention to beauty and order is thus another possible index of the contribution of moral theology to his learning.

Llull's explanations of order in rhetoric or preaching typically concern three levels of discourse: sentence construction, the plan of a speech, and the circumstances of speaking. He achieves this comprehensive view of order most often through distinctional exposition, that is, he simply assembles under the rubric of "order" precepts regarding a diverse range of concerns for orderliness in speaking.

117

Occasionally he makes this collation of concerns more explicit. For example, the *Rethorica nova* (1.4) suggests that correct word order must precede correct arrangement according to the order of form, matter, and end, which presumably constitute more fundamental levels of discursive order. Similarly, the *Liber de praedicatione* (2.A.3.4) explains how the preacher must be ordered (*ordinatus*) through good behavior and saintly living. Taken together, Llull's recommendations seek to render discourse "orderly" in the widest sense of the word. This comprehensive view of order implies his larger ideal of communication as a relationship of *ordinatio* in the Anselmian sense of a creature's disposition to fulfill its moral finality. This chapter reviews outstanding examples of Llull's precepts concerning each kind of order in eloquence. In general, his recommendations all contribute to orderly discourse insofar as they help maximize the efficiency of communication with God and neighbor.

Word Order

In chapter 5 I reviewed the techniques of word order that Llull recommends for purposes of verbal ornament, in the manner of conventional poetic doctrines concerning *determinatio*. He also treats the collocation of words strictly as a function of syntagmatic sequence, without necessarily claiming to foster beauty as well. Unlike the passages cited in chapter 5, which usually treat word order in terms of number of syllables or agreement in grammatical gender, these precepts on order abandon any reference to linguistic features and simply seek to replicate syntagmatically the hierarchies of society or being in general. For example, the first distinction of the *Rethorica nova* explains that

> no word should be indifferently placed before another. Hence someone who is going to speak about a queen and a handmaid should put the queen before the handmaid, and say "The queen and the handmaid have great beauty." However, one should not say "The handmaid and the queen are adorned with great beauty." For this word "lady" or "queen" is lovelier and nobler than the word "handmaid," because the word "lady" or "queen" signifies high rank and lordship, but the word "handmaid" indicates subjection and servitude. And therefore the noun "queen" is placed before the noun "handmaid," because the worthier should be placed before the less worthy. (1.2)[4]

As I noted already in chapter 5, suggestions like these would be very difficult to implement in vernacular discourse, where syntax determines word order so heavily. Furthermore, their adoption in Latin would require abandoning most conventional poetic or rhetorical techniques of style, especially those involving prosody. Perhaps this is one of Llull's reasons for proposing such usage: to replace Scholastic displays of verbal artifice with more orderly ways of speaking that overtly serve the moral finality of language. As a device of construction or style, this Lullian *gradatio* would substitute for the use of climax recommended by school manuals such as Vinsauf's *Poetria nova* (ll. 1148–50) or John of Garland's *Parisiana poetria* (1.349–54). Llull might have found some inspiration for his technique in preaching or devotional literature. For example, Robert of Basevorn likewise notes that "a word is not indifferently placed before a word" when explaining why a preacher should explicate a theme following the word order of the scriptural text (chap. 33). Moreover, even though Llull's examples mention his usual courtly personages, the sensitivity to connotations of the word "handmaid" may derive from exegesis of the Annunciation narrative (Luke 1.38). Hence, Llull's comparison of this term to "queen" may derive from some homiletic or devotional exposition of the Virgin's roles as "handmaid of the Lord" and "Queen of Heaven."[5] In any case, Llull's view of preaching as the paramount exercise of eloquence would authorize this and other attempts to extend techniques of sermon composition as general rules for all discourse.

Beginning, Middle, and End

Llull introduces the passage just cited from the *Rethorica nova* as an example of arranging discourse according to its beginning, middle, and end. This simple conception of a speech's organization constitutes one of his most frequent recommendations regarding order. Nearly all Llull's accounts of the arts of language, from the *Doctrina pueril* (73.1) to the *Ars generalis ultima* (10.86), mention this basic tripartite division.[6] Since Llull's customary distinctional exposition often exploits verbal correspondences, this attention to beginning, middle, and end may easily result from applying his own Relative Principles of Beginning, Middle, and End. Nonetheless, poetic authorities like Vinsauf (*Poetria nova* ll. 112–202) do offer extensive instruction about arranging the beginning, middle, and end of a composition. Even so, Llull's accounts seem to draw little from these doctrines, since his precepts recognize only a simple "natural" arrangement of beginning, middle, and end, without exploring the "artful" rearrangements suggested by the grammarians. For example, the *Doctrina pueril* (73.10–11) simply claims that rhetoric teaches "which words one should say first or which last or in the middle" and tells its reader to "give beautiful examples of beautiful things in the beginning of your speech; and let the best material of your speech be last."[7] This advice on beginning evidently alludes to commonplace doctrines regarding introductory proverbs or exempla (as described in chapter 6), while the recommendation to put the best material last perhaps echoes precepts from the *Rhetorica ad Herennium* (3.10.18). Llull rarely says anything more about the ornamentation of beginning, middle, and end; equally brief precepts appear in the *Rethorica nova* (3.11.1) and *Liber de praedicatione* (2.A.3.2).

Plans of Arrangement from the *Rethorica nova*

Indeed, the admonition to organize properly the beginning, middle, and end of a discourse is Llull's most frequent advice concerning the traditional rhetorical division of arrangement. His most noteworthy statements of more elaborate dispositional techniques appear in his two major treatises on eloquence, the *Rethorica nova* and

the *Liber de praedicatione.*[8] This increased attention to arrangement, in works written
after his first visits to Paris, is another possible indicator that his interest in the
language arts grew thanks to his contact with centers of Scholastic learning.
Nonetheless, the doctrine presented in these later works still does not exceed the
basic information available from enyclopedic accounts that Llull might have studied
anywhere. Especially striking is his complete lack of reference to the traditional
Ciceronian plan of exordium, narrative, partition, confirmation, refutation, and per-
oration *(De inv.* 1.14.19; *Rhet. ad Her.* 3.9.16). Indeed, the instruction that Llull does
offer appears to depend principally on models used outside the schools, such as the
arts of civic oratory and popular preaching.

The *Rethorica nova* surveys a wide range of disparate information in its distinctional exposition of the rubric "order." Llull's fullest remarks summarize
dispositional schemes evidently adapted from the *ars arengandi.* This art of political
oratory appeared in northern Italy by the early thirteenth century as an oral counterpart to the *ars dictaminis,* and subsequently reached the court of Aragon by
Llull's day.[9] The Italian preceptists of *arengae* claim wide application for their
skills; Guido Fava, for example, promises eloquence in affairs "not only of the
courts but also in judgments and in schools."[10] Llull's *Rethorica nova* (1.3.0) proposes its use in speeches of request, accusation, defense, and counsel. Like many
other features of the *ars arengandi,* these distinctions in genre probably simplify
existing categories from the *ars dictaminis.* For example, Baldwin's *Liber dictaminum* (chap. 7) distinguishes the function of a letter with labels such as entreating
(*precatoria*), interceding (*deprecatoria*), commanding (*inperatoria*), threatening
(*comminatoria*), exhorting (*exhortatoria*), dissuading (*dehortatoria*), admonishing
(*ammonitoria*), commending (*commendatoria*), counseling (*consultoria*), consulting (*consultatoria*), and reproving (*correptoria*). Manuals of diplomatic discourse,
like the *Dicerie volgari* of Matteo dei Libri da Bologna, include an equally wide
range of types of speech for the political adviser or ambassador. Some of these
types develop from the tradition of ethical literature based ultimately on Cicero and
Seneca. The basic categories of counsel, accusation, and defense appear in the
popular moral compendium attributed to William of Conches, the *Moralium dogma
philosophorum* (1.B.2.b), which adapts them in turn from Cicero's *De officiis*
(2.14.49–19.68). They are the basic divisions of judicial oratory in the *De inventione* (1.5.7), and Brunetto Latini adapts them as genres of courtly counsel (*Tresor*
3.2.11). It is impossible to know whether Ramon Llull was aware of the wide use
of these divisions, but their broad application might have encouraged him to regard
them as especially basic principles of secular discourse.

The first distinction of the *Rethorica nova* explains and illustrates each genre of
speech in turn, beginning immediately with requests. For example, if a poor knight
wants the king to provide a dowry for his daughter, he should begin "with praises
and commendations, inserting among them examples about charity and the subject
of liberality," which will move the king's spirit to giving (1.3.1).[11] Llull advises recounting the often-repeated exemplum of a soldier who refused Alexander the
Great's gift of a city, objecting that it was too grand for him. However, Alexander insisted, declaring that royal gifts must reflect the dignity of the giver, rather than of

the recipient. This anecdote ultimately derives from Seneca's *De beneficiis* (2.16.1), appears in ethical compendia such as the *Moralium dogma philosophorum* (1.B.2.a.), and is common in collections of exempla.[12] After this story, the poor knight should mention his economic problems and the peril that these pose for his daughter's future welfare. Next, he should state his request that the king provide a dowry for his daugther. Finally, he should conclude by emphasizing how this munificence will enhance the king's honor and reputation among his vassals. Llull's advice regarding a conclusion recalls conventional dictaminist recommendations that the letter writer emphasize the usefulness or disadvantage of the action requested, as advised in the *Rationes dictandi* (chap. 9) and Baldwin's *Liber dictaminum* (chap. 8). Although the circumstances and presentation of this request may appear somewhat contrived, it is not far removed from examples in the chronicle and memoir literature of later medieval aristocrats.[13]

The *Rethorica nova* continues with an example of how to compose an accusation, presenting once again a complete outline for such a speech. The speaker should begin with "some opening words condemning injustice and sin," then "recount the offense itself and finally state the allegation" (1.3.2).[14] Llull exemplifies this procedure with the speech of a knight who accuses his lord of betraying him by committing adultery with the knight's wife. The knight begins by condemning the sin of betrayal and explains how betrayal of vassals is especially disgraceful. Then he "sufficiently and systematically" explains his lord's misdeed, "vehemently" emphasizing his own anger at his lord and arguing that such a faithless lord should no longer enjoy the loyalty of his vassal. This last statement presumably constitutes the conclusion of the speech, although Llull does not specify this. His account does stress the vigor and emotion that the speaker should display. The knight's final comments may insinuate a recommendation of action or threat of consequences, which the *artes arengandi* often suggest as effective closing strategies. The *Aplicació de l'art general* (1. 842) also mentions making accusations with "lovely comparisons," advice that echoes Ciceronian precepts about using comparisons to sharpen praise or blame (*Rhet. ad Her.* 4.49.62) and impugning the accused through analogies *(De inv.* 2.10.32).

The subsequent explanation of a speech of defense is briefer, chiefly because Llull does not illustrate its complete procedure. Instead, he simply advises those defending themselves to follow the scheme already described: begin with praise and commendation of the audience; continue by denouncing the deception or mistake that caused the act in question; and finally conclude by promising never to commit such an act again for any reason (1.3.3). This last suggestion recalls Ciceronian doctrine regarding inferences drawn from the person of the accused *(De inv.* 2.9.28–14.47), but overall this scheme offers only a very compressed version of the plan typically recommended in the *artes dictaminis* or *arengandi*.

The last type of speech analyzed in the *Rethorica nova* is counsel. Although included here as a subtype of secular oratory, the courtly duty of offering counsel comprises a virtual art unto itself, treated in separate *artes consulendi*. Some of these, like the first book of Molinier's *Leys d'amors* (a fourteenth-century Provençal compendium of poetics), fuse advice on conduct and rhetoric. Llull's doctrine is less ambitious. He recommends that a counselor ornament a speech by first recounting the "order of things that one will recommend, in order to show where one wishes to begin and how one can obtain the desired result" (1.3.4).[15] Llull emphasizes how this prior explanation of one's argument renders the counsel more comprehensible and thus more beautiful to the Intellect, which more readily grasps "whatever expedites undertaking, continuing, and completing the affair." These suggestions appear to adapt various traditional precepts. For example, the exposition of recommended action is the fifth part of an *arenga,* according to Giovanni Fiorentino's *Somma d'arengare* (chap. 1). Llull's stress on explaining one's order and attaining one's objectives perhaps derives ultimately from Cicero's dictum that a narrative be brief, clear, and plausible *(De inv.* 1.20.28), which often appears in *artes dictaminis* such as Baldwin's *Liber dictaminum* (chap. 6). The general focus on achieving a goal corresponds to the emphasis on utility that the *Rhetorica ad Herennium* (3.2.3) defines for speeches of counsel.

Despite their abbreviated character, these precepts on organizing types of *arenga* constitute the most practical and the most derivative advice from any section of the *Rethorica nova.* Llull's reliance on this secular, vernacular art of eloquence certainly demonstrates his knowledge, and perhaps his particular appreciation, of its basic precepts. It is impossible to tell whether he views the *ars arengandi* as an alternative to the rhetorical erudition of the schools, although his general antiacademic stance might favor this inference. In any case, this presentation of techniques from an art of civic oratory provides a secular counterpart to the devices of sacred eloquence that the *Rethorica nova* adapts from the *ars praedicandi.* By including features from both profane and divine arts of discourse, Llull's treatise attempts to create a general art of communication suitable for discourse on all mundane and spiritual affairs.

Sermon Arrangement in the *Liber de praedicatione*

Ramon Llull's review of sermon theory in the *Liber de praedicatione* offers his other principal account of arrangement in artful speaking. Like the *Rethorica nova,* the *Liber de praedicatione* presumably benefited from Llull's visits to Paris in 1288–1289 and 1297–1299. Certainly, he would have had abundant opportunities both to hear and to study skilled preachers in the city whose theology schools were virtually the hub from which new sermon methods and styles radiated throughout Western Christendom. In considering Llull's methods, it is useful to remember the diversity of preaching genres current in his day. His contemporaries used the homily, the sermon, and the collation alike as functional genres of sacred eloquence.[16] The patristic homily provided both form and content for monastic preaching well into the twelfth century. The homilies of Gregory the Great served as resources for centuries of later writers.[17] The sermon and the collation became especially popular in the schools of Paris.[18] The chief difference between homily and sermon was generally that between literal commentary of the entire pericope and exposition of divisions in a one-line theme. However, in popular preaching the homily also functioned as general moral exhortation while the sermon provided (often extravagant) allegorical exposition of doctrine.[19] Some differentiation of the two genres clearly existed by the end of the twelfth century. For example, Innocent III begins one sermon by deliberately rejecting the use of "divisions and distinctions" in favor of "admonitions and exhortations."[20] By Llull's day, the homily and the sermon defined the broad types of Christian popular preaching that he could have imitated in his own proposals regarding discursive arrangement. The following features from each genre seem particularly relevant to his designs.

The homily represented the simplest form of popular preaching, which consisted merely in paraphrasing the pericope for the day. Robert Grosseteste gives an idea of this minimal level when he advises the parish priest to repeat during the week the Gospel for the coming Sunday, in order to narrate the story to his congregation in his own words. Using this method, he can learn for himself all the lessons, epistles, and saints' lives within a few years. If his Latin is inadequate to read the texts, he should seek out another cleric to explain them to him.[21] A century after Llull, Saint Vicent Ferrer enthralled six thousand lay listeners at Toulouse for six hours on Good Friday, recounting the Passion in a highly embellished exposition of every moment from the Gospel narrative.[22] Somewhat more developed than the practice suggested by Grosseteste is the method employed in a collection of Provençal sermons from around 1200, where the paraphrase leads to a minimal moral explication, usually presented allegorically.[23] Most Cathar preaching evidently consisted of this limited allegorical interpretation of Scripture.[24] Llull's *Libre de Blaquerna* (92.1) describes this method of scriptural paraphrase and accompanying moral lesson. Though simple in conception, the homiletic method of moral exhortation with paraphrase of the pericope remained an effective pulpit strategy throughout the later Middle Ages. In 1228 the learned Schoolman Philip the Chancellor preached a sermon to the Franciscans of Vauvert in which he simply pursued a miscellaneous development of various related issues, in the manner of a homily or of the "moral exhortation" favored by the early Friars Minor themselves.[25] The "criers" of comparisons proposed in the *Libre de Blaquerna* perhaps attempt to imitate the inspired, largely unstructured preaching that Thomas of Celano attributes to Saint Francis, but even the methods of the *Poverello* might have owed something to the *ars arengandi*.[26]

The defining feature of the later medieval sermon is of course its tactic of expounding a scriptural theme. Scarcely less obvious is its development of increasingly complicated techniques for dividing and subdividing this exposition. Prior to the thirteenth century, both homilies and sermons often displayed very loose organization. By Llull's day, the learned or so-called university sermon almost always employed some variation on a definite and complex plan. Theologians from different schools and generations favored different designs, but their underlying format usually follows this scheme, recognized by Thomas of Salisbury in the early thirteenth century:

1. Opening prayer
2. Protheme (antetheme; with its own divisions and development)
3. Statement of the theme (the Scriptural passage analyzed in the sermon proper)
4. Division of theme and statement of its (usually three) parts

5. Development of each part
    Development of part one
    Development of part two
    Development of part three
6. Conclusion (optional).[27]

Preachers in the schools acquired a reputation for nearly obsessive preoccupation with the methods of dividing a theme and developing those divisions. The more elaborate plans of thirteenth-century university sermons must have required careful attention and considerable ingenuity in order to achieve the full integration and corre- lation of their parts. Not surprisingly, Robert of Basevorn (chap. 34) comments that correspondence of divisions is one of the aspects of sermon composition most often handled unartistically. At the same time, many less ambitious *artes praedicandi* adapt and disseminate the university format for popular preaching.[28] Some preachers use very simple schemes consisting of only a few divisions.[29] For example, the works of Jean Halgrin d'Abbeville popularized division of a sermon into two complementary parts: (1) exposition, and (2) application.[30] The sermons of Maurice of Sully, which enjoyed wide circulation in dozens of (often anonymous) manuscripts, typically dis- play a tripartite division: (1) statement of the theme, (2) spiritual interpretation, and (3) moral exhortation.[31] Other preachers use other bipartite plans. For example, Jean de la Rochelle's sermons in honor of Saint Anthony of Padua expound the two major divisions of "life" and "doctrine."[32] A somewhat more ambitious format appears in the sermons of Servasanto da Faenza. He explicitly distinguishes between the *sermo solemnis*, which always requires a protheme, and the *sermo planus*, which does not. His development of the divisions usually comprises the body of his discourse, and varies in length depending on the requirements of the division proposed.[33] Servasanto's sermon on the Circumcision of Christ typifies his complete basic plan:

> STATEMENT OF PARTS: His name was called Jesus (Luke 2:21).
> INTERPRETATION OF THEME: His naming is celebrated and solemn with respect to (1) the most high authority of the one naming (with confirming authori- ties); (2) the most generous nobility of the one named; (3) the most fitting quality of the name given; . . . therefore let us say "His name . . . etc."
> DIVISION OF THEME: The name Jesus has five letters—J, E, S, U, S—desig- nating five virtues and grace.
> PROOF OF PARTS, each with confirming scriptural authorities and ending with a literary reference or exemplum: (1) for J; (2) for E; (3) for S; (4) for U; (5) for S.
> FINAL INVOCATION AND PRAYER.[34]

Servasanto's divisions are often more numerous, and his initial interpretations of the theme frequently less elaborate, than those shown here. Especially noteworthy for purposes of comparison to Llull's sermons is the Italian preacher's construction of the body of the sermon around a single coherent division and the ubiquitous appeal to scriptural authorities for confirmation of every term or sense adduced. Servasanto's format displays the efficacious merger of inventional and expositional functions that characterizes the medieval thematic sermon, but which most challenges Llull's expertise.

Ramon Llull's proposals regarding sermon arrangement describe a format that is definitely more complex than a homily, but not as sophisticated as the university sermon. His hostility to the schools and his popularizing objectives evidently limited his enthusiasm for the more complex academic model. In fact, the *Liber de praedicatione* and his other works offer far fewer precepts from Scholastic preaching doctrine than we might expect. Most of those that Llull mentions probably derive from *artes praedicandi* designed to teach procedures for addressing popular audiences. Llull submits these precepts to his usual distinctional exposition. Thus, the *Liber de praedicatione* distributes its advice regarding arrangement under the three conditions of division (*divisio*), organization (*ordinatio*), and prayer (*deprecatio sive oratio*).

Even though prayer is the last condition treated in this section of the *Liber de praedicatione,* it deals with the element that comes first in a typical sermon. Llull explains how

> [w]ith the theme done and the sermon divided, the preacher should make a prayer with the others, in order to obtain grace and assistance from God and the blessed Virgin, and thus be capable of proffering the word of God for the praise and honor of God and the blessed Virgin Mary. And this [should be done] artfully, that is, so that the request suits *(conveniat)* the subject of the sermon. (2.A.9)[35]

The ablative absolute construction and term "theme" employed in the first line of this passage are both very rare in Llull's writings, which suggests that he has borrowed this precept verbatim from some authority on preaching, such as Waleys (chap. 3). As it happens, none of the sermons collected in the *Liber de praedicatione* use opening prayers. Nonetheless, the suggestion to compose a prayer that suits the subject matter of the sermon is an interesting recognition of the need for discursive unity as well as an appeal to agreement that is quintessentially Lullian. The rest of his comments on prayer concern the preacher's obligation to teach audiences how to pray both orally and mentally. This collation of advice on constructing a sermon and pastoral duties illustrates well his facility in distinctionally expounding a term like "prayer."

Llull's comments on the condition of organization (*ordinatio*) recommend another important structural element of a sermon, namely, an introductory metaphor, proverb, or exemplum. He notes that this device should suit (*conveniat*) the subject matter of the sermon. He illustrates this practice by suggesting as subject matter the cardinal virtues and then recounting a long allegorical story about the four elements, personified as four friends who resolve their mutual conflicts by exercising virtue (2.A.3.1). Although Llull frequently recommends this introductory use of exemplary devices (as analyzed above in chapter 6), his vague appeal to the decorum of likeness in the verb *conveniat* provides his only explanation of its function here. By contrast, the sermon theorist Basevorn reviews the types of suitable material (chap. 31), while the grammarian Vinsauf (*Poetria nova* ll. 126–54) specifies the brilliance, appeal to general truth, distinction, elegance, and other qualities that those devices give to the beginning of a discourse. Llull's general resistance to Scholastic artifice perhaps determines his broad characterization of the match between introductory device and overall theme. The rest of Llull's remarks on organization deal with the circumstances of speaking, as discussed below.

Finally, Llull's comments on division also offer several recommendations regarding arrangement in preaching. These describe the correct segmentation of a sermon's scriptural theme in order to find topics to expound, as I explained above in chapter 4. Of course, the divisions of the theme also establish the sermon's basic structure, but Llull does not discuss the "prosecution" of that structure through subdivisions, as do the sermon theorists Basevorn (chap. 33–40) or Waleys (chap. 6–8). Moreover, Llull's advice on developing the exposition of these divisions consists merely of a reference to "the instruction previouly given," which evidently means his comments on the condition of "exposition."[36] Perhaps he prefers to ignore the complex prosecution of numerous subdivisions used in university sermons. In any case, he concludes his comments on division with two general recommendations on arrangement. First, he simply observes that division employs the two modes of exposition and application (2.A.2.4). This scheme recalls the model popularized by Jean Halgrin d'Abbeville. However, where Jean's sermons offer a literal exposition and a moral application, Llull's compositions typically employ a literal exposition and moral as well as doctrinal applications.[37] In the sermons from the *Liber de praedicatione,* the exposition and application usually have corresponding divisions.[38] The number of these divisions tends to exceed those found in popular preaching. However, more elaborate schemes do appear in sermons collected as pious readings, where they serve as the distinctional framework for contemplative programs.[39] Llull's texts may well imitate the latter purely literary genre. Finally, Llull's comments on division recommend that the preacher "recollect or recapitulate in a few words" the material from the sermon (2.A.2.5).[40] This advice seems best suited to the circumstances of actual oral delivery, especially to popular audiences not trained to follow the complex outlines of university sermons. Recapitulation of course occupies an important place in Cicero's theory (*De inv.* 1.52.98; *Rhet. ad Her.* 1.3.4), but does not always interest medieval sermon theorists. Robert of Basevorn (chap. 47) gives it unusually detailed attention.

Llull's distribution of his remarks on arrangement under three different conditions in the *Liber de praedicatione* displays more zeal for distinctional exposition than concern for the organization of a sermon as a complete discourse. Nonetheless, from his disconnected remarks, we can construct the following ideal plan for a sermon:

1. Statement and division of the theme
2. Opening prayer
3. Introductory metaphor, proverb, or exemplum
4. Exposition (of divisions of the theme)
5. Application (of divisions of the theme)
6. Recapitulation

The simple organization of this scheme places it somewhere between the model of Jean Halgrin d'Abbeville and that of Servasanto da Faenza. In Llull's own sermons, the exposition and application depend far less on the prosecution of divisions, which more sophisticated *artes praedicandi* typically emphasize. Instead, both the divisions and their exposition or application consist chiefly in applying those exegetical devices of amplification that Thomas Waleys aptly calls "connections" (chap. 9). In short, Llull regards the sermon chiefly as allegorical discourse, which was a common feature of much popular preaching in his era. The sophistication and organization of that discourse in his own work usefully gauges the level of learning that he attained and that he expected his audience to possess. Overall, the model sermons that he offers would probably have satisfied the listeners of Servasanto da Faenza or of Giordano da Pisa.

Orderly Circumstances of Discourse

Just as Ramon Llull's treatment of order extends within the complete discourse to include techniques of sentence construction, so it also extends beyond the structure of a speech to include the circumstances of speaking. Most of these circumstances properly pertain to the traditional rhetorical division of delivery and to the *ethos* of the speaker, which I will cover in detail in chapters 8 and 9. In order to demonstrate Llull's comprehensive view of order, I will review here one example that displays his broad perspective especially well. Recognizing Llull's extension of order from the organization of discourse to the circumstances of speaking is critically important to understanding how he presents word and deed as corollary modes of exemplary discourse.

Llull's analysis of organization as a condition of preaching in the *Liber de prae-dicatione* (2.A.3) superlatively illustrates how he extends its scope from the organization of a speech to the circumstances of speaking. His remarks are an almost paradigmatic example of his use of distinctional exposition. This section expounds the sense of "organization" by broadening it through real and verbal concordances to include location, social rank, and time. Thus the first precept recommends placing a metaphor, proverb, or exemplum in the beginning of a sermon, as explained above. The second precept extends this focus on placement with advice about choosing a suitable place to speak, matching the subject matter of a sermon to the social rank of the audience (*magnates* or *maiores, mediocres,* and *minores* or *populares*), and keeping each part of a sermon in its place (beginning, middle, or end). Llull's use of the transitional phrase "in another way" (*alio modo*) to connect these three recommendations neatly demonstrates his distinctional method. The third precept advises choosing a suitable time for speaking and extends this to include a warning about speaking too protractedly or too briefly. Since place and time conventionally appear together as circumstances of speaking, the second precept perhaps cues mention of the third here. Finally, Llull's fourth precept returns to a more explicit focus on order by discussing the preacher's obligation to keep his life well ordered (*ordinatus*). The wording of this last precept offers an outstanding example of Llull's debt to conventional ideas and sources:

> The fourth mode concerns the honorableness of the preacher. He should be so well ordered, that he maintains good behavior and a saintly life. He should be a light and mirror illuminating listeners in word and deed. It is a great disgrace and a great disorder when preachers set forth the good and the honorable to others from their own mouths, but the opposite appears in their personal deeds. Whence the poet: "It befouls teachers, when their faults contradict them." (2.A.3.4)[41]

The obligation to teach through word and deed is an ancient Christian ideal that Llull often recommends, as in his *Lectura super artem inventivam et tabulam generalem* (3.2.847, 849, 955–96). He might have known commonplace images of this ideal from a wide range of literature on ecclesiology, moral theology, and preaching.[42] Saint Ambrose declares in his commentary on the First Epistle to the Corinthians that exempla persuade more easily than words. Gregory the Great's reiteration of that maxim provides the epigram for at least three thirteenth-century sermon treatises.[43] Augustine likewise offers an extensive defense of the Christian teacher's obligation to edify through word and deed (*DC* 4.27.59–29.62). This duty inspired the rules for Augustinian canons that appeared in the eleventh and twelfth centuries,[44] and became a cornerstone of the charge given by Saint Francis to his first followers, as related in the *Legenda trium sociorum* (chap. 3). It is a commonplace of the *artes praedicandi* from Alan of Lille (chap. 38) to Thomas Waleys (chap. 1). Llull may especially esteem this ideal from its association with the theme of the *vita apostolica*. This connection appears very succinctly in a letter of Honorius III, which commends the early Franciscans to all Catholic bishops as "sowing the seeds of the Word with the example of the apostles."[45] Llull often cites the example of the early apostles (e.g., *Doctrina pueril* 83.12) and especially denounces the pretended apostles of his era who fail to practice what they preach (e.g., *Libre de meravelles* chap. 56). Overall, Llull emphasizes the coordination of word and deed because it furthers the general cooperation between the body and spirit that he deems necessary for effective communication, as I explained in chapter 3. Nearly everything that he says regarding this ideal assumes a context of moral theology or spiritual psychology. As a norm of conduct, it evidently replaces or subsumes the more worldly virtues of discursive behavior (such as *affabilitas* or *urbanitas*) expounded in contemporary courtesy literature.[46]

The reference to "the poet" in this passage, one of Llull's very rare citations of secular authority, clearly demonstrates the debt of his precepts to received doctrines. It introduces a citation from one of the best-known primers of the Middle Ages, the *Disticha Catonis* (1.30). Like the reference to "Seneca" in the prologue to the *Rethorica nova,* this citation of Cato demonstrates the contribution of basic ethical precepts to Llull's program for the arts of eloquence. Indeed, extracted from the context of his idiosyncratic diction, the body of moral advice on speaking that he offers would be nearly indistinguishable from similar material in florilegia such as the Pseudo-Senecan *De verborum copia* (chap. 3). Still, it seems most likely that Llull knew most of these precepts from contemporary manuals on the training of preachers. For example, the ancient commonplace of the preacher as *speculator* appears in Humbert of Roman's treatise (2.13), as well as in many inventories of biblical *distinctiones,* such as the *Allegoriae* of Pseudo-Rabanus.

Conclusion

Though limited, Llull's accounts of order illustrate especially well how he handles the aspects of eloquence that he deems most important. He insists on the importance of order in nearly every reference to the arts of discourse. He also consistently links it to the other major aspects that he recognizes, verbal ornament and propriety in speaking. Llull's most developed explanations of order typically extend its scope to include sentence construction and the proper circumstances of speaking, rather than exploring more fully the arrangement of complete discourses. Consequently, neither his *Rethorica nova* nor his *Liber de praedicatione* provides a broadly applicable scheme for rhetorical disposition. Their most complete instructions describe only certain types of *arengae* and popular sermons. Moreover, the plans for secular orations from the *Rethorica nova* must compete with structures based on Llull's tripartite hylemorphic categories or with moralized devices of word order. In the *Liber de praedicatione,* the integrity of the structural elements suggested for sermons is difficult to discern, thanks to their treatment under diverse conditions of preaching. Despite the dispersion of its components, Llull's plan for a sermon involves more structure than the simple instruction in faith and morals offered in the most popular preaching of his era.

Finally, Llull's extension of order to include the arrangement of individual words and propriety in speaking demonstrates especially well his concern for the comprehensive rectification of language. He creates a general art, as it were, for order. This art embraces conventional concern for arrangement within two wide types of order that reflect Llull's special concerns. On the one hand, Llull's idiosyncratic techniques of word order clearly manifest his concern for achieving verbal *rectitudo.* These tend to discourage concern for Ciceronian plans for the complete discourse in favor of treating speech as a virtually symbolic microcosmus, in the manner of some ancient Neoplatonic authorities.[47] Llull's rectification of words might even obviate the need for organizing discourse beyond the level of sentences, by subsuming rhetorical or homiletic language into the predicational mechanics and expositional strategies of his own Great Art. His proposals for word order, like the devices of style I analyzed in chapter 5, ultimately serve the contemplative apprehension of language as mystical Logos. At the same time, Llull's extension of order to include the proper circumstances of speaking associates arrangement with pragmatic considerations of time, place, audience, and the speaker's behavior. These all serve the active pursuit of evangelism and reform that largely define the *vita apostolica* for Llull. Thus his wide-ranging treatment of order displays, perhaps better than his treatment of any other topic, his integration of received rhetorical and homiletic doctrine into a general art of eloquence in word and deed.

8

Propriety in Speaking

In addition to beauty and order, the other major aspect of eloquence that Llull mentions most often is propriety. This typically consists of regard for the appropriate conditions or occasions of speaking. These usually include the three occasions of time, place, and audience best known from Isidore of Seville (*Etym.* 2.16.1), as well as miscellaneous aspects of delivery and appeal to the audience. Enumerating these conditions of propriety in speaking is a commonplace in moral literature on speech and in preaching manuals. Superlative illustrations of each genre's treatment are Albertano da Brescia's *Ars loquendi et tacendi* and Humbert of Roman's *De eruditione praedicatorum*.

Llull's accounts of the proper conditions of speaking are often extensive but rarely systematic. They usually display his distinctional methods in an almost pure form: he collects under one heading numerous senses for that term, in such a way that the collection itself serves to reinforce the recognition of a common factor in all the senses enumerated. His reviews of the conditions thus approximate the treatments of speech in ethical *florilegia*. For example, Bartolomeo da San Concordio's *Di studio* uses maxims like "a speech should keep to its subject" or "speaking briefly is better than speaking at length" (11.5–6) as rubrics for lists of biblical, classical, and patristic sententiae. Lists of similar pronouncements comprise a large part of Llull's comments on rhetorical beauty and knowledge in the *Rethorica nova*. His distinctional procedure there often leads him to repeat the same precepts or to collate very disparate elements under a single condition. Occasionally the traces of well-known doctrines are evident, as when the *Rethorica nova* (3.9.1) cites the Aristotelian dictum "all things seek the good" (*Eth.* 1.1 1094a2–3) in its explanation of the goodness of glorious speech. This distinctional exposition of heterogeneous conditions of speaking helps Llull to achieve a general guide to propriety in any Christian exercise of discourse. These conditions involve three chief areas: the traditional occasions of time, place, and audience; tactics of *captatio benevolentiae*; and delivery.

Time, Place, and Audience

Llull's enumerations of the proper conditions of speaking almost always mention the circumstances of time, place, and audience. The best-known authority for this traditional grouping is the succinct precept of Isidore: "Now truly in speaking one must proceed as the subject matter, place, time, and character of the listener demand" (*Etym.* 2.16.1). Llull's lists often omit subject matter, probably because the inventive methods of his own Great Art adequately handle this circumstance. For Llull, his Great Art surely provides all the subject matter necessary for effective persuasion, through contemplation of the *liber naturae* and attention to the *intentio* of human existence. Moreover, this exclusion of subject matter from the circumstances of eloquence follows a precedent established long before in patristic authorities. For example, Augustine urges only that "careful attention be paid to what is proper to places, times, and persons" (*DC* 3.12.19). The sententia of Christian discourse is predetermined and simply requires adequate adaptation to particular circumstances. The ancient precedents for attention to these circumstances also extend beyond rhetorical doctrine. Neoplatonist scholiasts commonly include discussions of the propriety of character, time, and place in their textual commentaries, in an effort to find relationships of correspondence, harmony, or concord among the circumstances of discourse.[1] Later medieval authorities develop these considerations even further. For example, Albertano da Brescia draws upon an especially wide range of moral literature when discussing these occasions (3.1–6; 4.1–5; 6.1). Since Albertano organizes his treatise according to the ancient rhetorical scheme of circumstantial questions (what, when, where, who, etc.), his review of moral precepts regarding time, place, and audience acknowledges and reinforces the union of ethics and eloquence implied in the general concern for propriety. Llull's collation of miscellaneous advice on the conditions of speaking constitutes a popularizing attempt to define a similarly holistic model of the communicative situation, in which both speech and speaker are as appropriate as possible to their circumstances.

The insistence on observing the proper subject, time, place, and audience for speaking defines a broad relationship of decorum, suitability, or fitness. From his earliest writings, Llull presents this relationship as a mode of affinity and even resemblance. His *Libre de contemplació* justifies paying attention to the proper circumstances with a naturalistic analogy: some words are more pleasing at one time than another, just as some birds and animals are fatter at some times, and just as some fruits and creatures appear only in certain seasons (359.22).[2] Arguments like this perhaps constitute theoretical analogues to the "nature introductions" practiced widely in the troubadour lyric.[3] Some of his precepts appeal to naturalistic forces, as when he observes that words are appropriate to a given place according to the audience present, just as some species of trees grow better than others in a particular place (359.24).[4] These general pronouncements would fit in any guide to courtly or clerical conduct, which commonly emphasize the paramount value of decorum.[5] Llull offers a more metaphysical argument when he explains that words spoken opportunely are more beautiful than those spoken inopportunely since the former are nearer to being than the latter (359.25).[6] This explanation is obviously schoolish: it applies Aristotle's association of chance and the accidental with non-being, indefiniteness, and disorder (*Metaph.* 6.2 1026a34–7a27; 11.8 1064b15–5b4). Llull's very allusive reference to this doctrine here suggests that he has borrowed it from some source where it appeared as a corroborative *auctoritas* for the discussion of opportune speech.

Brief references to the occasions of time and place are fixtures of Llull's comments on eloquence in his later writings, such as the *Aplicació de l'art general* (ll. 873–87), the *Rethorica nova* (3.5.1, 3.6.1), and the *Liber de praedicatione* (2.A.3.2–3).[7] These references employ the same general terminology, repeatedly urging speakers to seek a time or place that is opportune *(opportunum)*, fitting *(congruum)*, suitable *(conveniens)*, or otherwise appropriate, but without specifying exactly what factors determine this characteristic. Llull does not imitate authorities on preaching like Humbert of Romans (4.18), who often review extensively the proper and improper locations or moments for speaking.

Ramon Llull's later works generally provide the most detailed explanation for the circumstance of audience. The diversity of audience types, usually expressed in lists of social or economic groups, is a traditional precept of sermon theory.[8] Gregory the Great's *Regula pastoralis* (3.1) was still the locus classicus for these lists in Llull's era. The *Rethorica nova* (3.5.1, 3.6.1) and the *Liber de praedicatione* (2.A.3.2) mention only the three broad divisions of inferior (or *populares*), middle, and superior (or *magnates*) audiences. Alan of Lille likewise recommends simply "greater things to the greater, lesser things to the lesser" (*Summa* chap. 38).[9] Such distinctions evidently apply the ancient classification of "humble," "mediocre," and "grand" styles, whether adapted from the *Rhetorica ad Herennium* (4.8.11–11.16), from Augustine's citation of Cicero (*DC* 4.17.34), or from the schemes of medieval poetical authorities such as John of Garland (1.116). These divisions probably held particular appeal for Llull because they closely match his own Relative Principles of Inferiority, Equality, and Superiority. At the same time, the reference to "magnates" and "common people" in the *Rethorica nova* may intimate a specifically secular context for Llull's advice. Brunetto Latini offers similar precepts regarding courtly audiences of lower and higher status in his *Tresor* (2.64.10–11). His comments in turn probably adapt Albertano da Brescia's remarks (3.6–7) on the same issue. Such broad categories were perhaps the narrowest divisions that popular preachers needed to make when facing large assemblies of listeners from many social levels.[10] Nonetheless, Llull's *Ars generalis ultima* also offers more specific examples of audience types, following the Gregorian tradition:

> The rhetorician ornaments words according to the profession of the people. Thus one speaks of learning, liberality, and chastity to the clergy, and so forth. And similarly in warfare there is rhetoric, when one speaks of courage, excellence, and nobility, about a horse, sword, etc. And in the art of commerce one speaks about silver, gold, and precious goods, and so forth. And in agriculture one speaks about the land, garden, and plants and animals. For just as speaking about gold, etc. is beautiful speech for a merchant, so for the peasant a beautiful word is speaking about the land or iron or so forth. (10.86)[11]

Some of Llull's other writings, such as the *Libre de contemplació* (187.10–11), also specify differences in intellectual capacity when describing the aptitude of students or participants in a disputation.[12] However, this passage follows the conventional method of distinguishing sermon audiences by social rank or occupation, perhaps adapting the traditional division of society into clergy, nobility, and third estate.[13] The list provided by Gregory continued to serve sermon theorists from Alan of Lille (*Summa* chap. 40–47) to Francesc Eiximenis (3.6), but new classifications also appeared in Llull's era.[14] Advice about different audience types occurs too in secular guides to conduct, such as Francesco da Barberino's *Documenti d'amore* (1.6).[15] Such doctrines assume that each vocation or class possesses its own idiolect or "rhetoric" based on its special interests and status in society. A fourteenth-century French compendium of *distinctiones* especially notes the difference in manners and speech between rustics and courtiers.[16] In this respect, the enumerations of preaching audiences *ad status* create new social models as alternatives to the traditional division into three estates.[17] Insofar as the listings created by sermon theorists impose a new system of norms for all social roles and ranks, it is interesting to see how Llull moralizes that model as a basis for an ideal Christian community of true and loving discourse. He would have found a ready precedent for that moralization in the commonplace tactic of selecting a typological representative—a saint or personage from sacred history—for each audience *status*. For example, the *Libro de las confesiones* of Martín Pérez (from the early fourteeenth century) classifies a long list of vocations according to the harm or benefit that they bring to society.[18] Llull's social model of communication universalizes these types as mutual exempla: each interprets to the other the general *caritas* that informs them all.

Llull does not explicitly cite one very common distinction in audience types that is most relevant to his popularizing objectives. This is the division between the elaborate sermon *ad intra* given to clerics and the simpler sermon *ad extra* given to laymen, which *artes praedicandi* mention beginning at least as early as Guibert of Nogent (25B). For example, Thomas of Celano praises Saint Francis for his ability to employ concrete and coarse things (*materialia et rudia*) when preaching to the masses, but stimulating and profound things (*vivifica et profunda*) when addressing clerics or other more capable listeners.[19] Even popular ethical authorities recognize this division. For example, Bartolomeo da San Concordio lists eight scriptural and patristic authorities, as well as Aristotle, to support the tenet that one "ought not to preach high things to coarse people" (*Di studio* 11.7). Although Llull does not explicity elaborate this commonplace distinction, he often simply assumes the division between learned and unlearned audiences. For example, a scene from his *Libre de Blaquerna* attempts to explain the most effective way of preaching to rustics. The monk who wants to evangelize shepherds receives cursory instruction in homiletics from his abbot, who advises him to use "necessary, probable reasons" rather than *auctoritates,* because "shepherds are people more disposed to understanding through reasons than through *auctoritates*" (66.4).[20] Later, however, the monk appears preaching to the shepherds "with exempla, in order to incite best their devotion" (66.22),[21] which implies an identification of exempla and necessary reasons as devices of popular preaching. This coincidence of probative arguments and exemplary stories probably reveals the difficult appropriation that Llull's Great Art seeks as a program of learning: it strives to achieve in discourse with lay, even uneducated, audiences the level of demonstrative proof attained in the philosophical and theological disputations of the schools. Indeed, his commitment to the popular dissemination of higher philosophical and theological truths probably reflects his own acute dissatisfaction with the privileged access to this knowledge that the clergy of cathedrals, classrooms, and cloisters enjoyed.

Captatio benevolentiae

Llull's concern for engaging audiences appropriately is clear from his attention to various devices that serve the traditonal rhetorical function of *captatio benevolentiae*. He does not describe them using this term, although some of his precepts probably derive ultimately from Ciceronian doctrine regarding the need to win an audience's favor (*De inv.* 1.15.20–18.26; *Rhet. ad Her.* 1.4.6–7.11). Llull's attention to this condition of speaking is hardly surprising, since one of the advantages that he claims for his Great Art is its ability to gain a receptive hearing for Christian doctrine among nonbelievers. His accounts of the arts of eloquence mention a range of specific techniques, most of them known from classical or medieval authorities, for instilling a favorable response and ultimately conviction in an audience. These techniques concern the traditional *captatio benevolentiae* itself, demonstrating the feasibility of one's objectives, making promises to the audience, praising the audience, and narrating great deeds.

Llull's *Rethorica nova* often alludes to the characterization of *captatio benevolentiae* found in many works of medieval rhetorical theory that describe an effective exordium. Most authorities present this function in terms that recall the *Rhetorica ad Herennium*: "[I]t straightaway renders the spirit of the listener ideal for listening to us. It is thus used so that we might have attentive, docile, and well-disposed listeners" (1.4.6). This concern becomes a shibboleth of the *artes dictaminis*, which recognize it as an actual part of the letter, as in the *Rationes dictandi* (chap. 4). Llull's *Rethorica nova* uses the phrase "render words more pleasing to the listeners" in its prologue; the second distinction repeats it frequently when discussing the principles of beautiful speech. These passages offer another excellent illustration of how Llull discursively develops material gathered together in a *distinctio*. For example, he explains how the principles of truth, courage, goodwill, and humility "render the speakers loveable"; "fortify and render ready the spirit of the speaker"; render "the audience . . . well-disposed and interested"; or "humble the listeners and render them well-disposed and attentive" (2.2.1–4).[22] The last two phrases clearly recall the common Ciceronian source of all these precepts. Llull's distinctional exposition leads him to apply this formula to both the audience and the speaker. As applied to the preacher, this "benevolence" becomes one of the personal virtues necessary for effective evangelizing. Extending these formulas to both speaker and audience certainly serves the treatise's implicit goal of creating a comprehensive model of communication.

Llull's acquaintance with conventional accounts of *captatio benevolentiae* evidently inspires his recommendation from the *Rethorica nova* that a "speech be applied to a feasible *(possibilis)* end" (3.5.1). Functionally, this advice perhaps corresponds to Ciceronian precepts about how speakers secure goodwill from themselves by offering pertinent arguments (*De inv.* 1.16.23; *Rhet. ad Her.* 1.5.8). However, from Llull's brief allusion it is not clear whether this requirement refers to the speaker's own purposes or to the audience's ability to realize them. His recommendation most closely recalls the admonitions to advise feasible actions, which often appear in contemporary *artes consulendi*, courtesy literature, and *artes arengandi*. For example, it is the first rule of good counseling in Giles of Rome's *De regimine principum* (3.2.16) and also appears in Giovanni Fiorentino's *Somma d'arengare* (chap. 1).

In the *Rethorica nova* Llull also advises a speaker to make promises to the audience: "[W]hen a speaker promises an audience many gifts, indulgences, and favors, the speech becomes very pleasing to those listeners" (3.9.1).[23] Again, this recommendation may echo classical instruction: both Cicero (*De inv.* 1.16.23) and the *Rhetorica ad Herennium* (1.4.7) suggest promising to discuss important or urgent issues, and to speak briefly. Alan of Lille applies this precept to preachers (*Summa* chap. 1). Later sermon treatises, like the *De faciebus* (chap. 11–12) attributed to William of Auvergne or Robert of Basevorn's *Forma praedicandi* (chap. 50), specify the promise of heavenly rewards. This spiritual sense of reward perhaps motivates Llull's recommendation of these promises as a condition of "glory," understood as eternal blessedness.

More clearly derived from traditional conceptions of *captatio benevolentiae* is Llull's advice to praise one's audience. The *Rethorica nova* explains that speech becomes glorious when speakers "pronounce those whom they address praiseworthy, since if the speech appears insulting, it will lack glory and pleasantness" (3.9.1).[24] Praise of the audience is a principal device for securing goodwill for both Cicero (*De inv.* 1.16.22) and the *Rhetorica ad Herennium* (1.4.7–5.8). Consequently, it appears frequently in discussions of *captatio benevolentiae* from *artes dictaminis* such as the *Rationes dictandi* (chap. 5–6) or *artes arengandi* such as Giovanni Fiorentino's (chap. 1–2). Among the sermon theorists, however, Eiximenis (3.6) and Waleys (chap. 1) advise caution in flattering or praising the audience. Llull's remarks evidently reflect secular rather than religious precepts. His distinction between praise and reproach echoes the ancient definition of the two subjects of epideictic and demonstrative rhetoric, already canonical for Cicero (*De inv.* 2.59.177) and the *Rhetorica ad Herennium* (2.2.2). Llull's allusions to these traditional doctrines are so basic that they might derive from almost any Latin or Arabic encyclopedia.

Finally, the *Rethorica nova* appears to adapt some received instruction about engaging an audience in the counsel to "narrate the lovely deeds of the great" (*magnorum pulcra gesta narrantur*) (3.9.1).[25] Since this appears as a means of achieving the Lullian Principle of Glory in speech, it suggests a spiritual sense for "lovely deeds of the great." This phrase probably refers to the saints' lives or Scripture mentioned elsewhere in the *Rethorica nova* (3.3). The appearance of the term *gesta,* rare in Llull's Latin vocabulary, might tempt us to infer a reference to heroic deeds such as those recounted in the chansons de gestes. However, the term also applies to broadly moralized historical anecdotes, such as the famous *Gesta romanorum*. Thus, Giles of Rome uses the phrase *laudabilia gesta* to identify the histories and hagiographies suitable as mealtime entertainment for princes (*De reg.*

princ. 2.3.20). In any case, Llull's notion of suitable *materia praedicabilis* grants only a limited place to stories told simply for entertainment, as I noted already in chapter 6. For him, the deeds of the saints are by definition "great" because spiritually edifying. Humbert of Romans likewise observes that the inherent greatness of God's word as a subject matter is sufficient reason for hearing it (6.29).

Delivery

Delivery is another aspect of conventional rhetorical and preaching doctrine that Llull occasionally mentions in his remarks on propriety in speaking. His precepts regarding delivery are far more limited than his comments on the other conditions of speaking, but are detailed enough to indicate some debt to traditional doctrines. These precepts, most of which appear in the *Rethorica nova*, concern the control of voice, body, and appearance in speaking.

Precise diction is the aspect of delivery that Llull explains most fully. His analysis of the Relative Principles of Difference, Concord, and Contrariety explicitly advises a speaker

> to distinguish between one word and another so that in each one the proper syllables
> are wholly maintained, and so that they are pronounced with the proper accentuation.
> In this way the difference in words shines forth in speaking. Anyone saying to some-
> one "ama ardenter" should not pronounce these two words so fast that the "a" ending
> the first word (namely "ama") and the "a" beginning the second (namely "ardenter")
> run together in speaking. Otherwise the words would be confused, with clipped syl-
> lables and wrong accentuation, which renders speech ugly. (3.10.1)[26]

The *Rhetorica ad Herennium* (4.12.18) recommends that one avoid such difficult combinations of sounds altogether, but Llull evidently regards them as unalterable challenges that a speaker must simply surmount through special care in diction. Llull's solution is to impose a kind of hiatus, which most medieval poetic authorities regard as a stylistic defect. Geoffrey of Vinsauf views it thus (*Poetria nova* ll. 1923–27), but also mentions accent and word separation as functions of delivery (ll. 2034–35). Llull's advice and example probably come from the *artes praedicandi*, since sermon theorists from Guibert of Nogent (24CD) to Eiximenis (3.3) commonly emphasize careful, even slow, diction. Llull also recommends continuity in diction, "without shortening or lapse in speaking" (*sine detruncatione et vocis cessatione*), because this ensures the continuous attention of the audience's Imagination, Intellect, and Memory. By contrast, discontinuous delivery causes the listeners to regard the speech as unimportant and worthless (2.2.5).[27] This passage illustrates well how likeness functions in the basic psychological model described in chapter 3. A simple homology causes the style and inflection of a speech to reappear in the listeners' minds. Llull does not explain the more interesting question of how particular features of style or inflection acquire a positive or negative value for the audience. This evaluation of course depends on the vagaries of cultural tastes or traditions, which he must ignore. Llull insists on explaining the affective force of speech directly from its reception *similiter*. Consequently, he describes one invariable approach to this aspect of delivery, where classical authorities like the *Rhetorica ad Herennium* (3.12.20–14.25) and Cicero's *De oratore* (3.44.173–51.198) describe several options. Llull's precepts probably derive from the limited remarks on continuity found in *artes praedicandi*, such as the manual attributed to William of Auvergne (chap. 5) and Humbert's *De eruditione praedicatorum* (2.10). Similarly limited precepts regarding the importance of continuity also appear in contemporary *arts de trobar*, such as Ramon Vidal's *Razos de trobar* (ll. 451–54) and Terramagnino da Pisa's *Doctrina d'acort* (ll. 737–52). It is interesting to note that the vernacular preceptists sometimes identify continuity in speaking or the expert joining of words with the coherence of literal and moral sense in a poem.[28] Llull's arguments suggest an equally direct correlation between continuous articulation and favorable reception of a speech's message by the audience.

Finally, the *Rethorica nova* also offers specific advice regarding gesture and dress. Since the precepts on these topics from the *Rhetorica ad Herennium* (3.11.19–15.27) remain definitive for nearly all medieval arts of eloquence, Llull's comments indicate very well how he handles received doctrine. An excellent standard of comparison for his treatment is this concise passage from the anonymous *Dicta beati Bernardi*:

> When you give a sermon, you should not rail in the face of the people, your hands projecting with your words, or with eyes closed or fixed on the ground, or stand with face uplifted, or shake your head like one gone mad, or twist your mouth in different directions, but as rhetoric teaches—speak with a proper expression, form words humbly and carefully, proffering sad things with a sad voice, joyful things with a happy voice, harsh things with a sharp voice, and humble things with a quiet voice, so that it seems to the listeners that they are watching these things, rather than hearing you represent them verbally.[29]

Llull evidently takes precepts like these and presents them more plainly. He simplifies the terminology, emphasizes the general feature of beauty, and recasts some of the doctrine as an example about speaking before a king, his favorite illustrative figure in the *Rethorica nova*:

> One who speaks with beautiful gestures greatly ornaments a speech. Just as when someone speaking to the king, turning to the king's face, keeps a joyful expression and avoids coughing or spitting, so that in this way the words will be continuous and maintained in a unified voice. No less should one keep the body straight, hands still, and feet still, displaying toward the king the humility of reverence and honor that ought to be exhibited to the king and lord by any subject.
>
> Beautiful and decent apparel, which one who speaks knows well to wear, are beautiful ornaments for making words appear beautiful, while foul and vile apparel on the other hand degrades rather than adorns, since it insinuates the speaker's poverty and indigence. (2.5.3–4)[30]

Llull repeats similar precepts more briefly in his *Liber de praedicatione* (2.A.8.4). The *Aplicació de l'art general* (ll. 944–49) also recommends different demeanors for different circumstances: contrition for devotion, laughter for entertainment, and humility for confession. The latter advice seems most likely to come from authorities on preaching, such as Thomas Waleys (1.8), Humbert of Romans (2.1; 4.18), or Robert of Basevorn (chap. 50). However, the example of speaking before a king suggests an emphasis on regard for the status of one's audience and the dignity of the occasion, which commonly appears in secular authorities such as Brunetto Latini (*Tresor* 2.64.11) and Giovanni Fiorentino (chap. 3–6).

The synthesis or at least the combination of lay with clerical doctrine is most apparent in Llull's recommendation that a speaker dress well. His own *Libre de meravelles* (chap. 7, prol.) urges humble dress for those preaching the Faith, a standard that reflects his own commitment to the example of Saint Francis, which moved Llull to adopt a "humble habit" at the time of his conversion, according to his *Vita* (par. 9–11).[31] His attitudes appear to reflect the stricter standards urged by advocates of clerical poverty. In fact, Llull associated during the 1290s with some partisans of the Spiritual Franciscans, the chief antagonists in the dispute about poverty, but his own writings usually avoid this issue altogether. Satirists of ecclesiastical conduct frequently lampoon the excesses of clerical dress in and out of the pulpit.[32] Consequently, it is hardly surprising that the sermon theorist Thomas Waleys treats the question of humble dress as especially problematic (chap. 1). Llull, on the other hand, presents the issue as unambiguous: he states flatly that elegant clothes enhance a speech while poor clothes invite scorn for the speaker. This view follows advice regarding courtly decorum commonly found in manuals of courtesy, such as the Provençal *ensenhament*. His preference for this standard in the *Rethorica nova* indicates his effort to create a program of eloquence suitable for general use by laypeople living in the world at large. Even in Llull's native Majorca, the increasing attention to dress as an index of social status was a factor of public discourse that no layperson could afford to ignore.[33]

Conclusion

Ramon Llull's precepts regarding the conditions of speaking comprise some of his most pragmatic and conventional advice about the arts of eloquence. Even when simplified or phrased in his idiosyncratic terminology, they demonstrate his attempt to create a viable program of communication and the debt of his work to received doctrines. It is important to remember, however, that he usually does not isolate or identify these precepts as I have in this survey. Instead, they frequently appear interspersed among his many other recommendations on beauty, order, invention, or virtue in speaking. Thus it is difficult to know whether he gleaned his knowledge of the conditions of speaking from diverse texts, or found them already organized as he presents them. In any case, Llull tends to treat all his precepts as equivalent elements of knowledge, which he freely mingles and associates according to his habits of distinctional exposition. In this way he establishes their common function as individual rhetorical truths in the service of one universal practice of verbal *caritas* and *rectitudo*.

Llull's accounts of the proper conditions of speaking display two interesting general characteristics. First, they include far less of the moralization that appears in his treatments of beauty or order. That is, his comments on time, place, and audience or delivery rarely try to reinterpret these conditions in order to make them serve more directly the moral finality of language. Llull never proposes, for example, to abbreviate or lengthen one's discourse solely according to the status of the listener. This lack of moralization perhaps reflects his pragmatic regard for the conditions of speaking. A more likely explanation is that he already finds received doctrine concerning the conditions invested with sufficient moral import because it depends so heavily on relationships of decorum. That is, most conventional advice about time, place, and audience or delivery already urges a speaker to match a speech to the social, moral, or political character of these circumstances. Second, and more importantly, Llull's treatment of the proper conditions of speaking supports his view of communication as a kind of bond between speaker and audience. His precepts focus on the circumstances that foster this verbal participation. Llull's special dedication to evangelizing unbelievers and inspiring the faithful of course assures his keen interest in the pragmatic factors that govern preaching. At the same time, his eagerness to spread moral reform throughout Christian society leads him to include many precepts from vernacular moral and courtesy literature. Thanks to this collation of secular and sacred precepts, Llull's proposals regarding the conditions seek to make all eloquence speak with one voice.

9

Virtue in Speaking

Ramon Llull's accounts of the arts of language display an intriguing attempt to assert a new medieval Christian understanding of the ancient ideal of uniting eloquence and wisdom. Llull's zeal for retracing the arts to theology encourages him to follow the traditional perspective established since the earliest patristic apologists.[1] Augustine's *De doctrina christiana* comprehensively defines this view: the first three books substitute Christian truth for pagan philosophy as wisdom, while the fourth book recommends adapting traditional skills of rhetoric to Christian evangelism as eloquence. Nonetheless, Llull never recognizes the union of eloquence and wisdom as a fundamental spiritual or intellectual good, probably because he lacks the training in the arts curriculum that would have familiarized him with the *auctores*—especially the famous opening paragraphs of Cicero's *De inventione*—that expound this ideal. Indeed, he never seems to recognize that his own insistence on virtue in speaking might share some of the same goals as the Scholastic curricula that he so often denounces. As I explained in chapter 1, his antiacademic arguments usually lament the neglect of Christian truth in the schools. Therefore Llull's plan for uniting eloquence and wisdom is to rectify all uses of language by reestablishing their moral finality. In short, he seeks to moralize secular and sacred eloquence alike as verbal exercises of virtue.

The resources available to Llull for this purpose included a vast and diverse body of ethical and theological literature concerning speech: *summae* of moral theology, compendia of classical ethical *sententiae*, catalogues of virtues and vices, monastic rules, clerical conduct guides, and courtesy literature.[2] Their treatment of the ideal of wisdom and eloquence is equally diffuse and varied. Some twelfth-century authorities use it as a master concept to organize entire programs of learning.[3] This produces an extensive collation of ethical and rhetorical *auctores*, which encyclopedias like Vincent's *Speculum doctrinale* (bks. 4–5) continued to disseminate. Patristic and early Scholastic treatises on ethics typically distribute precepts regarding speech under all four cardinal virtues. Some authorities give very specific advice about

140

speaking in connection with one virtue, as Hildebert of Tours does with justice in his *Libellus de quattuor virtutibus vitae honestae.*[4] The introduction of Aristotelian moral science in the thirteenth century renewed attention to the relationship of rhetoric to ethics, inspiring analyses like Giles of Rome's *De differentia rhetoricae, ethicae et politicae.*[5] Even popular enyclopedias like Brunetto Latini's *Tresor* (4.6) cite Aristotle's accounts of virtue in speaking (*Eth.* 2.7, 4.6–8). Ramon Llull's *Rethorica nova* follows their approach in its conflations of the traditional cardinal virtues with other skills of speaking.

Some of Llull's precepts on virtue in speaking clearly express the ideals of decorum, moderation, and discretion commonly recommended in guides to courtesy.[6] Although earlier clerical critics of courtly conduct denounced the growing preoccupation with these ideals as effete, Llull advocates them alongside other more spiritual standards of verbal behavior, perhaps because he accepted them from his own experience or perhaps because by his day they no longer seemed problematic.[7] In any case, his zeal for general reform led him to seek a model of eloquence applicable to laypeople and clergy alike. Of course, his remarks on the virtues of secular eloquence still emphasize those ideals of conduct, such as honorableness and calmness, that most directly serve the pursuit of spiritual virtues, such as love and humility.

Many of Llull's other suggestions regarding the virtuous use of language seem directly indebted to manuals of clerical conduct and especially to guides for training preachers. However, his presentation of these virtues is usually much simpler than the account offered by authorities such as Humbert of Romans. Instead, Llull's maxims typically recall the more succinct advice offered by Saint Francis in his early Rule for his followers: "[I]n the preaching that they do, let their speech be well weighed and chaste for the benefit and edification of the people, announcing to them the vices and virtues, punishment and glory, with few words" (chap. 9).[8] Writers on the training of preachers typically discuss these virtues not only in regard to preaching, but with respect to the whole range of behavior. Saint Francis devotes a chapter of his early Rule to the friars' conduct in "admonition and correction" of laypeople, warning particularly against the vices of detraction and gossip (chap. 10). The early fourteenth-century Dominican Philip of Ferrara provided a compendious *Liber de introductione loquendi* (*Liber mensalis*) with detailed directions for behavior in every conceivable pastoral and social situation.[9] This broad concern for virtuous communication best matches Llull's own general program. He considers the exercise of language part of an all-encompassing discipline of thought, word, and deed, as in the scheme proposed by the Dominican William of Tournai.[10] Indeed, Llull most often treats the union of eloquence and virtue as a manifestation of the ancient injunction to edify through word and deed. But even this venerable ideal serves a higher purpose, namely, the union of speakers and audiences in love for one another and for God. This common affection is, for Llull, the truest communication.

This chapter surveys the major virtues of speech that Llull mentions, beginning with those found in secular moral literature, such as the caution to think before speaking, and concluding with the supreme Christian principle of love. The latter enjoys tremendous importance in Llull's rhetorical program because it defines the charitable union of speaker and audience. As many subsequent passages will show, this union establishes a common and ultimate objective for all exercise of secular and sacred eloquence. For Llull, the arts of communication achieve their moral finality in Christian *caritas*.

Conduct

Previous chapters have indicated various precepts concerning eloquence that Llull probably incorporated from secular ethical and conduct literature, especially guides to courtesy. His *Libre de l'orde de cavalleria*, which offers a completely moralized program of knighthood, is one of the best-known medieval treatises on chivalry.[11] His *Mil proverbis* of 1302 is also an excellent compendium of adages regarding courtesy, ethics, and moral theology applied to lay life. In 1309 Llull sent a shorter version of this work, entitled *Proverbis d'ensenyament,* as a gift to King James II of Aragon, for use in educating the royal offspring.[12] The format and purpose of both these proverb collections resemble the *Libre de doctrina* attributed to King James I of Aragon, while the title of the 1309 text literally imitates the Provençal courtesy manuals called *ensenhament.* The chapter of the *Mil proverbis* devoted to speech offers a nearly paradigmatic listing of the advice on speaking typically found in this kind of literature:

1. Speak willingly about what you know, [but only] when required about what you do not know.
2. Since what you know is less than what you don't, use few words.
3. Deliberate much and speak little.
4. Think before you speak.
5. Learn to be silent and to talk from one who speaks.
6. In speaking one appears a fool.
7. Think about the purpose of speaking before talking.
8. If in speaking you put what is proper in the beginning, middle, and end, you speak rhetorically.
9. Speech is the image and likeness of thought.
10. Thought moves speech, and speech moves the feet and hands.
11. In bad words you travel bad roads.
12. Through good words you will be good.
13. Say many good words, and you will have many good friends.
14. With delight you will speak many good words, and with effort bad ones.
15. Do not speak many words about yourself.
16. Bad speech is fearful.
17. Good words, good habits.
18. Speak often with your peer, and rarely with your superior.
19. Do not try to speak unless usefully.
20. Speech requires proportion *(proporció)* in itself, the time, the place, the speaker, and the listener. (chap. 48)[13]

Many similar pearls of gnomic advice appear in virtually every medieval collection of moral sententiae or guide to courtesy, such as the widely diffused Pseudo-Senecan *De verborum copia* or the *Facetus*.[14] These works sometimes combine elementary ethical and rhetorical precepts, and thus implicitly urge the union of virtue and eloquence within the context of instruction on conduct.[15] Llull's maxims from the *Mil proverbis* are noteworthy for their explicit references to rhetoric and psychology. This appeal to other knowledge is hardly unusual, and Llull's own methods of distinctional exposition probably enhance it. Nonetheless, it suggests his effort to establish a broad basis for defining the use of language. In the final maxim cited above, the sweeping claim about proportion in a speech and the proper conditions of speaking clearly indicates Llull's interest in imposing a comprehensive order on eloquence.

From the many precepts about speech available in popular ethical or courtesy literature, Llull borrows several pragmatic ideals that he repeats often or develops in particular detail. By far the most common is the ancient admonition to observe the correct occasions for speaking and for listening. The question of when to speak and when to remain silent effectively defines the virtue of discretion in gnomic wisdom literature (as in the famous verse of Ecclesiastes 3.7) and provides the title for Albertano da Brescia's *Tractatus de arte loquendi et tacendi*. It often appears as a separate topic in vernacular conduct literature, such as the thirteenth-century Castilian mirror for princes, *Flores de filosofía* (chap. 13). Llull likewise devotes a complete chapter to it in his *Libre de contemplació* (chap. 210), entitled "How One Is Conscious of Speaking or Being Silent Too Much." Like so many chapters from this vast text, it includes or insinuates virtually everything that he subsequently wrote on its topic. His account begins with the broad recommendation to keep silent regarding vile or worthless matters, and to speak only regarding the useful: "[T]hings worthy of being said should be said, those not worthy of mention, left unmentioned" (210.2).[16] Similar advice appears in the Senecan sententiae *(Ep. ad Luc.* 4.18–27; 5.18–22) collected in the widely circulated *De verborum copia* (3.14–19; 4.12). Such commonplaces function in Llull's texts largely as *distinctiones*: they provide a string of ethical ideals whose meaning for Christian verbal conduct he expounds according to his doctrine of first and second intentions. None of his remarks explicitly recall the more generalized secular concern for discretion. Instead they enumerate the things that Llull the sinner has rightly or wrongly proffered in his own speech: praise of God, accounts and proofs of God, truth, oaths, blasphemy, vanity and flattery, humility, and devotion. The *Libre de contemplació* notes in several instances that God gave humans the power of speech in order for them to express truth, utility, moral exhortation, and proofs of God. It concludes (210.26) that these topics all pertain to the first intention or "movement" by which humans verbally orient themselves toward God. *Rectitudo* thus aligns the virtue of speaking or remaining silent with the other virtues of speaking enumerated in later texts such as the *Rethorica nova*. As the following analysis shows, those other virtues all help to foster the bond between speaker and listener through active discourse; silence and quietism do not readily serve Llull's evangelizing goals.

Another traditional practical counsel that Llull frequently repeats is the need to avoid both extreme brevity and extreme prolixity. This advice is one of the most common precepts in ethical and courtesy literature. At the same time, the explicit warnings of Cicero (*De inv.* 1.20.28) and the *Rhetorica ad Herennium* (1.9.14) ensure that it became a commonplace of medieval poetics and rhetoric as well.[17] Augustine adds a somewhat moralizing perspective (*DC* 4.8.22–10.25) that certainly suits Llull's concerns. However, Llull's claims are so rudimentary that they resemble the pronouncements of authorities from any of the language arts, such as Alberic of Montecassino (7.7), John of Garland (5.20–44), and Humbert of Romans (1.7; 2.9).[18] For instance, the *Doctrina pueril* (73.10) notes simply that rhetoric makes long words seem short. Likewise, the *Libre de contemplació* declares that "[l]ong words make [speech] ugly, and short words render unintelligible what one wishes to make understood" (359.10).[19] The *Rethorica nova* restates this advice in several passages: wisdom in speech requires the speaker to avoid excessive brevity or excessive superfluity in order to "maintain a discreet medium" (3.5.1); speech that is too long or too brief cannot be loveable (3.6.1); and, finally, a speaker must exercise care in using "simple and compound words," because excessive prolixity or brevity renders the words displeasing (*ingrata*) to listeners (3.18).[20] The *Liber de praedicatione* explains that prolixity generates tedium, and brevity obscurity, in the hearts of listeners (2.A.3.3).

All these precepts display an implicit concern with pleasing the audience, but the reference to "simple and compound words" is almost the only phrase that suggests specific techniques for achieving that pleasure. Llull rarely follows authorities on poetics or rhetoric in considering brevity and prolixity as ornaments, rather than vices, of speech. As compositional devices, brevity and superfluity correlate easily with the two broad stylistic functions of abbreviation and amplification. Techniques to achieve these ends appear in most rhetorical arts, as Alberic (7.7), Eiximenis (chap. 3), and Vinsauf (*Poetria nova* ll. 206–10) show. Llull's precepts also do not really distinguish the diverse considerations that govern attitudes toward brevity and prolixity in lay or clerical conduct. For example, the early Rule of Saint Francis (chap. 9) insists that friars preach "with brief speech," while Humbert of Romans (1.7) denounces ornamentation as a major cause of overblown sermonizing. Ethical and courtesy manuals also extol the virtue of brevity as an index of the speaker's self-control and moderation, as in the *Secretum secretorum*[21] or Giles of Rome's *De regimine principum* (2.3.20). Yet, popular preachers such as Saint Vicent Ferrer earned praise from contemporary chroniclers for their ability to hold an audience's attention for hours.[22] Similarly, the ability to deliver full, well-composed addresses was considered to be fundamental to successful exercise of courtly eloquence.[23] Llull's own Great Art seems to embody this larger tension that opposes the ornaments of abbreviation and amplification to the defects of excessive brevity and prolixity. On the one hand, his program promises to reduce the terms of all learning, while on the other hand his own discourse is often very lengthy and repetitive.

Llull also repeatedly cites the traditional warning to weigh one's words before speaking, which guides to conduct regularly include. Llull easily adapts this advice to several of his own Principles in the *Rethorica nova*. Thus, Wisdom requires that the "speaker, before beginning to speak, meditate diligently on what to say" (3.5.1). The Relative Principles of Beginning, Middle, and End require that "someone intending to speak, before starting, should diligently ponder and determine what to say in the beginning, what in the middle, and what last of all" (3.11.1). By considering the

Rule of How? "before speaking, the wise and discrete speaker has a mode of form-
ing in thought the speech addressed to others" (3.22).²⁴ Similarly, the *Aplicació de
l'art general* (ll. 962–67) urges that "[b]efore you wish to speak, begin to consider
the words that you wish to say, and how you might make them pleasing through
beautiful composition and true speech."²⁵ Such advice most often resembles maxims
from ethical compendia such as Albertano da Brescia's *Ars loquendi et tacendi*
(intro.). It also has parallels in discussions of invention by classical literary authorities from Cicero *(De inv.* 1.14.19) to Horace (ll. 289–94). Similar cautions appear
in medieval preceptists from Geoffrey of Vinsauf *(Poetria nova* ll. 43–59) to Robert
of Basevorn (chap. 50). Some of Geoffrey's remarks especially suggest a parallel
with the distinction between the "inner and outer man" from traditional spiritual psy-
chology.²⁶ Hence, concern for prior deliberation may also bear psychological import
for Llull as a means of explaining the transferral of ideas between speaker and listener, and therefore the mechanics of communication, viewed as verbal "influence."
Consequently, his psycholinguistic theories, which I discussed in chapter 3, allude to
prior deliberation several times.

Finally, an interesting, though singular example of how Llull's doctrines on eloquence adapt wisdom literature appears in his attempt to formulate advice about good
princely government as a norm of discourse. The *Rethorica nova* uses the Lullian
Rule What Kind? in order to categorize types of speech according to the commonplace Scholastic distinction between proper and appropriated characteristics (usually
expressed as *per se* and *per aliud).* Llull illustrates their difference thus:

> Proper speech is when one speaks thus: "The king speaks to his people urging them
> to prepare for war." And it is appropriated when one speaks thus: "The vizier urges
> the people on behalf of the king to be continually ready for war." Now if the proper
> speech is good, it is more beautiful and excellent than the appropriated. If, however,
> it is bad, it will be otherwise, because then the proper will be more foul and unworthy
> than the appropriated. (3.19)²⁷

Llull thus presents as a problem of communication the relationship between sove-
reigns and their subjects, which is also the chief focus of his maxims on princely
ethics in the *Mil proverbis* (chap. 3). Medieval mirrors for princes—such as Vincent
of Beauvais's *De regimine principum,* and its two better known adaptations,
Guillaume Peyraut's *De eruditione principum* and Giles of Rome's *De regimine principum*—commonly urge great care in delegating authority to royal officials. Llull's
somewhat cryptic advice perhaps adapts these cautions about entrusting to aides great
endeavors like war. For example, Giles's text specifically urges a prince to delegate
minor affairs to subordinates so that the prince himself will be free to concentrate on
major issues such as war and peace (2.3.19). Similarly, the *Secretum secretorum* em-
phatically warns the prince not to set advisers in his place as ruler.²⁸ At the very least,
Llull's remarks concern this general princely obligation to retain direct management
of the affairs of state.²⁹ Several texts widely circulated in the Iberian Peninsula also
emphasize this responsibility, usually following their Oriental sources.³⁰ For example,
special concern for a ruler's handling of advisers *(privados),* along with advice about
rhetoric and courteous speech, appears in the thirteenth-century Castilian *Libro de
los cien capítulos* (chap. 19–31) and its abridgement, the *Flores de filosofía.* Llull's

text, no less than these compilations, demonstrates how one body of basic lore is capable of supporting popular theories of ethics, government, and eloquence alike. The widespread circulation and avid consumption of these works in lay court culture perhaps defines the market that Llull imagined for his own *Rethorica nova*.[31] Ultimately, the appearance of these commonplace precepts in such a wide range of lay and clerical conduct literature probably justifies to Llull their use as general principles for a broad art of discourse.

The Cardinal Virtues of Speech

Ethical treatises and *florilegia* based on classical *auctores* and the vast patristic and Scholastic literature of moral theology also suggest a number of the virtues that Ramon Llull associates with the arts of language. His discussions of rhetoric or preaching regularly mention a fairly constant group of moral values for speech: advantage, justice, honorableness, truth, courage, goodwill, humility, goodness, and—above all—love. Several of these recall at least nominally the basic divisions of utility, honorableness, and the four cardinal virtues, which were well known from the *Rhetorica ad Herennium* (3.2.3) and Cicero's *De inventione* (2.52.157). These authorities establish not only a vocabulary, but also theoretical models for much medieval moral literature. To the basic core of the cardinal virtues, later writers freely add others drawn both from Christian precept and courtly norms: an excellent illustration of this synthesis is the dramatization of the Council of Nature from the opening scene of Alan of Lille's *Anticlaudianus*.[32] Just as Christian tradition recognizes a definite group of major virtues, so Islamic tradition offers similar schemes, especially the lists of mystical virtues developed by Sufi authorities and, following them, Algazel, whom Llull certainly read.[33]

Nearly any treatment of virtue and vice from medieval moral theology accords a prominent place to the so-called sins of the tongue. Numerous scriptural verses (the locus classicus is James 3.5–14) as well as Aristotle's extended discussion (*Eth.* 4.6–8 1126b11–8b9) provided a large and diverse corpus of precepts about vices in speaking, which some Scholastic authorities eventually synthesized into an eighth capital sin.[34] In the fourteenth century, the Dominican devotional writer Domenico Cavalca devoted two entire treatises to the sins of the tongue: *Frutti della lingua* and *Pungi lingua*. Attention to specific vices of speech was also strong in the Islamic theological tradition, especially from the legacy of Sufi authorities, as the work of Algazel shows.[35] Not surprisingly, Ramon Llull likewise treats them as an eighth sin in many of his writings: the *Liber de praedicatione* (2.B.2.83.2.2), the *Liber de virtutibus et peccatis*, the *Mil proverbis* (chap. 48), and the *Medicina de peccat*.[36] Despite the vast range and scope of the texts that mention virtues in speaking, their terminology usually remains fairly consistent, regardless of whether it appears in moral treatises such as Albertano da Brescia's (1.2–2.10) or *florilegia* of classical maxims such as the *De verborum copia* (e.g., 1.19–22; 3.14–31). The same terms even occur in more technical treatises on the arts of discourse, such as the works of Alberic of Montecassino (3.1), Giovanni Fiorentino da Vignano (chap. 2, 4, 5), and

Humbert of Romans (4.18). Consequently, it is not surprising that Llull uses a fairly limited and constant selection of terms to name the moral virtues of speaking. Their consistent nomenclature conveniently reinforces his effort to define these virtues as general principles of ethics.

The virtue that most obviously derives from classical ethical and rhetorical authorities is the one known variously as advantage, benefit, or utility *(utilitas)*. Llull's *Mil proverbis* (48.19) succinctly avers that one should never speak "unless usefully" *(sens alcuna utilitat)*.[37] Just as he does with other virtues of speaking, Llull often distinctionally explicates advantage according to his own Absolute Principles, Relative Principles, and Rules. These expositions sometimes create unusual collations of commonplace precepts. For example, the *Rethorica nova* (3.5.1) briefly asserts that wisdom in speaking requires words that are useful, "since what lacks utility cannot be beautiful."[38] This direct association of utility and beauty evidently assumes that speech beneficial to listeners pleases them and thus appears beautiful thanks to this pleasure. The psychology underlying this argument is unclear. It probably associates utility, beauty, and pleasure through a tacit appeal to the Lullian first intention of language, rather than with any assumptions about the affective force of certain arguments.[39] The *Rethorica nova* (3.9.1) also claims that glory in speaking arises from words "about something useful, since the usefulness of the narrative renders the listeners favorable and attentive."[40] Llull thus combines allusions to Ciceronian doctrines regarding the introduction that earns the audience's goodwill, the narrative that expounds a case, and the utility sought in deliberative oratory. This passage exemplifies his highly synthetic collation of received elementary terminology.

However, Llull most often presents the virtue of utility as the speaker's specific obligation to seek the good of the audience rather than personal aggrandizement or display. Devotion to the good of the audience manifests Christian love for one's neighbor. For example, the *Ars generalis ultima* explains that

> [j]ust as preachers artfully train the Intellect in teaching, so they should artfully train the Will in loving the advantage *(utilitatem)* of the audience, so that the sermon is worth as much in existence as it is worth in appearance. This is from the definition of equality between the Intellect and the Will, so that the Intellect and Will will find repose *(requiem)* in the sermon. Otherwise preachers become accustomed to vainglory in the sermon. (10.98)[41]

Despite its appeal to Llull's view of the necessary cooperation between mental faculties, this explanation invokes a commonplace warning from authorities on preaching, such as Eiximenis (3.5) or the *De faciebus* attributed to William of Auvergne (chap. 6), who regularly require a preacher to offer useful words. Humbert of Romans (6.29) even avers that a sermon's usefulness is the principal reason to hear it. Llull evidently identifies this utility with the didactic function of a sermon, and hence refers to preachers as "teaching." This reference also echoes the commonplace definition of preaching as "public instruction," regarded as axiomatic already by Alan of Lille *(Summa* chap. 1). The distinction between "existence" and "appearance" and mention of vainglory evidently imply the frequent disapproval of verbal ornament in preaching. Practitioners of the elaborate university sermon often incurred criticism of their ostentatious oratorical display, as did university masters of their self-serving disputations.[42]

Although Llull follows the *artes praedicandi* in his insistence on delivering useful sermons, he departs significantly from them in his attitude toward the function of pleasure in preaching. The sermon theorist Alan of Lille specifically denounces attempts to please the audience (chap. 1), as do Humbert of Romans (3.14), Thomas Waleys (chap. 1), and Francesc Eiximenis (chap. 1) after him. Ramon Llull insists that pleasure and beauty are essential to effective preaching. For example, his *Libre de contemplació* (359.27) explicitly argues that a speaker should "allow more occasions for the pleasure of those that hear the words than for the pleasure of the one who speaks the words, because where the occasion for pleasing the listeners matters most, the speaker will more avidly seek words pleasing to hear and retain."[43] This exchange between Raymond and Peter, the interlocutors of Llull's treatise *Phantasticus*, best explains his justifications for this view:

> Peter says: I delight in speaking many eloquent words, because this activity naturally causes delight; and I am delighted *per accidens,* because I consider how many praise me for what I say. Therefore since I am able to procure this delight for myself, I would be crazy not to accept it.
>
> Raymond says: The good eloquence and knowledge that you possess are for you a means for acquiring merit or punishment. You acquire merit if you praise those things worthy of praise from the habit of prudence, justice, or the other virtues. So it is permissible to justify your delight through such speech. But you truly speak otherwise and therefore ought to feel great pain and sadness, because you are crazy. (term. 4)[44]

It is clear that Llull does not advocate the sensational or provocative delight condemned by sermon theorists. Rather, his criteria of beauty and pleasure depend directly on the moral finality of language that he expects every human mind to recognize. That is, any audience should find beauty and feel pleasure in a discourse that describes their salvation. The progression from natural to spiritual delight is paradigmatic for Llull. It defines broadly the obligation of all the soul's powers to promote the first *intentio* of human existence.

Along with utility, truth is another major virtue of speaking for Ramon Llull. He lists it as the first beautiful principle of speech in the second distinction of the *Rethorica nova.* The role of Truth as an Absolute Principle from Llull's Great Art already determines its universal applicability to language. Consequently, the *Aplicació de l'art general* (ll. 850–57) suggests that truth simply appears in speech, if it includes the ornament of discoursing through the Lullian Rules, explaining the significance of each. Outside of Llull's own system, many authorities from various fields present truth as a virtue of speaking. Albertano da Brescia (2.1) and the Pseudo-Senecan *De verborum copia* (1.22) treat truth as a general condition of all discourse. Preaching theorists from Alan of Lille (*Summa* chap. 1) and Humbert of Romans (2.10; 4.20) to Eiximenis (3.6) insist on it. Manuals of conduct like the *Facetus* (nos. 24, 159) typically contrast truth with the social evil of mendacity. Llull evidently combines terms or ideals drawn from the whole range of these contexts, sometimes producing intriguing but vague associations, just as he does with utility. For example, the *Rethorica nova* (3.9.1) recommends that speech be "true or at least verisimilar."[45] The term "verisimilar" is rare in Llull's Latin vocabulary. It is impossible from this brief mention to know whether the word involves Ciceronian doctrine regarding the qualities of an effective narrative (*De inv.* 1.20.28; *Rhet. ad Her.* 1.9.14). Likewise, the *Rethorica nova* (3.6.1) avers that "false words are hateful to the wise," an aphorism that recalls well-known maxims from the Book of Proverbs (e.g., 13.5; 15.26). All these brief precepts about truth presumably refer to Christian belief, rather than to the ethos of the speaker, and thus require little further explanation. In Llull's view, properly receptive listeners will always accept truth, since this is the "proper object" of the human Intellect.

A few passages from Llull's accounts of rhetoric and preaching also acknowledge the manipulation of truth as a discursive problem in the arts of eloquence, but without separating it completely from his usual moral perspective. For example, the *Arbre de sciència* ("Arbre questional" 5.5.j.184) explicitly asks whether "[r]hetoric is as beautiful through humble and pious words as through true ones"? Llull replies that rhetoric is an art through which the natural human power of language seeks truth as its ultimate end; consequently "it often happens that rhetoric moves people to piety and love with the false words that they are given to understand."[46] This question perhaps alludes to the problem of whether to encourage untrained, but devout teachers of the Faith, which Augustine poses (*DC* 4.28.61). However, the "false words" are probably fictions and incredible stories, whose use Llull rarely recommends, as I explained in chapter 6. Hence this passage evidently argues the commonplace criticism of rhetoric as an art of deceptive persuasion, probably as an implicit contrast to the wholly rectified art of discourse that Llull seeks. His explanation of truth as a beautiful principle of speech in the *Rethorica nova* gives one of his most detailed arguments regarding these problems. It relates this virtue to the beauty of moral finality already noted in connection with utility:

> For when anyone speaks true words, the beauty of the truth makes the form, matter, and end of speech clearly apparent to the audience. Thanks to this the listeners clearly understand, and feel love for the speakers, because truth understood in words renders speakers loveable. Likewise the converse: from falsehood and malice words become obscure and hateful, because no beauty of form, matter, or end shines in them, nor do they display any reason for loving them. Similarly also if words are true and bad, because neither in false and bad nor in true and bad words can any beauty of form, matter, and end shine, since these lack a good end. (2.2.1)[47]

The tripartite hylemorphic model of language that Llull imposes in this analysis seems incidental to his conviction that the beauty of true words depends chiefly on their end. Clearly, discourse that does not maintain the Lullian first *intentio* of communication—that is, love of God and neighbor—cannot be beautiful. The references to "malice" and to "bad" words perhaps indicate generally any speech that lacks a good intention, which treatises on moral theology typically specify as separate sins of mendacity, backbiting, hypocrisy, and so forth. Llull may also be alluding to the problems, commonly mentioned in conduct and courtesy literature, of giving advice to peers or superiors. His comments perhaps apply as well to the traditional clerical duty of correcting and reprehending the laity, which preaching authorities such as Humbert of Romans (7.35–37) often treat in detail. Saint Francis's biographer lauds his zeal in speaking the truth frankly and his willingness to censure an audience's failings.[48] This sense of truth as "frank speaking" or *parrhesia* attains increasing prominence in the moral and social literature of the thirteenth century, evidently as a virtue specially opposed to the flattery and deception of court politics.[49] Llull's *Libre de contemplació* (chap. 118) bitterly denounces the mendacity and misrepresentation promoted by minstrels who serve nobles. Thus, his references to "true but bad words" may allude as well to abuses treated in the copious anticourtly literature of the period.[50] Ultimately, his remarks provide a general principle for all situations in which a speaker uses language for an evil purpose.

The *Rethorica nova* also lists the virtue of courage (*audacia*) in speaking as another beautiful principle of speech. Llull suggests a correlation between bold delivery and spiritual strength in the courage that

> fortifies and renders resolute the spirit of the speaker and exalts and invigorates the voice. For beautiful speech forms in those words that most powerfully affect the spirit of the audience, which desires and craves hearing things that receive beauty and loveliness from courage. But when someone proffers a speech with fear and without courage, the speech loses its power and is considered worthless by the audience. Because it is spoken with fear, it insinuates to the audience that it lacks a good end; or if it has a true end, it is deemed of little or no benefit. (2.2.2).[51]

These remarks are most relevant to the situation of the evangelist or the apologist, and almost certainly derive from authorities on preaching such as Humbert (4.18, 20) and Eiximenis (3.2).[52] In general, conduct and courtesy literature tend to recommend restraint, rather than zeal, in speaking, following the tenor of the ancient precepts compiled in the *De verborum copia* (20.19). For example, Albertano da Brescia (2.2; 5.1) urges gravity and moderation, while Francesco da Barberino (1.5) lists boldness as a defect in speaking. These authorities probably discourage overly zealous speech because it contravenes the self-control so esteemed in courtly ethics.[53] The battlefield is the place to display zeal and courage: "[K]nights should strike high and speak low" advises *Le roman des ailes* of Raoul de Houdenc.[54] Since Llull generally seeks to moralize all eloquence as an exercise of Christian virtue, it is not surprising that he recommends the courage of the evangelist as a virtue for all speakers.

The virtue of affection or goodwill (*affectio*) is the third beautiful principle of speech in the *Rethorica nova*. Just as he does with other virtues of speaking, Llull relates this goodwill to the speaker's commitment to a higher purpose:

> [W]hen someone speaks with great affection, it renders the audience benevolent and more interested in the things said. And it inclines more easily to those things that the speaker seeks to achieve in speaking. But when one delivers a speech without affection, the suspicion immediately arises in the mind of the listener that the speaker has litttle interest in the end for which the speech is composed. So lack of affection in speaking indicates scant desire for one's end; the speech is thus rendered ugly and deemed worthless or unimportant in the minds of the listeners. Therefore someone who speaks should, if seeking beautiful speech that achieves the desired end, at the outset of a narration deliver the words with a fervent spirit and great affection. (2.2.3)[55]

The Ciceronian formula of *captatio benevolentiae* and reference to narration suggest that Llull is again freely combining diverse elements of rhetorical and ethical doctrine. Sermon theorists such as Humbert of Romans (6.25–30) also emphasize the importance of establishing goodwill before an audience, but Llull's explanation is too vague and simplified to allow any exact coincidence with terms or themes from the guides for preachers. At most, his comments confirm the importance that *affectus* had attained in the psycholinguistic models of contemporary moral theology.[56] The same conclusion seems applicable to Llull's remarks on the virtue of humility, the fourth beautiful principle of speech from the *Rethorica nova* (2.2.4). Again, he justifies it by invoking the formula of *captatio benevolentiae*: "[T]he beautiful power of humility renders the speech beautiful and exalts it. And the exaltation *(exaltatio)* of the speech humbles the listeners, renders them benevolent, and makes them listen attentively to the speech."[57] Arrogance and pride, on the other hand, generate an impression of unimportance and worthlessness. The latter warning again parallels similar advice from sermon theorists such as Humbert (2.8, 11) or Eiximenis (2; 3.5). However, secular authors such as Albertano da Brescia (2.9) or the *Facetus* (nos. 77, 111) also caution against arrogance, especially boasting. Llull's precepts create a very generalized principle, suitable to the very broad exercise of eloquence that the *Rethorica nova* describes.

The *Rethorica nova* also includes brief references to the virtues of justice, honorableness, and goodness in speaking. Llull's use of the first two terms (3.5.1) offers little indication of whether they allude to any conventional ethical and rhetorical doctrines.[58] However, his brief mention of goodness (3.9.1) includes a very famous *auctoritas*: "[G]lorious speech also requires words that are good, and thus pleasing as well, because the good is what all things desire."[59] This unacknowledged quotation from Aristotle (*Eth.* 1.1 1094a2–3) is another of the very rare citations of philosophical authority in Llull's work. The fact that it appears anonymously suggests that it probably comes from some compilation of *distinctiones* or *florilegium* where it appears without attribution. But it also simply reflects the fundamental moral finality of all Christian communication, which Llull repeatedly invokes in the *Rethorica nova* in his claims that the virtues of speaking promote the union of speaker and listener. Llull would in any case understand the Aristotelian maxim as a reference to the Divine Dignity of Goodness, and thus a corollary of the Lullian first intention, which governs language just as it does all other beings. This quest for the Supreme Good undoubtedly guides Llull's overall selection of virtues in speaking. Where courtesy and conduct literature surveys the urbanity, wit, grace, sweetness, modesty, and joy that constitute elegant behavior *(elegantia morum)*, Llull limits his attention to the honorableness, utility, justice, goodness, benevolence, courage, and truth that define upright behavior *(probitas morum)*.[60] Llull's fundamentally instrumental view of beauty and pleasure in speaking suggests that the former secular values will derive, if they exist at all, from the latter spiritual virtues.

Love

If there is one general and paramount virtue of speaking in Llull's program for eloquence, it is unquestionably love. It constitutes a sort of master virtue that embraces all the other virtues described in the preceding section of this chapter. Indeed, one recent study finds in love a primary principle of Llull's entire metaphysics.[61] Its fundamental and comprehensive role in Llull's program for eloquence is obvious from its use to name the fourth distinction of the *Rethorica nova,* which consists of ten stories that illustrate practical uses of loving speech. Llull shares the zeal for exercising *caritas* through evangelical action that characterizes many aspects of later medieval popular spirituality, especially those associated with Franciscan groups.[62] If love for one's neighbor is the basis of all Christian community and language is the medium of that community, then the exercise of love virtually coincides with communication. Since Llull regards the moral finality of human existence as part of human nature, this discourse of love is a major justification for his proposal of speech as a sixth sense. Both the theory of *affatus* and the role of love in the *Rethorica nova* are readily comprehensible as contributions to the tradition of moral philosophy that includes Cicero's well-known claims (*De inv.* 1.2.2–3)[63] about the role of eloquence in founding human society and Augustine's emphatic definition (*DC* 1.35.39–40.44) of love as the objective of all Christian learning and discourse. Hence, a Scholastic contemporary like Grosseteste argues that love of Christ as truth necessarily leads to preaching, as imitation of the divine Verbum in all its aspects.[64] Contemporary preaching authorities such as Humbert (2.11; 6.29), Eiximenis (2; 3.5), and Thomas Waleys (chap. 1) unanimously insist on Christian love as the goal of any sermon.

Ramon Llull's treatment of love as the paramount virtue in speaking effectively extends the Schoolmen's view of preaching to any good use of language. Eloquence thus becomes indistinguishable from loving speech in general. The most succinct illustration of this broad view is a passage from Llull's *Libre de Blaquerna* (88.4), which recommends his *Libre de amic e de amat* as a model of devout speech for the diverse purposes of making sermons more pleasing and of reducing contention among litigants. The most comprehensive illustration is the fourth distinction on love from the *Rethorica nova.* This section of Llull's treatise displays perfectly his methods of exemplary instruction, setting forth ten proverbs on loving speech and illustrating each proverb with an appropriate exemplum. These anecdotes show how loving speech deters lust, humbles the proud, calms anger, achieves justice, edifies audiences, maintains friendship, consoles the dejected, corrects the mighty, encourages self-denial, or adorns the homely. To each proverb and its exemplum Llull adds a brief indication of an appropriate audience before which to use them, thus imitating the commonplace classification of preaching materials *ad status.* Llull's treatment of these exempla illustrates superlatively how *materia praedicabilis* becomes conduct literature. The *Rethorica nova* takes material originally collected for preachers to use in exhorting their audiences, and offers it as a guide for loving communication in general. Thus, the preacher's special imperative of *docere verbo et exemplo* becomes a general Christian obligation of *diligere verbo et exemplo.* Llull's text both describes and teaches the exercise of verbal *caritas.* The proverbs and exempla with their expositions impart simultaneously love, knowledge, and memory of God as a unified spiritual and intellectual experience, based of course on the interpretative methods of Llull's Great Art. This dual moral and intellectual function, probably developed through intensive meditation upon devotional and contemplative literature, distinguishes Ramon Llull the moralizer from a moral preacher such as

Bernardino of Siena. Llull's program does not seek simply to persuade, but to inform and to reform. His reliance on a metaphysics of participated resemblance especially promotes the soul's participation in truth by facilitating its assimilation of true forms. Llull's arguments do not attempt, in the manner of Cicero, to persuade a particular secular audience to accept the best response to a specific material controversy, but rather, in the manner of Augustine, to teach all Christians the one right answer for every spiritual question.[65]

The final proverb and exemplum (4.10) in Llull's treatise illustrate exceptionally well the broad moral ground that he seeks to establish for the virtuous exercise of speech. The tenth maxim avers that "Whoever has love, makes ugly words beautiful."[66] The corresponding anecdote dramatizes the recognition of spiritual truth and beauty in speech as a kind of *allegoria per contraria*. It tells how a poor woman regularly prays to God with great love, offering to "sweep God's house, wash dishes, and prepare food to eat," as well as "lay out God's bed and wash God's feet with warm water." An old man overhears the woman, and reprehends her, denouncing her prayers as "foul and fatuous" because "God truly has no need of such services. God's house is brighter than the sun. God's life is eternal. God therefore has no need of corporeal food, nor requires dishes washed, nor needs a bed or home."[67] When the woman explains that these chores are the only way in which she can imagine serving God, the old man suddenly recognizes her devotion, and her prayers then seem beautiful to him. Llull recommends recounting this proverb and exemplum "to those who judge words foolish without considering the spirit in which they are offered," in order to teach them that "one must consider the spirit in which words are said and to what end or purpose they are directed."[68]

This explanation of an appropriate audience implies that the fundamental lesson of this story is the need to achieve correspondence between a speaker's moral intentions and an audience's spiritual *intentio*. By Llull's day, the scrutiny of intentions had become a preeminent concern of the penitential manuals that taught confessors how to analyze "cases of conscience."[69] The burgeoning literature in this field of moral theology, especially treatises from Dominican authors, probably constitutes another ready source of exemplary material for Llull. His perspective readily matches Scholastic doctrine. For example, Aquinas (2a.2ae.83, 15–16) observes that prayer involves both merit and some satisfaction as its future effects; hence, even a sinner can request something worthy. At the same time, the emphasis on the audience's *intentio* recalls Llull's evangelical preoccupation with promoting the "supposition" of faith in unbelievers.[70] Numerous contemporary exempla concern the importance of pure intentions as prerequisites of effective prayer.[71] The character of the poor woman especially recalls the poor widow from the Gospels who donates all that she has (Mark 12:42; Luke 21:2), as well as conventional figures of women whose simple divine wisdom confounds those who vaunt the subtleties of human knowledge.[72]

Moreover, Llull's deliberately homely illustration of "foul" speech aptly fulfills Saint Vicent Ferrer's advice to preach or exhort using simple speech and "domestic conversation for explaining individual acts," because such discourse best engages the individual listener.[73] Since the poor woman's speech presumably functions, like all language, by virtue of the Lullian Principles inherent in it, we might imagine that the old man's sudden illumination occurs through transmission of her loving Will to his soul through her loving words. As a result, he and she become united through their common love of God. In this story, that communication evidently occurs through *dis-similia* rather than *similia*. The poor woman's prayer presents the old man with a sort of living *allegoria per contrarium*. The old man exercises a moral interpretation authorized by the ancient Christian ideal of *sermo humilis:* he ignores the rough outer appearance of the old woman's speech in order to find the sublime inner truth that it conceals. Llull's exemplum would ultimately authorize the universal exercise of humble Christian discourse, in the sense defined by Auerbach: communication available to everyone uniformly in loving submission.[74] It is fitting that Llull's *Rethorica nova* end with this anecdote, since the rough diction of his own discourse troubled later humanist devotees of his work, such as Jacques Lefevre d'Étaples. Although some of Llull's early Renaissance enthusiasts praised him as a *doctus idiota,* others composed a new rhetorical treatise to circulate under his name.[75]

Other sections from the *Rethorica nova* and Llull's other accounts of eloquence also emphasize the comprehensive connection between love and the various virtues in speaking. The third distinction of his treatise on rhetoric (3.6.1, 3.9.1) cites love between speaker and audience as the basis of utility in speaking and as a means to achieve *captatio benevolentiae*. These incidental references indicate well how love as a virtue in speaking combines with other rhetorical functions such as utility or securing goodwill to found Llull's overall program for an art of eloquence. Of course, this larger scheme assumes that virtues like love necessarily cooperate with the devices of his own Great Art. Thus, the *Liber de praedicatione* (2.A.7.3) declares that the combinational discourse of the Lullian Great Art generates "love and devotion in the hearts of the listeners."[76] The *Ars generalis ultima* especially emphasizes this artful handling of virtue in speaking:

> The preacher should work artfully *(artificiare)* on the listeners' Memory with the instrument *(artificio)* of an artful sermon. Thus, if predicates naturally joined to a subject are proposed *(praedicantur)* about the subject—as in "The justice of God is great" or "The mercy of God is great"—and one of these is as great as the other, then thanks to this the preacher should show joy and awe, by means of justice, prudence, and hope. Moreover, the audience's disposition to fear and love is highly memorable and loveable, just as it is highly intelligible. (10.98)[77]

The reference to "subjects" and "predicates" invokes the presumed logical and metaphysical truth of Lullian discourse, even while depending on the wordplay of the double meaning in the verb *praedicare* ("to preach" and "to predicate"). The argument of these lines illustrates very aptly Llull's view of communication as fundamentally participational. His comments offer an analogy that in fact has causal value as an explanation: a sermon's audience will develop a "disposition to fear and love," not simply in the same manner as, but also to the degree that, a natural conjunction exists between the subjects of the sermon. This natural conjunction in communication is homologous with the willingness to grant an opponent's premises that Llull requires as a basis for fruitful disputation, and also with the doubt that stands between affirmation and negation in his program for logic.[78] Far more important, however, is the encouragement of the soul's "disposition to fear and love." Although this passage initially mentions only the audience's Memory, the last line stresses the mutual cooperation of all three mental faculties, as I explained in chapter 3. Their response constitutes the virtue of love in listening, as it were, that results from the preacher's virtue of love in speaking. By instilling this love in the listeners' souls, the preacher enhances their moral finality, that is, their Lullian first intention of knowing, loving, and serving God. This love in listening is Llull's version of the "goodwill" or "purity of heart" that Augustine requires for right argument and interpretation of Scripture.[79] Ultimately, this disposition consists in the willingness to understand all things in this world as signs of higher truths. This innate disposition to spiritual insight is fundamental to the entire program of natural theology offered in Llull's Great Art. Hence, loving communication is the necessary instrument of his entire evangelical enterprise.

Conclusion

Ramon Llull recognizes a variety of virtues in speaking, ranging from pragmatic ideals of discretion to qualities of moral character to the fundamental obligation of Christian *caritas.* Because he does not mention these as insistently as he does beauty, order, or propriety, and because he often associates their manifestation with devices of style or arrangement, it would be easy to overlook their importance in his scheme. Nonetheless, their broad contribution to his program for an art of eloquence becomes obvious if we consider the range of moral literature from which he draws them. His precepts echo advice from *florilegia* of classical ethical *sententiae*, courtesy manuals, guides to clerical conduct, and treatises of moral theology. The scope of these sources indicates, better than almost any other aspect of Llull's work on rhetoric and preaching, his effort to create a general art of secular and sacred discourse that unites virtue and eloquence.

Consequently, the virtues of speaking tend to function in Llull's program as common principles, just as do the many other basic notions of beauty, order, or propriety that he cites. He presents and develops them all at a level of generality that presumably facilitates their application to particular situations. Although this free collation of moral ideals with technical precepts results largely from Llull's moralizing objectives, he is certainly not the only writer of his era to explore the coincidences of rhetorical and ethical doctrines. A later fourteenth-century rhetorician, Nicolaus Dybinus, expounds a program of "ornate affable eloquence" that also seeks the convergence of technical and moral instruction.[80] However, Dybinus, like other academic authorities of the period, grounds his efforts explicitly on received Ciceronian doctrine. Despite their dissimilarities, the projects of Dybinus and Llull both offer precedents for the humanists' subsequent campaign to reintegrate eloquence and wisdom.

Llull expounds the virtues of speaking distinctionally, as he does most topics. This method of treatment tends to approximate the procedures of his own *ars combinatoria,* which greatly facilitates collation of these virtues with other technical precepts. However, this constant association and reassociation of terms also tends to make the different virtues of speaking lose their value as names for specific ethical qualities. The third distinction of the *Rethorica nova* especially displays this result. There, truth is beautiful when it is honest, beauty is honest when it is true, honesty is true when it is beautiful, and so forth for all the virtues. The virtues thus come to display the same mutual coessentiality found among the Principles of Llull's Art. Nonetheless, this practical effect of Llull's methods in fact realizes the theoretical ideal that he seeks to expound. That is, the mutual inherence of all the virtues of speaking both constitutes and explains communication.

This communication corresponds ultimately to the loving union that Llull considers the purpose of all Christian eloquence. Love organizes all communication in human society, just as it organizes the participation of all being in creation. Both that communication and that participation depend upon and manifest the Goodness, Greatness, and other Divine Dignities that Llull regards as the fundamental constituents of creation. Whether one finds in Llull's work a recognizably Augustinian or Franciscan "philosophy of love," it is clear that he treats love as the fruit of all Christian communication with God and neighbor.

10

Llull's Sermons

In addition to the many preceptive and descriptive accounts of eloquence that appear in Ramon Llull's oeuvre, his writings also include many collections of model discourses that illustrate his own practical application of rhetoric and preaching. Virtually all of these model discourses are sermons. Hence, although they do not display the general exercise of artful communication proposed in the *Rethorica nova,* we might expect them to illuminate Llull's conceptions of sacred eloquence. However, even as specimens of the preacher's art his collections of model sermons present two broad limitations.[1]

The first limitation is a problem common to all studies of medieval preaching, namely, the extremely fragmentary knowledge that we possess regarding actual homiletic practices, as opposed to the theories expounded in the *artes praedicandi.* Although new researches continue to extend this knowledge, many of the questions about medieval preaching raised by Murith fifty years ago still remain insufficiently explored.[2] The sermon was unquestionably the single most practiced oratorical genre of the Middle Ages.[3] Nonetheless, the restricted literacy of the medieval West virtually guarantees that the available documents in no way offer a complete or comprehensive sample of that oral practice. Records of preaching, produced for various reasons, are available. The transcription *(reportatio)* of sermons by an amanuensis already existed during the twelfth century, as the collected sermons of Maurice of Sully testify. In the late thirteenth century, Pierre de Limoges hired a recorder to visit churches and take notes on sermons. At the beginning of the fourteenth, devout listeners of Giordano da Pisa made their own copies.[4] Obviously, these transcriptions do not come from the hand of the cleric preaching the sermon.[5] The laypeople or other clerics who made *reportationes* did so for a variety of reasons, few of which correspond to the interests of modern scholars. The effort to preserve models for future consultation, the attempt to collect materials for compilation, or a desire to record the authoritative words of a great teacher does not necessarily match the concerns of historical investigation or literary criticism.

Different collections of sermons by one author might serve different purposes, as happens with the Sunday and holiday sermons of Saint Anthony of Padua.[6] Depending on their purpose, reporters might omit materials irrelevant to their interests, or even suppress commonly repeated structural elements such as the protheme, opening prayer, or closing. This lack of complete information, frustrating though it might seem to modern scholars, remains unavoidable even today: only a tiny fraction of the sermons delivered this coming Sunday in Christian churches around the world will survive fully recorded in any form. By definition, preaching is a mode of public speaking, not of public writing. Consequently, Michel Zink concludes, in his exhaustive study of French popular sermons from the twelfth and thirteenth centuries, that very few extant vernacular or Latin texts provide verbatim transcripts of sermons as they were actually delivered.[7] The texts preserved range instead from polished revisions to models for development to rough notes on a preacher's best material. There is, Zink argues, a fundamental difference between texts created before or "upstream from" and those created after or "downstream from" actual delivery.[8] Moreover, both types of text commonly served another use, namely, adaptation as literature for spiritual edification. This ancillary sermon literature comprises a wide range of related material, from manuals of clerical instruction to devotional guides for laypeople.[9] Finally, the implied audiences for sermons and the literature based on them ranged from university scholars skilled in Latin to illiterate rustics speaking vernacular dialects. The work of Ramon Llull evidently assumes an intermediate audience composed of secular or regular clergy outside the schools and of educated laypeople who attend or patronize them. Such groups typically appear in the courts and towns, as happened at Paris from the time of Maurice of Sully and Stephen Langton.[10] Llull perhaps experienced a similar level of spiritual and intellectual culture during his early years of study and contemplation. Our piecemeal knowledge of that culture in Llull's era is one of the major obstacles to understanding the entire development of his career: both the composition of his audiences and their norms of piety and learning remain incompletely understood.

This general problem leads directly to the second and more specific limitation that constrains our understanding of Ramon Llull's model sermons: the evidence regarding his own preaching practices is very scant. The only extant third-party record of his homiletic, apologetic, or disputational efforts are episodes from his *Vita* (par. 26–28, 36–38) that describe his debates with Islamic authorities in Tunis. His own references to his activities, such as the prologue to his *Disputatio Raimundi christiani et Hamar saraceni,* tell us little about the circumstances of those adventures. Passages from his writings that describe lay preachers or evangelists perhaps offer idealized representations of the tactics that Llull himself employed.[11] His *Vita* characterizes him as a kind of latter-day prophet, while his lay status and frequent travels suggest parallels with some celebrated itinerant preachers of the twelfth century.[12] Nonetheless, the absence of other contemporary testimony about his activities make him appear as a very lonely voice crying in the wilderness. The internal evidence from his homiletic writings is also frustratingly limited. The texts that Llull collects as sermons ignore most of the common preaching techniques used by his contemporaries, and even fail to illustrate many of the devices recommended in his own *Rethorica nova* and *Liber de praedicatione.* Many of his so-called sermons simply constitute applications of his Great Art, and differ little from any other Lullian demonstration. Their discursive method is as idiosyncratic as the methods of his Great Art or his proposals about rhetoric or preaching in general. Moreover, few of Llull's model sermons or sermon plans readily lend themselves, in the form that he offers them, to delivery from the pulpit. None bear any traces of dictation or transcription from an actual public address. Most seem designed for consultation in reading only. Ultimately, his sermons seem to serve the same purposes as his Art: they provide schemes of argument for use in disputations about the Faith with unbelievers, and they provide texts for meditation according to the contemplative methods taught by the Great Art. As contributions to the *ars praedicandi*, they perhaps offer *materia praedicabilis* for the preacher willing to adapt or adopt their peculiarly Lullian diction and organization.[13]

Llull's oeuvre includes vastly more model sermons than precepts regarding the *ars praedicandi*. Their number alone demands that we consider them in analyzing his proposals about the arts of rhetoric and preaching. Ultimately, however, the value of the discourses that Llull calls sermons lies chiefly in their illustration of how much his views of eloquence depend on the system of his own Great Art. This chapter analyzes in detail several typical sermons from the various homiletic collections that he composed. By demonstrating the dependence of Llull's sermons on the methods of his Great Art, this analysis in effect returns us to the point where this study began, namely, the recognition that Llull's system functions as an art of arts.

Llull's Sermon Collections

The overwhelming bulk of Ramon Llull's contribution to the arts of eloquence consists of sermon collections. The *Rethorica nova* is his only treatise on rhetoric or preaching devoted exclusively to theoretical precepts. Some of his collections, such as the *Liber de praedicatione,* do contain incidental comments on theory, but most include only model discourses. A few of Llull's writings also have titles, such as *Sermones contra errores Averrois*, that use the term "sermon" metaphorically to indicate their function of promoting Christian truth, although their discursive form is no different from any other Lullian argumentation. The works that most clearly offer model sermons for preaching are the following: *Liber de praedicatione* or *Ars magna praedicationis* (1304), *Liber predicationis contra Judeos* (1305), *Sermones de decem praeceptis* (1312), *De septem sacramentis ecclesiae* (1312), *De septem donis Spiritus Sancti* (1312), *Sermones de Pater Noster* (1312), *Sermones de Ave Maria* (1312), *Liber de virtutibus et peccatis* (1313), *Ars abbreviata praedicationis* (1313), and *Sermones de operibus misericordiae* (1313). Taken together, these works contain nearly four hundred separate sermons or sermon plans. Their titles broadly reflect Llull's two major lifelong concerns: proselytizing unbelievers and reforming Christian society. The works on the Pater Noster, Ave Maria, Decalogue, sacraments, and morals especially attempt to provide Lullian explanations of the rudimentary catechetic instruction that most popular preachers or parish priests of this era expounded.[14] Llull's accounts of these subjects are strictly orthodox. They usually provide full distinctional expositions of their topics, which could make them equally useful as compilations of *materia praedicabilis* for preachers or as works of meditation for pious readers.[15]

Some insight into Llull's view of his collections' use appears in a passage from the *Libre de Blaquerna* (93.3), which tells how the pope and cardinals order the composition of "as many sermons as days in the year, containing the best material fit to preach, of suitable length, and intelligible to people, since through ignorance their hearts often lack devotion; these 365 sermons should be general and preached in order one after another each year."[16] This short passage alludes to a number of issues and practices. To begin with, the term "general" suggests that these are schematic models in which many particular sermons are "implicit," just as individual arts are implicit in Llull's Great Art. A collection of 365 model sermons would certainly be useful to a friar required to preach regularly, but could also function as a guide for daily meditation, like the 365 chapters of Llull's own *Libre de contemplació* or *Libre de amic e de amat*. The stress on intelligibility to the people evidently assumes a largely popular audience, as well as Llull's epistemological theories regarding the proper objects of the Intellect. The specification of "best material" undoubtedly refers to the selection of topics from the nine Subjects of Llull's Great Art, following his criteria of beauty. Thus, even a passage that seems to propose a fairly simple scheme for disseminating *materia praedicabilis* nonetheless involves a number of specific Lullian concerns and methods. The latter clearly determine the composition of the sermons analyzed below.

The Sermons of the *Liber de praedicatione*

Indeed, the preface to Llull's *Liber de praedicatione* explicitly stresses their reliance on the method of his Art, declaring that they omit the "authorities, histories, miracles of saints, prayers, and interpretations" customarily found in the Sacred Page (2.b.praef.).[17] The term "Sacred Page" probably indicates the theology of the schools. Hence, this declaration expresses the deliberately nonacademic character of Llull's sermons and their reliance on the necessary reasons that he favors.[18] This disclaimer is very apt. Half of the *Liber de praedicatione* consists of a review of Llull's Great Art.[19] The 108 sermons that follow offer chiefly dogmatic and moral theology, all expounded with exempla from natural science or metaphysics in typically Lullian fashion.[20] The *Liber de praedicatione* offers fifty-two sermons for the Church year *(sermones de tempore)* and fifty-six more on Christ, Mary, and selected saints *(sermones de sanctis)*. The *sermones de tempore* use a sequence of Scripture texts that matches, with only a few exceptions, those prescribed for the Dominican liturgy.[21] Each *sermo de sancto* curiously begins by explicitly refusing to deal with any hagiographical details from the saint's legend, but does invoke them generally as cues for the moral instruction that it offers. For example, one section of the sermon on Saint Peter (2.B.2.65) begins: "Blessed Peter was one of the faithful who constitute the Church. His legend explains his faithfulness. But bad prelates and other bad clergy pretend to be faithful."[22] A long diatribe against hypocritical clergy follows this somewhat vague reference to the saint's exemplary faithfulness. All the sermons from the *Liber de praedicatione* employ the simple twofold division into exposition and application, which he also recommends in his own precepts.[23] The statement of the theme and the exposition of its parts is often very brief, sometimes only a single sentence, while the dogmatic and moral application of the parts constitutes the rest of the sermon. The two sections of application often use lengthy distinctional explications to amplify their topics, but employ no other subdivisions.

In short, the 108 sermons from the *Liber de praedicatione* consist chiefly of doctrinal and moral *distinctiones,* a design that gives them a conspicuously didactic and schematic character. They are presumably most useful as models to expand into full-length sermons. Many of them acknowledge this purpose by including occasional brief instructions to the preacher. This advice often consists simply of references to relevant sections of the Great Art. Llull thus imitates a common practice of many preaching manuals and model sermon collections.[24] These works, designed to allow the widest possible application, typically omit details that depend on the particular circumstances of delivery. This omission occurs even in the texts of sermons delivered about specific events. For example, the surviving text of Eudes de Chateauroux's sermon on the Paris university strike of 1229 gives only the *distinctiones* and supporting scriptural citations, but includes no reference to the violence that prompted his pleas to the people.[25] The initial sermon in Llull's collection, for the first Sunday in Advent, contains lengthy and numerous digressions directed to the preacher. Unfortunately, these interruptions confuse the organization and development of the sermon's parts, which are not as neatly parallel as in other sermons from the collection. Thus, while it attempts to include useful suggestions about its practical application, it also creates a flawed model to follow. The first of these digressions interrupts the exposition of the theme in order to explain the purpose of its own intrusion into the text of the sermon:

> In the first part we want to mention points from the Great Art in this book, so that they will be subject matter for the presentation of the sermon. We do not mean to say that the preacher should mention points of this Art or book in preaching, as we do. We mention these points in order to inform the preacher and also to teach how one ought to use this Art. Nevertheless, from the points mentioned by us the preacher should extract the sense and apply the meaning to the sermon in due fashion. For example: if the sermon is about God, and the preacher wishes to speak copiously about God, the preacher should go to the chapter on God deduced through Principles and Rules. (2.B.1.1)[26]

The warning against repeating these instructions in the sermon itself seems unnecessary, but aptly recognizes the degree to which all the sermons depend on Llull's Great Art. The instructions in this first sermon are the most extensive of any in the 108 sermons from the *Liber de praedicatione.* This first sermon thus serves an exemplary didactic function, even if the practices recommended in the instructions do not describe Llull's actual procedures in the body of the sermons. At least it establishes the overall function of these sermons as a collection of models.

Llull's sermon for Christmas Eve (2.B.2.53), the longest in the *Liber de praedicatione,* best illustrates the structure typically used in his collection. It develops most fully all of the distinctions that it initially proposes. Llull's exposition of the theme from Matthew 1:20—"for that which is conceived in her is of the Holy Ghost"—divides this verse into three segments: "which is conceived in her," "Holy Ghost," and "is." He explains that the first segment refers to the Mother of God and to the Son of God. To understand this relationship he proposes nine modes of filiation. The segment "Holy Ghost," Llull notes, indicates God and the human spirit. He does not develop this distinction further, except insofar as subsequent contrasts between divine and human nature imply it. He expounds the segment "is" by introducing five modes of being (absolute, potential, effective, habitual, and privative), adapted from Aristotle's standard enumeration of eight (*Phys.* 4.3 210a32–b31). In the application, these nine modes of filiation and five modes of being constitute a fourteenfold *distinctio* for reviewing Catholic dogma about Christ's divine nature and for presenting moral instruction about the life of sin. The doctrinal application focuses on the doctrine of the Incarnation that a proselytizer would have to argue before unbelievers, while the moral application holds up the Incarnate Word as the object of devotion for the believer. In general, these two sections of application utilize amplificational techniques that correspond only broadly to the specific theoretical devices that Llull recommends as conditions of preaching in the *Liber de praedicatione*. Instead, they develop their subjects as follows.

The application of the first mode of filiation to Christ begins with a reminder, presumably directed to the preacher consulting Llull's text, that this doctrine is suggested (*figuratum*) in the chapter on God from the Great Art. Applying the five modes of filiation to Christ's nature requires some interpretative work, since filiation is a natural, rather than a divine relationship. Consequently, most of Llull's remarks involve some contrast or comparison between natural and divine relationships of filiation, using the adverbs "just as" *(sicut)* or "likewise" *(a simili)*. For example, Eve was born of Adam as flesh from flesh, and "likewise" *(a simili)* Christ was born of Mary. Llull's discourse mixes obligatory references to Scripture or Christian dogma with more general terms from his own Art. Thus, he illustrates several types of natural filiation with beings that clearly correspond to some of the nine Lullian Subjects, such as the elements, plants, the senses, and God. An especially interesting feature of Llull's exegetical discourse is his designation of three natural varieties of filiation as figural relationships. According to the first, Adam was made from the mud of the earth, and therefore "he was allegorically born of the four elements" (2.B.2.53.2.1.1).[27] This use of synecdoche does not demand any revaluation of the nature of the terms involved in the light of the interpretation suggested, but does require some redefinition of the term "allegory." The composition of human nature from the elements refers to the commonplace doctrine of the human being as a microcosmus.[28] Second, "speech is born figurally from the mind" (2.B.2.53.2.1.5).[29] Llull uses the verb *figurare* broadly to name various functions of displaying, showing, or signifying. Its utilization here illustrates well how the manifestation of thought in speech is simply one variety of universal signification, as I described previously in chapter 3. Third, the action of loving, "metaphorically speaking, is born of the lover and the beloved, just as an action from a [sense] power and its object" (2.B.2.53.2.1.1).[30] This comparison is ambiguous. It presumably indicates that the action of loving is "metaphorically" comparable to the action of sensation.

However, it could also indicate that loving is "metaphorically" born between the lover and the beloved just as sensation is "metaphorically" born from the sense power and its object. The latter interpretation rather incongruously makes sensation a metaphorical product of the sense power and its object. This amphibolous passage illustrates superlatively how Llull's moralizing discourse tends to recast all knowledge as a vast discourse of resemblance. Constant exercise of this procedure probably facilitated Llull's discovery of unusual arguments such as his theory of *affatus*. In general, Llull's treatment of these various physical or metaphysical relationships as figural associations reorganizes those relationships as a structure of wholly figurative connections. Ultimately, the terms "figural," "metaphorical," and "allegorical" used here serve the same function as the term "signify" in the *Libre de contemplació*: they all serve as interpretative warrants for reading the language of creation.

Llull turns next to the moral application (2.B.2.53.2.2), which explains the nine modes of filiation and five modes of being in the life of the sinner. His exegetical methods consist of the same broadly allegorical procedure used to expound the application concerning Christ's nature. These fourteen applications include five comparisons of similarity (nos. 1–4, 8) and six of dissimilarity (nos. 5, 6, 9–11, 13) between Christ and the sinner, as well as three noncomparative statements of moral doctrine (nos. 7, 12, 14). One of these noncomparative statements (no. 12) may simply be a defective comparison, in which Llull's recursive style has obscured the logic of his argument. Because his method consists in correlating associations, he often conflates or elides the stages or connections in these when presenting them discursively. The other two noncomparative statements employ the only figural interpretations in the moral application. These illustrate neatly Llull's facility in moralizing discourse. The first (no. 7) argues that a rose is born from a rosebush and Jesus from his mother; hence, Christ is the "fruit of the whole universe," the end to which all creatures should strive (2.B.2.53.2.2.7).[31] The definition of Christ as the perfection of the Creation is the traditional doctrine expounded in summaries of dogma like Bonaventure's *Breviloquium* (4.3.5, 4.4). Llull's argument depends on two commonplace associations of the term "fruit": its exegesis as a reference to "Christ the Redeemer," noted in the Pseudo-Rabanus's *Allegoriae;* and the Gospel metaphor of Christ as the fruit of Mary's womb (Luke 1:42). His comments in effect offer a small *distinctio* on the term "fruit" itself.[32] The second figural interpretation (no. 14) affirms that the privative mode of being "figures" how the sinner is stripped (*denudatus*) of any hope of salvation. This argument appears to employ simple metaphor as much as any figural understanding of "privation" (2.B.2.53.2.2.14).[33] However, some etymological connection may well authorize understanding the term "privation" to mean the sinner "deprived" (in the sense of "denuded") of salvation. The moral application in this sermon ends with a reminder for the preacher to consult the chapters of Llull's Great Art in order to investigate or multiply discourse concerning "Christ, the virtues and sins, and many other things."[34]

Finally, the sermon's conclusion briefly recalls the distinctions of filiation and being, along with their application to Christ and sinners. It begins with a sentence that combines Llull's usual concluding apostrophe to the audience with instructions to the preacher: "And thus, beloved, summarizing briefly, you have many things

touched upon in this sermon, which the preacher can briefly set forth."[35] The confusion of audience and preacher in this remark neatly indicates how Llull's sermons
from the *Liber de praedicatione* stand somewhere between models for a preacher
to develop and complete texts for the edification of an audience. Llull's frequent
advice to recapitulate may indicate that he considers this audience challenged by the
structure of his sermons. Nonetheless, the recorded versions of Giordano da Pisa's
sermons suggest that his listeners possessed the capacity both to follow and to appreciate his sometimes complex divisions and concordances.[36] At the same time,
sermons collected as pious literature for reading audiences often provide little more
than a series of allegorical distinctions.[37] The schematic character of Llull's sermons
imply this use as well.[38]

Where Llull's sermon for Christmas Eve pursues a separate doctrinal and a separate moral application of the same fourteen distinctions, his sermon for the Second
Sunday in Advent (2.B.1.2) offers one combined doctrinal and moral application of
its distinctions.[39] This more integrated treatment illustrates extremely well Llull's expertise in moralizing diverse material. The sermon begins with the theme from
Luke 21:25—"And there shall be signs in the sun, and in the moon"—followed by a
statement of the sermon's division into an exposition and application of this theme.
The exposition commences immediately by restating the theme and then expounds
its literal meaning as a prophecy of the Last Judgment. Then it declares the allegorical sense of the theme: "the sun metaphorically represents Christ" and "the moon
metaphorically signifies the life of this world."[40] Both interpretations are traditional,
appearing in Pseudo-Rabanus's *Allegoriae*, and nominally employ one of the four
methods of exposition that Llull prescribes (2.A.1). He then proposes to elaborate
these metaphorical comparisons according to five natural properties of the sun and
moon, selected from basic astronomical and astrophysical lore like that found in
Isidore (*Etym.* 3.47–59, 71). Much more sophisticated interpretations of these basic
properties are certainly possible, as Jean de la Rochelle shows in his sermons on
Saint Anthony of Padua.[41] In any case, this exposition of the senses of sun and moon
really explicates only two terms from the theme, rather than the customary three.

The introductory paragraph of this application announces that "we will deal with
the sun, and immediately afterward with the moon in the same paragraph. And we
do this because juxtaposed opposites seem greater and are perceived more clearly, as
white appears to be more so, juxtaposed with black."[42] This explanation evidently appeals to Llull's previous precepts (2.A.8.2–3) regarding "ornamentation" of the
mental faculties with their proper objects in order to justify the contrast of virtue and
vice commonly used in popular preaching. To Llull's Scholastic peers this explanation would seem to contradict Aristotelian doctrine regarding the impact of
constrasting sensations (*De sensu et sens.* 7 447a13–9a32). The following list summarizes the five bipartite comparisons between Christ as sun and this life as moon
that Llull offers as a combined doctrinal and moral application:

Sun
1. Always shines without increasing or decreasing
2. Causes day and night
3. Possesses light in itself

4. Is hot, and naturally radiates heat
5. Is in the middle of the planets, communicating to those below the influence of those above it

   Christ
1. Remains unchanged, unaltered, uncorrupted, unhurt
2. Causes the day of eternal life and the night of Gehenna
3. Possesses strength and virtue in himself
4. Is generous and loving, sharing all good things
5. Stands between us and God

   Moon
1. Waxes and wanes with variable brightness
2. Causes neither day nor night
3. Shines at night with light received from others
4. Is cold and retentive or avaricious, allegorically speaking
5. Occupies the lowest place among the planets, receiving influences from all those above it; metaphorically speaking it is avaricious and slow, not giving freely, but by compulsion

   Life of This World
1. Is changeable and mutable
2. Causes neither eternal day nor perpetual infernal night
3. The sinner cannot receive Christ's light
4. Is comparable to the miser or worldly person
5. Likewise the sinner bitterly and greedily holds back, not giving freely, but timidly and when compelled and is set in the lowest place

The discourse of the sermon justifies each comparison concerning natural or moral properties with a reference to the relevant sections of Llull's Great Art in the first half of the *Liber de praedicatione*. Of course, virtually all of the moralized interpretations of these properties are exegetical commonplaces: for example, day is eternal life, the Incarnation, and good works, while night is hell, spiritual darkness, and sin in Pseudo-Rabanus's *Allegoriae*. In fact, Jean de la Rochelle lists the opposition of the night of sin to the day of grace as the epitome of an allegory based on time, while Grosseteste creates from them an allegory of preaching itself.[43] After the exposition of these five bipartite comparisons, the sermon concludes with a recapitulation that includes Llull's customary advice to the preacher about the need to summarize the sermon's distinctions.

The explicit role played by the exegetical devices that Llull calls "comparisons" and "metaphors" in this sermon illustrates well his understanding of these interpretative techniques and their utilization in popular preaching. For his Scholastic peers they raise urgent questions concerning the adequacy of theological language and the analogical value of Divine Names, but Llull's writings almost never acknowledge these issues.[44] He asserts without qualification that the allegorical exposition in which the sun represents Christ and the moon signifies the life of this world functions metaphorically by reason of the five properties found "in their own way" in the sun, moon, Christ, and this life. That is, analogous natural accidents or properties allow comparison of one being to another, but this explanation begs the question of exactly how the same kinds of accidents exist in different types of being. The first, third, and fifth comparisons all attribute certain natural accidents or characteristics to the sun, moon, Christ, and this life alike: these include permanence, change, hierarchical rank, the transmission of received influences, and the reception of those influences. Llull's realist metaphysics undoubtedly regards these as simply the same accidents functioning in different substances, which obviates any need to invoke analogy. His superrealist conception of the diffusion of the Divine Dignities as Principles of all knowledge and being easily accommodates such an explanation. Yet Llull scarcely invokes his Principles as master categories embracing those characteristics. At no point does he consider the theological consequences of attributing these characteristics either analogically or really to God. Perhaps few popular preachers of his era would worry their audiences with these problems of theological language, but his contemporaries in the schools certainly analyzed them carefully. By formalizing in his Great Art the popular rather than the academic handling of such problems, Ramon Llull evidently sought to validate the moralized theological arguments disseminated among laypeople as legitimate spiritual understanding.

The treatment of sun and moon in this sermon especially illustrates how Llull's models for homiletic discourse propound a kind of popular natural theology. For example, the second comparison from Llull's joint doctrinal and moral application is noteworthy for its explicitly metaphorical attribution of an eschatological sense to an astronomical phenomenon. He achieves this substitution discursively through the verbal structure of an extended simile: "Christ can be compared to the sun, because just as the sun causes the day by its presence, and causes the night by its absence, so Christ by his presence causes the day, that is glorious eternal life, where the greatest brightness is found, and by his absence causes the night, that is Gehenna and horrible infernal death where the greatest darkness is found."[45] Having equated day with salvation and night with damnation, Llull argues that the moon does not cause day or night and "likewise" the sinner of this world does not cause salvation or damnation. This broadly exegetical technique is equally explicit in Llull's fourth comparison, which also names its metaphorical method: the sun is hot, "and because it is characteristic of the hot to be expansive, to give, and to be generous, we say that Christ can be called the sun by virtue of similitude because he is generous and charitable."[46] Likewise "the moon is cold, and because it is possessive *(restrictiva)*, allegorically speaking, it is avaricious, and thus the moon is comparable to the avaricious worldly person."[47] Thus, where the first, third, and fifth comparisons analogously invoke the same natural characteristic in different beings, the second and fourth figurally interpret the terms "night," "day," "hot," and "possessive." The discussion of the moon in the fifth analogizing comparison also includes a figural exposition: all the superior celestial influences pass to the sublunar realm through the sphere of the moon, which "metaphorically speaking, is unwilling and avaricious in itself, and does not give freely" and similarly the sinner is avaricious and ungenerous.[48]

Ultimately, Llull employs for the same persuasive purposes various devices that he calls "metaphor," "allegory," "simile," and "comparison," but without distinguishing one device from another according to their use of figural interpretation or analogy of natural characteristics. This undifferentiated use allows him to apply the terms "metaphor" and "allegory" to the comparison of Christ and the sun through natural properties that each possesses "in its own way," as well as to the anthropomorphic description of the moon as avaricious. Llull's constant use of *distinctiones* to develop his sermons in the *Liber de praedicatione* certainly encourages these results, but he relies on distinctional exposition no more than a contemporary like Ranulph d'Homblières.[49] Llull's broad conflation of purely typological associations with analogous relationships among actual beings arises so easily because it involves a realist exemplarism that ignores the metaphysical and epistemological distinctions recognized by his peers in the schools. Thus, his moralization ranges freely from exegesis in the strict typological sense to the loosest sort of spiritual interpretation. Llull's work shares this expansive exercise of moral interpretation with many twelfth- and thirteenth-century popular sermons.[50] By 1200 these had already conflated the four exegetical senses into a sort of general "spiritual sense." Thus Odo of Cheriton simply terms "mystical" the exposition added to many of the fables in his collection (e.g., nos. 90–91).[51] This broadly conceived moralization, often confused or incoherent, became the predilect recourse for popularizing difficult theological issues,[52] even while strict tropological exposition remained in vogue among Franciscans such as Bonaventure.[53] Comparison of the Seraphic Doctor's *Collationes in Hexaëmeron* with Llull's sermons from the *Liber de praedicatione* readily discloses how the Catalan layman exercises popular moralization as his normative mode of discourse. His model discourses do not "transgress and supplant" the contemporary *ars praedicandi*,[54] so much as they level and unify it.

Sermons from the *Liber predicationis contra Judeos*

An especially clear measure of the distance between Llull's methods and the techniques of the schools appears in the fifty-two sermons of his *Liber predicationis contra Judeos*. This text probably marks the limits of his ability to apply the devices of his Great Art and tactics of popular moralization to the more demanding scholarly tasks of scriptural exegesis and controversial disputation. Composed in 1305 at Barcelona, an important site of debate with Jewish theologians, this stridently apologetic work really concerns preaching only insofar as Llull extends the term to include apologetic argumentation. Each sermon is brief, rarely longer than five hundred words, and consists of three parts, according to the work's introduction: "[F]irst we will state the scriptural text *(auctoritatem)*, and then we will prove what we say, and in the end of the chapter we will prove the proposition, namely, that the Jews are wrong."[55] This error is their refusal to understand the allegorical sense of the Old Testament. Jewish scholars enjoyed an acknowledged reputation in the thirteenth century as experts on the literal sense of Scripture.[56] At the same time, they commonly incurred the charge of misinterpreting the Divine Word, which was tantamount to heresy, as Aquinas acknowledges (2a.2ae.11, 2). They remain the "slaves to the letter" condemned by Saint Paul (2 Cor. 3.14–17) and Augustine (*DC* 3.5.9–11.13). For Llull no less than Saint Thomas the need to escape this servitude is an axiom of exegesis.[57] Consequently, in 1267, when James I of Aragon directed mendicant friars to examine and correct Hebrew texts, the king's decree stated that its principal objective was the elimination of "falsehoods and corruptions that [the Jews] had inserted in many places of the Bible in order to hide the mysteries of the Passion and many other sacraments of the Faith."[58] Similarly, in the *Libre de mera-velles* (chap. 11), Blaquerna warns Felix that the Jews "have made many glosses contrary to the texts."[59] Llull's sermons in the *Liber predicationis contra Judeos* prove the existence of these deliberate attempts to impugn Christian truth in Scripture. Although the introduction to the work refers only to this willful error of the Jews, Llull consistently mentions the need to refute Jews and Muslims alike throughout his treatise.

Llull states that the *Liber predicationis contra Judeos* offers sermons for all the Sundays of the year (Sermo 1). Consequently, the text's modern editor suggests that its purpose was to provide a guide for the weekly preaching that various decrees of the period required Jews and Moors to attend.[60] Llull had already advocated some kind of forced instruction in his early *Libre de contemplació* (346.18). The *Liber predicationis contra Judeos* perhaps compiles arguments that Llull himself employed when exercising the licenses to proselytize unbelievers granted to him at Naples in 1294 or in Aragon in 1299.[61] However, we know as little about this proselytizing ac-tivity as we do about Llull's other evangelical endeavors. He presumably attempted to imitate the tactics of the mendicant friars engaged in controversial encounters with Jewish scholars. Their arguments generally try to prove the fundamental tenets of Christian dogma by explicating messianic texts from the Old Testament, supporting these interpretations with other texts from the Prophets and Talmudic authorities.[62] Llull's sermons from the *Liber predicationis contra Judeos* explicate Scripture, but include almost no clear references to rabbinic literature. The first forty-nine sermons are all devoted to proving the Incarnation and the Trinity, the two tenets of Christian belief least acceptable to Jews. These are the same basic issues argued by Friar Pau Crestià in his famous debate with Rabbi Moses at Barcelona in 1263. Llull's last sermon, which is so short that it hardly deserves the name, simply posits the superi-ority of the Christian faith. It thus states as a general conclusion what Llull proves in the preceding forty-nine examples: namely, that the Christian faith best interprets Scripture, and is therefore the better and truer faith.[63] The *Liber predicationis contra Judeos* says nothing about requiring Jewish or Muslim advocates to reply to these arguments, although some of Llull's other apologetic works, like the *Liber de novo modo demonstrandi*, do insist on this response.[64] The last lines of Llull's *Liber predi-cationis contra Judeos* recommend using it to preach against Jews and Saracens as well as to argue with philosophers who contradict Christian dogma (Sermo 52). Because this method of preaching is generally useful, he suggests combining the *Liber predicationis contra Judeos* with his *Liber de demonstratione per aequiparan-tiam* (Montpellier, March 1305) and *Liber de incarnatione* (this is probably the *Liber de trinitate et incarnatione* composed at Barcelona in October 1305). This conclud-ing advice clearly shows that Llull regards these fifty-two sermons as part of his larger program for apologetic argument. The *Liber predicationis contra Judeos* may in fact simply constitute an attempt to recast arguments from the *Liber de trinitate et incarnatione* in the form of discourses, rather than apologetic arguments. These lines just as readily support the inference that Llull did not clearly distinguish the two practices.

Llull's sermons expound three types of themes: nineteen are passages from the Old Testament; eighteen are Lullian philosophical axioms or propositions, which he calls *problemata;* and fifteen are precepts from the Decalogue and customary law. The theme of the fourth sermon—"Abraham however saw three and adored one"— is actually a line from the liturgy for Quinquagesima Sunday. The English Dominican Thomas Waleys, when denouncing the use of nonscriptural themes (chap. 2), mentions the case of a "great preacher" who used this same theme. It is tempting to imagine that the "great preacher" was Llull himself, although this seems chronologically unlikely.[65] Llull's method in each sermon of the *Liber predicationis contra Judeos* is deliberately schematic. He explains that his sermons contain many implicit arguments (*rationes*) from which a preacher can create many explicit sermons, especially by observing the method of the Lullian Art (Sermo 1). Each sermon is in effect only the nucleus of a complete discourse.[66]

The argumentation that Llull does offer employs his usual moralizations of physical or metaphysical categories, as well as appeals to the Lullian correlatives, proof *per aequiparantia,*[67] and superrealist exemplarism. These tactics are certainly necessary in order to interpret the incarnational or trinitarian sense of some Old Testament passages. Llull's twentieth sermon, whose theme is Isaiah 66.9, typifies his methods. It begins with this exposition of the theme:

"SHALL I, WHO INSTILL GENERATION IN ALL THINGS, BECOME STER-ILE?" SAYS THE LORD
> This is a true prophecy, since without the Divine Trinity it could not be true, and I prove this in the following way: This pronoun *I* signifies the first person, because it says *I;* and because it says *who instill generation in all things* it signifies divine action; and because it says *become sterile* it signifies the Divine Person regarded in itself, not as acting; therefore, since the Divine Person is active and is not sterile, as the aforesaid signifies, thus one concludes that the aforesaid person is intrinsically active. Now a personal product follows produced from a person, which is certainly not sterile, since it produces from itself something personal and generated; and the producer and product breath forth the Holy Spirit through love. Now since the Jews and Saracens deny this product, they imply a contradiction, and are therefore in error.[68]

Llull divides his theme into the customary three parts, using the kind of parsing of grammatical *partes orationis* recommended by the sermon theorist Basevorn (chap. 33–34). The subsequent declaration serves both to state Llull's overall argument, and to create the "universal whole" that Basevorn deems necessary to any proper declaration (chap. 34). As usual, Llull cites no concordant authorities, but relies solely on necessary reasons, which he casts here in the style of a syllogism. In typically Lullian fashion, however, the syllogism presented in this passage at best constitutes an enthymeme whose implied minor premise is "activity is intrinsic." This implied minor premise depends in turn upon the activism of Llull's coessential correlatives and his insistence on the Neoplatonic axiom of *bonum diffusivum sui.* Llull's recourse to his innate correlatives renders his exposition of the trinitarian sense somewhat elliptical. Nonetheless, the selection of scriptural passages to use as themes in the *Liber predicationis contra Judeos* undoubtedly follows contemporary apologetic literature. The *Glossa ordinaria* for this passage interprets it as a reference to the creation of the "living Church."[69] However, by Llull's day the trinitarian interpretation had evidently become commonplace, even though Nicholas of Lyre deemed this reading "more mystical than literal."[70]

The remainder of the sermon constitutes a kind of fivefold "proof of parts" that defends the necessary reasons cited initially. This proof does not explain those reasons so much as it provides further corollary arguments. Although these reasonings would presumably be useful to the apologist in need of material, their unadorned enumeration hardly constitutes a finished sermon. At best they offer a distinctional exposition of metaphysical categories, based heavily on the Lullian innate correlatives. The first explains that God is pure form and actuality, which therefore requires the production of any product (i.e., Christ) that potentially exists in God. The second avers that God is nature and must therefore be giving nature to something natural (i.e., Christ). The third explains that because divine Power is infinite and eternal, God must therefore have generated some infinite, eternal effect (i.e., Christ). The fourth argues the same for divine Goodness and Greatness, which therefore require infinite and eternal good and great results (i.e., Christ). The fifth explains that since the Divine Intellect must also be intelligible and intelligent, therefore God must be triune as well. These arguments do not follow any discernible pattern of subdivisions suggested in the declaration of parts. In fact, they all expound the same principle, namely, the necessary threefold activism of Divine Nature. The repetition of "therefore" lends a syllogistic tenor to Llull's discourse that implies the demonstrative validity of his appeals to that activism. Despite his confidence in their force, these corollary arguments do not *prove* that the generation mentioned in the passage from Isaiah necessarily corresponds to the production of the Persons in the Trinity. At best, this "prophecy," as Llull calls it, merely implies his trinitarian conclusion, perhaps in the same way that the general truths of his Great Art regularly imply more specific truths.

Llull's appeal to his innate correlatives in effect creates a very abstract exercise of figural interpretation, whose foundations are patent elsewhere in the *Liber predicationis contra Judeos*. Eight of Llull's other sermons (34, 35, 37, 38, 40, 44, 47, and 50) explicitly invoke figural interpretation as their principal argument, using terms such as "figured," "signified," "metaphorically," or the four exegetical senses. Sermons 35, 37, 40, 44, and 50 all justify the application of figural interpretation with the ancient Christian doctrine—as old at least as Origen—that "the literal sense is not sufficient for salvation."[71] Since Llull rarely cites this precept so concisely, he has probably borrowed it, along with the scriptural passages to interpret and many of his supporting examples, from some apologetic authority. He explains how this doctrine is true even for literally valid biblical injunctions, like the prohibition against sowing a field with more than one type of seed (Deut. 22:9). Llull interprets this law allegorically and anagogically in order to demonstrate the ignorance of the Jews, who follow only the literal meaning (Sermo 50). In the case of laws forbidding consumption of pork, animals that do not chew the cud, or scaleless fish, Llull adds that the literal sense of these precepts goes against the end and purpose of the Creation, which is to serve humans (Serm. 40, 44). Llull thus generalizes the criterion of sufficiency into two axioms that posit the a priori truth and plenitude of scriptural sense: "the law is true that more truly and clearly explains the precepts" (Sermo 37) and "the literal and figural senses say more by virtue of Goodness, Greatness, and the other Principles than what is said from the literal sense alone" (Sermo 35).[72] Where Augustine appeals to the teaching of love as a warrant for the figural interpretation of Scripture, Llull appeals to the teaching of Christian truth as truth. That is, Augustine proposes to corroborate a truth expressed figurally with its literal expression elsewhere and accepts the literal meaning as self-sufficient according to historical circumstances (*DC* 3.26.37; 3.12.18–14.24). Llull, on the other hand, corroborates a figural interpretation with the truth that it expresses, and accepts the sufficiency of that truth by virtue of its function in providential history, as known from Christian tradition. His appeal to his own Divine Dignities implies the somewhat circular character of this argument.

Ultimately, Llull's reliance on demonstrating this truth through necessary reasons and claims for the preeminence of the figural sense make little attempt to use arguments or doctrines familiar to Jewish or Muslim audiences.[73] Llull evidently knew well some works of Islamic theology, although his acquaintance with rabbinic literature appears far more limited.[74] Certainly, his habitual exposition of *distinctiones* through necessary reasons and frequent appeal to categories from his Great Art display little effort to imitate styles of preaching practiced by Jews or Muslims. For example, he might have known two traditional types of Muslim preaching. The *khutba* (official brief sermon preached on Fridays) was the work of special preachers using classical Arabic in a highly stylized presentation. Far more influential at the popular level were the *quṣṣāṣ*, itinerant storytellers whose later name of *wāʿiẓ* ("one who admonishes") or *mudhakkir* ("one who reminds") aptly indicates their role as freelance reformers, social critics, and evangelists. Although few of these preachers were probably practicing in Spain or North Africa by Llull's era,[75] his *Libre de Blaquerna* (88.4) perhaps refers to them in its description of certain Barbary "scoundrels" who preach so beautifully that they move Muslim audiences to tears. Llull clearly approves of their efficacy, but not of their vocation. Various techniques of Jewish preaching would also have been easily adaptable to Christian usage. The sermon typically delivered with the reading of the Pentateuch during services or festivals consisted in artfully relating a Scripture passage (its *thema*, as it were) to the occasion, using stories, illustrative anecdotes, etymology, numerology, puns, and acrostics. Although not recognized everywhere as an independent literary genre, the sermon enjoyed a special vogue among Spanish and Provençal Jews in the twelfth and thirteenth centuries. This preaching was heavily philosophical in orientation but also treated devotion and penitence.[76] Both of these emphases should have interested Llull, but he makes no explicit reference to Jewish preaching. Indeed, his constant joint references to Jews and Muslims in the *Liber predicationis contra Judeos* and his reliance on the Great Art to create sermons for both audiences suggests that he probably considers its methods superior to any techniques available from either Jewish or Muslim preaching.

The *Summa sermonum* of 1312

Ramon Llull's last major collection of sermons comprises his most ambitious program for the exercise of preaching. While residing on Majorca between October 1312 and February 1313 he composed the group of texts known collectively as his *Summa sermonum*: these are the *Liber de sermonibus factis de decem praeceptis*, the *Liber de septem sacramentis Sanctae Ecclesiae*, the *Liber de Pater Noster*, the *Liber de Ave Maria*, the *Liber de virtutibus et peccatis*, the *Liber de septem donis Spiritus Sancti*, and *Sermones de operibus misericordiae*. After completing this cycle of works, he prepared the *Ars abbreviata praedicandi* as an epitome, just as he condensed the massive *Ars generalis ultima* into the *Ars brevis*.[77] The treatise on vices and virtues is very long, but all the others are fairly short. Along with the *Liber qui continet confessionem* (composed in September 1312), they offer a complete program for practice of the basic pastoral duties of preaching, confession, and catechetical instruction. Llull perhaps wrote these texts for circulation among the group of reformers gathered around King Frederick of Sicily. He visited the Sicilian ruler from 1313 to 1314, seeking new patronage for his schemes.[78] In this period Frederick's court boasted a multilingual culture in secular and divine letters that Llull perhaps considered particularly receptive to his plans.[79]

The titles of these works clearly identify their concern with the moral exhortation and catechetical instruction offered by most popular preachers or parish priests in this era. Numerous manuals of pastoral care tell clergy how to instruct the faithful in the Creed, the articles of faith, the Lord's Prayer, the gifts of the Spirit, the virtues and vices, and the sacraments.[80] Despite the fundamental importance of these concerns, few collections of model sermons use them to organize their material.[81] Perhaps Llull conceives this simple topical organization as an especially helpful strategy for educating parish clergy. Several other nonhomiletic works from this same period, such as the *Liber de quinque principiis* (August 1312) and the *Liber de novo modo demonstrandi* (September 1312), also present their arguments through simplified schemes. The introduction to the *Liber de decem praeceptis* explicitly advertises its popular method: "[W]e intend to make these sermons clearly. We will flee and avoid great subtlety so that these sermons can be understood by the people. For a sermon not understood offers no benefit or advantage."[82] The rejection of oversubtle argument echoes the obvious antiacademic tenor found throughout Llull's writings. Despite the popular focus of those comments, the conclusion to the *Liber de virtutibus et peccatis* suggests a wide range of tactics and audiences:

> The sermons in this book are of three types. [There are] sermons easily understood by simple people without great learning. Other sermons are more subtle and should be preached to people possessing knowledge in the comparative degree. And there are other sermons, which are higher and ought to be preached to people possessing knowledge in the superlative degree. And thus the sermons of this book are sufficient for all people according to the aforesaid comparison.[83]

The commonplace division of positive, comparative, and superlative degrees is one of Llull's favorite expository devices.[84] It does not define here any specific categories of audience, as other conventional divisions *ad status* do, and perhaps serves simply to insinuate how this collection is general, just as the Great Art is universal. The conclusion adds that the sermons in the *Liber de virtutibus et peccatis* employ both philosophy and theology, so that the preacher can use the light of philosophy to lead the people to theology, which allows them to achieve their Lullian *intentio* of knowing, adoring, serving, and praising God. Apart from these remarks, the several texts of the *Summa sermonum* offer little advice about adapting their copious material to a preacher's audience.

The works that comprise the *Summa sermonum* organize their sermons in two ways. The catechetical works assign one sermon to each doctrinal topic treated: hence the *Liber de sermonibus factis de decem praeceptis* offers one sermon on each of the Ten Commandments, the *Liber de septem sacramentis Sanctae Ecclesiae* devotes one sermon to each of the seven sacraments, and so forth. The *Liber de virtutibus et peccatis* employs a more elaborate scheme. It provides one sermon for each of the eight individual virtues and vices that Llull recognizes, and one sermon for each possible combination of two virtues, two vices, or one virtue and one vice: this expository procedure generates a total of 136 sermons. Each sermon in the *Summa sermonum* evidently attempts to be complete, but they nonetheless display very disparate degrees of elaboration. Some are quite short, like the last two in the *Sermones de operibus misericordiae*. Many from the *Liber de virtutibus et peccatis* require the preacher to supply the initial theme, definition, and division. Most of the last fifteen sermons from this text (as well as sermons 4, 5, and 7 from the *Liber de septem donis Spiritus Sancti*) abandon full discursive development and simply end by giving lists of topics to develop. Full exposition of these ideas would considerably lengthen each sermon, so these lists perhaps appear as examples or even proverbs to use in other sermons on similar issues.[85] This application of the *Liber de virtutibus et peccatis* is implicit in various directions to the preacher. For example, the first sermon on the virtue of justice ends its exposition of each species of justice by suggesting that the preacher use other exempla taken from the subject of the treatise. The tenth sermon on lust ends by mentioning the possibility of using other exempla omitted for the sake of brevity. These details certainly suggest that the *Summa sermonum* should provide a comprehensive collection of model sermons, readily adaptable to the needs of the individual preacher. The sermons in the *Summa sermonum* all employ the same basic format: this consists of a statement of the theme, an opening prayer, exposition (sometimes with multiple divisions), and a closing prayer. Two aspects of this format, the selection of a theme, and the development of the exposition, receive somewhat diverse treatment. Llull's handling of these two aspects ultimately substitutes his Great Art for the *ars praedicandi* as a system of invention and amplification.

Preaching authorities of Llull's era usually insist that the theme of a proper sermon come from Scripture. This is easy to accomplish for sermons preached on Sundays or other occasions for which the liturgical calendar provides fixed scriptural readings. However, the selection of a theme for sermons not based on the liturgical calendar could pose a problem. The petitions of the Lord's Prayer, lines of the Ave Maria, or the Ten Commandments of the Decalogue are all based on actual scriptural texts available for use as a theme in the usual fashion. By contrast, the seven sacraments lack this literal scriptural basis. Llull's solution is to employ a definition of the topic itself for the theme, as in the *Liber de septem sacramentis,* or simply to advise the preacher to supply such a definition, as in the *Liber de septem donis Spiritus Sancti*. The *Sermones de operibus misericordiae* make definitions through the combinational device of defining each work of mercy as the union of a particular virtue and a particular Lullian Principle. For example, the first sermon begins: "Giving food to the poor should be done with Justice and Goodness, so that food is justly and well given to the poor."[86] The remaining sermons begin by advising the preacher to create similar definitions for the combinations that they expound.

The *Liber de virtutibus et peccatis* employs a more complex and comprehensive means of creating themes for its sermons. In its prologue, Llull notes the need to provide a scriptural theme for every sermon and therefore offers the Great Commandment (Deut. 6.5) as a universal theme for "selecting and picking" all the particular themes in the collection.[87] Thanks to this general procedure,

> To the sermons contained in this book one can apply all the other sermons and themes chosen and taken from Holy Scripture. And the preacher can do this because this book has a general subject, as we said above. Moreover, in each sermon and theme of this book, the subject is God, who is the general subject for maintaining all virtues and destroying all vices.[88]

This general subject thus substitutes for the scriptural theme usually expounded in a sermon.[89] This substitution obviously facilitates the application of Llull's Great Art to preaching. Moreover, the relationship of universal to particular authorizes this application because that relationship is based on real metaphysical participation. Just as God really sustains all virtue and resists all vice, so the Great Commandment really sustains all other moral teaching. Llull's departure from the exposition of scriptural themes taught by the *artes praedicandi* does not completely reject medieval Christian homiletic method.[90] Since the virtues and vices are the chief subject of the *Liber de virtutibus et peccatis*, Llull may simply be adapting the looser methods typical of the informal kind of preaching usually called "moral exhortation." Moreover, since laypeople were more likely to receive permission to exercise this kind of preaching (in the manner of the "criers" described in Llull's *Libre de Blaquerna*), his adoption of a general theme perhaps served to make Llull's treatise attractive to lay as well as clerical users.

In practice, the sermons of the *Liber de virtutibus et peccatis* create themes by using an expanded form of the combinatory definitions from the *Sermones de operibus misericordiae*. The first sermon on the virtue of justice presents its theme thus:

> In the beginning of the sermon we state the theme, which is this: Because God is just, you should have justice. The definition of justice is this: Justice is the habit through which someone just does just works. From this definition one knows what justice is, since it happens that the definition and the thing defined are one and the same. Justice has two species and is a genus. The first of these is equal measure. The second is proportionate measure. (1.1.1)[91]

The axiom regarding definition is a cornerstone of Llull's logical doctrine,[92] which he cites here as a virtual *auctoritas*. The *distinctio* regarding two types of justice is the first of many used for dividing the sermons in this work. This reliance on division into species facilitates Llull's habitual distinctional exposition. Each subsequent sermon on the individual virtues and vices begins with a theme, a definition, and a division of species for the virtue or vice that the sermon treats. The statement of the theme usually comes first, before the opening prayer. However, later sermons on combinations of virtues and vices merely advise the preacher to provide a theme, definition, and division into species, without examples.

The sermons in the *Liber de virtutibus et peccatis* include several further incidental instructions about using a theme, definition, and division. The opening lines of the sermon on justice and prudence (3.1.1.17) remark that the theme, definition, and division provide the material for the form of the sermon and allow the people to know the end of the sermon.[93] These terms distantly recall the tripartite hylemorphic scheme of the *Rethorica nova,* although their exact role is unclear. The sermon on justice and temperance (3.1.3.19) recommends abstracting words from the text of these virtues in order to create a "concordance in words" that will be contrary to injury and immoderation.[94] The reference to "concordance in words" of course suggests the "verbal concordances" used by contemporary preachers. However, since it appears here associated with the term "contrary," it more likely invokes the Lullian Relative Principles of Concord and Contrariety. At best, the term itself appears simply as a verbal concordance between Llull's Principle and the homonymous technical device from the *ars praedicandi.* Sermon 29 notes that stating a theme, definition, and division guides the sermon with the preacher's sense and intellectual faculties, perhaps in the manner suggested originally in chapter 359 of the *Libre de contemplació.* Sermon 30 advises selecting unspecified arguments and similitudes from the subject of the book. All subsequent sermons lack these additional suggestions, probably because they rely more and more on the combinatory expositional techniques explained below. In any case, these further incidental instructions all involve devices based on the methods of Llull's Great Art.

The expositional methods and plans of the sermons in the *Summa sermonum* vary considerably, especially since the *Liber de virtutibus et peccatis* and the catechetical texts employ somewhat different methods of exposition. Some sermons from the latter group, like those in the *Liber de septem sacramentis Sanctae Ecclesiae,* employ no overt divisions of any kind, but simply explain dogma from start to finish, embellishing their explanations with simple comparisons or brief *distinctiones* based on Lullian terminology. Most of the other catechetical sermons announce some initial division, although they develop this in various ways and often add further, unannounced divisions. For example, the fairly brief *Sermones de operibus misericordiae* announce an initial distinction between the corporeal and spiritual or between the literal and allegorical senses of their subjects. The subsequent exposition of each variety almost always digresses to other aspects. Similarly, the sixth sermon from the *Liber de sermonibus factis de decem praeceptis* begins its treatment of the commandment "Thou shalt not commit adultery" by defining three species of lust, in the Senses, in the Imagination, and in the Intellect. It expounds this distinction by reviewing how lust arises in each of the six Senses, noting in each case that this subsequently affects the Imagination and the Intellect. The sermon concludes somewhat inappropriately that this exposition shows "in what way sensation, imagination, and the mind are three species of lust."[95] A loose association organizes the third sermon from the *Liber de Pater Noster,* which expounds the petition "Thy kingdom come." It initially states five kinds of kingdom or rule, which the first half of the sermon then explains. The second half describes the stupidity of those who fail to rule in themselves each of the eight mortal sins. The only common element between the first and second halves is the term "ruling," and the sermon makes no effort to synthesize or correlate the five sections of the first half with the eight sections of the second half. The two halves evidently constitute separate doctrinal and moral distinctions on their common term. Finally, the fifth sermon from the *Liber de sermonibus factis de decem praeceptis,* which expounds the commandment "Thou shalt not kill," begins with a distinctional exposition of how someone kills another person through the Senses, Imagination, and Intellect. The remainder of the sermon then introduces a series of briefer, loosely connected, distinctions. First it notes that people kill themselves through their own minds when they fail to serve God. Then it defines the Church as the congregation of the faithful that one rejects by practicing the vices, which constitutes killing onself with one's mind. Next it distinguishes three principal things that one knows in the Church (the articles of faith, the Ten Commandments, and the seven sacraments) and explains how those who fail to preach and teach these things kill themselves. The sermon concludes with the same argument about the virtues and vices, and a closing prayer. This treatment insinuates an overall correspondence between killing others through misuse of the Senses or Intellect and killing oneself through failure to propagate the Faith. However, this parallel remains implicit at best, since Llull nowhere states it explicitly and does not clearly organize the sermon's divisions to develop it. Despite the lack of coherence in these sermons, any preacher consulting Llull's texts could presumably remedy their awkward development of distinctions and divisions. Still, Llull's collection includes virtually no internal rubrics or other devices to assist in this task. The only guidelines for consultation are the topical titles of each sermon. Since so many of Llull's sermons offer material that is already developed, but not always well associated, it is possible that they are based on prearranged distinctions and divisions that he adapts from some other compilation of model sermons.

The expositional method of the *Liber de virtutibus et peccatis* differs from the catechetical texts because it attempts to apply exhaustively ten general divisions defined in its prologue: these are the ten Lullian Subjects; the ten Lullian Principles; the fourteen articles of faith; the seven sacraments; the Ten Commandments; the ten Aristotelian *praedicamenta;* the ten sensitive, imaginative, and mental faculties; the four Aristotelian causes; the two species of fortune; and the liberal and the mechanical arts. These divisions never appear explicitly announced in the sermons of the *Liber de virtutibus et peccatis,* but they appear repeatedly as implied distinctions for expounding or amplifying any topic, argument, or example. Sometimes the terminology of a paragraph reveals which division it applies, but in many passages the division employed (if any) is difficult to discern. The following passage from the sermon on fortitude and temperance typifies Llull's use of these distinctions and divisions:

> When you are at a table well arranged with corporeal victuals, furnish then your soul
> with the spiritual victuals of fortitude and temperance. These will be the forms to
> inform your eating and drinking, which are the material of health. And if you do con-
> trariwise, you will eat and drink by chance, and you can suffer indigestion and

drunkenness and you will clothe your memory, understanding, and desire with mortal sin. (3.3.1.30)[96]

The initial instructions in this sermon advise the preacher to recall the "themes, definitions, species, and text of fortitude and temperance. And through this process make a sermon composed of fortitude and temperance, and collect arguments and similitudes from the subject of this book."[97] The term "text" especially suggests that this sermon somehow incorporates and combines material taken from the two earlier sermons on fortitude and temperance. Both Sermon 3 on fortitude and Sermon 4 on temperance discuss inculcating these virtues in the three powers of the soul. There is little else, however, from Sermon 3 that would justify the mention of fortitude in the passage quoted here. On the other hand, these lines clearly cite various details from Sermon 4, which defines temperance as moderation in eating and drinking, discusses the importance of digestion for health, and mentions attention to table etiquette. Sermon 4 says nothing, however, about the orderly arrangement of these processes. The mention of order evidently serves to create a contrast with the disorder of indigestion and drunkenness. The *Liber de virtutibus et peccatis* often uses the commonplace distinction between corporeal and spiritual health, and its application here to victuals demonstrates well its wide utility as an inventional topic. The reference to fortitude and virtue as forms and to eating and drinking as the matter of health obviously attributes hylemorphic roles to them. In this way the passage perhaps invokes the four Aristotelian causes suggested as general inventional divisions in the prologue. The order created by these causes contrasts with the disorderly chance caused by their opposite vices, and this reference to chance thus invokes another of the general inventional divisions recommended in the prologue. Finally, the reference to clothing the three powers of the mind may indicate the predicamental category of habit, whose various senses (such as "disposition" or "garment") Llull's writings often conflate.[98] As a result, this reference to habit illustrates the Aristotelian *praedicamenta* recommended in the prologue. We cannot definitely know if these sermons owe their genesis to exercise of a Lullian *ars combinatoria* involving the ten sets of terms mentioned in the prologue, but the consistent appearance of examples associated with those sets makes it highly likely. In short, the sermons from the first half of the *Liber de virtutibus et peccatis* demonstrate the fullest exercise of Llull's Great Art as a homiletic "machine of discourse."[99]

Where the passage from Sermon 30 reveals no explicit pattern of distinctional terms, the sermons from the latter half of the *Liber de virtutibus et peccatis* more often display their organization very overtly. For example, Sermons 42 through 45 all analyze pairs of virtues through the Lullian Principles. Sermon 58 discusses how lust and pride relate to each of the Dignities. Sermon 82 describes how prudence governs gluttony in the Intellect, Imagination, and Senses. Sermon 116 reviews how hope combats the effects of pride in each of the sensual and intellectual faculties. The increasingly obvious divisional framework of the later sermons—and especially the appearance of undeveloped lists of topics in the last sermons—probably resulted from Llull's own waning interest in expounding the complicated combinational plan announced for the *Liber de virtutibus et peccatis*. The increasingly schematic expositional style of this text never gives way, however, to simple statements of inventional method. The *Liber de virtutibus et peccatis* shows much, but tells little, about its compositional procedures. Nowhere does it offer any detailed comments about the mechanics that might be guiding the association and derivation of terms or categories within each sermon. Nonetheless, the sermons in this work demonstrate Ramon Llull's extraordinary ability to combine and expound repeatedly a limited group of abstract terms and categories. In short, it reveals the ultimate reduction of the *ars praedicandi* to the methods of his own Great Art.

Conclusion

The schematic assemblies of *materia praedicabilis* that Ramon Llull offers as model sermons might well seem almost irrelevant to contemporary popular preaching.[100] Their idiosyncrasy does not arise simply from the fact that few of these models constitute full-blown sermons, since many extant sermons from this era survive only in summary *reportationes*. Nor is their theology too idiosyncratic: the catechetical instruction provided in Llull's *Summa sermonum* corresponds exactly to the simple education in faith and morals offered by many other popular sermons. Certainly, their nearly exclusive dependence on techniques of moralization and repeated use of basic *distinctiones* would be readily familiar to lay audiences. Instead, what makes Llull's model sermons seem so different from those of his contemporaries is simply their attempt to link all their methods to those of his Great Art. The *Liber de praedicatione* only partially achieves this assimilation of preaching and Llull's own system by offering a complete, separate exposition of the Great Art and then referring subsequent model sermons to its procedures. The *Liber de virtutibus et peccatis* more successfully generates all of its sermons through combinatory procedures that imitate those of the Great Art.

The model discourses that result from these efforts include much *materia praedicabilis* that would be useful to preachers seeking guidance. Nonetheless, several other features of Llull's sermons might make them less attractive as resources for consultation. First, they include none of the hagiographic legends or astonishing exempla typically used by popular preachers. They likewise lack the regular scriptural references and concordances necessary for more sophisticated sermons based on collation of authorities. The philosophical erudition included in many of Llull's models probably suited a fairly limited range of "semilearned" lay or clerical audiences: masses in the marketplace would find it incomprehensible, while students and masters in the schools would consider it simplistic, if not mistaken. The danger of error in the theology taught through popular preaching eventually led English authorities to seek restrictions on the content of preaching to the laity.[101] Later attacks on Lullism may reflect similar fears. Finally, Llull's sermon collections suffer the considerable disadvantage of employing his idiosyncratic terminology. Sermons that rely heavily on his vocabulary of innate correlatives or Absolute and Relative Principles are only intelligible to audiences already trained in the system of his Great Art.

Despite these peculiarities and limitations, Llull's model "sermons" aptly indicate the moral edification and doctrinal instruction that he evidently expected popular preaching to provide. Even where his own methods complicate fulfillment of these goals, his plans for pulpit discourse demonstrate the utility, power, and fecundity invested in sacred eloquence for laypeople in the later thirteenth century. Indeed, the novelty and idiosyncracy of Llull's homiletic oeuvre offers extraordinary and perhaps singular testimony to the creative vigor that popular piety and learning had already attained in his era.

Conclusion

In this study I have sought to show how Ramon Llull's proposals about the arts of eloquence arise from and contribute to the broad level of late medieval learning and piety that we call "popular." This thesis involves two contingent issues of reception that require consideration now that I am concluding. The first is the dissemination of his works on rhetoric and preaching among later medieval readers. The second is the prevailing modern view of Llull as an influential contributor to the academic, political, and spiritual affairs of his era. Each reception of Llull's achievement offers certain lessons about our understanding of his enterprise.

The Late Medieval Reception of Lullian Rhetoric and Sermons

In the preceding chapters I have tried to show how Ramon Llull synthesized elements from his Great Art with commonplace precepts regarding eloquence and ethics in order to produce plans of rhetoric and preaching that differed substantially from those taught by his Scholastic contemporaries. Llull not only insisted on employing the idiosyncratic terminology and categories of his own system, but touted his programs as simpler and more righteous alternatives to the elaborate discourse of his Scholastic contemporaries. Since rhetoric and preaching by definition teach skills for practical use, we might imagine that Llull's precepts regarding eloquence, however idiosyncratic, would attract some serious attention. After all, Llull does insist that his tactics are especially appropriate for engaging popular audiences and for finding material to utilize in preaching. Of course, this same practical use also fosters the improvisation that enables readers to adapt Llull's works for their own purposes. The manuscript transmission of his writings on rhetoric and preaching suggests that some later medieval readers did indeed recognize the value of these works for certain interests.[1] Copies of Llull's treatises on eloquence from before 1500 typically appear in three codicological contexts: they are copied with other Lullian texts in a compendium of Lullian doctrine; they are copied individually as independent works of reference or study; or they are copied along with other, conventional medieval treatises on the arts of language.[2] Each context probably implies a different type of interest in Llull's work, as the following examples show.

The least popular of Llull's works on rhetoric or preaching appears to be his *Liber predicationis contra Judeos*, which survives in only two copies from the sixteenth and seventeenth centuries (the former is incomplete). These manuscripts obviously offer little testimony to the work's medieval circulation, apart from demonstrating its mere survival.[3] The deficiencies of this treatise (explained above in chapter 10) make its limited popularity easy to understand. Its very heavy reliance on Lullian doctrine, especially his theory of innate correlatives, offers little material of use to an apologist. Moreover, most trained controversialists were probably capable of creating for themselves far more sophisticated exegetical arguments regarding the Old Testament and the Talmud.

The huge cycle of model sermons that modern editors have dubbed Llull's *Summa sermonum* survives in only one medieval copy: Munich, Bayerische Staatsbibliothek, MS Clm. 10495.[4] This fourteenth-century Catalan manuscript is perhaps a transcription of one of the compilations of Llull's works that his will ordered to be made after his death. In addition to the *Summa sermonum*, this volume includes the *Ars abbreviata praedicandi*, the *Liber qui continent confessionem*, the *Liber per quem potest cognosci quae lex sit magis bona*, the *Liber de virtute veniali atque vitali*, the *Liber de trinitate et incarnatione*, the *Liber de quinque principiis*, the *Liber de participatione christianorum et saracenorum*, the *Liber differentiae correlativorum divinarum dignitatum*, and the *Liber de locutione angelorum*. Several of these works survive only in this manuscript. If this massive volume has a common theme, it appears to be evangelism in general, of both Christians and unbelievers. The texts included obviously serve the needs of catechizing and perhaps serve the needs of proselytizing as well. Unfortunately, the manuscript includes no indications of its provenance, although it may be identical with a "book of sermons" listed in the library of the fifteenth-century Lullist school at Barcelona. The *Liber de virtutibus et peccatis* also survives alone in two additional manuscripts from the fourteenth or fifteenth centuries: Rome, College of San Isidoro MS I.i, and Toledo, Biblioteca Capitular, MS 22–23 Zelada. These two manuscripts evidently are copies of the Munich volume, though with very disparate accuracy. Both copies are basically quarto-sized volumes and each includes an additional folio of anonymous theological material. These single copies perhaps served as manuals of sermonizing for some Lullist. The highly mechanical design of this work might even favor their use as a guide to contemplation. However, their schematic, even incomplete treatment of material (described in chapter 10) may also be responsible for their limited circulation. Even less attractive is their very poor Latin usage, which is evidently due to the text's inept translation from Llull's Catalan original.[5] One copy of this vernacular version, entitled the *Art major de predicació*, is extant. It appears after a vernacular version of the *Ars abbreviata predicationis* (discussed below) in the early fifteenth-century MS 2021 of the Biblioteca de Catalunya in Barcelona. This volume, which apparently belonged to the Lullist school of Barcelona, clearly constitutes a Lullian guide to preaching. Nonetheless, it would appear that the *Summa sermonum* achieved only limited diffusion even among Lullists before 1500.

Llull's *Rethorica nova* evidently generated more interest. At least six copies of the Latin text are extant from the fourteenth and fifteenth centuries.[6] One of these appears in the notebooks that Nicholas of Cusa compiled while studying at Paris in 1428. Codex Cusanus 83 includes the complete text of the *Rethorica nova* along with all or part of dozens of other Lullian writings. Cusanus clearly found enough interest in Llull's rhetorical treatise to copy its entirety, but not enough to add the marginal comments that he made on many other Lullian texts in his notebooks. The extraordinary range of Lullian texts that he reproduced readily demonstrates his broad interest in the Catalan thinker's project, but his copy of the *Rethorica nova* does not reveal any special attention to Llull's proposals about rhetoric or preaching. By contrast, a less capacious interest in Llull's program apparently guided the design of MS lat. 6443c from the Bibliothèque Nationale in Paris.[7] The oldest part of the manuscript dates from the fourteenth century and offers these texts: *Brevis practica tabulae generalis*, *Lectura brevis practicae tabulae generalis*, *Liber ad probandum aliquos articulos fidei catholicae per syllogisticas rationes*, *Logica nova*, and *Rethorica nova*. This group of works offers a concise introduction to Lullism and the Lullian arts of language, based on the simplified version of the Great Art provided by the *Tabula generalis* and on Llull's treatises about logic and rhetoric.[8] It is very tempting to regard this group of texts as a kind of Lullian preuniversity arts curriculum,[9] perhaps like the one taught later at the Lullist school in Barcelona.[10] In the sixteenth century someone bound this material together with a fifteenth-century copy of the *Ars generalis ultima* and the *Liber de demonstratione per aequiparantiam*, thereby creating a comprehensive guide to Lullian argumentation. The older portion of this volume contains regular marginal comments and various scattered notes, which indicate its actual use by at least one owner. Finally, MS Clm. lat. 10529 from the Bayerische Staatsbibliothek in Munich displays the deliberate use of Llull's *Rethorica nova* in conjunction with more conventional arts of language. A quarto-size volume of forty-two folios copied around 1400, it contains numerous marginal and interlinear emendations in a later hand. It begins with the paragraphs on rhetoric from Llull's vernacular *Doctrina pueril*, followed by the *Rethorica nova* itself. Next comes a series of brief, unattributed treatises (at least one incomplete) on the cursus and other aspects of the *ars dictaminis*. The same hand is responsible for all of the texts copied into this manuscript. It is impossible to know whether the compiler of this volume considered Llull's treatise as useful as the guides to letter writing or simply regarded it as an edifying Christian introduction to the *ars dictaminis*. However, the latter perspective may well have appealed to some lesser clergy or laypeople studying the trivial arts. For them, the *Rethorica nova* could offer a valuable spiritual foundation for more technical applications of grammar, the *artes dictaminis* and *poetriae*, or logic. Devotees of Llull's system continued to make manuscript copies of the *Rethorica nova* into the sixteenth century, but the great printed collections of Lullian texts from the early modern era excluded it, preferring to disseminate instead the apocryphal *Isagoge in rhetoricen* composed by Parisian Lullists in the early sixteenth century. This choice probably reflects the tastes of readers trained according to humanist standards of eloquence. For them, Llull's poor Latin and popularized Scholastic techniques surely seemed unattractive.[11]

Like the *Rethorica nova*, Llull's *Liber de praedicatione* also seems to have enjoyed some popularity in the later Middle Ages. At least eight copies made before 1500 are extant.[12] One of these comes from the ample Lullian library created by the fifteenth-cenury Venetian physician Nicholas Poli: Innichen, Stiftsbibliothek MS VIII C.13, combines the *Liber de praedicatione* with the *Logica nova*, the *Disputatio Raimundi christiani et Hamar saraceni*, the *Ars abbreviata praedicandi*, the *Liber novus physicorum*, the *Metaphysica nova*, the *Ars demonstrativa*, and the *Ars generalis ultima*. This collection evidently offers a kind of Lullian encyclopedia of the arts and sciences. Another volume, MS lat. 15385 from the Bibliothèque Nationale in Paris, contains the *Liber de praedicatione*, with many explicit revisions, as well as the *Liber de demonstratione per aequiparantiam* and the *Liber ad probandum aliquos articulos fidei per syllogisticas rationes*. Once the property of a certain Abbot Jacques de Verdun, this volume more obviously forms a guide to Lullian preaching and apologetics. One of the notebooks gathered by Nicholas of Cusa, Codex Cusanus 118, is patently a manual of sermons aids: it contains the *Liber de praedicatione* and two preaching works by William de Lavicea, the *Dieta salutis* and the *Themata dominicarum*. Use as a resource for preaching is also the apparent function of MS 1034 from the Biblioteca Pública of Majorca, which includes only the *Liber de praedicatione* (and some concluding theological notes). This manuscript appears to be a copy of Bayerische Staatsbibliothek MS Clm. 10521, a volume that also includes the same theological notes on the first folio and the *Liber de praedicatione* alone. Similarly, preparing sermons is the indisputable function of MS 1020 from the Biblioteca Pública of Majorca, since it contains the *Liber de praedicatione* copied out and corrected in a single hand along with a short anonymous collection of sermons. The testimony of these several manuscripts clearly shows that some later medieval readers found the *Liber de praedicatione* useful as an aid to preaching. The second half of the work may also have served as a text of devotional reading. It is interesting that the work rarely appears copied or bound with sermon or preaching treatises by other authors, suggesting either that its contents were sufficient in themselves for the readers who consulted it or that they found it hard to integrate with other materials.

The most popular of Ramon Llull's works on rhetoric or preaching was evidently his *Ars abbreviata praedicandi*. Two manuscripts of the Catalan version and eight of the Latin text are extant from before 1500. Moreover, the Latin text exists in three different renderings, so at least that many readers found it valuable enough to merit revision or retranslation. The title of this text varies considerably in Llull's own work and he occasionally ascribes to it the broad inventive and discursive functions of his entire Great Art, perhaps because its focus is not simply preaching but all edifying communication.[13] Appreciation of this wider application may explain the disparity, which the text's modern editors find puzzling, between its diffusion in multiple copies or versions and its apparent lack of influence on actual homiletic practice.[14] Indeed, some later readers may simply have used the *Ars abbreviata praedicandi* as a convenient epitome of the entire Lullian system. Hence, it appears in several later medieval manuscripts that offer a miscellany of Llull's texts or a Lullian encyclopedia (like some of those containing the *Rethorica nova*). The most obvious is the fourteenth-century Munich manuscript (Clm. 10495) mentioned above, an omnibus volume created to fulfill Llull's desire for posthumous distribution of his writings. As I noted already, the *Ars abbreviata praedicandi* forms part of the comprehensive Lullian collection found in the fifteenth-century manuscripts from Innichen. Two fifteenth-century manuscripts from Majorca—MS 994 from the Biblioteca Pública and MS 7 from the Franciscan convent—likewise exemplify how later readers deliberately included Llull's treatise within a general scheme of Lullian knowledge. MS 994, which is copied in one hand, begins with various lists of the Lullian Principles and Rules, followed by the *Ars brevis*, an anonymous exposition of the Great Art, the *Ars iuris*, the *Ars abbreviata praedicandi*, the *Arbor philosophiae desiderata*, and the *Principia artis inventivae* (a section of the *Ars inventiva veritatis*).[15] The inclusion of the treatise on law is an intriguing extension of the volume's concentration on homiletic and devotional interests. MS 7 from the Franciscan convent combines complete texts of the *Ars iuris particularis*, the *Arbor philosophiae desideratae*, the *Principia artis inventivae*, the *Ars abbreviata praedicandi*, the *Liber de lumine*, and the *Ars compendiosa inveniendi veritatem*, intermingled with brief definitions of Lullian categories, extracts from the *Liber de praedicatione*, lists of virtues and vices, and summaries of the "articles" in Christian, Jewish, and Muslim belief. The last folio includes an account of the Dominican doctrines that caused a rift between the order and the University of Paris, until settled by royal intervention in 1403. The latter material and the extracts from the *Liber de praedicatione* strongly suggest some application to devotion and preaching, evidently by a member of the Order of Preachers. This homiletic use is apparent in manuscripts that combine the *Ars abbreviata praedicandi* with some of Llull's sermon collections. MS 2021 of the Biblioteca de Catalunya is an excellent example. Its combination of the vernacular *Art abreujada de predicació* and the *Art major de predicació* (the only known Catalan copy of the *Liber de virtutibus et peccatis*) raises interesting questions about the level of education of its owner. Most intriguing of all are those manuscripts that combine Llull's treatise with homiletic works by other authors, since these imply some attempt to integrate his doctrines into conventional preaching practice. For example, MS Mar. F. 309 from the Biblioteka Polskiej Akademii Nauk in Gdansk is evidently a personal notebook of sermon material and theology compiled in the fifteenth century by one Augustinus Dirsschaw, "canon and preacher."[16] The *Ars abbreviata praedicandi* is the eleventh of at least twenty-eight separate items in this volume, which gathers a variety of material: sixteen Lullian treatises ranging from the *Tabula generalis* and the *Liber novus animae rationalis* to the *Ars iuris* and the *Tractatus de astronomia*; an exegetical treatise by Llull's contemporary Peter John Olivi; an index to the writings of Aquinas and extracts from his works; and an ambitious treatise (perhaps by Augustinus Dirsschaw himself) called *Liber virtutum moralium omnium et vitiorum de arte maiori praedicandi et memorandi*. Finally, Vatican MS Ottob. lat. 396 is a fourteenth-century volume, probably from Majorca, that combines Llull's *Ars abbreviata praedicandi* with exegetical and homiletic works by Francesc Eiximenis, Jean de la Rochelle, and John of Chatillon.[17] Here the integration of Llull's doctrines with conventional preaching aids is unmistakable.

Nonetheless, MS Ottob. lat. 396 is somewhat exceptional. Many other copies of the *Ars abbreviata praedicandi* do not demonstrate so clearly its application to preaching during the later Middle Ages. The treatise's appearance in omnibus volumes of Llull's writings suggests that it more often served as a facile summary of his methods or component in some Lullian encyclopedia of learning. Still, some regular or secular clergy certainly did find it helpful as an aid to preaching, and this use of Llull's *Ars abbreviata praedicandi* thus constitutes precious testimony to the circulation of his doctrines among certain classes of clerical readers. It seems inevitable that Llull's works on rhetoric and preaching would be among his most interesting writings for clerical audiences, which formed a ready market for all types of sermon aids. Indeed, their ancillary use as guides to devotion would make them likely choices to include with copies of his Great Art. Understanding the circumstances that created those choices remains one of the most urgent tasks facing current research on later medieval Lullism.[18]

Ramon Llull, Illuminated Doctor: Lay Cultural Authority and the Pastoral Transformation of the Christian Self

Understanding the reception of Ramon Llull's works on rhetoric and preaching requires comprehensive analysis of their relation to contemporary doctrines of eloquence. I have sought to advance that analysis in this study. Many specific aspects of Llull's doctrines still await further investigation, especially the difficult question of how Llull or later Lullists applied those doctrines in practice. In addition, any effort to understand Llull's role in the spiritual and intellectual culture of his era must also confront a more general and obdurate problem, namely, evaluating critically the views of his role that prevail in current scholarship. Two perspectives have lately become prevalent: the first tends to regard Llull as the singularly inspired creator of a unique intellectual system, while the second regards him as a great Scholastic thinker on a par with Bonaventure, Aquinas, or Duns Scotus. Both views subtly perpetuate, I suspect, two ancient traditions of pious and occult esteem for Llull's achievements. The pious tradition celebrated him as the "Illuminated Doctor," an unofficial saint venerated in Majorca virtually from his own lifetime until the present century. The occult tradition, which flourished in the Renaissance, prized his Great Art as a potent key to cabbalistic, Hermetic, alchemical, or numerological wisdom. Numerous apocryphal legends—such as the story of his martyrdom or his alchemical experiments in the Tower of London—supported each tradition.

Whatever their debt to these older traditions, the two modern views of Llull as singular genius and Scholastic giant both overlook the overwhelmingly commonplace character of the doctrines expounded in the Great Art. Llull himself insists that his system employs general principles common to Christian, Muslim, and Jewish learning alike, and comprehensible to "simple people." Indeed, his ideas rarely exceed the basic doctrines found in any Latin or Arab encyclopedia. Hence, the first common view of Llull's work, which regards it as unique, vastly overestimates the contribution of his idiosyncratic terminology and methods, perhaps from deference

to his claims of divine revelation. Arguments that Llull's system disguises highly sophisticated but little-known Greek, Christian, or Islamic doctrines—or even that his
Great Art consitutes a medieval precursor to modern computer science—are histo-
riographically very problematic, to say the least. The former make study of Llull's
work a fanciful exercise in philological allegory, whose conclusions refuse corrob-
oration from historical evidence. The latter force us to view his enterprise with the
kind of ironic, condescending hindsight that regards all past undertakings as quaint
aspirations to modern triumphs. These arguments tend to "dehistoricize" Llull, an inclination unfortunately reinforced in twentieth-century philology by a persistent
romantic esteem for the transcendency of genius.[19] The second common view of
Ramon Llull's achievement, which places him among the great Schoolmen, certainly
recognizes his historical role, but inflates it by projecting modern esteem for his
achievements into the thirteenth century. Many modern scholars have affirmed un-
equivocally that Llull was a university master.[20] This claim ignores the special
dispensations that he needed in order to teach or preach,[21] the negligible value of
his Great Art to students pursuing a university education, and his own professed antagonism toward the schools in general. Nonetheless, celebration of Llull's
achievements by modern Catalan nationalists, and perhaps even the academic vocation of most historians who study him, continue to nourish the conviction that Llull
was a highly influential Scholastic philosopher and theologian. The feeble historiographical value of the relationship called "influence"—surely one of the most abused
explanations in modern philology—becomes most obvious in arguments about
Llull's importance for the evolution of Scholastic thought around 1300.

  In this study I have sought to avoid these two common views of Llull's enterprise
by adopting two broad assumptions that will probably seem unnecessary, if not perverse, to partisans of those two views. Neither of my assumptions depends on
sophisticated arguments from historiographical theory or the philosophy of history.
They are instead chiefly pragmatic strategies that I have adopted in order to render
Ramon Llull more interesting and more comprehensible to someone besides Lullists.
Perhaps Llull himself would have approved this ambition.

  The first broad assumption is that most of Ramon Llull's work reprises spiritual
or intellectual practices already known to us from his era. Llull was hardly the only
layman who taught, preached, or wrote learned works in Western Europe around
1300. Moreover, very few of the theories or methods that he advocates are original.
This study has repeatedly suggested conventional sources for his precepts on rhetoric
and preaching.[22] For this reason, Tomás y Joaquín Carreras i Artau concluded over
fifty years ago, in the first comprehensive modern scholarly study of Llull's work,
that he was "the most typical representative of popular Scholasticism."[23] Ruedi
Imbach has lately revived appreciation of this popularizing function in his survey
of *Laien in der Philosophie des Mittelalters*. Llull's constant recourse to distinctional
exposition and moralization demonstrates his own profound internalization of the discourses used to disseminate theology from the classroom and cloister in the thirteenth
century: sermon collections, handbooks on pastoral care, manuals of preaching or
apologetics, guides to meditation or contemplation, and so forth. Indeed, this discourse is the paradigm of eloquence for Llull. His own writings both promote that
vast enterprise of dissemination and demonstrate the tremendous value of these

genres as generative models.[24] Llull's adaptations of ideals or techniques cultivated in monastic spirituality especially illustrate the transfer of religious culture *de cella in saeculum* that characterizes so many developments in popular devotion during the late Middle Ages.[25] Not enough recent scholarship explores the place of Ramon Llull in popular religious movements. The relationship of his work to the lay spirituality or vernacular aesthetics promoted by Franciscans remains unclear.[26] In general, he resembles many other twelfth- and thirteenth-century reformers who valued public preaching and charity over communal devotion and study, sought to renew the spirit of Christendom, stressed poverty as a guarantee of their own sincerity as much as a social ideal, and departed very little from orthodox norms of piety.[27] The popular passion for renewal and reform of Christian society was central to Llull's enterprise.[28] He pursues reform not only as a spiritual, but also as an intellectual ideal. Thus, the innovations propounded in his claims to discover a new fallacy, a new sixth sense, or a new mode of demonstration, and in the whole series of works called *Rethorica nova*, *Logica nova*, or *Metaphysica nova*, all assert this dual ideal of spiritual and intellectual reform.

The originality that does appear in Ramon Llull's innovations offers us important insights into the general processes of cultural transmission, circulation, and exchange in the so-called popular culture of the late Middle Ages. Llull's proposal of speech as a sixth sense or his broad treatment of rhetoric as loving communication in the *Rethorica nova* illustrate very strikingly how lay learning and piety could produce doctrines that differed substantially from the philosophy and theology of the schools. The same difference is obvious between devotional works created for lay audiences and Scholastic theological literature. Hence, Llull's work may give us some exceptional tools for refining our still rough concepts of "popularization" in late medieval culture. His revision of philosophical and theological doctrines should especially encourage us to develop new models of description, like the relationships of "appropriation" that Roger Chartier proposes for explaining how diverse sectors of a society use the same cultural materials in different ways.[29]

My second broad assumption in studying Llull's work is that the extant evidence from his career sufficiently manifests its "true" nature or identity. (It is certainly not sufficient in quantity, but that is a different problem.) In other words, I assume that Llull's writings and the documents regarding his affairs are not enigmas in themselves, although the circumstances of their production may remain obscure. Hence, we do not need to redefine their "real" nature or function in order to understand them,[30] but rather to investigate the cultural, social, or political relationships, practices, or institutions responsible for their existence. I see little value in claiming that Llull's Great Art actually is or even resembles a Scholastic summa or that his letters of commendation and permissions to proselytize actually constitute university degress or admission to holy orders. The validity of such claims evaporates as soon as we compare Llull's writings to the work of any Schoolman or the letters concerning his affairs to similar documents of the period. At best, these claims serve to illuminate the diverse kinds of recognition available to laypeople such as Llull who sought to practice skills usually exercised by clerics.

Above all, this presumption of truth obviates the need to qualify the sincerity of Llull's own convictions. It allows us to accept that his vocation probably made sense to him, that he regarded it as worthwhile, and that it was not merely camouflage for other political or academic enterprises. Of course, Llull's sense of his vocation is inseparable from the visions and revelations that prompted his original conversion to penitence and the design of the Great Art. Such mystical events are difficult for modern historical and critical analysis to accommodate.[31] Nonetheless, claims of divine inspiration or revelation were common among those laypeople, lesser clergy, or religious women who sought recognition as prophets.[32] Llull's *Vita* uses scriptural allusions to suggest a similar role for him. These claims legitimized knowledge or views that would otherwise lack institutional sanction or authority. Hence, there is a manifest parallel between Llull's claims of divine revelation and his reliance on necessary reasons instead of authorities. It is not necessary to separate these as unrelated issues of religious psychology and dialectical method. Indeed, there is a broader parallel between Llull's claims to illumination by God, his repudiation of *auctoritates* in argumentation, and his estrangement from the ecclesiastical and academic institutions of his day. Llull's work manifests a constant tension between his Great Art and Scholastic curricula and between his evangelical plans and Church policy on missions. On the one hand, he offers his system as a divinely inspired alternative to the flawed human sophistications of the schools. On the other hand, he often begins or ends his writings with invitations for their correction by Church and university authorities. His *Vita* displays the same double stance: it presents him as a latter-day prophet who wins applause from Parisian scholars, financial support from pious Genoese widows, and admiration from a Franciscan friar appointed to inspect his writings; yet it also tells how popes ignore him, the mendicants refuse to accept him, and the practices of the schools discourage him. Through this conflict Llull exercised the kind of de facto "mixed life" that many *laici religiosi* and *conversi* of his era evidently lived. Their ambiguous status is apparent in the question that Saint Louis, according to John of Joinville (5.32), posed to Robert of Sorbon on one occasion: the king asked his chaplain to consider whether a good and wise layperson was better than a *béguin*. The unclear meaning of the term "beguine" neatly suggests the problems involved in defining the relative spiritual identities of laity and clergy.[33] Their relationship depended on diverse considerations of personal virtue, public regard, social class, institutional authority, and religious vocation, all of which must have affected Ramon Llull as well.

Llull adumbrates a radically simple solution to this complex problem in his proposals regarding eloquence—especially his broad conception of rhetoric in the *Rethorica nova* and his tendency to identify preaching with the methods of his Great Art. His proposals advocate the general exercise of righteous discourse: all Christians, laity and clergy alike, bear the obligation to communicate love and truth. The application of Llull's Great Art to eloquence strives to ensure the ethical basis of all discourse, especially by conforming word and deed. His plans for meditation and evangelism in effect constitute a universal rule for Christian life. Perhaps better than any other aspect of his work, Llull's accounts of rhetoric and preaching demonstrate the "pastoral transformation" of the self achieved through new practices of preaching, confession, and devotion in the later Middle Ages.[34] Hence, Michel Zink very suggestively places Llull's work in the development of a literary subjectivity where "the formalized stereotypes of lyric poetry, the rhetorical rules of spiritual literature, the requirements of penance, and the regimen of confession are all assimilated, fused, and reconceived by a consciousness that makes them as much instruments of contemplation as of self-expression."[35] Llull's dual goals of contemplation and self-expression foster consciousness of a personal and a social as well as a literary subjectivity. Thus, his accounts of rhetoric or preaching insist on the proper ordering—the "rectification"—of the discursive subject as a condition of successful discourse. As the basis for improved communication with God and one's neighbor, that perfection defines the subjects necessary for full integration of the Christian commonwealth. Llull's hostility to heterodoxy in the schools and his zeal to convert unbelievers perhaps signals a new impetus for developing the concern with perfection of the self into policies for the "formation of a persecuting society."[36]

All these questions await further study. For now, it is sufficient to recognize that we do not denigrate Ramon Llull's stature by doubting whether he vanquished Parisian masters in public disputation, led debate at the court of Philip the Fair, or dictated Church policy to the Council of Vienne. In fact, judged by the very modest results that Llull achieved from those interventions, his contribution would seem negligible. Nonetheless, Ramon Llull's private devotion to evangelism and reform unquestionably merits our notice and even admiration, not because it won the attention of great princes, prelates, or philosophers, but simply because it exemplifies so fully the intensity of intellectual and spiritual experience possible among Christian laypeople in Western Europe around 1300.

Notes

Introduction

1. Research on this topic grows steadily. Major studies to date include Bäuml,"Varieties and Consequences of Medieval Literacy"; Clanchy, *From Memory to Written Record*; Coleman, *Medieval Readers and Writers*; Graff, *Legacies of Literacy*; Parkes, "Literacy of the Laity"; Saenger, "Silent Reading"; and Stock, *Implications of Literacy.*
2. Research on literacy in medieval Spain remains limited. Some useful recent studies are Faulhaber, *Libros y bibliotecas*; Hillgarth, *Readers and Books*; and Lawrance, "Spread of Lay Literacy."
3. Ed. Rubió, *Documents per l'història de la cultura,* 2:4–5.
4. Utterback, *Pastoral Care and Administration,* 40, 131.
5. Hillgarth, *Readers and Books,* 45, 50, and table II. I exclude the fifty-eight Jews or *conversos* who owned 802 books, since they involved less representative linguistic, professional, and social situations. Nonetheless, the concentration of books in this sector of the population is, if anything, even more striking than among the Christian owners.
6. On the problematic definition of the "popular," see Aers, "Rewriting the Middle Ages"; LeGoff, *Time, Work, and Culture,* 225–36; Paul, "La religion populaire au Moyen Age"; or Vauchez, *Laity in the Middle Ages,* 27–38.
7. As suggested by Fumagalli Beonio Brocchieri in "The Intellectual," 194–96, in an effort to revise LeGoff's *Intellectuals in the Middle Ages.*
8. E.g., Delcorno, "Predicazione volgare e volgarizzamenti."
9. The best English summaries of Llull's life are Bonner's *Doctor Illuminatus,* 1–45, and the *Selected Works,* 3–52. In Catalan, the most useful account is Batllori and Hillgarth's *Vida de Ramon Llull.* The most comprehensive account in any language remains Hillgarth's *Ramon Lull and Lullism.*
10. See the characterization in Paterson's *World of the Troubadours,* 100–114.

11. Llull's writings are one of the most important historical witnesses to the development of Old Catalan. For general accounts of his language, see Badia and B. de Moll, "La llengua de Ramon Llull," or Martí i Castell, *El català medieval*; for more detailed studies, see Bonner and Badia, *Ramon Llull*, 182.

12. The topic of lay education in the medieval Crown of Aragon still needs a study like Davis's "Education in Dante's Florence"; Goñi Gaztambide's "La formación intelectual de los navarros"; Orme's *From Childhood to Chivalry*; or Petti Balbi's *L'insegnamento nella liguria medievale*. Some details about the educational opportunities available to Llull emerge from Hillgarth's *Readers and Books*, 35–77.

13. E.g., his *Doctrina pueril* (73.2), *Blaquerna* (chap. 2), or *Libre de meravelles* (chap. 18–19). On his proposals regarding education, see Genovart Servera, "El Cavaller i el Vell Savi"; Llinarès, "Algunos aspectos de la educación"; Tusquets, *Ramon Llull pedagogo de la cristiandad*; L. Vidal, "Esbozo comparativo"; or Viera, "Les idees pedagògiques."

14. Torre y del Cerro, *Documentos para la historia de la Universidad de Barcelona*, 185–86.

15. On the latter, see Martínez Val, "Contribución al estudio."

16. On the significance of this phrase, see Johnston, "Ramon Llull's Conversion to Penitence."

17. Records from the Cistercian house of La Real mention "magistri" of unspecified functions as early as 1233; students of theology from the church of Saint Eulalia appear in 1278. See Mora and Andrinal, *Diplomatari del Monestir de Santa Maria la Real*, nos. I and 102.

18. Bonner, "L'aprenentatge intel.lectual" and "Ramon Llull and the Dominicans."

19. This is one of the few extant documents regarding Llull's early years. See Rubió, *Documents per l'història de la cultura*, 1:3–4, and the comments of Hillgarth in *Ramon Lull and Lullism*, 5n20.

20. Chapter 1 explains the operation of Llull's Great Art.

21. Hillgarth, in "Una biblioteca cisterciense medieval," 116, oddly describes this collection as "inadequate."

22. See the often-cited list from Carreras y Artau, *Historia de la filosofía española*, 1:268–69.

23. On the subjects taught at this level, see Capdevila, "Les antigues institucions escolars"; Revest Corzo, *La enseñanza en Castellón;* or Sanchís Rivera, "La enseñanza en Valencia."

24. Ed. Keicher, 221.

25. On Llull's polemic against Parisian "Averroists," see Vansteenberghen, "La signification de l'oeuvre anti-Averroiste," and Moreno Rodríguez, *La lucha de Ramon Llull contra el averroísmo*.

26. A modern editor wrongly identifies the scriptural allusion as Numbers 31.20 (RLOL 5:150).

27. Curtius, *European Literature*, 86–87.

28. Newman, "Hildegard of Bingen: Visions and Validation," and *Sister of Wisdom*, 39–41, 254–57.

29. Ed. Denifle and Châtelain, *Chartularium universitatis Parisiensis*, 2:148–49 (no. 691), but with corrections from Hillgarth, *Ramon Lull and Lullism*, 119n304.

30. His most extensive complaint appears in his poem *Desconhort*. He appears as "Ramon the Fool" in his novel *Blaquerna*.

31. Llull's work and the later spread of Lullism parallel earlier cases analyzed by Stock in *Implications of Literacy*, 132–49, 217–40.
32. Our understanding of Llull's "wise foolishness" would benefit tremendously from analysis as detailed as that devoted to Jacopone da Todi by Peck in *Fool of God.* On the traditional image of the "divine jongleur," see Leclercq, "Jonglerie," and Szittya, *Antifraternal Tradition*, 251–57. On this type in Llull, see Corominas, "El juglar a lo divino," and González Casanovas, "Writer and Preacher as *juglar de Déu.*"
33. The longest, though still problematic, account of medieval lay preaching is Zerfass's *Der Streit um die Laienpredigt.* Schneyer reviews the best-known medieval cases in "Die Laienpredigt im Mittelalter." See also the briefer assessments in Bériou, "Femmes et prédicateurs"; D'Avray, *Preaching of the Friars*, 25–29; Schneyer, *Geschichte der katholischen Predigt*, 176–78; and Spencer, *English Preaching*, 49–57. In a forthcoming study on Llull as lay preacher and teacher I hope to give these facets of his career the careful analysis that Powell gives to similar activities in the life of Albertano da Brescia.
34. The best overall account of Llull's activities in France and Italy remains Hillgarth's *Ramon Lull and Lullism*, chap. 2–4. On his exploits in Pisa, see Domínguez Reboiras, "In civitate pisana," which suggests that he perhaps served as a kind of secret agent for the Aragonese Crown.
35. See the letters requesting their aid, printed in RLOL 2:402–5.
36. Hillgarth, *Ramon Lull and Lullism*, 100.
37. Delcorno, "Predicazione volgare i volgarizzamenti," 679; Lazzerini, "Per latinos grossos," 226; Roberts, *Stephanus de Lingua-Tonante*, 52–56.
38. Bennett, *Early Dominicans*, 91–93; D'Avray, *Preaching of the Friars*, 90–96; Hinnebusch, *History of the Dominican Order*, 1:291–99; Moorman, *History of the Franciscan Order*, 272–77.
39. Cantini, "S. Antonio da Padova," 419; Lecoy, *La chaire française*, 36.
40. See the discussion in chapter 5.
41. Kedar, *Merchants in Crisis*, 38–39.
42. Lazzerini, "Per latinos grossos," 225, 229.
43. Bofarull i Sans, "El testamento de Ramón Lull," 454, 456.
44. The problematic perception of Llull's own "voice" or "persona" in his writings illustrates well the arguments of Foucault in "What Is an Author?"
45. Servera, in "Utopie et histoire," distinguishes and discusses superbly these broad aspects of Llull's enterprise.

Chapter 1

1. For a summary introduction, see Johnston, *Spiritual Logic*, 3–7 and 15–27, or Bonner, *Selected Works*, 55–70. Still valuable as complete surveys are the first volume of Carreras y Artau's *Historia de la filosofía española* and Platzeck's *Raimund Lull.*
2. Rouse and Rouse, "*Statim invenire.*"
3. E.g., Platzeck, "Raimund Lulls Auffassung von der Logik."
4. Johnston, *Spiritual Logic*, 117–20; see also the important studies by Pring-Mill: "Analogical Structure," *El microcosmos lul.lià,* and "Trinitarian World-Picture." On Llull's understanding of these "necessary reasons," see Eijo Garay, "Las 'razones necesarias'"; Garcías Palou, "Las 'rationes necessariae'"; Gracia, "La doctrina luliana de las razones necesarias" and "Structural Elements of Necessary Reasons";

and Mendía, "En torno a las razones necesarias." On the general character of Llull's "rationalism," see Decorte's "Het middeleeuwse rationalisme."

5. An excellent summary is Pépin's "Aspects"; for detailed discussion, see Gersh, *From Iamblichus to Eriugena;*. On the literary basis, see Whitman, *Allegory*. This basic characteristic of Llull's work became clear from the analyses of Carreras y Artau, in *Historia de la filosofía española*, 1:637.

6. Developed in stages over the course of Llull's career, his theory of "innate correlatives" establishes trinitarian *vestigia* as minimal metaphysical constituents in all beings. For example, his Principle of Bonitas causes the correlatives of *bonificans*, *bonificatum*, and *bonificare*. This very "activist" metaphysics helps Llull explain the Neoplatonic axiom of *bonum diffusivism sui*. On the details of this theory, see Gayà Estelric, *La teoría luliana de los correlativos*, and Pring-Mill, "Trinitarian World-Picture." On its role in language, see my remarks below in chapters 4 and 5.

7. Bataillon, "Intermédiaires entre les traités de morale et les sermons"; and Rouse and Rouse, "Biblical Distinctions."

8. The fundamental study of this function is J. B. Allen's *Ethical Poetic*, to which my own analyses in this study are greatly indebted.

9. J. B. Allen, *Ethical Poetic*, 148.

10. ORL 15:52.

11. Concisely analyzed by Bataillon, in "Early Scholastic and Mendicant Preaching." On exegesis, see also the conclusions of Smalley, in *Study of the Bible*, 371, and *Gospels in the Schools*, 275–78; on popular preaching, see also Zink, *La prédication en langue romane*, 443–50.

12. Heath, *Allegory and Philosophy*, 3–17, 147–86.

13. See especially the sermon on Saint Agnes studied by Zink in *La prédication en langue romane*, 217–19, 244–51.

14. Stock, *Implications of Literacy*, 148–49, 218–19.

15. J. M. Vidal, "Doctrine et morale," 37–46. Like Lullism, Joachimism owed part of its ongoing popularity precisely to its reliance on allegoresis and use of *figurae*; see Reeves, *Influence of Prophecy*, 4–27, 100.

16. From the extensive scholarship on this activity, some useful studies include: Bozóky, ed., *Le livre secret des Cathares*; Dossat, *Les crises de l'Inquisition* and *Église et hérésie en France*; Emery, *Heresy and Inquisition in Narbonne*; Griffe, *Le Languedoc cathare et l'Inquisition*; Lee, Reeves, and Silano, *Western Mediterranean Prophecy*, 47–74, 89–100; Mundy, *Repression of Catharism;* A. Oliver, "Heterodoxia en Mallorca"; Thouzellier, *Catharisme et Valdéisme;* and Ventura Subirats, "La valdesía en Cataluña" and "El catarismo en Cataluña."

17. With this phrase he introduces the exhaustive "Tree of Examples" in his *Arbre de sciència* of 1296; see Cabré et al., " 'Conèixer e haver moralitats bones.' "

18. As recognized by Carreras y Artau, in *Historia de la filosofía española*, 1:610–14.

19. These include Augustine's distinction between use and enjoyment *(DC* 1.3.3) as well as Anselm's principles of *caritas ordinata, ordinatio,* and *rectitudo (Monol.* 68; *De ver.* 7; *Cur Deus* 11). Still useful is Rohmer's survey, *La finalité morale;* on twelfth-century precedents, see esp. Pelikan, *Growth of Medieval Theology*, 139–40, and Javelet, *Image et ressemblance*, 1:409–27.

20. Urvoy, "La place de Ramon Llull," 212.

21. Rohmer, "Sur la doctrine franciscaine des deux faces de l'âme," and Marrone, *William of Auvergne and Robert Grosseteste*, 36. The commentary on Ecclesiasticus ascribed to William of Middleton, OFM, speaks of "two ends" that the soul seeking rectification must observe; see Smalley, "Some Thirteenth-Century Commentaries," 3:55.

Llull's "first and second intentions" have nothing to do with the similarly named logical distinctions; see Johnston, *Spiritual Logic,* 46–47.

22. For a summary of this question, see Grieve, "Ramon Llull i la càbala."
23. Hillgarth, *Ramon Lull and Lullism,* 19–20; Urvoy, "La place de Ramon Llull," 218–19.
24. Taylor, "Juan Manuel's Cipher."
25. Yates, in "Ramón Llull y Johannes Scotus Eriugena," noted parallels between Llull's work and basic categories from Eriugena's *De divisione naturae,* but their affinities extend as well to the whole system of aesthetical and metaphysical doctrines analyzed by De Bruyne in *Études d'esthétique médiévale,* 1:343–70.
26. On his debt to Algazel, see Johnston, *Spiritual Logic,* 31–44. On his readings in the apologists, see Burman, "Influence of the *Apology of Al-Kindi.*"
27. Gilson, *Philosophy of St. Bonaventure,* 114.
28. But without denying the sufficiency of belief. Llull's arguments regarding the relationship of faith and reason are often difficult to follow; see Johnston, *Spiritual Logic,* 120–33, and 296–308.
29. Kaster, *Guardians of Language,* 70–95; Evans, *Old Arts,* 34; Delhaye, "'Grammatica' et 'Ethica,'" 60–67; and Morrison, "Incentives for Studying the Liberal Arts."
30. On Augustine's argument, see Robertson, *Preface to Chaucer,* 340–41.
31. ORL 14:301–2.
32. RLOL 17:253. D'Allerit analyzes well the presentation of this ideal in the *Doctrina pueril;* see "Pensée métaphysique et orientation morale."
33. Fakhry, "Liberal Arts in the Medieval Arabic Tradition"; Gómez Nogales, "Las *artes liberales* y la filosofía hispano-musulmana"; Lomba Fuentes, "Sentido y alcance del catálogo de las ciencias de al-Fârâbî."
34. Johnston, *Spiritual Logic,* 32–35. Urvoy, *Penser l'Islam,* remains the best account of Llull's debt to Islam.
35. However, the *Libre de meravelles* (chap. 18) does claim that experience leads to philosophy and philosophy to theology in the manner that the active life leads to the contemplative life.
36. On Adelard, see Bultot "La Chartula", 791–2; on Godefroy see the comments in Synan's translation, 26.
37. On the ideal of apostolic life, see Dereine, "La 'vita apostolica' dans l'ordre canonial"; Lapsanski, *Evangelical Perfection*; McDonnell, "*Vita Apostolica*: Diversity or Dissent?"; and Vicaire *The Apostolic Life.*
38. The best discussion to date is Servera, "Utopie et histoire."
39. On Bonaventure's exercise of this ideal, see Allard, "La technique de la *reductio.*"
40. ORL 16:111–12.
41. As Gayà suggests in his introduction to Llull's *Ars notatoria,* 23.
42. As argued, e.g., by Bonner, in "Les arts de Llull com a paradigmes cientìfics"; Colomer, "De Ramon Llull a la moderna informàtica"; and Gayà, ed., *Ars notatoria,* 7–10.
43. Bonafede, in "La condanna di Stefano Tempier," studies Llull's attitudes.
44. On the earlier prohibitions of Aristotle, see Wippel, "Condemnations of 1270 and 1277."
45. He does not specifically represent the great Greek philosopher. Llull perhaps uses the name "Socrates" in imitation of the numerous Scholastic texts that employ it simply as a representative personal name.

46. Evans, *Old Arts,* 49.
47. ORL 9:333.
48. Evans, *Old Arts,* 50–51.
49. Evans, *Old Arts,* 14.
50. Johnston, *Spiritual Logic,* chap. 18.
51. On this vice, see Newhauser, "Augustinian *vitium curiositatis.*"
52. Corti, "Modelli e antimodelli," 5–6.
53. Murray, *Reason and Society,* 266–70; see also Borst, *Medieval Worlds,* 167–81.
54. Evans, *Old Arts,* 56.
55. Evans, *Old Arts,* 29.
56. Elder, *From Cloister to Classroom,* and Sommerfeldt, *Erudition at God's Service.* Davy, in *Les sermons universitaires,* 292–95 offers especially good examples of arguments from preaching.
57. Bougerol, "Les sermons dans les 'Studia,'" 264.
58. Lawrence, "Stephen of Lexington and Cistercian University Studies."
59. On those prefatory schemes, see Hunt, "Introductions"; Quain, "Medieval *Accessus*"; Minnis, *Medieval Theory of Authorship,* 9–39; and Copeland, *Rhetoric, Hermeneutics, and Translation,* 63–86. On Saint Thomas's division, see Maurer's "Introduction" to his edition of the commentary.
60. Evans, *Old Arts,* 28; Ward, "Date of the Commentary," 247.
61. ORL 1:130.
62. On Llull's classifications, see Colomer, "Las artes liberales." On Scholastic schemes, see esp. Giacone, "Arti liberali e classificazione delle scienze"; Gandillac, ed., *La pensée encyclopédique;* Rossi, "La classificazione delle scienze"; Wagner, *Seven Liberal Arts;* and Weisheipl, "Classification of the Sciences."
63. Colom, in *Glossari,* 4:278, notes one appearance of the vernacular term *quadruvi.*
64. Duby, *Three Orders,* 313.
65. ORL 20:11.
66. ORL 20:233–34.
67. On the legal learning that Llull describes elsewhere, see Monserrat Quintana, *La visión luliana del mundo del derecho.*
68. Useful general studies of Llull's views on language include Llovet, "Ramon Llull: Nostàlgia de la lletra"; Trías Mercant, *El pensamiento y la palabra* and "Raíces augustinianas"; and Tusquets, "El lenguaje, como argumento."
69. On Llull's theory of fallacy, see Johnston, *Spiritual Logic,* 264–82. Chapter 3 discusses his proposal of speech as a sixth sense; chapters 5 and 7 analyze his recommendations regarding word order.
70. L. Badia, "Et hoc patet per regulam C," 83.
71. Méla, "*Poetria nova et Homo novus.*"
72. Cf. similar arguments of Llull's editors in RLOL 18:31.
73. Murphy, *Rhetoric in the Middle Ages,* 91–92, and Alfarabi, *Deux ouvrages inédits sur la réthorique,* 30–34.
74. Johnston, "Parliamentary Oratory."
75. ORL 8:532.
76. Murphy, *Rhetoric in the Middle Ages,* 159–60, 192.
77. On Llull's elaboration of these parallels, see Bonner and Badia, *Ramon Llull,* 98–102.
78. ORL 1:131–32.
79. The passage from the *Ars generalis ultima* adds only a few new details to this characterization; for a summary analysis of that passage, see L. Badia, "Et hoc patet per regulam C." Compare also his brief account in *Arbre de sciència* ("Arbre humanal" 5.5.j.).

80. For a detailed analysis of this work's design, see the introduction to my edition and translation of the *Rethorica Nova.*
81. Alfarabi, *Deux ouvrages inédits sur la réthorique,* 3–121; Averroes, *Three Short Commentaries,* 57–78. Faulhaber, *Rhetoric in Thirteenth-Century Castile,* surveys the Latin school tradition in contemporary Spain.
82. The *Liber de memoria* (1304) and the *Liber de memoria Dei* (1314) are works of spiritual psychology. The *Ars memorativa* and the *Liber ad memoriam confirmandam* are apocryphal. Bonner, in *Selected Works,* 1283, still lists the latter work as genuine; on its non-Lullian origins, see Domínguez Reboiras, "'In civitate pisana,'" 397–400.
83. Rossi, *Clavis universalis,* and Yates, *Art of Memory,* 173–98.
84. Powell, in *Albertanus of Brescia,* 61–69 analyzes this treatise in detail.
85. Ed. Johnston, 1.
86. Ed. Johnston, 2.
87. On Seneca as moral authority, see Meersseman, "Seneca maestro di spiritualità." This particular aphorism appears to remit ultimately to Isocrates's oration *Ad Demonicum* (33). Among Llull's contemporaries, Albertano da Brescia includes it in his *Ars loquendi et tacendi* (5.5) and Brunetto Latini after him in his *Tresor* (2.66.7).
88. Powell, *Albertanus of Brescia,* 65.
89. Faulhaber, in "Las retóricas hispanolatinas medievales," 34, lists Llull as the first Iberian author of an *ars praedicandi.*
90. ORL 9:344.
91. Bynum, *Docere verbo et exemplo,* 77–93.
92. ORL 9:239.
93. Ed. Johnston, 51.
94. RLOL 3:140.
95. RLOL 3:106. Cf. also the characterization of L. Badia, in "Ramon Llull i la tradició literària," 134.
96. RLOL 3:141.
97. Spencer, *English Preaching,* 101–4.
98. RLOL 3:395.
99. E.g., 1.A.1, 1.A.2, 1.A.2.9, 1.A.3, 1.A.5, 1.A.6, or 1.B.1; RLOL 3:143, 153, 154, 165, 168, 174–75.
100. E.g., 1.B.3, 1.B.4; RLOL 3:233, 257.
101. E.g., 1.C.1.2.Quid.4; RLOL 3:307.
102. 1.C.1, 1.C.2, 1.C.3; RLOL 3:282, 338, 367.
103. RLOL 3:394.
104. Perhaps for this same reason Llull often calls the preacher a *sermocinator,* in the sense of "speaker." This term is a peculiar deviation from the more common use of *praedicator;* see Longère, "Le vocabulaire de la prédication."
105. Spencer, *English Preaching,* 45–46.
106. Sugranyes, *Raymond Lulle Docteur des Missions,* 15.
107. As Murray, *Reason and Society,* 270–81, suggests.
108. On the campaign against the Lullists, see Roura i Roca, *Posición doctrinal,* and Puig i Oliver, "La *Fascinatio lullistarum* " and "El procés dels lul.listes valencians." On the circumstances of Arundel's prohibitions, see Spencer, *English Preaching,* 159–82.
109. Delcorno, in "Rassegna di studi," 262, cites a treatise from 1400 that analyzes the common rules of preaching and *arengae.*

110. Fakhry, "Liberal Arts in the Medieval Arabic Tradition," 94–96.
111. Gehl, "Mystical Language Models," surveys well these doctrines.

Chapter 2

1. Curtius, *European Literature*, 319–26; Gellrich, *Idea of the Book*, 29–50; Stock, *Implications of Literacy*, 315–25.
2. Among the many studies of Lullian metaphysics, especially pertinent to my analyses are Artus, "Man's Cosmic Ties" and "Ramon Llull, the Metaphysician"; Canals Vidal, "El principio de la conveniencia"; T. Carreras i Artau, "Fonaments metafísics"; Carreras y Artau, *Historia de la filosofía española*, 1:480–94; Ruiz Simon, "De la naturalesa com a mescla"; and Viñas Delgado, "Relación entre la ideología ejemplarista."
3. I use the English terms "participated resemblance" because they best approximate the Latin and Catalan vocabulary used by Llull and his contemporaries, and this usage facilitates translation of passages where the metaphysics of participated resemblance plays a critical role in Llull's arguments.
4. Allen, *Ethical Poetic*, chap. 4–5; Chenu, *Théologie au douzième siècle*, chap. 7; and Foucault, *Order of Things*, chap. 2. On the role of resemblance in social ritual, see esp. Bloch, *Etymologies and Genealogies*, intro.
5. Geiger's *La participation dans la philosophie de S. Thomas d'Aquin* exhaustively analyzes its role in Aquinas's metaphysics.
6. Foucault, *Order of Things*, 43.
7. I.e., of the faculty or capacity that produces it.
8. ORL 14:163–64.
9. Heidegger, "Onto-theo-logical Constitution of Metaphysics."
10. PL 34:242.
11. PL 175:980A.
12. On their theories, see Zinn, "Book and Word."
13. *Arbre de filosofia desiderat* 1.3.2.17; ORL 17:421.
14. *Libre de demostracions* 4.47; ORL 15:585. Aquinas typically quotes the more concise Latin maxim *omne agens agit sibi simile* (every agent does something similar to itself); e.g., *Summa contra gentiles* 2.45.
15. Accounts like the *Libre de meravelles* (chap. 30–31, 96) expound the Augustinian doctrine of the *regio dissimilitudinis*. This was a favorite topic of monastic and early Scholastic authorities, see Châtillon, "Les régions de la dissemblance," and Javelet, *Image et ressemblance*, 1:412–13.
16. Gersh, *From Iamblichus to Eriugena*, 141–76.
17. RLOL 16:27.
18. ORL 15:169.
19. ORL 15:131.
20. RLOL 16:27.
21. RLOL 2:302; cf. *Disputatio Raimundi et Averroistae* 3 (RLOL 6:14).
22. On Cusanus's interest, see Pindl-Büchel, "Relationship between the Epistemologies."
23. ORL 14:183–84.
24. RLOL 5:484.
25. ORL 14:168.

26. Ed. Galmés, 1:136.
27. ORL 12:252.
28. ORL 21:341.
29. ORL 14:169.
30. RLOL 14:339–40.
31. On this work, see Johnston, *Spiritual Logic,* 162–75.
32. RLOL 10:17, 18.
33. Pépin, "Linguistique et théologie."
34. Amsler, in *Etymology and Grammatical Discourse,* offers a very complete account of these doctrines.
35. ORL 8:532.
36. ORL 8:539–40.
37. On Augustine's theories of signs, see: Baratin and Desbordes, "Sémiologie et métalinguistique"; Jackson, "Theory of Signs", Markus, "St. Augustine on Signs"; and Swearingen, *Rhetoric and Irony,* 175–214.
38. Dronke, *Fabula,* 28.
39. As recognized by L. Badia, "Ramon Llull i la tradició literària," 128.
40. ORL 8:537.
41. See chapter 7 for further discussion of this scheme in Llull's work.
42. ORL 14:3.
43. Stock, *Implications of Literacy,* 254–59.
44. PL 150:423A.
45. Johnston, *Spiritual Logic,* 264–75.
46. One passage from the second distinction of the *Rethorica nova* refers to "form, matter, and conjunction," which is one of the sets of correlative terms used in Llull's early *Libre de demostracions* (3.13.2).
47. Coulter, *Literary Microcosm,* 123.
48. Cf. Woods, *An Early Commentary on the* Poetria nova, xxviii.
49. Ed. Fredborg, "Commentaries on Cicero's *De inventione*," 7.
50. Dist. 2 intro.; ed. De Rijk, *Logica modernorum,* 1:415.
51. Alford, "Grammatical Metaphor" and "Literature and Law."
52. Ed. Johnston 4.
53. RLOL 14:365.
54. Ed. Johnston, 4.
55. E.g., Russell, *Criticism in Antiquity,* 86, 96–97, 107, 116, 126; Coulter, *Literary Microcosm,* 77; or the many examples collected by Minnis and Scott, *Medieval Literary Theory*, indexed under "intention."
56. Ed. Johnston, 10.
57. RLOL 14:340.
58. Ed. Johnston, 39. Similar claims appear in the sections on Glory (3.9.2), Beginning, Middle, and End (3.11.0); and Superiority, Equality, and Inferiority (3.12).
59. E.g., Fortunatianus 1.5–7. On this poetic doctrine, see De Bruyne, *Études d'esthétique médiévale,* 1:47–50.
60. Ed. Johnston, 33. The analysis of Wisdom likewise explains that this larger form of beauty, "like light," renders the speaker's account pleasing and decorous (3.5.2).
61. Lindberg, *Theories of Vision,* 95.
62. E.g., *Libre de meravelles* 17; *Libre de demostracions* 1.28–29; or the *Liber de lumine.* On the latter work, see esp. Carreras y Artau, *Historia de la filosofía española,* 1:488–90.
63. De Bruyne, *Études d'esthétique médiévale,* 3:3–29, esp. 22.

64. For examples, see Cigman, "*Luceat lux vestra,*" and Levy, *Nine Verse Sermons by Nicholas Bozon,* 25–33.
65. Ed. Johnston, 32.
66. Ed. Johnston, 35, 36.

Chapter 3

1. Pring-Mill, "Ramon Llull y las tres potencias del alma"; Capánaga, "San Agustín y el lulismo."
2. Well summarized by Harvey, in *Inward Wits,* or Heath, in *Allegory and Philosophy,* 60–65. Still useful is Wolfson, "Internal Senses."
3. Aos Braco, in "La imaginación en el sistema de Ramon Llull," reviews the relevant passages from Llull's oeuvre, but without discussing their sources or implications.
4. See especially the *Philosophy of Aristotle* 1.2–3, 11.88; trans. Mahdi 72–81, 121. Haddad's *Alfarabi's Theory of Communication,* 171–76, summarizes Alfarabi's psychology.
5. Pépin, *Ex platonicorum persona,* chap. 5.
6. Harvey, *Inward Wits,* 37. On the problems of assessing literary adaptation of Victorine theories, see White, "Langland's Imaginatif."
7. McGinn, *Golden Chain,* 208–27. On these schemes generally, see Michaud-Quantin, "La classification des puissances de l'âme."
8. Javelet, *Psychologie des auteurs spirituels;* Rahner, "Le début d'une doctrine des cinq sens spirituels" and "La doctrine des 'sens spirituels.'"
9. Johnston, "*Affatus:* Natural Science as Moral Theology," 30:9–12.
10. E.g., Perarnau, in "*Lo sisè seny,*" compares Llull to contemporary authorities such as Jean de la Rochelle, rather than to monastic or earlier Scholastic writers on spiritual psychology.
11. See the summary of these developments in the *Cambridge History of Later Medieval Philosophy,* 595–628.
12. Allers, "Microcosmus from Anaximandros to Paracelsus"; D'Alverny, "L'homme comme symbole"; Rico, *El pequeño mundo del hombre.*
13. ORL 21:188.
14. The best investigations of this question are Ruiz Simon, "De la naturalesa com a mescla"; and Yates, "Art of Ramon Lull" and "La teoría luliana de los elementos."
15. E.g., the cases in ed. Buschinger and Crepin, *Les quatres elements dans la culture médiévale.*
16. McEvoy, "Microcosm and Macrocosm."
17. De Bruyne, in *Études d'esthétique médiévale,* 1:26, analyzes this function especially well.
18. ORL 4:373.
19. ORL 5:4.
20. On this traditional image, see Bradley, "Backgrounds of the Title *Speculum,*" "Mirror of Truth," and "Speculum Image"; also see Javelet, *Image et ressemblance,* 1:376–90.
21. ORL 17:41–42. The final phrase begins "e les substancies e les semblances que lespill pren," but I follow the Latin version printed in the Mainz edition, which says "de."
22. Leupin, *Barbarolexis,* 33–8.

23. ORL 21:193.
24. Johnston, *Spiritual Logic,* 169–72.
25. ORL 14:83.
26. ORL 4:376.
27. ORL 16:292.
28. Tusquests, *Ramon Llull pedagogo de la cristiandad,* 327.
29. Cited by J. B. Allen, in *Ethical Poetic,* 98. On other senses of "signify" as used by Llull, see chapter 2.
30. Mastrelli, "Reflessi linguistici." The same remains true of his logical terminology, even though he attempts to refine it much more extensively in the course of his efforts to offer a moralized version of Scholastic logic as a remedy against the spread of error in the *studia*; see Johnston, *Spiritual Logic,* 150.
31. ORL 8:506.
32. Coulter, *Literary Microcosm,* 89; Lubac, *Exégèse médiévale,* 1:425–681.
33. ORL 8:506.
34. ORL 8:510–11.
33. Pépin, "L'absurdité, signe de l'allégorie."
34. Ed. Galmés, 1:117.
35. Ed. Galmés, 1:142.
36. On the various literary, philosophical, and theological developments of this justification, see Chenu, "Involucrum"; Jeauneau, "Usage de la notion d'integumentum"; Robertson, *Preface to Chaucer,* 341–60; Stock, *Myth and Science,* 49–62; and Wetherbee, *Platonism and Poetry,* 36–48.
37. Shapiro, "Word-Weaving," 356–59.
38. Paterson, *Troubadours and Eloquence,* 96.
39. Heath, *Allegory and Philosophy,* 177–87.
40. It is amusing to imagine writing Llull into the pages of a critique like that in Eagleton's *Literary Theory,* 143–44. Llovet attempts something like this in "Ramon Llull: Nostàlgia de la lletra."
43. As argued lately by Derrida, in *Of Grammatology,* 11.
44. Pépin, "Linguistique et théologie," 97–98.
45. O'Daly, *Augustine's Philosophy of Mind;* Lonergan, "Concept of *Verbum.*"
46. *Liber de ente* 6.6; RLOL 8:242.
47. Pépin, "Linguistique et théologie," 97.
48. ORL 4:329.
49. ORL 4:329.
50. ORL 4:146. The latter claim may recall Aristotelian explanations of how the Senses, though unerring in the perception of their proper objects (color, flavor, odor, etc.) can nonetheless err in perception of general features (shape, size, weight, etc.) or in the identity of the thing clothed in sensible characteristics *(De an.* 3.3 428b18–24). The Intellect, however, never errs with regard to its proper object, the quiddity of things, but does err in the operations of combination and separation *(De an.* 3.6, 10 430b29, 33a26).
51. ORL 4:147.
52. ORL 4:148.
53. On the identification of the mouth or tongue with particular sins, see Bloomfield, *Seven Deadly Sins,* 124.
54. Smalley, *Study of the Bible,* 1–2; Ripanti, "L'allegoría o l'*intellectus figuratus.*"
55. Coulter, *Literary Microcosm,* 29; Smalley, *Study of the Bible,* 3, 41–47, 86–87.
56. Stock, *Implications of Literacy,* 19–87.

57. ORL 4:333.
58. ORL 4:333–34.
59. Ed. Mainz, 4:76; cf. *Compendium artis demonstrativae* 2.1.5 (ed. Mainz 3:75–6).
60. Trías Mercant, in *El pensamiento y la palabra,* 17, relates it to the Platonic dialogue of the soul with itself.
61. PL 64:407B. On the significance of Boethius's famous formula, see Stock, *Implications of Literacy,* 366–72.
62. On this literature, see Gehl, "Mystical Language Models" and "Philip of Harveng on Silence."
63. Cf. 1a.34, 1; 79, 11 ad 3; 107, 1. Klubertanz, in *Discursive Power,* exhaustively analyzes the role of this discourse in Aquinas's scheme of the internal senses.
64. Cf. *Medicina de peccat,* l. 3412, and *Libre de meravelles,* chap. 16.
65. Tusquets, "El lenguaje como argumento," 173.
66. McKeon, "Rhetoric in the Middle Ages," 280–88.
67. Minnis, *Medieval Theory of Authorship,* 122–29.
68. On the contribution of Augustine's ideal to medieval rhetorical doctrine, see Murphy, *Rhetoric in the Middle Ages,* 290–91.
69. Cf. a similar account in *Libre de demostracions* 1.49.
70. On Albert's theories, see Steneck, "Albert on the Psychology of Sense Perception," and Dewan, "St. Albert, the Sensibles, and Spiritual Being."
71. Bultot, "La *Chartula,*" 791.
72. The strongest arguments remain Platzeck's "Descubrimiento y esencia"; Bonner, in *Selected Works,* 63–65, adds some helpful and necessary qualifications. On Llull's use of number symbolism in general, see Wittlin, "Numerological Structures."
73. Pring-Mill aptly notes their quasi-mathematical tenor in "Ramon Llull y las tres potencias del alma," 123.
74. On the distinction between "symbolic" and "figural" reading of signs, see Auerbach, "Figura," 57.
75. On God as the *primum cognitum* or *primum desideratum,* see Johnston, *Spiritual Logic,* 122, 292.
76. ORL 8:534.
77. Dal Pra, "Studi sul problema logico del linguaggio" 328.
78. ORL 8:535.
79. The remaining paragraphs of chapter 359 from the *Libre de contemplació* offer a miscellany of elementary rhetorical precepts, examined individually in subsequent chapters of this study.
80. Johnston, "Ramon Llull's Language of Contemplation and Action."
81. *Distinctiones,* s.v. "virtus"; PL 210:1007A.
82. Cit. Callaey, "La vie belge," 128.
83. Ed. Johnston, 37.
84. See the comments by Berlioz in "Le récit efficace," 127, following Yates, *Art of Memory,* 64.
85. Coincidentally, section 2.2.5 of the *Rethorica nova* does use the term "fantasy," which Scholastic authors like Aquinas (1a.78, 4) often employ as a synonym for the Avicennan internal sense of imagination.
86. ORL 16:397–98.
87. Llull cites this distinction again in his *Ars brevis quae est de inventione iuris* 5.5.
88. RLOL 3:405.
89. Ed. Johnston, 38.

90. Alfarabi, *Deux ouvrage inédits sur la réthorique,* 30–60.
91. Fredborg, "Commentaries on Cicero's 'De inventione,'" 23; Evans, "*Argumentum* and *argumentatio.*"
92. Johnston, *Spiritual Logic,* 305–12.
93. RLOL 3:402.
94. The *Lectura super artem inventivam* (3.2.851–52) offers an earlier version of this same argument.
95. The editors of Llull's *Ars abbreviata praedicandi* treat this conception of eloquence as a radical rejection of Ciceronian tradition; RLOL 18:26–28.
96. Johnston, "*Affatus:* Natural Science as Moral Theology," 5–12, and "*Affatus* and the Sources of Llull's Latin Vocabulary." Although Llull "discovered" his sixth sense of speech called *affatus* around 1294, it is curious that he barely mentions it in his *Liber de praedicatione* of 1304 and ignores it completely in his *Rethorica nova* of 1301/1303. Several reasons are possible for its omission from his treatise on rhetoric: Llull saw no need to repeat doctrines treated elsewhere (an economy he rarely observes); he deemed the psychology of *affatus* too complex for the intended readers of the *Rethorica nova;* he had already composed much of the rhetorical treatise before his discovery of the sixth sense around 1294; or perhaps his composition of the *Rethorica nova* while traveling to Cyprus prevented him from consulting the background texts necessary to develop more elaborate analyses.
97. The *Liber de affatu* of 1294 and contemporary writings offer much more detail regarding the physiology of speech than does the earlier *Libre de contemplació.* Consequently, it is difficult to resist the conclusion that Llull has gained some new familiarity with medical authorities. Most of these sources—Razes, Haly Abba, Costa ben Lucca, Platearius, Constantinus Africanus, and above all, Avicenna—were based ultimately on Aristotle and Galen; see Harvey, *Inward Wits,* 28. Moreover, their teachings circulated widely in manuals such as the famous compendium prepared in 1301 by Bernard of Gordon for his medical students at Montpellier; Bernard's text even appeared in vernacular translations.
98. Gieben, "Robert Grosseteste on Preaching," 122.
99. Cf. *Lectura super artem inventivam* 3.2.240 (ed. Mainz 5:325). Similar claims appear in *Proverbis de Ramon* 262.2–3; "Arbre sensual," 3.3.6.
100. Cf. "Arbre elemental," 7.89; *Arbre de filosofia desiderat* 1.3.17; *Lectura super artem inventivam* 3.2.240; *Proverbis de Ramon* 184.12; and "Arbre questional," 7.1.89.366.
101. Cf. *Arbre de filosofia desiderat* 1.3.17. Llull often uses *figuratum,* meaning "given form" or "formed"; see Colom, *Glossari,* 1:49 (s.v. "*affigurar*").
102. As Perarnau suggests in "*Lo sisè seny,*" 61. Cf. Aquinas 1a.85, 2; Avicenna, *De anima* 5.6; or Vincent of Beauvais *Spec. nat.* 27.29–60.
103. Aquinas refers in one case to a "speech of the Imagination" (1a.34, 1). See Lonergan, "Concept of *Verbum,*" 7:351.
104. For a full review of the moral theology that justifies *affatus,* see Johnston, "*Affatus:* Natural Science as Moral Theology," 139–59.
105. Cf. *Liber de affatu* 296; "Arbre sensual," 3.3.6; *Medicina de peccat* 3. 16 (ll.1519–21); *Liber de praedicatione* 2.B.1.36.2.1; *Metaphysica nova* 2.5.2.1.6; *Liber de divina existentia et agentia* 4.2.6.61; *Liber de possibili et impossibili* 4.2.1.6.67; *De experientia realitatis artis generalis* 5.6.8.
106. Ripanti, "Il problema della comprensione," 93–94.
107. Ripanti, "L'allegoria o l'*intellectus figuratus.*"

Chapter 4

1. See esp. the section "De Figura Y" of part 1; ed. Mainz, 1:4–5.
2. ORL 20:240.
3. Ed. Johnston, 9.
4. Delcorno, "L'exemplum nella predicazione volgare," 17.
5. Cf. Dante's adaptation in *De vulg. eloq.* 2.2. On classical authorities, see Russell, *Criticism in Antiquity,* 137–40.
6. Copeland, "Richard Rolle and Rhetorical Theory."
7. L. Badia, "Et hoc patet per regulam C," 95.
8. RLOL 14:364.
9. L. Badia, "Ramon Llull i la tradició literària," 129.
10. A basic authority for associating poetic invention with the Imagination is probably Augustine, *De Gen. ad litt.* 12.6ff. On the development of this doctrine, see Bloomfield, *Piers Plowman as a Fourteenth Century Apocalypse,* 170–74; Bundy, *Theory of Imagination,* chap. 5, p. 276; Kelly, *Medieval Imagination,* 26–56; and Murphy, *Rhetoric in the Middle Ages,* 92.
11. L. Badia, in "Et hoc patet per regulam C," argues that this passage from the *Ars generalis ultima* demonstrates Llull's recognition of separate literary and logical "rhetorics" corresponding to the diverse operations of sensation and intellection.
12. RLOL 14:385–86.
13. RLOL 14:386.
14. RLOL 3:401.
15. Ed. Cantini, 266–67.
16. Johnston, *Spiritual Logic,* 76–93, 238–47.
17. RLOL 3:404.
18. Trans. Krul, in Murphy, *Three Medieval Rhetorical Arts,* 143.
19. On these, see Stump, "Dialectic" and "Topics."
20. Johnston, *Spiritual Logic,* 256–58. The discussion of preaching in the *Ars generalis ultima* (10.98) does treat three "places" (*loci*) but explicates these as this world, heaven, and hell.
21. Traditionally attributed to Hermagoras. A typical late antique example is the Pseudo-Augustinian *De rhetorica* 141–42. On their history and use in the Middle Ages, see Copeland, *Rhetoric, Hermeneutics, and Translation,* chap 3.
22. A freedom emphasized by Bataillon in "Les instruments de travail" and "De la *lectio* à la *praedicatio*."
23. Murphy, *Rhetoric in the Middle Ages* 326–29.
24. As explained above in the introduction.
25. Chapter 6 below reviews the whole range of the figures of likeness that Llull recommends.
26. RLOL 3:396.
27. Owen, *Doctrine of Being,* 123–25, 180, 265–68, 320.
28. Johnston, *Spiritual Logic,* 153–55.
29. RLOL 3:396.
30. RLOL 3:397–98.
31. Ed. Cantini, 257.
32. RLOL 3:399.

33. Even when Llull uses more formal structures of syllogistic argument, he almost always adapts them to the limited terminology of his Great Art, and frequently reduces relationships of deduction to correlations of likeness. See Johnston, *Spiritual Logic,* chap. 6, 17.
34. RLOL 14:387.
35. Its editors' assessment; RLOL 18:16.
36. Ed. Wittlin, 39.
37. The *Glossa ordinaria* simply notes "Mysterium trinitatis" (PL 113:1243D). Nicholas of Lyre notes the Jewish exegesis that this repetition serves only "ad excitandum maiorem attentionem" and the additions to his gloss refute this explanation in detail; See *Postilla super totam Bibliam,* vol. 2, ff. BBiv^v–BBv^r.
38. On the exempla collected in this text, see Cabré et al. "'Conèixer e haver moralitats bones'"; Knabe, "Der enzyklopedische Gedanke"; and Pring-Mill, "Els recontaments."
39. ORL 12:341.
40. ORL 12:341–42.

Chapter 5

1. Delhaye, "L'enseignement de la philosophie morale," 91.
2. C. Davis, "Education in Dante's Florence," 161.
3. Murphy, *Rhetoric in the Middle Ages,* 43–61.
4. Michel, *La parole et la beauté,* 151–52.
5. Kovach, "The Transcendentality of Beauty"; Pouillon, "La Beauté, propriété transcendentale." Unlike some contemporaries, Llull never asks whether the transcendentals might exist in reason alone; on their doctrines, see De Bruyne, *Études d'esthétique médiévale,* 3:161–73.
6. Gauthier, "*Pulcher* et *formosus.*"
7. On this famous aspect of Llull's enterprise, see Coll, "Escuelas de lenguas orientales"; Colomer, "Ramon Llull y Ramon Martí"; Cortabarría, "Originalidad y significación de los *Studia Linguarum* "; Garcías Palou, *El Miramar de Ramon Llull,* 30–32, 50–51.
8. References to Miramar in Llull's writings are too idealized, vague, or inconsistent to characterize the house's operations: see, e.g., *Doctrina pueril* 83.7; *Blaquerna* 65, 80.3; *Cant de Ramon* 13–18; *Desconhort* 649–57; *Libre de contemplació* 346.10, 26; or *Petitio ad Celestinum V papam.* See Garcías Palou, *El Miramar de Ramon Llull,* 5–6, 116.
9. ORL 9:367.
10. ORL 9:365: cf. sections 80.3 and 85.2.
11. On medieval arguments about Babel, see D. C. Allen, *Legend of Noah;* Dubois, *Mythe et langage;* Mazzocco, *Linguistic Theories in Dante,* 159–79; Niederehe, *Alfonso X el Sabio y la lingüística,* 85–95; and Weignad, "Two and Seventy Languages."
12. On Dante, see Mazzocco, *Linguistic Theories in Dante,* 108–58. On the French translators, see Batany, *Approches langagières,* 77–94, and Lusignan, *Parler vulgairement;* on the Italian, see Gehl, *A Moral Art.*
13. Apel, *L'idea di lingua,* 87–93, 136–40.
14. For a different view of this problem, see L. Badia, "A propòsit de Ramon Llull i la gramàtica."
15. Contrary to the claims of some modern scholars; see Gayà, ed., Llull, *Ars notatoria* 22; Platzeck, "La Figura T." On the linguistic issues raised in Scholastic theology, see

Chenu's classic essay "Grammaire et théologie" and Evans's *Earlier Middle Ages* or his *Old Arts.*

16. Ed. Gayà, 19–21.
17. Kaster, in *Guardians of Language,* 11–4, neatly characterizes their narrow interests.
18. On these treatises, see Johnston, "Literary Tradition and the Idea of Language in the *artes de trobar.*"
19. RLOL 16:313.
20. Ed. Marshall, 14.
21. The *Siete Partidas* of Alfonso the Wise also use a variable grammatical metalanguage; see Niederehe, *Alfonso X el Sabio y la lingüística,* 55.
22. Elsewhere, this illustrative use evidently leads to some very loose or even mistaken citations of grammatical terminology. For example, the *Arbre de sciència* applies the label "adverb" to the Catalan nouns "bonificament" and "magnificament" ("Arbre questional" 5.10.2.360; ORL 13:284). Llull apparently confuses the nominal and adverbial meanings of the vernacular suffix "-ment."
23. E.g., section 3.8.2 uses it to explain how discourse must organize events temporally with the appropriate tenses in verbs.
24. ORL 8:541–42.
25. Paterson, *Troubadours and Eloquence,* 89–117, 147–93 (esp. 100, 131).
26. ORL 20:245.
27. See the examples in the introduction above.
28. Ed. Mainz, 3:160.
29. As noted by L. Badia, "Ramon Llull i la tradició literària," 128.
30. Platzeck, in "La combinatoria luliana," 136–40, reviews the range of Greek, Latin, and Arabic precedents. See also the comments of Badia and Moll in "La lengua de Ramon Llull," 1355–58 or Pring-Mill, in *Microcosmos lul.lià,* 143–47.
31. Shapiro, "Word-Weaving."
32. Gehl, *"Competens Silentium,"* 147.
33. Leclercq, *Recueil d'études sur Saint Bernard,* esp. "L'art de la composition," 150.
34. Gamboso, "Sermoni festivi," 17.
35. On these rhyming word lists, see D'Avray, "Wordlists," and *Preaching of the Friars,* 248. Wenzel in *Preachers, Poets,* reviews the whole spectrum of lyrical and rhythmic devices.
36. Ed. Charland, 321.
37. Spencer, *English Preaching,* 110–18.
38. Levy *Nine Verse Sermons by Nicholas Bozon*; Wenzel, *Preachers, Poets,* 75–76, 99; Zink, *La prédication en langue romane,* 266, 288–90.
39. Wilmart, "Sermons d'Hildebert," 45.
40. Saenger, "Silent Reading," 382.
41. Lazzerini, "Per latinos grossos," 281; Nolan, *Now through a Glass Darkly,* 219–41; Spencer, *English Preaching,* 118–32.
42. Bonnes, "Un des plus grands prédicateurs."
43. Lazzerini, "Per latinos grossos," 327.
44. Lazzerini, "Per latinos grossos," 243.
45. E.g., Richard Rolle in English; see R. Allen, "Singuler Lufe."
46. Johnston, "Reception of the Lullian *Art,*" 36–39.
47. On related techniques, see Purcell, *"Transsumptio."*
48. Ed. Johnston, 3.
49. Ed. Johnston, 3.

50. Ed. Johnston, 13.
51. Ed. Johnston, 13.
52. Ed. Johnston, 40.
53. Robins, *Short History of Linguistics,* 19.
54. I.e., saying "rex bonitas" instead of "rex bonus."
55. Ed. Johnston, 38.
56. Similarly, the *Arbre de sciència* briefly cites "beautiful adjectives, participles, and verbs" without explaining how these function ("Arbre humanal" 5.5.j; ORL 11:216).
57. Bursill-Hall, *Speculative Grammars,* 286–326.
58. For a bibliography, consult Horner, *Present State of Scholarship*; the best guide to Renaissance devices remains Lanham, *Handlist of Rhetorical Terms*; an ambitious modern reformulation is Dubois et al., *General Rhetoric.*
59. Ed. Johnston, 45.
60. Johnston, *Spiritual Logic,* 223–26.
61. Johnston, "Treatment of Speech."
62. Ed. Furnivall, ll. 244–48.
63. Ed. Johnston, 25.
64. Trans. Preminger, Hardison, and Kerrane, p. 331.
65. Cited in Alford, "Grammatical Metaphor," 42–43.
66. Lubac, *Exégèse médiévale,* 1:479.
67. Spencer, *English Preaching,* 142–3. On less exalted analogies of this kind, see Ziolkowski, *Alan of Lille's Grammar of Sex.*
68. Gellrich, *Idea of the Book,* 29–39.
69. Ed. Johnston, 14.
70. The manner in which substantives signify both substance and quality is a commonplace problem, as the opinions gathered by Vincent of Beauvais indicate (*SD* 2.21).
71. As noted by Rubió i Balaguer, in "La 'Rhetoriea nova' de R. Llull," 271.
72. Ed. Johnston, 41.
73. Ed. Keil, 1:141.
74. Ed. Bursill-Hall, 178.
75. Heffernan, *Sacred Biography,* 111–13.
76. Spencer, *English Preaching,* 70.
77. Hatzfeld, *Estudios literarios sobre mística española,* 48–51.
78. Excellently surveyed by Schnapp in "Virgin Words."

Chapter 6

1. Jordi Rubió i Balaguer noted that in the *Rethorica nova* proverbs, exempla, similes, and fables mingle indifferently as devices serving similar functions; see "La 'Rhetorica nova' de R. Llull," 265.
2. Biglieri, *Hacia una poética del relato didáctico,* 39.
3. Almazán, "L'exemplum chez Vincent Ferrier," 299–300.
4. Roberts, *Stephanus de Lingua-Tonante,* 84, 89.
5. McInerny, "Metaphor and Analogy," 90–91.
6. Ed. Mainz, 1:5.
7. Ed. Mainz, 1:39.
8. The curative or preventive function of these truths recognized *per similia* and *per contraria* suggests that this "metaphor" comprehends the cures from similarity and

contrariety mentioned in Llull's other accounts of medicine, such as the review in the *Doctrina pueril* (78.7–8).

9. Agrimi and Crisciani, *Medicina del corpo e medicina dell'anima.*

10. Curtius, *European Literature,* 57–61; Walther, *Proverbia sententiaeque.*

11. Ageno, "Premessa a un repertorio" and "Tradizione favolistica"; Hassell, *Middle French Proverbs;* Mettman, "'Proverbia Arabum'"; Morawski, "Les recueils d'anciens proverbes français"; Pfeffer, "'Eu l'auzi dir un ver reprover,'" "The Riddle of the Proverb," and "'Ben conosc e sai que merces vol so que razos dechai'"; and Segre, "Le forme e le tradizioni didattiche."

12. Zink, *La prédication en langue romane,* 272.

13. ORL 14:1.

14. ORL 14:327.

15. Vecchi, "Il 'proverbio' nella pratica letteraria dei dettatori."

16. Vincenti, "Sentenze e spirito sentenzioso in Matteo," in Matteo dei Libri, *Arringhe,* cviii–vxxv.

17. Bonner and Badia, in *Ramon Llull,* 149, note his affinity for this device.

18. Ed. Johnston, 28.

19. Zink, *La prédication en langue romane,* 308.

20. Ageno, "Tradizione favolistica."

21. Johnston, *Spiritual Logic,* chap. 16.

22. Johnston, *Spiritual Logic,* 31–44.

23. ORL 5:399.

24. ORL 5:393–94.

25. Ed. Johnston, 13.

26. This use is sheerly an instance of an applied *distinctio,* and not the foundation of a new theory of demonstration, as E.-W. Platzeck argued in "La combinatoria luliana," 598–600, or a doctrine borrowed from the speculative grammarians, as L. Badia suggested in "Et hoc patet per regulam C," 95. Also see Johnston, *Spiritual Logic,* 253–56.

27. Ed. Cantini, 255.

28. E.g., Alan of Lille, *Distinctiones,* s.v. "amygdalus," and Ps.-Rabanus *Allegoriae,* s.v. "rosa." Cf. Bonaventure's treatment in Schumacher's "Mysticism in Metaphor."

29. Cf. the similar analysis of rhetorical language through the Relative Principles of Superiority, Equality, and Inferiority, in the *Rethorica nova* (3.12.2). There Llull very clearly uses his Relative Principles as a *distinctio* to organize different relationships between substances (e.g., God and an angel), substances and accidents (e.g., human nature and vision), or accidents (e.g., understanding and loving).

30. RLOL 3:403–4.

31. RLOL 3:404n57.

32. RLOL 3:404n59.

33. See Johnston, *Spiritual Logic,* 46–47, 153–55.

34. Berube and Gieben, "Guibert de Tournai et Robert Grosseteste," 647–49.

35. Ed. Johnston, 40.

36. The Aristotelian laws of contrariety and opposition play little role in Llull's logical doctrines; see Johnston, *Spiritual Logic,* 239.

37. Ed. Johnston, 10.

38. Ed. Johnston, 41.

39. Ed. Johnston, 41.

40. RLOL 14:364.
41. Ed. Galmés, 1:90.
42. ORL 9:356.
43. ORL 9:357.
44. For examples of the former, see Goering, *William de Montibus,* 304–471; for the latter, see Rouse and Rouse, *Preachers, Florilegia, and Sermons.*
45. ORL 9:357.
46. ORL 9:359.
47. Bolton, "Innocent III's Treatement of the *Humiliati,*" 177; Gratien, *Histoire de la fondation,* 127; and Nantes, "La première prédication franciscaine" 372–75.
48. ORL 9:380.
49. ORL 16:117.
50. I apply the term "thick resemblance" to this recourse of spiritual inquiry as a deliberately anachronistic echo of the term "thick description" that Clifford Geertz proposes for certain practices of modern cultural anthropology; see Geertz, "Thick Description." Or viewed more historically, Llull's use of these devices achieves that "prose of the world" based on likeness, which Foucault attributes to late medieval and Renaissance learning, see his *Order of Things* 17–45.
51. Useful guides to the ample scholarship on exempla include Berlioz and Polo de Beaulieu, *Les exempla médiévaux,* and Brémond et al., *L'exemplum.* Especially suggestive are the essays collected in *Rhétorique et histoire: L'exemplum et le modèle de comportement.*
52. McCall, *Ancient Rhetorical Theories,* 60–61, 78–79, 180–94.
53. On the various functions played by exempla in medieval preaching, see Bataillon "Les images dans les sermons" and "Similitudines et exempla"; Berlioz, "Le récit efficace"; D'Avray, *Preaching of the Friars,* 64–70; Delcorno, *L'exemplum nella predicazione volgare;* Longère *La prédication médiévale,* 194–95; Mosher, *Exemplum;* Murphy, *Rhetoric in the Middle Ages,* 341; Owst, *Literature and Pulpit;* Roberts, *Stephanus de Lingua-Tonante,* 79–89; Rouse and Rouse, *Preachers, Florilegia, Sermons,* 96; Schenda, "Stand und Aufgaben"; Schmitt, *Prêcher d'exemples;* and Welter, *L'exemplum.*
54. Berlioz, "Le récit efficace," 116.
55. Almazán, "L'exemplum chez Vincent Ferrier," 291.
56. Welter, *L'exemplum,* 477–502; Schmitt, "Recueils."
57. E.g., Terry, *Catalan Literature,* 14.
58. Almazán, "L'exemplum chez Vincent Ferrier," 295.
59. Gratien, *Histoire de la fondation,* 81–89.
60. ORL 9:345.
61. Hillgarth suggests that Llull refers to epic poetry in *Ramon Lull and Lullism,* 39–40. On the traditional image of "divine jongleur," see note 32 to the introduction.
62. ORL 9:232, 239.
63. Cit. Almazán, "L'exemplum chez Vincent Ferrier," 306.
64. Jacobs, *Fables of Odo of Cheriton,* 26–28.
65. Roberts, *Stephanus de Lingua-Tonante,* 86; Delcorno, *L'exemplum nella predicazione volgare,* 31.
66. Gamboso, "Sermoni festivi," 18.
67. Lazzerini, "Per latinos grossos," 271.
68. Zink, *La prédication en langue romane,* 291.
69. ORL 9:11.

70. See the "Index nominum locorum et personarum" for the *Summa Sermonum* in RLOL 15:474.
71. Piana, "Sermoni di F. Visconti."
72. Roberts, *Stephanus de Lingua-tonante,* 92–93.
73. Olson, *Literature as Recreation,* 128–63.
74. ORL 12:341.
75. Ed. Johnston, 35.
76. Rubió i Balaguer, in "La 'Rhetorica nova' de R. Llull," 269, suggests the parallel to oral epic. On perpetuation through literature, see Curtius, *European Literature,* 476–79.
77. Even the sermons devoted to specific saints in his *Summa sermonum* say little about their holy subjects; see the examples in chapter 10.
78. ORL 10:9.
79. Suggested by L. Badia, in "No cal que tragats exempli dels romans."
80. These correspond to items 4989 and 100 in Tubach's *Index exemplorum.*
81. Ed. Singleton, 210–12.
82. All extant manuscripts of the *Rethorica nova* give this unusual and somewhat garbled version: "sicut de quodam imperatore romano narratur, qui cum magnum exercitum ad eundum in indiam preparasset, ea die qua progredi ad bellum iter acceperat, sustinuit ut quedam paupercula mulier eum acciperet per habenas, ab eo de filii sui occisione iusticiam petitura. Unde cum mulier diceret se imperatorem numquam dimittere, nisi de filio suo et de eo (qui ei filium suum occiderat) iusticiam faceret, rex, ut erat veraciter iustus, secundum iusticiam filium suum capiens mulieri in carcerali custodia mancipandum tradidit donec de India rediit" (ed. Johnston, 34).
83. On methods of narrative adaptation, see Berlioz, "La mémoire du prédicateur"; Gregg, "Exempla of Jacob's Well"; Kahrl, "Allegory in Practice"; Stierle, "Story as Exemplum"; Suleiman, "Le Récit exemplaire"; Tubach, "Exempla in the Decline"; and Zink, "Le traitement des 'sources exemplaires.'"
84. Ed. Johnston, 19.
85. Galley, "*Calila e Digna.*"
86. Bohigas, ed., *Libre de les bèsties*; Deyermond, *Middle Ages,* 98; Llinarès, ed., *Le Livre des Bêtes*; and Neugaard, "Sources of the Folk Tales." For Raymond of Béziers's Latin version, see Hervieux, *Les fabulistes latins,* 5:379–775.
87. Minnis, *Medieval Theory of Authorship,* 131–45; Spencer, *English Preaching,* 78–80.
88. ORL 13:251.
89. The *Cilium oculi sacerdotis,* cited by Owst in *Preaching in Medieval England,* 328.
90. Ed. di Luca, 81.
91. On the tension between these two developments, see Hanning, "I Shal Finde It in a Maner Glose."

Chapter 7

1. De Bruyne, *Études d'esthétique médiévale,* 1:36–57.
2. De Bruyne, *Études d'esthétique médiévale,* 1:5–34, remains the best summary of the Boethian doctrines.
3. Ed. Pouillon, "La Beauté, propriété transcendentale"; also see Marrone, *William of Auvergne and Robert Grosseteste,* 34–37.
4. Ed. Johnston, 5.

5. For a popular account of these Marian titles, see Warner, *Alone of All Her Sex*; on Llull's Marian literature, see Bétérous, "Ramon Llull et le renouvellement"; Caldentey, "La asunción de la virgen María," 431–36; Cascante Dávila, "El culto a María"; Vidal i Vendrell, "La mediación universal" and "Maternidad de María."

6. A notable exception is chapter 359 of the *Libre de contemplació,* which repeatedly mentions "beautiful and orderly" speech, but says nothing about arrangement. Here all consideration of dispositional order cedes to the task of defining the spiritual ordering of the Senses and Intellect. In contrast to this, the *Aplicació de l'art general* (ll. 830–83) seems to regard division of discourse as an ornament.

7. ORL 1:131–32.

8. The early *Ars notatoria* (1.1) mentions a "proem" and "narration" in its discussion of the proper plan for recording readings or lectures, but does not explain them (ed. Gayà, 27–29).

9. Johnston, "Parliamentary Oratory." The earliest extant reference to an *ars dictaminis* in a Catalan library list dates from the late thirteenth century; see Faulhaber, "Rhetoric in Medieval Catalonia." However, since Catalan students were attending the schools of Bologna from at least 1218, knowledge of the epistolary art had surely returned to Catalonia with them; see Miret i Sans, "Escolars catalans al Estudi de Bolonia."

10. Cited in Rockinger, *Briefsteller und formelbücher,* 1:178n3.

11. Ed. Johnston, 6.

12. Tubach, *Index exemplorum,* no. 100. The un-Lullian quality of the diction in this passage implies that this exemplum, like others in the *Rethorica nova,* comes from some source text, perhaps already linked with a suitable topic, such as God's generosity. The sententious character of Alexander's response, which effectively states the entire lesson of the exemplum, also recalls the cultivation of proverbs in the *artes dictaminis.*

13. E.g., the English case discussed by Green in *Poets and Princepleasers,* 42–43.

14. Ed. Johnston, 7.

15. Ed. Johnston, 7.

16. Bataillon, "Approaches to the Study," 28. Spencer, in *English Preaching,* 230–47, summarizes well the features of homily and sermon.

17. Roberts, *Stephanus de Lingua-Tonante,* 39–40.

18. Perhaps thanks to the example of the Victorine writers who cultivated them in the twelfth century; see Châtillon, "Les écoles de Chartres et de Saint-Victor," 823.

19. Bataillon, "Approaches to the Study," 28.

20. Cantini, "*Processus negociandi,*" 250.

21. Gieben, "Robert Grosseteste on Preaching," 112.

22. Brunel, "Le sermon en langue vulgaire."

23. Chabaneau, "Sermons et préceptes," 18:110.

24. J. M. Vidal, "Doctrine et morale," 37–46.

25. Vorreaux, "Un sermon de Philippe"; on Philippe's work, see Schneyer, *Die Sittenkritik in den Predigten Philipps des Kanzlers.*

26. Delcorno, "Predicazione volgare e volgarizzamenti," 680–81.

27. From Murphy, *Rhetoric in the Middle Ages,* 325.

28. Wenzel, *Preachers, Poets,* 100.

29. Zink, *La prédication en langue romane,* 233–34.

30. Bataillon, "Early Scholastic and Mendicant Preaching," 172–74; Lecoy, *La chaire française,* 60–64; Zink, *La prédication en langue romane,* 222–23.

31. Robson, *Maurice of Sully,* 46, 27.

32. Amsterdam, "Tres sermones inediti."
33. Gamboso, "Sermoni festivi" 17–18.
34. Gamboso, "Sermoni festivi," 76.
35. RLOL 3:406.
36. Analyzed above in chapter 4. One manuscript of the *Liber de praedicatione* adds the phrase "that is, through multiple senses," thus specifying Llull's treatment of these in his previous section on exposition (RLOL 3:399).
37. See the comments of Soria Flores in RLOL 3:104.
38. See the specimen sermons analyzed below in chapter 10.
39. Zink, *La prédication en langue romane,* 225–50, and Spencer, *English Preaching,* 259–61.
40. RLOL 3:399.
41. RLOL 3:401.
42. On the image of preacher as light, see the references cited in chapter 2, note 64.
43. Just as his own writings provide numerous narrative exempla for later preachers. For Ambrose's letter, see PL 17:254. On Gregory, see Berlioz, "La récit efficace," 128. On later authorities, see Roberts, *Stephanus de Lingua-Tonante,* 81.
44. Bynum, *Docere verbo et exemplo,* 77–98.
45. Nantes, "La première prédication franciscaine," 371.
46. Jaeger, *Origins of Courtliness,* 147. Llull does recognize these virtues in his section on courtesy from the *Mil proverbis* (chap. 37; ORL 14:359–60).
47. Coulter, *Literary Microcosm,* 128.

Chapter 8

1. Coulter, *Literary Microcosm,* 122.
2. ORL 8:540.
3. Damon, "Modes of Analogy," 299–313.
4. ORL 8:541.
5. Often based on study of Cicero's and Ambrose's treatises *De officiis*; see Jaeger, *Origins of Courtliness,* chap. 7–8, and esp. 139, 173.
6. ORL 8:541.
7. The *Ars generalis ultima* notably omits any reference to the three traditional occasions.
8. Murphy, *Rhetoric in the Middle Ages,* 294–96.
9. On Alan's theory of audience levels, see esp. Zink, "Rhétorique honteuse."
10. As suggested by Spencer in *English Preaching,* 65–68.
11. RLOL 14:364.
12. Johnston, *Spiritual Logic,* 135–37.
13. L. Badia, "Et hoc patet per regulam C," 95, sees this passage as Llull's audaciously original revision of the traditional *Rota Vergilii.*
14. Casagrande, *Prediche alle donne;* D' Avray, *Preaching of the Friars,* 127; D' Avray and Tausche, "Marriage Sermons"; Ferruolo, "Preaching to the Clergy and Laity"; LeGoff, *Time, Work, and Culture,* 107–21; and Zafarana, "La predicazione ai laici."
15. Ed. Egidi, 84–96.
16. Chaurand, "Latin médiéval et contexte social."
17. As argued by Batany, in *Approches langagières,* 117–266; Corti, in "Modelli e anti-modelli," 11–13; and Duby, in *Three Orders,* 314–21.

213

18. Hernando, "Els moralistes i l'alimentació," 287–90.
19. Thomas of Celano, *Vita secunda*, chap. 73; see Nantes, "La première prédication franciscaine," 370.
20. ORL 9:232.
21. ORL 9:239.
22. Ed. Johnston, 11–12.
23. Ed. Johnston, 39.
24. Ed. Johnston, 39.
25. Ed. Johnston, 39.
26. Ed. Johnston, 40.
27. Ed. Johnston, 12.
28. Paterson, *Troubadours and Eloquence,* 71–72.
29. Cit. Leclercq, "L'art de la composition," 150.
30. Ed. Johnston, 24–25.
31. On the impact of Francis's example, see Nantes, "La première prédication franciscaine," 363–65, and Bériou, "Saint François, premier prophète."
32. Owst, *Literature and Pulpit,* 277–80.
33. On dress and social status, see Cateura Bennasser, *Sociedad, jerarquía y poder,* 114–31.

Chapter 9

1. On its classical and early Christian treatments, see Kennedy, *Art of Persuasion in Greece,* 14–25; S. Bonner, *Education in Ancient Rome,* 64–89; and Kennedy, *Art of Rhetoric in the Roman World,* 607–14.
2. On literature regarding virtues of speech specifically, see Johnston, "Treatment of Speech." On classifications of the virtues generally, see Bloomfield, *Seven Deadly Sins,* or Lottin, *Psychologie et morale,* 3:99–252.
3. Delhaye, "L'enseignement de la philosophie morale" and "'Grammatica' et 'Ethica' au XIIe siècle."
4. Delhaye, "L'enseignement de la philosophie morale," 86; Johnston, "Treatment of Speech," 26.
5. Murphy, *Rhetoric in the Middle Ages,* 97–101.
6. Jaeger, *Origins of Courtliness,* 129–68; Nicholls, *Matter of Courtesy,* 15–16, 39, 123. The etiquette of table conversation was also an important aspect of courtesy literature on speech; see the studies in Menjot, ed., *Manger et boire.*
7. Jaeger, *Origins of Courtliness,* chap. 9.
8. Ed. Esser, 234.
9. Creytens, "Manuel de conversation."
10. Ed. Corbett, 48.
11. Johnston, "Literacy, Spiritual Allegory, and Power."
12. See the accompanying letter of transmission in Rubió, *Documents per l'història de la cultura,* 1:41, and the dating suggested by Hillgarth, in *Ramon Lull and Lullism,* 69n70.
13. ORL 14:368–69.
14. Johnston, "Treatment of Speech," 23–25.
15. It is interesting to see how this objective becomes explicit in later humanist manuals, such as J. L. Vives's *De ratione dicendi*, which often present the same precepts as their medieval predecessors. On the Renaissance ideal, see Grassi, *Rhetoric as*

Philosophy; Kristeller, *Renaissance Thought II,* 27–32; Seigel, *Rhetoric and Philosophy,* chap. 3; and Struever, *Language of History,* 144–63.

16. ORL 5:354–55.
17. On brevity as a literary ideal, see Curtius, *European Literature,* 487–94.
18. The *Libre de contemplació* specifically mentions the *arengador* who neglects brevity (359.27); this term may simply indicate the long-winded speaker, but probably refers as well to the orator of the *ars arengandi.* Colom notes only the literal sense: see *Glossari,* s.v. "arengador." On sermon theorists' concern about long-winded preaching, see Spencer, *English Preaching,* 92.
19. ORL 8:535–36.
20. Ed. Johnston, 36, 37, 45.
21. *Secretum secretorum,* 1501 ed., f. 15vb.
22. Brunel, "Le sermon en langue vulgaire."
23. Jaeger, *Origins of Courtliness,* 38, 145.
24. Ed. Johnston, 36, 41, 46.
25. ORL 20:245.
26. De Bruyne, *Études d'esthétique médiévale,* 2:27–28.
27. Ed. Johnston, 45.
28. *Secretum secretorum,* 1501 ed., f. 14vb.
29. Jaeger, *Origins of Courtliness,* 92.
30. The Castilian *Bocados de oro* offers an especially full compendium of such lore.
31. The arguments of Green, in *Poets and Princepleasers,* 140–43, regarding the circulation of such texts in English aristocratic culture probably apply to Spain as well.
32. Delhaye, "L'enseignement de la philosophie morale," 87.
33. Abul Qasem, *Ethics of al-Ghazali,* 147–53.
34. Bloomfield, *Seven Deadly Sins,* 124; Johnston, "Treatment of Speech," 28–30; and above all Casagrande and Vecchio, *I peccati della lingua.*
35. Abul Quasem, *Ethics of al-Ghazali,* 106, 112–18.
36. On Llull's schemes of vices, see Brummer, "Die vitia principalia."
37. ORL 14:369.
38. Ed. Johnston, 36.
39. See chapter 3 regarding Llull's scant attention to techniques of rhetorical affectivity.
40. Ed. Johnston, 39.
41. RLOL 14:386.
42. Gabriel, "Ideal Master of the Medieval University," 32.
43. ORL 8:542.
44. RLOL 16:25.
45. Ed. Johnston, 39.
46. ORL 13:251.
47. Ed. Johnston, 11; cf. the briefer mentions in 3.5.1 and 3.6.1.
48. Thomas of Celano, *Vita prima,* chap. 15; see Nantes "La première prédication franciscaine," 368.
49. Murray, *Reason and Society,* 394–98.
50. Jaeger, *Origins of Courtliness,* chap. 3, 9.
51. Ed. Johnston, 11; cf. the similar, brief remarks in section 3.2.6.
52. Rubió i Balaguer, "La 'Rhetorica nova' de R. Llull," 265, refers this advice to the vernacular *arts de trobar* that urge troubadours to speak ardently in their poetic pleas. Llull's dislike of minstrels militates against this allusion, unless it constitutes an attempt to include all secular arts of language in a general program for eloquence.
53. Jaeger, *Origins of Courtliness,* 46–48, 129–33.

54. Ed. Scheler, 20. "Speak softly and carry a big stick" would evidently be the corresponding modern American idiom.
55. Ed. Johnston, 11.
56. For recent discussions of this topic, see Dreyer, "'Affectus' in St. Bonaventure's Theology," and Minnis, *Medieval Theory of Authorship,* 49–52.
57. Ed. Johnston, 12.
58. See chapter 7 on the discussion of honorableness as "orderly living" in the *Liber de praedicatione.*
59. Ed. Johnston, 39.
60. On these broad categories of courtly virtues, see Jaeger, *Origins of Courtliness,* chap. 8.
61. Sala-Molins, *Philosophie de l'amour,* 68, 236–47.
62. Oliver, "Ramón Llull en sus relaciones con la escuela franciscana," 9:155.
63. Well analyzed by Grassi in *Rhetoric as Philosophy,* chap. 4 ("Rhetoric as the Ground of Society").
64. Gieben, "Robert Grosseteste on Preaching," 109–10.
65. Fortin, "Augustine and the Problem of Christian Rhetoric."
66. Ed. Johnston, 53.
67. Ed. Johnston, 53.
68. Ed. Johnston, 54.
69. Chenu *L'éveil,* 41–61; Lottin, *Psychologie et morale,* 4:309–486; and Tentler, *Sin and Confession,* 95–124, 148–62.
70. The role of this supposition, which corresponds functionally both to the "benevolence" that Augustine deemed necessary to understand Scripture and to the *synderesis* (natural inclination to good) recognized by Scholastic theologians, is critical in Llull's arguments about the interaction of faith and understanding. On the disposition to understand, see Ripanti, "Il problema della comprensione," 90; on *synderesis*, see the *Cambridge History of Later Medieval Philosophy,* 687–704, or more fully, Lottin, *Psychologie et morale,* 2:103–350; on Llull's "supposition" of faith, see Johnston, *Spiritual Logic,* 128–33, 296–301.
71. E.g., Tubach, *Index exemplorum,* nos. 3877, 3890, 3897–98, 3901.
72. Newman, *Sister of Wisdom,* 39–41, 254–57, and "Hildegard of Bingen: Visions and Validation," 171–75.
73. Cit. Almazán "L'exemplum chez Vincent Ferrier," 306.
74. Auerbach, *"Sermo humilis,"* 52, 68.
75. Johnston, "Reception of the Lullian Art," 41–43.
76. RLOL 3:405.
77. RLOL 14:386.
78. Johnston, *Spiritual Logic,* 91, 141–43.
79. Ripanti, "Il problema della comprensione."
80. Ed. Jaffe, 117.

Chapter 10

1. On the general problems involved, see Bataillon, "Approaches to the Study," and Zink, *La prédication en langue romane,* 151–71, 335–40.
2. Murith, "Pour l'histoire de la prédication." Delcorno, "Rassegna di studi," offers many incisive suggestions for further research. Spencer, *English Preaching,* 1–19, reviews well some of the problems that still arise.

3. The best general survey is Longère, *La prédication médiévale;* the indispensable inventory remains Schneyer's *Repertorium.* Other useful general studies include Amos et al., *De l'homélie au sermon* and *De ore domini*; Bataillon, *La prédication au XIIIe siècle en France et Italie*; D'Avray, *Preaching of the Friars*; Davy, *Les sermons universitaires*; Longère, *Oeuvres oratoires des maîtres parisiens*; Martin, *Le métier de prédicateur*; and Zink, *La prédication en langue romane.* On Spain in particular, see the brief surveys by Deyermond, in "Sermon and Its Uses," and Rico, in *Predicación y literatura.*

4. Roberts, *Stephanus de Lingua-Tonante,* 56–57; Bériou, "Prédication au béguinage," 114; Delcorno, "Predicazione volgare e volgarizzamenti," 684.

5. Bataillon, "Sermons rédigés"; D'Avray, *Preaching of the Friars,* 97–98, 103; and Hamesse "'Collatio' et 'Reportatio.'" See esp. the interesting case studied by Bougerol, in "Le sermon de Saint Bonaventure sur le royaume de Dieu."

6. Cantini, "S. Antonio da Padova," 420. On the main types of collections, see Spencer, *English Preaching,* 20–33.

7. Zink, *La prédication en langue romane,* 212.

8. As distinguished by Zink, in *La prédication en langue romane,* 209.

9. Spencer, *English Preaching,* 33–42.

10. Roberts, *Stephanus de Lingua-Tonante,* 47–48.

11. On Llull's efforts to evangelize Jewish or Muslim audiences in Christian lands, see Johnston, "Ramon Llull and the Compulsory Evangelization of Jews and Muslims."

12. Leclercq, "Prédicateurs bénédictins" and "Recherches sur d'anciens sermons monastiques"; Meersseman, "Eremitismo e predicazione itinerante."

13. The conclusion reviews evidence for this use by later medieval readers of Llull's works.

14. Zink, *La prédication en langue romane,* 431; Domínguez Reboiras, RLOL 15:9–34.

15. On this use in reading, see Gallick, "Artes praedicandi," and Zink, *La prédication en langue romane,* 301.

16. ORL 9:362.

17. RLOL 4:11.

18. The term "Sacred Page" as a designation for study of theology is more typical of the mid-thirteenth century, but slightly anachronistic usage of this kind is common in Llull's work.

19. See the discussion above in chapter 4.

20. Rico, in *Predicación y literatura,* 12, characterizes Llull's general method in this work as "true syllogisms *sui generis.*"

21. O'Carroll, "Lectionary."

22. RLOL 4:298.

23. See the discussion above in chapter 7.

24. Zink, *La prédication en langue romane,* 477.

25. Callebaut, "Sermon historique," 105.

26. RLOL 4:13–14.

27. RLOL 4:208.

28. D'Alverny, "L'homme comme symbole," 172–73.

29. RLOL 4:209.

30. RLOL 4:209.

31. RLOL 4:211.

32. The various exempla concerning fruit in the *Rethorica nova* (e.g., 2.4.17) rely on similar allegorical interpretations.

33. RLOL 4:212.

34. RLOL 4:212.
35. RLOL 4:213.
36. Delcorno, "Giordano da Pisa e la tecnica del sermone," 330–38, and *Giordano da Pisa e l'antica predicazione volgare,* 156.
37. Zink, *La prédication en langue romane,* 237–38.
38. On later medieval circulation of the *Liber de praedicatione,* see the discussion in the conclusion below.
39. This more synthetic treatment apparently has prevented the text's modern editor from recognizing and marking the sermon's expositional and applicational divisions in the printed edition.
40. RLOL 4:18.
41. Amsterdam, "Tres sermones inediti."
42. RLOL 4:18.
43. *Processus negociandi,* ed. Cantini, 257; Gieben, "Robert Grosseteste on Preaching," 103.
44. See the previous discussion in Chapter 2.
45. RLOL 4:19.
46. RLOL 4:20.
47. RLOL 4:20.
48. RLOL 4:20.
49. Bériou, "L'art de convaincre."
50. Or simply with most patristic and early medieval allegoresis; see Wailes, *Medieval Allegories,* 11.
51. Ed. Hervieux, *Les fabulistes latins,* 4:388–89.
52. Zink, *La prédication en langue romane,* 279–87.
53. Cantini, "S. Bonaventura da Bagnorea," 48.
54. L. Badia, "Ramon Llull i la tradició literària," 134.
55. Ed. Millás Vallicrosa, 71.
56. Minnis, *Medieval Theory of Authorship,* 85; Smalley, *Study of the Bible,* 338–55.
57. On this "error" of the Jews, see Lubac, *Exégèse médiévale,* 2:287, or Pelikan, *Growth of Medieval Theology* 17–19.
58. Cited in Coll, "Escuelas de lenguas orientales," 19:230.
59. Ed. Galmés, 1:119.
60. Riera i Sans, "Les llicències reials."
61. Their texts appear in Rubió, *Documents per l'història de la cultura,* 1:13–14, and Egidi, *Codice diplomatico,* 32–33.
62. For a summary of these tactics, see Coll, "Escuelas de lenguas orientales," 19:232–33. Chazan provides detailed analyses of these encounters in *Daggers of Faith* and *Barcelona and Beyond.*
63. Like many of his arguments, this one appears already in his *Libre de contemplació* (188.22).
64. RLOL 16:376.
65. Waleys was much younger than Llull; he died after 1349, but not before he probably visited Italy, thanks to his connections with the archbishop of Palermo.
66. Millás Vallicrosa summarizes each argument well in his introduction to the text (34–57).
67. Millás Vallicrosa calls this an "ontological" argument (53) although it more accurately corresponds to Llull's "coessential predication"; see Johnston, *Spiritual Logic,* 114–17, 306.
68. Ed. Millás Vallicrosa, 105.

69. PL 113:1313B.
70. *Postilla super totam Bibliam* vol. 2, f. LLii^r.
71. Smalley, *Study of the Bible,* 10.
72. Ed. Millás Vallicrosa, 128, 126.
73. Cf. the conclusions of Millás Vallicrosa, 19, 24–27, 60, and Cohen, *Friars and the Jews,* 214–21.
74. On Llull's generally limited knowledge of Jewish theology, see the comments of Millás Vallicrosa, 22–31, 60, and Burman, "Anti-Islamic Preoccupation."
75. Swartz, "Islamic Preaching and Sermons."
76. Signer, "Jewish Preaching and Sermons," 75, and Saperstein, *Jewish Preaching,* 26–79; see the exemplary case analyzed by Horowitz, in *Jewish Sermon.*
77. Chapter 4 analyzes a model sermon from the *Ars abbreviata praedicationis.*
78. Suggested by Domínguez Reboiras (RLOL 17:9–26).
79. Roccaro, "I *Sermones* di Ruggero da Piazza."
80. The best introduction to this literature is Goering's study of William de Montibus. See also Boyle, "Aspects of Clerical Education" and "The *Summa confessorum* of John of Freiburg"; the Castilian catechism of Pedro de Cuéllar, edited by Martín and Linage Conde as *Religión y sociedad medieval*; and Spencer, *English Preaching* 196–227.
81. D'Avray, *Preaching of the Friars,* 82–90.
82. RLOL 15:6.
83. RLOL 15:432.
84. Cf. the example cited in chapter 6 above.
85. "Entries in a thematic index," according to L. Badia, in "Ramon Llull i la predicació," 574.
86. RLOL 15:460.
87. Prol. 2; RLOL 15:115.
88. RLOL 15:115.
89. L. Badia, "Ramon Llull i la predicació," 571–73.
90. As claimed by the editors of Llull's *Ars abbreviata praedicandi*; RLOL 18:23.
91. RLOL 15:116.
92. Johnston, *Spiritual Logic,* 223–26.
93. RLOL 15:162.
94. RLOL 15:166.
95. RLOL 15:19.
96. RLOL 15:193.
97. RLOL 15:191.
98. Johnston, *Spiritual Logic,* 70, 206–19. An especially noteworthy moralization of this ambiguity appears in the *Liber de virtutibus et peccatis,* where the habit of faith contrasts with the clothing of infidelity (3.1.4.20; RLOL 15:169).
99. Many of Llull's writings from his last five years are short treatises on theological issues, all expounded in the manner of these sermons. They evidently are products of Llull's own use of his system as a compositional method.
100. The conclusion of L. Badia, "Ramon Llull i la tradició literària," 137.
101. Spencer, *English Preaching,* 199.

Conclusion

1. I consider here only manuscripts created before 1500, because the advent of new humanist ideals of oratory significantly altered esteem for Llull's arts of eloquence. The

work of Jacques Lefèvre d'Étaples, Bernardo de Lavinheta, and other Parisian Lullists in the period 1499–1516 marks the beginning of Renaissance Lullism; see Johnston, "Reception of the Lullian *Art,*" 39. After this period, only Neo-Scholastic Lullists, like those on Majorca, continue to use his writings on rhetoric or preaching.

2. On the difficulties of the Lullian manuscript tradition, see Rubió i Balaguer, "Notes sobre la transmissió"; Reidlinger's comments in his introduction to RLOL 5:1–257; and Bonner, *Selected Works,* 1257–1304.

3. See the remarks of Millás Vallicrosa in his introduction to the text, pp. 62–67.

4. Described and analyzed in RLOL 15:lxxxiii–lxxxiv, xcix–cv. See also Perarnau, "Consideracions diacròniques."

5. Analyzed in RLOL 15:lxxxix–xciv.

6. There is no extant copy of the Catalan version mentioned in the treatise's colophon (ed. Johnston, 54).

7. For a full description of this manuscript, see ed. Johnston, xxxii–xxxv.

8. An even more limited Lullian arts curriculum perhaps appears in Manuscript 413 of the Biblioteca Universitaria in Pavia, which combines a fourteenth-century copy of the *Rethorica nova* with a fifteenth-century copy of the Pseudo-Augustinian *De dialectica*; on this volume, see Batllori, "Relíquies manuscrites," 140.

9. On the education provided by this level of instruction, see Gabriel, "Preparatory Teaching in the Parisian Colleges," and on some Spanish examples, see Arco Garay, "Un estudio de artes en Barbastro"; Capdevila, "Les antigues institucions escolars," 86–89; Duran i Sampere and Gómez Gabernet, "Las escuelas de gramática en Cervera"; and Vega y de Luque, "Un centro medieval de enseñanza."

10. Johnston, *"Sacrum studium."*

11. Johnston, "Reception of the Lullian *Art,*" and RLOL 18:32–34. The best guide to early printed texts of Llull is Rogent and Duran, *Bibliografia de les impressions lul.lianes.*

12. RLOL 3:43–66.

13. As suggested by the text's modern editors (RLOL 18:6).

14. Our knowledge of this practice is, of course, very limited, for the reasons noted at the beginning of chapter 10. The text's editors confuse this question further by arguing that the schematizing zeal of Llull's treatises on preaching reflect the calculating, formalistic habits of the later medieval money economy, but that they nonetheless contributed to new humanist views of preaching that challenged mechanical, rigidly structured preaching methods (RLOL 18:34–37). The revisions and apocryphal versions of Llull's preaching works that appeared in the Renaissance manifest the humanist enthusiasm for artful discourse precisely in their efforts to improve Lullian style.

15. Described completely in RLOL 12:xxviii–xxix.

16. Described in RLOL 1:29–32.

17. Barcelona, "L'*Ars praedicandi* de Francesc Eiximenis," 302. Described also in Pérez Martínez, "Los fondos lulianos," 372–73.

18. Groundbreaking work in this area appears in several essays by Perarnau: "Un altre testimoni"; "Indicacions esparses sobre lul.lisme"; and "Sobre mestre Antoni Sedacer."

19. Secular veneration for Llull as the "universal Majorcan" implies this transcendence of historical circumstance. On the cultural ideology expressed in such philological judgments, see Patterson, *Negotiating the Past,* 41–74, or Spiegel, "History, Historicism, and the Social Logic of the Text" (esp. 74–75). Contemporary research on Llull could profit considerably from more attention to the issues raised in recent

debate on historiographical method, e.g., Lacapra and Kaplan, *Modern European Intellectual History.*

20. E.g., Hillgarth, *Ramon Lull and Lullism,* 153. Glorieux confidently lists Llull among the Parisian masters of both arts and theology; see *La Faculté des Arts,* 300–313, and *Répertoire des Maîtres en Théologie,* 2:146–91.
21. Johnston, "Ramon Llull and the Compulsory Evangelization of Jews and Muslims."
22. Faulhaber, "Las retóricas hispanolatinas medievales," 35, judges Llull the most original medieval writer on rhetoric from Iberia, and perhaps all of Europe.
23. Carreras y Artau, *Historia de la filosofía española,* 1:268 (my translation).
24. L. Badia, "L'aportació de Ramon Llull," 278–90, and Durieux, "La catéchisme occitane."
25. Constable, "Twelfth-Century Spirituality," and Sargent, ed., *De cella in saeculum.*
26. Llull especially merits comparison to the practices described by Despres, in *Ghostly Sights,* 5–54, or Jeffrey, in *Early English Lyric and Franciscan Spirituality,* 1–117, and to the authors surveyed by Fleming, *Introduction to Francisco Literature.* Oliver's "Ramón Llull en sus relaciones con la escuela franciscana" remains the best survey of this topic. Webster, in *Els Menorets,* 220–89, offers the best review of Franciscan activity in Aragon during Llull's era.
27. Lambert, *Medieval Heresy,* 39–46.
28. Compare the ideals surveyed by Constable in "Renewal and Reform."
29. Chartier, "Text, Printing, Readings," 171–73.
30. Study of Lullism would benefit greatly from the refusal of allegory and interpretation advocated by Foucault in *Archaeology of Knowledge,* 135–40.
31. On this general problem, see P. Moore, "Christian Mysticism and Interpretation."
32. Vauchez, *Laity in the Middle Ages,* 219–64.
33. McDonnell, *Beguines and Beghards,* 120–40. The king's question perhaps contrasts beguines to virtuous laypeople as an alternate mode of mixed life or as examples of devout hypocrisy. This negative reputation becomes widespread in the early fourteenth century, as Juan Manuel's *El Conde Lucanor* (ex. 42) shows.
34. I borrow this phrase from Vauchez, *Laity in the Middle Ages,* 95–106.
35. Zink, *La subjectivité littéraire,* 247 (my translation).
36. Cf. R. I. Moore's provocative study with this title and the suggestive comments on Llull's "theology of colonization" in Barceló's "Ramon Llull i el seu viatge banal a l'Islam."

Works Cited

The initial "Note on References and Quotations" explains the system of citations employed throughout this book. The following list gives the full bibliographical information for each work cited. Works appear listed by author (including traditional attributions) or by title only, in the case of anonymous writings.

This list does not include general secondary bibliography or other works consulted but not cited. The indispensable guide to scholarship in medieval rhetoric is James J. Murphy, *Medieval Rhetoric: A Select Bibliography*, 2d ed. (Toronto: University of Toronto Press, 1989); see also the relevant chapters in Winifred B. Horner, ed., *The Present State of Scholarship in Historical and Contemporary Rhetoric*, rev. ed. (Columbia: University of Missouri Press, 1990). Still useful as a guide to late medieval philosophy is Norman Kretzmann, Anthony Kenny, and Jan Pinborg, eds., *The Cambridge History of Later Medieval Philosophy* (Cambridge: Cambridge University Press, 1982). The modern literature and scholarship on Ramon Llull is very extensive and of vastly disparate quality. The most comprehensive listings are Rudolf Brummer, *Bibliographia Lulliana: Ramon-Llull-Schrifttum 1870–1973* (Hildesheim, Germany: Gerstenberg, 1976) and Marcel Salleras i Carolà, "Bibliografia lul.liana (1974–1984)," *Randa* 19 (1986): 153–98. The journal *Studia Lulliana* (formerly *Estudios Lulianos*) also reviews new Lullian scholarship in each issue.

Works of Ramon Llull

Collected Works

Doctor Illuminatus: A Ramon Llull Reader. Edited amd translated by Anthony Bonner. Princeton, N.J.: Princeton University Press, 1993.
Nova edició de les obres de Ramon Llull. 2 vols. to date. Majorca: Patronat Ramon Llull, 1990– . Continues the ORL. [NEORL]

Obres originals del Illuminat Doctor Mestre Ramon Lull. 21 vols. Edited by M. Obrador y Benassar (vols. 1–3), Comissió Editora Lulliana (vols. 4–6), Salvador Galmés (vols. 7–20), and Miquel Tous Gayà and Rafel Ginard Bauçà (vol. 21). Majorca: Comissió Editora Lulliana, 1906–1917 and Diputació Provincial de Balears and Institut d'Estudis Catalans, 1923–1950. [ORL]

Opera Latina. 18 vols. to date. Majorca: Maioricensis Schola Lullistica del CSIC, 1959–1967, and Turnhout, Belgium: Brepols, 1978–   . Since vol. 6 appearing in the Corpus Christianorum, Continuatio Mediaevalis. [RLOL]

Opera omnia. 9 vols. Edited by Ivo Salzinger. Mainz, 1721–1740. Reprint, Frankfurt am Main: Minerva, 1965. Each work is paged separately in the original edition; the reprint adds continuous paging for each volume. [ed. Mainz]

Selected Works of Ramon Llull. Translated by Anthony Bonner. Princeton, N.J.: Princeton University Press, 1985.

Individual Works

Aplicació de l'art general. ORL 20:209–54.

Arbre de filosofia de amor. ORL 18:67–227.

Arbre de filosofia desiderat. ORL 17:399–507.

Arbre de sciència. ORL 11–13.

Ars abbreviata praedicandi. RLOL 18:1–158.

Ars brevis. In *Opera parva.* Vol. 1. Majorca, 1744. Reprinted as *Opuscula.* Vol. 1. Hildesheim, Germany: H. Gerstenberg, 1971. Paged separately.

Ars brevis, quae est de inventione iuris. Published as "*Ars brevis, quae est de inventione iuris,*" edited by E. Wohlhaupter. *Estudis Franciscans* 29 (1935): 161–250.

Ars compendiosa inveniendi veritatem. Ed. Mainz 1.

Ars generalis ultima. RLOL 14.

Ars mystica theologiae et philosophiae. RLOL 5:259–466.

Ars notatoria. Edited by Jordi Gayà. Madrid: CITEMA, 1978.

Art abreujada de predicació. Edited by Curt Wittlin. Barcelona: Edicions del Mall, 1982.

Art amativa. ORL 17:1–398.

Art demostrativa. ORL 16:1–288.

Brevis practica tabulae generalis. Ed. Mainz 5.

Cant de Ramon. ORL 19:255–60.

Cent noms de Déu. ORL 19:77–170.

Compendium artis demonstrativae. Ed. Mainz 3.

Declaratio Raymundi. Edited by Otto Keicher. Beiträge zur Geschichte der Philosophie des Mittelalters, vol. 7, pt. 4–5. Munster: Aschendorff, 1909.

Desconhort. ORL 19:219–54.

Disputatio fidei et intellectus. Ed. Mainz 3.

Disputatio Raimundi christiani et Hamar saraceni. Ed. Mainz 4.

Disputatio Raimundi et Averroistae. RLOL 7:1–17.

Doctrina pueril. Edited by Greta Schib. Barcelona: Barcino, 1972. Also ORL 1:1–199.

Lectura super artem inventivam et tabulam generalem. Ed. Mainz 5.

Lectura super figuram artis demonstrativae. Ed. Mainz 3.

Liber ad memoriam confirmandam. In "Enciclopedismo e combinatoria nel secolo XVI," by Paolo Rossi. *Rivista critica di storia della filosofia* 13 (1958): 243–79 (text 273–79).

Liber correlativorum innatorum. RLOL 6:117–52.

Liber de affatu, hoc est de sexto sensu. Published as "Affatus," edited by Armand Llinarès and Alexandre Jean Gondras. *Archives d'Histoire doctrinale et littéraire du Moyen Age* 51 (1984): 269–97.

Liber de ascensu et descensu intellectus. RLOL 9:20–199.

Liber de astronomia. RLOL 17:63–218.

Liber de Ave Maria (Sermones de Ave Maria). RLOL 15:79–102.

Liber de convenientia fidei et intellectus in obiecto. Ed. Mainz 4.

Liber de demonstratione per aequiparationem. RLOL 9:216–32.

Liber de divina existentia et agentia. RLOL 8:103–37.

Liber de ente reali et rationis. RLOL 16:31–131.

Liber de experientia realitatis artis generalis. RLOL 11:169–222.

Liber de geometria nova et compendiosa. Edited by José María Millás Vallicrosa. Barcelona: CSIC, 1953.

Liber de inventione maiore. RLOL 2:300–302.

Liber de lumine. In *Opera medica.* Majorca: Pere Antoni Capó, 1752. Paged separately.

Liber de modo naturali intelligendi. RLOL 6:188–223.

Liber de novo modo demonstrandi. RLOL 16:339–77.

Liber de Pater Noster (Sermones de Pater Noster). RLOL 15: 51–78.

Liber de perversione entis removenda. RLOL 5:467–506.

Liber de possibili et impossibili. RLOL 6:375–466.

Liber de praedicatione. RLOL 3–4.

Liber de principiis medicinae. Ed. Mainz 1.

Liber de quinque principiis. RLOL 16:281–314.

Liber de septem donis Spiritus Sancti (Sermones de septem donis Spiritus Sancti). RLOL 15:433–53.

Liber de septem sacramentis Sanctae Ecclesiae (Sermones de septem sacramentis Ecclesiae). RLOL 15:31–50.

Liber de sermonibus factis de decem praeceptis. RLOL 15:1–30.

Liber de significatione. RLOL 10:11–100.

Liber de virtutibus et peccatis (Liber de virtutibus et vitiis, Ars maior praedicationis). RLOL 15:103–432.

Liber lamentationis philosophiae. RLOL 7:85–126.

Liber novus physicorum. RLOL 6:53–83.

Liber predicationis contra Judeos. Edited by José María Millás Vallicrosa. Madrid and Barcelona: CSIC, 1957. Also in RLOL 12:1–78.

Liber qui continet confessionem. RLOL 16:379–96.

Libre de amic e de amat (An intercalated "appendix" to the *Libre de Blaquerna*). ORL 9:379–431.

Libre de anima racional. ORL 21:161–304.

Libre de Blaquerna. ORL 9.

Libre de contemplació en Déu. ORL 2–8.

Libre de demostracions. ORL 15.

Libre de home. ORL 21:1–159.

Libre de les bèsties (Book 7 of the *Libre de meravelles*). Edited by Pere Bohigas. Barcelona: Edicions 62, 1965. French translation, *Le Livre des Bêtes.* Translated by Armand Llinarès. Paris: Klinsieck, 1964.

Libre de l'orde de cavalleria. ORL 1:201–47.

Libre de meravelles. 4 vols. Edited by Salvador Galmés. Barcelona: Barcino, 1931–1934.

Libre de Sancta Maria. ORL 10:1–228.

Libre dels àngels. ORL 21:305–75.

Logica del Gatzel. Published as "La Lògica del Gazzali, posada en rims per En Ramon Lull," edited by Jordi Rubió i Balaguer. *Anuari de l'Institut d'Estudis Catalans* 5 (1913–1914): 311–54.

Logica nova. Published as *Die neue Logik—Logica nova*, edited by Charles Lohr. Hamburg: Felix Meiner, 1985.

Medicina de peccat. ORL 20:1–205.

Metaphysica nova et compendiosa. RLOL 6:10–51.

Mil proverbis. ORL 14:325–72.

Petitio ad Celestinum V papam. Ed. Mainz 2.

Petitio Raymundi in Concilio Generali (Sixth Distinction of the *Liber de ente* or *Liber de perseitate et finalitate Dei*). RLOL 8:239–45.

Phantasticus (Liber disputationis Petri et Raimundi). RLOL 16:11–30.

Proverbis d'ensenyament. ORL 14:373–89.

Proverbis de Ramon. ORL 14:1–324.

Quaestiones per artem demonstrativam solubiles. Ed. Mainz 4.

Regles introductòries. ORL 20:289–94.

Rethorica nova. Published as *Ramon Llull's New Rhetoric: Text and Translation of Llull's Rethorica nova*, edited by Mark D. Johnston. Davis, Calif.: Hermagoras Press, 1994.

Sermones contra errores Averrois. RLOL 7:245–62.

Sermones de operibus misericordiae. RLOL 15:455–70.

Lo sisè seny, lo qual apel.lam affatus. Published as "*Lo sisè seny, lo qual apel.lam affatus*, de Ramon Llull. Edició i estudi," edited by Josep Perarnau i Espelt. *Arxiu de Textos Catalans Antics* 2 (1983): 23–121.

Taula general. ORL 16:295–522.

Vita coetanea. Published as *Vida de Ramon Llull: Les fonts escrites i la iconografia coetànies*, edited by Miguel Batllori and J. N. Hillgarth. Barcelona: Associació de Bibliòfils de Barcelona, 1982.

Other Original Sources

Adelard of Bath. *De eodem et diverso.* Edited by Hans Willner. Beiträge zur Geschichte der Philosophie des Mittelalters, vol. 4, pt. 1. Munster: Aschendorff, 1903.

Alan of Lille. *Anticlaudianus.* Edited by R. Bossuat. Paris: J. Vrin, 1955.

―――. *Distinctiones dictionum theologicalium.* PL 210:685–1012.

―――. *De planctu naturae.* Edited by Nikolaus M. Häring. *Studi Medievali,* 3d ser., 19 (1978): 797–879.

―――. *Summa de arte praedicatoria.* PL 210:109–98.

Alberic of Montecassino. *Flores rhetorici.* Edited by D. M. Inguanez and H. M. Willard. Miscellanea Cassinese, vol. 14. Montecassino, Italy: Abbadia di Montecassino, 1938.

Albertano da Brescia. *Sermones quattuor.* Edited by Marta Ferrari. Brescia and Lonato: Fondazione "Ugo da Como," 1955.

―――. *Tractatus de arte loquendi et tacendi.* In *Della vita e delle opere di Brunetto Latini,* by Thor Sundby. Florence: Le Monier, 1884.

Albertus Magnus. *De anima.* In *Opera omnia.* Vol. 7, pt. 2. Munster: Aschendorff, 1968.

Alcher of Clairvaux (attrib.). *De spiritu et anima.* PL 40:779–832.

Alexander of Villadei. *Doctrinale.* Edited by Dietrich Reichling. Monumenta Germaniae Paedagogica, vol. 12. Berlin: A. Hofmann, 1893.

Alfarabi. *Alfarabi's Philosophy of Plato and Aristotle.* Rev. ed. Translated by Muhsin Mahdi. Ithaca, N.Y.: Cornell University Press, 1962.

―――. De ortu scientiarum. In *Alfarabi über den Ursprung der Wissenschaften (De ortu scientiarum),* by Clemens Baeumker. Beiträge zur Geschichte der Philosophie des Mittelalters, vol. 19, pt. 3. Munster: Aschendorff, 1916.

―――. *De scientiis.* Published as *Catálogo de las ciencias,* edited by Angel González Palencia. Madrid: CSIC, 1953.

―――. *Deux ouvrages inédits sur la réthorique.* Edited by J. Langhade and M. Grignaschi. Beirut: Dar El-Machreq, 1971.

Alfonso X the Wise, King of Castile. *Siete Partidas.* Madrid: Academia de la Historia, 1807.

Algazel. *Logic.* Published as "Logica Algazelis: Introduction and Critical Text," edited by Chales H. Lohr. *Traditio* 21 (1965): 223–90.

Alighieri, Dante. *De vulgari eloquentia.* Edited by A. Marigo. Florence: Le Monnier, 1957.

―――. *The Divine Comedy.* 6 vols. Edited and translated by Charles S. Singleton. Princeton, N.J.: Princeton University Press, 1970–1975.

―――. *Epistola ad Canem Grandem.* In *Dantis Alagherii Epistolae,* edited by Paget Toynbee. Oxford: Clarendon Press, 1920.

Amaneo Des Escás. *Ensenhamen del escudier.* In Manuel Milà y Fontanals, *De los trovadores en España,* edited by C. Martínez and F. R. Manrique. Vol. 2 in *Obras de Manuel Milà y Fontanals,* edited by Martín de Riquer. Barcelona: CSIC, 1966.

Ambrose. *Commentarium in epistolam B. Pauli ad Corinthos primam.* PL 17:193–290.

―――. *De officiis ministrorum.* PL 16:25–194.

Anselm of Canterbury. *Cur Deus Homo. De veritate. Monologion.* In *Opera omnia,* 2 vols., edited by Franciscus S. Schmitt. Edinburgh: T. Nelson, 1946.

Arbor amoris der Minnebaum: Ein Pseudo-Bonaventura-Traktat herausgegeben nach lateinischen und deutschen Handschriften des XIV. und XV. Jahrhunderts.

Edited by Urs Kamber. Philologische Studien und Quellen, vol. 20. Berlin: Erich Schmidt, 1964.

Aristotle. *Analytica posteriora. De anima. Categoriae. Ethica. De generatione et corruptione. Metaphysica. Physica. Poetica. De sensu et sensibilibus. De sophisticis elenchis. Topica.* In *The Complete Works of Aristotle: The Revised Oxford Translation*, 2 vols., edited by Jonathan Barnes. Princeton, N.J.: Princeton University Press, 1984. (Cited by book, chapter, and Bekker pages.)

Augustine, Aurelius. *Confessiones.* Edited by M. Skutella, revised by H. Juergens and W. Schaub. Stuttgart: B. G. Teubner, 1981.

———. *De civitate Dei.* 5th ed. Edited by A. Kalb and B. Dombart. Stuttgart: B. G. Teubner, 1981.

———. *De doctrina christiana.* Edited by William Green. Corpus Scriptorum Ecclesiasticorum Latinorum, vol. 80. Vienna: Hoelder-Pichter-Tempsky, 1963.

———. *De Genesi ad litteram.* PL 34:245–486.

———. *De Genesi liber imperfectus.* PL 34:219–45.

———. *De magistro.* Edited by G. Weigel. Corpus Scriptorum Ecclesiasticorum Latinorum, vol. 77. Vienna: Hoelder-Pichter-Tempsky, 1961.

———. *De musica.* PL 32:1081–1194.

———. *De ordine.* Edited by P. Knoll, Corpus Scriptorum Ecclesiasticorum Latinorum, vol. 63. Vienna: Hoelder-Pichter-Tempsky, 1922.

———. *De trinitate.* Edited by W. J. Mountain. Corpus Christianorum, Series Latina, 50–50A. Turnhout, Belgium: Brepols: 1968.

———. *Soliloquia.* PL 32:869–904.

———. (attrib.). *De dialectica.* Edited by B. Darrell Jackson. Dordrecht, Netherlands: D. Reidel, 1975.

———. (attrib.). *De rhetorica.* In *Rhetores latini minores*, edited by Karl Halm. Leipzig: B. G. Teubner, 1863.

Averroes. *Three short commentaries on Aristotle's "Topics," "Rhetoric," and "Poetics."* Translated and edited by Charles E. Butterworth. Albany: State University of New York Press, 1977.

Avicenna. *Liber de anima seu sextus de naturalibus, IV–V.* Ed. Simone van Riet. Leiden: E. J. Brill, 1968.

Bacon, Roger. *De signis.* Published as "An Unedited Part of Roger Bacon's 'Opus maius': 'De signis,'" edited by K. M. Fredborg. *Traditio* 34 (1978): 75–136.

Baldwin. *Liber dictaminum.* Published as "Il *Liber Dictaminum* de Baldwinus," edited by S. Durzsa. *Quadrivium* 13, no. 2 (1972): 5–41.

Bartolomeo da San Concordio. *Di studio.* In Scrittori di religione, vol. 1: *Prosatori minori del Trecento*, edited by Giuseppe di Luca. Milan and Naples: R. Ricciardi, 1954.

Bernardus Silvestris. *De mundi universitate (Cosmographia).* Edited by Carl S. Barach and Johann Wrobel. Bibliotheca Philosophorum Mediae Aetatis, vol. 1. Innsbruch: Wagner, 1876.

Bernold of Kaisersheim. *Summula dictaminis.* In *Briefsteller und formelbücher des eilften bis vierzehnten jahrhunderts*, edited by Ludwig Rockinger. Munich, 1863. Reprint, New York: Burt Franklin, 1961.

Biblia sacra cum glossis, interlineari & ordinaria, Nicolai Lyrani Postilla & Moralitatibus, Burgensis Additionibus, & Thoringi Replicis. Lyons: Anthoine Vincent and Gaspar Trechsel, 1545.

Bocados de Oro. Edited by Mechthild Crombach. Bonn: Romanisches Seminar der Universität Bonn, 1971.

Boethius. *De differentiis topicis. In "De interpretatione" editio secunda. Topicorum Aristotelis interpretatio.* PL 64:1173–217; 393–638; 909–1008.

———. *In "Isagogen" Porphyrii commentorum editio prima.* Edited by Samuel Brandt as *In "Isagogen" Prophyrii commenta.* Corpus Scriptorum Ecclesiasticorum Latinorum, vol. 48. Vienna: Tempsky, 1906.

Bonaventure, Saint. *Breviloquium. De reductione artium ad theologiam. Collationes in Hexaëmeron.* In *Opera omnia.* Vol. 5 Quaracchi: Collegium S. Bonaventurae, 1891.

———. *Determinationes quaestionum circa Regulam Fratrum Minorum.* In *Opera omnia.* Vol. 8. Quaracchi: Collegium S. Bonaventurae, 1898.

Boncompagno of Siena. *Rhetorica novissima.* Edited by Augusto Gaudenzi. Bibliotheca Iuridica Medii Aevi, Scripta anecdota glossatorum, vol. 2. Bologna: Angelo Gandolpho, 1892.

Bozóky, Edina, ed. *Le livre secret des Cathares* Interrogatio Iohannis: *Apocryphe d'origine bogomile.* Paris: Beauchesne, 1980.

Calila e Dymna. In *Escritores en prosa anteriores al siglo XV*, edited by Pascual de Gayangos. Biblioteca de Autores Españoles, vol. 51. Madrid: Real Academia Española, 1952.

Cassiodorus Senator. *Institutiones.* Edited by R.A.B. Mynors. Oxford: Clarendon Press, 1937.

Cavalca, Domenico. *Frutti della lingua.* Venice: Contrada di Santa Maria Formosa al segno della Speranza, 1563.

———. *Pungi lingua.* Venice: Marchio Sessa, 1540.

Cicero. *De amicitia.* In *De senectute. De amicitia. De divinatione.* Edited by W. A. Falconer. Loeb Classical Library, vol. 154. Cambridge, Mass.: Harvard University Press, 1971.

———. *De inventione. Topica.* Edited by H. M. Hubbell. Loeb Classical Library, vol. 386. Cambridge, Mass.: Harvard University Press, 1976.

———. *De officiis.* Edited by C. Atzert. *De virtutibus.* Edited by W. Ax. 4th ed. Leipzig: B. G. Teubner, 1963.

———. *De oratore.* Edited by K. F. Kumaniecki. Leipzig: B. G. Teubner, 1969.

Compendium speculi charitatis. PL 195:621–58.

Costa ben Luca. *De animae et spiritus discrimine.* Edited by Carl S. Barach. Bibliotheca Philosophorum Mediae Aetatis, vol. 2. Innsbruch: Wagner, 1878.

Cuéllar, Pedro de. *Catecismo.* In *Religión y sociedad medieval: El catecismo de Pedro de Cuéllar (1325)*, edited by José Luis Martín Rodríguez and Antonio Linaje Conde. Valladolid: Consejería de Cultura y Bienestar Social, 1987.

De disciplina scholarium. Edited by Olga Weijers. Leiden: E. J. Brill, 1976.

De verborum copia. Published as "Un apocryphe de Sénèque mal-connu: Le *De verborum copia*," edited by Jeannine Fohlen. *Mediaeval Studies* 42 (1980): 139–211.

Denifle, Heinrich, and Émile Châtelain, ed. *Chartularium universitatis Parisiensis*, vols. 1–2. Paris: Fr. Delalain, 1889–1891.

Disticha Catonis. Published as *The Distichs of Cato*, translated and edited by W. J. Chase. University of Wisconsin Studies in Social Sciences and History, vol. 7. Madison: University of Wisconsin, 1922.

Donatus. *Ars grammatica*. In *Grammatici latini*, edited by Heinrich Keil. Vol. 4. Leipzig: B. G. Teubner, 1855.

Dubois, Pierre. *De recuperatione terrae sanctae*. Edited by Ch.-V. Langlois. Paris: A. Picard, 1891.

Dybinus, Nicolaus. *Declaracio oracionis de beata Dorothea*. Edited by Samuel Jaffe. Wiesbaden, Germany: F. Steiner, 1974.

Eiximenis, Francesc. *Ars praedicandi*. Published as "L'*Ars praedicandi* de Francesc Eiximenis," edited by P. Martí de Barcelona. *Analecta Sacra Tarraconensia* 12 (1936): 301–40.

Étienne de Bourbon. *Tractatus de diversis materiis praedicabilibus*. In *Anecdotes historiques, légendes et apologues*, edited by Albert Lecoy de la Marche. Paris: Société de l'Histoire de France, 1877.

Facetus. In *Der deutsche Facetus*, edited by Carl Schroeder. Palaestra, vol. 86. Berlin: Mayer and Müller, 1911.

Ferrer, Vicent, Saint. *Quaresma de s. Vicent Ferrer predicada a Valencia l'any 1413*. Barcelona: Institució Patxot, 1927.

Fiorentino da Vignano, Giovanni. *Flore de parlare. [Somma d'arengare.]* In Matteo dei Libri, *Arringhe*, edited by Eleanora Vincenti. Milan: R. Ricciardi, 1974.

Flores de filosofía. In *Dos obras didácticas y dos leyendas sacadas de manuscritos de la Biblioteca del Escorial*, edited by Herman Knust. Madrid: Sociedad de Bibliófilos Españoles, 1878.

Formularius de modo prosandi. In *Briefsteller und formelbücher des eilften bis vierzehnten jahrhunderts*, edited by Ludwig Rockinger. Munich, 1863. Reprint, New York: Burt Franklin, 1961.

Fortunatianus, C. Chirius. *Ars rhetorica*. In *Rhetores latini minores*, edited by Karl Halm. Leipzig: B. G. Teubner, 1863.

Francesco da Barberino. *I Documenti d'amore*. Edited by Francesco Egidi. Rome: La Società, 1905.

Francis of Assisi. *Regula bullata*. In *Opuscula Sancti Patris Francisci Assisiensis*, edited by Caietanus Esser, O.F.M. Quaracchi, Italy: Collegium S. Bonaventurae, 1978.

Fulgentius. *Expositio virgilianae continentiae secundum philosophos moralis*. In *Opera*, edited by R. Helm. Leipzig: B. G. Teubner, 1898.

Geoffrey of Vinsauf. *Poetria nova. Documentum de arte versificandi*. In *Les arts poétiques du XIIe et du XIIIe siècle*, edited by Edmond Faral. Paris: E. Champion, 1923.

Géraud du Pescher. *Ars faciendi sermones*. Published as "L'*Ars faciendi sermones* de Géraud du Pescher," edited by Ferdinand M. Delormé. *Antonianum* 19 (1944): 169–98.

Gesta romanorum. Edited by H. Oesterley. Berlin: Weidmann, 1872.

Giles of Rome. *De differentia rhetoricae, ethicae et politicae.* Published as "The 'De differentia Rhetoricae, Ethicae et Politicae' of Aegidius Romanus," edited by Gerardo Bruni. *New Scholasticism* 6 (1932): 1–18.

———. *De regimine principum.* Venice: Bernardinus Vercelensus, 1502.

Glossa ordinaria (attrib. Walafrid Strabo). PL 113 and 114:9–752.

Godefroy of St. Victor. *Fons philosophiae.* Edited by Pierre Michaud-Quantin. Analecta mediaevalia Namurcensia, vol. 8. Namur, Belgium: Godenne, 1956.

———. *The Fountain of Philosophy: A Translation of the Twelfth-Century* Fons philosophiae *of Godfrey of Saint Victor.* Translated by Edward A. Synan. Toronto: Pontifical Institute of Medieval Studies, 1972.

Gregory the Great. *Regula pastoralis.* PL 77:12–128.

Grosseteste, Robert. *De artibus liberalibus.* In *Die philosophischen Werke des Robert Grosseteste,* edited by L. Baur. Beiträge zur Geschichte der Philosophie des Mittelalters, vol. 9. Munster: Aschendorff, 1912.

Guitmund of Aversa. *De corporis et sanguinis Christi veritate in eucharistia.* PL 149:1427–94.

Gundissalinus, Dominicus. *De divisione philosophiae.* Edited by L. Baur. Beiträge zur Geschichte der Philosophie des Mittelaters, vol. 4, pt. 2–3. Munster: Aschendorff, 1903.

Hervieux, Léopold, ed. *Les fabulistes latins.* 5 vols. Paris: Firmin-Didot, 1893–1899.

Hildebert of Tours. *Libellus de quattuor virtutibus vitae honestae.* PL 171:1055–64.

Hildegard of Bingen. *Scivias.* 2 vols. Edited by Adelgundis Führkötter and Angela Carlevaris. Corpus Christianorum, Continuatio Mediaevalis, vols. 43–43A. Turnhout, Belgium: Brepols, 1978.

Horace, *Ars poetica.* In *Epistles, Book II and Epistle to the Pisones (Ars poetica),* edited by N. Rudd. Cambridge: Cambridge University Press, 1989.

Hugh of St. Victor. *De sacramentis christianae fidei.* PL 176:173–618.

———. *Didascalicon de studio legendi.* Edited by Charles H. Buttimer. Washington, D.C.: Catholic University of America Press, 1939.

———. *Expositio in Hierarchiam coelestem.* PL 175:923–1154.

Humbert of Romans. *De eruditione praedicatorum.* In *Opera de vita regulari,* edited by Joachim-Joseph Berthier. Rome: A. Befani, 1888.

Interrogatio Iohannis. See Bozóky, Edina, ed.

Isidore of Seville. *Etymologiarum sive originum libri XX.* 2 vols. Edited W. M. Lindsay. Oxford: Clarendon Press, 1911.

———. (attrib.). *Sententiarum libri tres.* PL 83:537–738.

Isocrates. *Ad Demonicum.* In *Isocrates,* 3 vols., edited by George Norlin and Larue Van Hook. London: W. Heinemann, 1928–1945.

Jacques de Vitry. *Sermones vulgares. The Exempla or Illustrative Stories from the* Sermones vulgares (a partial version of the whole), edited by Thomas F. Crane. Publications of the Folklore Society, vol. 16. London: D. Nutt, 1890.

Jean de la Rochelle. *Processus negociandi themata sermonum.* Published as "Processus negociandi themata sermonum di Giovanni della Rochelle," edited by Gustavo Cantini. *Antonianum* 26 (1951): 247–70.

John of Garland. *Parisiana poetria*. Edited by Traugott Lawler. New Haven, Conn.: Yale University Press, 1974.

John of Joinville. *Histoire de Saint Louis*. In *Credo et Lettre a Louis X*, edited by Natalis de Wailly. Paris: Firmin Didot, 1874.

Juan Manuel. *El Conde Lucanor*. Edited by José Manuel Blecua. Madrid: Castalia, 1969.

Lanfranc of Canterbury. *De corpore et sanguine Domini*. PL 150:406–42.

Latini, Brunetto. *Li Livres dou Tresor*. Edited by Francis Carmody. University of California Publications in Modern Philology, vol. 22. Berkeley and Los Angeles: University of California Press, 1948.

———. *Tesoretto*. Edited by Julia Bolton Holloway. New York: Garland, 1981.

Legenda Trium Sociorum. Published as "Legenda tria Sociorum: Édition critique," edited by Théophile Desbonnets. *Archivum Franciscanum Historicum* 67 (1974): 38–144.

Liber de causis. Edited by Adriaan Pattin. Louvain: Tijdschrift voor Filosofie, 1967.

Liber exemplorum. Published as *Liber exemplorum ad usum praedicantium*, edited by A. G. Little. Aberdeen: University of Aberdeen, 1908.

Liber sex principiorum. In *Porphyrii Isagoge translatio Boethii et Anonymi Fragmentum vulgo vocatum "Liber sex principiorum,"* edited by Laurentius Minio-Pauluello and Bernard G. Dod. Aristoteles Latinus, vol. 2, pt. 6–7. Bruges: Desclée de Brouwer, 1966.

Libro de los cien capítulos. Edited by Agapito Rey. Bloomington: Indiana University Press, 1966.

Marbodus. *Liber de gemmis*. PL 171:1735–80.

Marius Victorinus. *De diffinitione*. In Boethius, *Opera omnia*. PL 64:891–910.

Matteo dei Libri da Bologna. *Arringhe*. Edited by Eleonora Vincenti. Milan: R. Ricciardi, 1974.

———. *Dicerie volgari*. Edited by Luigi Chiapelli. Pistoia: G. Flori, 1900.

Matthew of Vendome. *Ars versificatoria*. In *Les arts poétiques du XIIe et du XIIIe siècle*, edited by Edmond Faral. Paris: E. Champion, 1923.

Minnis, Alastair J., A. B. Scott, with David Wallace, eds. *Medieval Literary Theory and Criticism c. 1100–c. 1375: The Commentary Tradition*. Rev. ed. Oxford: Clarendon Press, 1991.

Molinier, Guilhem. *Leys d'amors*. Edited by Joseph Anglade. Bibliothèque Méridionale, vols. 17–20. Toulouse: E. Privat. 1919–1920.

Nicholas of Lyre. *Postilla super totam Bibliam*. In *Biblia sacra cum glossis, interlineari & ordinaria, Nicolai Lyrani Postilla & Moralitatibus, Burgensis Additionibus, & Thoringi Replicis*. Lyons: Anthoine Vincent and Gaspar Trechsel, 1545.

Odo of Cheriton. *Fabulae*. In *Les Fabulistes Latins*, 5 vols., edited by Léopold Hervieux. Paris: Firmin-Didot, 1893–1899.

Peter Damian. *Epistolarum libri octo*. PL 144:205–498.

———. *Liber qui appelatur Dominus vobiscum, ad Leonem eremitam*. PL 145:231–52.

Peter of Spain. *Summule logicales*. Edited by Lambertus M. De Rijk. Assen, Netherlands: Van Gorcum, 1972.

Peter the Chanter. *Verbum abbreviatum*. PL 205:23–370.

Philip of Ferrara. *Liber de introductione loquendi (Liber mensalis)*. Vatican MS Pal. lat. 960, f. 71ra–120vb.

Priscian. *Institutiones grammaticae*. Edited by Martin Hertz. In *Grammatici latini*, edited by H. Keil, vols. 2–3. Leipzig: B. G. Teubner, 1855–1859.

Pseudo-Dionysius. *De divinis nominibus*. Versio Johannis Scoti. PL 122: 1111–72.

———. *De ecclesiastica hierarchia*. Versio Johannis Scoti. PL 122: 1069–112.

Quintilian. *Institutio oratoria*. Edited by H. E. Butler. London: Heinemann, 1920–1922.

Rabanus Maurus (attrib.). *Allegoriae in Universam Scripturam*. PL 112:849–1088.

Raoul de Houdenc. *Le roman des ailes*. Published as *Li romans des eles*, edited by Auguste Scheler. Brussels: C. Muquardt, 1868.

Rationes dictandi. In *Briefsteller und formelbücher des eilften bis vierzehnten jahrhunderts*, edited by Ludwig Rockinger. Munich, 1863. Reprint, New York: Burt Franklin, 1961.

Recull de eximplis e miracles, gestes e faules e altres ligendes ordenades per A-B-C. 2 vols. Edited by Mariano Aguiló y Fuster. Barcelona: Alvar Verdaguer, 1881.

Rhetorica ad Herennium. Edited by Harry Caplan. Loeb Classical Library, vol. 403. Cambridge, Mass.: Harvard University Press, 1954.

Richard of St. Victor. *Benjamin maior*. PL 196:63–202.

Richard of Thetford. *Ars dilatandi sermones*. Printed as part 3 of *Ars concionandi* in Bonaventure, *Opera omnia*. Vol. 9 Quaracchi: Collegium S. Bonaventurae, 1901.

Robert of Basevorn. *Forma praedicandi*. In *Artes praedicandi: Contribution à l'histoire de la rhétorique au Moyen Age*, by Th. M. Charland. Paris: J. Vrin/Ottowa: Institut d'Études Médiévales. 1936.

Rockinger, Ludwig. *Briefsteller und formelbücher des eilften bis vierzehnten jahrhunderts*. Munich, 1863. Reprint, New York: Burt Franklin, 1961.

Secretum secretorum. In *Aristotelis philosophorum maximi secretum secretorum ad Alexandrum. . . .* Bologna: Impensis Benedicti Hectoris, 1501.

Seneca. *De beneficiis*. In *Moral Essays*, 3 vols., edited by John W. Basore. London: W. Heinemann, 1928–1935.

———. *Epistulae Morales*. 3 vols. Edited by Richard M. Gummere. London: W. Heinemann, 1925.

"Stans puer ad mensam." In Sir Humphrey Gilbert, *Queene Elizabethes Achademy. A Booke of Precedence. The Ordering of a funerall . . .* , edited by F. J. Furnivall. Early English Text Society, extra series, vol. 8. London: N. Trübner, 1869.

Sulpitius Victor. *Institutiones Oratoriae*. In *Rhetores latini minores*, edited by Karl Halm. Leipzig: B. G. Teubner, 1863.

Summa sophisticorum elenchorum. In *Logica modernorum: A Contribution to the History of Early Terminist Logic*, 2 vols., edited by L. M. De Rilk. Assen, Netherlands: Van Gorcum, 1962–1967.

Tabula exemplorum secundum ordinem alphabeti. Edited by J. Thomas Welter. Paris: Occitania, 1926.

Terramagnino da Pisa. *Doctrina d'Acort*. In *The* Razos de trobar *of Raimon Vidal and Associated Texts*, edited by J. H. Marshall. London: Oxford University Press, 1972.

Thomas Aquinas. *De veritate*. In *Quaestiones Disputatae*. Vol. 3. Turin and Rome: Marietti, 1927.

———. *The Division and Methods of the Sciences: Questions V and VI of His Commentary on the* De trinitate *of Boethius*. Translated and edited by Armand Maurer. Toronto: Pontifical Institute of Medieval Studies, 1963.

———. *In Aristotelis libros "Peri hermeneias" et "Posteriorum analyticorum."* Edited by Raimondo M. Spiazzi. Turin and Rome: Marietti, 1955.

———. *Summa contra gentiles*. Editio Leonina manualis. Rome: Libreria Vaticana, 1934.

———. *Summa theologiae*. Blackfriars Edition. 60 vols. New York: McGraw-Hill/London: Eyre and Spottiswoode, 1964–1976.

Thomas of Celano. *Vita prima Sancti Francisci. Vita secunda Sancti Francisci.* In *Legendae Sancti Francisci Assisiensis saeculis XIII et XIV conscriptae*, Analecta Franciscana, vol. 10. Quaracchi: Collegium S. Bonaventurae, 1926–1941.

Thomas of Erfurt. *Grammatica speculativa*. Edited by Geoffrey L. Bursill-Hall. London: Longman, 1972.

Torre y del Cerro, Antonio de la. *Documentos para la historia de la Universidad de Barcelona*. Barcelona: Universidad de Barcelona, 1971.

Vidal, Ramon. *Razos de trobar*. In *The* Razos de trobar *of Raimon Vidal and Associated Texts*, edited by J. H. Marshall. London: Oxford University Press, 1972.

Villanueva, Jaime, ed. "Acta disputationis R. Moysis Gerundensis cum Fr. Paulo Christiani, O.P." In *Viage literario a las iglesias de España*. Vol. 13. Madrid: Real Academia de la Historia, 1850.

Vincent of Beauvais. *Speculum doctrinale. Speculum morale (attrib.). Speculum naturale*. In *Bibliotheca mundi*, vols. 1–3. Douay, 1624. Reprint, Graz: Akademische Druck-u.-Verlagsanstalt, 1964–1965.

Vives, Juan Luis. *De ratione dicendi*. In *Opera omnia*. Vol. 2. Valencia, 1782. Reprint, London: Gregg, 1964.

Waleys, Thomas. *De modo componendi sermones*. In *Artes praedicandi: Contribution à l'histoire de la rhétorique au Moyen Age*, by Th. M. Charlend. Paris: J.Vrin/Ottawa: Institut d'Études Médiévales, 1936

William of Auvergne (attrib.). *De faciebus*. In "Un manuel de prédication médiévale," by A. De Poorter. *Revue Néo-Scholastique de Philosophie* 25 (1923): 192–209.

William of Conches (attrib.). *Moralium dogma philosophorum*. Published as *Das Moralium dogma philosophorum des Guillaume de Conches: Lateinisch, altfranzösisch und mittelniederfränkisch*, edited by John Holmberg. Paris: H. Champion, 1929.

William of Ockham. *Summa logicae*. Edited by Philotheus Boehner, Gedeon Gál, and Stephen Brown. St. Bonaventure, N.Y.: Franciscan Institute, 1974.

William of Sherwood. *Introductiones in logicam*. Published as *Introduction to Logic*, translated by Norman Kretzmann. Minneapolis: University of Minnesota Press, 1966.

232 *Works Cited*

William of Tournai. *De instructione puerorum.* Edited by James A. Corbett. Notre Dame, Ind.: University of Notre Dame, Mediaeval Institute, 1955.

Woods, Marjorie, ed. *An Early Commentary on the* Poetria nova *of Geoffrey of Vinsauf.* New York: Garland, 1985.

Secondary Studies

Abul Quasem, Muhammed. *The Ethics of al-Ghazali: A Composite Ethics in Islam.* Petaling Jaya, Malaysia: Universiti Kebangsaan Malaysia, 1975.

Aers, David. "Rewriting the Middle Ages: Some Suggestions." *Journal of Medieval and Renaissance Studies* 18 (1988): 221–40.

Ageno, Franca. "Premessa a un repertorio di frasi proverbiali." *Romance Philology* 13 (1960): 242–64.

———. "Tradizione favolistica e novellistica nella fraseologia proverbiale." *Lettere Italiane* 8 (1956): 351–84.

Agrimi, Jole, and Chiara Crisciani. *Medicina del corpo e medicina dell'anima: Note sul sapere del medico fino all'inizio del secolo XIII.* Milan: Episteme. 1978.

Alford, John A. "The Grammatical Metaphor: A Survey of Its Use in the Middle Ages." *Speculum* 57 (1982): 728–60.

———. "Literature and Law in Medieval England." *PMLA* 92 (1977): 941–51.

Allard, Guy-H. "La technique de la 'reductio,' chez Bonaventure." In *S. Bonaventura, 1274–1974,* edited by Jacques Guy Bougerol et al., vol. 2. Grottaferrata, Italy: Collegio S. Bonaventura, 1973.

Allen, Don Cameron. *Legend of Noah: Renaissance Rationalism in Art, Science, and Letters.* Urbana: University of Illinois Press, 1963.

Allen, Judson Boyce. *The Ethical Poetic of the Later Middle Ages: A Decorum of Convenient Distinction.* Toronto: University of Toronto Press, 1982.

———. *The Friar as Critic: Literary Attitudes in the Later Middle Ages.* Nashville, Tenn. Vanderbilt University Press, 1971.

Allen, Rosamund. "'Singular Lufe': Richard Rolle and the Grammar of Spiritual Ascent." In *The Medieval Mystical Tradition in England,* Papers Read at Dartington Hall, July 1984, edited by Marion Glasscoe. Cambridge: D. S. Brewer, 1984.

Allers, Rudolf. "Microcosmus from Anaximandros to Paracelsus." *Traditio* 2 (1944): 319–407.

Almazán, Vincent. "L'exemplum chez Vincent Ferrier." *Romanische Forschungen* 79 (1967): 288–332.

Amos, Thomas, et al., eds. *De l'homélie au sermon: Histoire de la prédication médiévale.* Louvain: Université Catholique de Louvain, 1993.

Amos, Thomas L., Eugene A. Green, and Beverly M. Kienzle, eds. *De ore domini: Preacher and Word in the Middle Ages.* Studies in Medieval Culture, no. 27. Kalamazoo, Mich.: Medieval Institute Publications, 1989.

Amsler, Mark. *Etymology and Grammatical Discourse in Late Antiquity and the Early Middle Ages.* Amsterdam: John Benjamins, 1989.

Amsterdam, Balduinus ab. "Tres sermones inediti Ioannis de Rupella in honorem S. Antonii Patavini." *Collectanea franciscana* 28 (1958): 32–58.

Aos Braco, Celestino. "La imaginación en el sistema de Ramon Llull." *Estudios Lulianos* 23 (1979): 155–83.

Apel, Karl Otto. *L'idea di lingua nella tradizione dell'umanesimo da Dante a Vico.* Translated by Luciano Tosti. Bologna: Il Mulino, 1975.

Arco Garay, Ricardo del. "Un estudio de artes en Barbastro en el siglo XIII." *Estudios de Edad Media de la Corona de Aragón* 3 (1947–48): 481–83.

Arts Libéraux et Philosophie au Moyen Age. Actes du Quatrième Congrès International de Philosophie Médiévale. Montreal: Institut d'Études Médiévales/ Paris: J. Vrin, 1969.

Artus, Walter W. "Man's Cosmic Ties within the Thought of Ramon Llull." *Estudios Lulianos* 25 (1981–1983): 25–46.

———. "Ramon Llull, the Metaphysician." *Antonianum* 56 (1981): 715–49.

Auerbach, Erich. "Figura." In *Scenes from the Drama of European Literature.* Minneapolis: University of Minnesota Press, 1984.

———. "Sermo Humilis." In *Lenguaje literario y público en la Baja Latinidad y en la Edad Media*, translated by Luis López Molina. Barcelona: Seix Barral, 1969.

Badia, Lola. "A propòsit de Ramon Llull i la gramàtica." *Estudis de Llengua i Literatura Catalanes* 18 (1989): 157–82.

———. "L'aportació de Ramon Llull a la literatura en llengua d'oc." In *Actes del Vuitè Col.loqui Internacional de Llengua i Literatura Catalanes.* Montserrat, Spain: Publicacions de l'Abadia, 1990.

———. "Et hoc patet per regulam C." *Quaderns Crema* 7 (1983): 79–98.

———. "No cal que tragats exempli dels romans. *Estudis de Llengua i Literatura Catalanes* 3 (1981): 87–94.

———. "Ramon Llull i la predicació." *Llengua i Literatura* 3 (1988–1989): 563–75.

———. "Ramon Llull i la tradició literària." *Estudios Lulianos* 28 (1988) 121–38.

Badia i Margarit, Antoni, and Francesc de B. Moll. "La llengua de Ramon Llull." In Ramon Llull, *Obres essencials*, edited by Miquel Batllori et al. Vol. 2. Barcelona: Selecta, 1960.

Baratin, Marc, and Françoise Desbordes. "Sémiologie et métalinguistique chez Saint Augustin." In *Signification et référence dans l'antiquité et au Moyen age. Languages* 65 (March 1982): 75–89.

———, eds. *Signification et référence dans l'antiquité et au moyen age. Languages* 65 (March 1982).

Barceló, Miquel. "Ramon Llull i el seu viatge banal a l'Islam." *L'Avenç* 61 (1983): 71–75.

Barcelona, P. Martíde. "*L'Ars praedicandi* de Francese Eiximenis." *Analecta Sacra Tarraconensia* 12 (1936): 301–40.

Bataillon, Louis J. "Approaches to the Study of Medieval Sermons." *Leeds Studies in English*, n.s., 11 (1980): 19–35.

———. "De la *lectio* à la *praedicatio*: Commentaires bibliques et sermons au XIIIe siècle." *Revue des Sciences philosophiques et théologiques* 70 (1986): 559–75.

———. "Early Scholastic and Mendicant Preaching as Exegesis of Scripture." In *Ad litteram: Authoritative Texts and Their Medieval Readers*, edited by Mark D.

Jordan and Kent Emery, Jr. Notre Dame, Ind.: University of Notre Dame Press, 1992.

———. "Les images dans les sermons du XIIIe siècle." *Freiburger Zeitschrift für Philosophie und Theologie* 37 (1990): 327–95.

———. "Les instruments de travail des prédicateurs au XIIIe siècle." In *Culture et travail intellectuel dans l'occident médiévale*, edited by Geneviève Hasenohr and Jean Longère. Paris: CNRS, 1981.

———. "Intermédiaires entre les traités de morale et les sermons, les *distinctiones* bibliques alphabétiques." In *Les genres littéraires dans les sources théologiques et philosophiques médiévales: Définition, critique et exploitation.* Louvain: Institut d'Études Médiévales, 1982.

———. *La prédication au XIIIe siècle en France et Italie.* Brookfield, Vt.: Ashgate Variorum, 1993.

———. "Sermons rédigés sermons réportés (XIIIe siècle)." *Medioevo e rinascimento* 3 (1989): 69–86.

———. "*Similitudines* et *exempla* dans les sermons du XIIIe siècle." In *The Bible in the Medieval World: Essays in Memory of Beryl Smalley*, edited by Katherine Walsh and Diana Wood. Oxford: Blackwell/Ecclesiastical History Society, 1985.

Batany, Jean. *Approches langagières de la société médiévale.* Caen, France: Paradigme, 1992.

Batllori, Miquel. "Relíquies manuscrites del lul.lisme italià." *Analecta Sacra Tarraconensia* 11 (1935): 129–41.

Batllori, Miquel, and J. N. Hillgarth, eds. *Vida de Ramon Llull: Les fonts escrites i la iconografia coetànies.* Barcelona: Associació de Bibliòfils de Barcelona, 1982.

Bäuml, Franz H. "Varieties and Consequences of Medieval Literacy and Illiteracy." *Speculum* 55 (1980): 237–65.

Bennett, R. F. *The Early Dominicans.* Cambridge: Cambridge University Press, 1937.

Bériou, Nicole. "L'art de convaincre dans la prédication de Ranulphe d'Homblières." In *Faire croire: Modalités, de la diffusion et de la réception des messages religieux du XIIe au XVe siècle.* Collection de l'Ecole Française de Rome, no. 51. Rome: Ecole Française de Rome, 1981.

———. "Femmes et prédicateurs: La transmission de la foi aux XIIe et XIIIe siècles." In *La religion de ma mère: Les femmes et la transmission de la foi*, edited by Jean Delumeau. Paris: Cerf, 1992.

———. "La prédication au béguinage de Paris pendant l'année liturgique 1272–1273." *Recherches Augustiniennes* 13 (1978): 105–229.

———. "Saint François, premier prophète de son ordre, dans les sermons du XIIIe siècle." *Mélanges de l'École Française de Rome, Moyen Age et Temps Modernes* 102 (1990): 535–56.

Berlioz, Jacques. "La mémoire du prédicateur: Recherches sur la mémorisation des récits exemplaires (XIIIe–XVe siècles)." In *Temps, mémoire, tradition au Moyen Age: Actes du XIIIe Congrès de la Societé des Historiens Médiévistes de l'En-*

seignement Supérieur, edited by Bernard Guillemain. Aix-en-Provence: Publications de l'Université de Provence, 1983.

––––––. "Le récit efficace: L'exemplum au service de la prédication (XIII–XV siècles)" *Mélanges de l'École Française de Rome, Moyen Age et Temps Modernes* 90 (1980): 113–46.

Berlioz, Jacques, and Marie Anne Polo de Beaulieu, eds. *Les exempla médiévaux: Introduction à la recherche, suivie des tables critiques de l'*Index exemplorum *de Frederic C. Tubach*. Carcassone, France: GARAE/Hesiode, 1992.

Berube, Camille, and Servus Gieben. "Guibert de Tournai et Robert Grosseteste: Sources inconnues de la doctrine de l'illumination." In *S. Bonaventura 1274–1974*, edited by Jacques Guy Bougerol et al. Vol. 2. Grottaferrata, Italy: Collegio S. Bonaventura, 1973.

Bétérous, Paule. "Ramon Llull et le renouvellement du thème des miracles mariaux au XIIe siècle." *Cultura neolatina* 38 (1978): 37–47.

Biglieri, Aníbal A. *Hacia una poética del relato didáctico: ocho estudios sobre* El Conde Lucanor. University of North Carolina Studies in Romance Languages and Literatures, no. 233. Chapel Hill: University of North Carolina Press, 1989.

Bloch, R. Howard. *Etymologies and Genealogies: A Literary Anthropology of the French Middle Ages*. Chicago: University of Chicago Press, 1983.

Bloomfield, Morton. *Piers Plowman as a Fourteenth Century Apocalypse*. New Brunswick, N.J.: Rutgers University Press, 1961.

––––––. *The Seven Deadly Sins: An Introduction to the History of a Religious Concept, with Special Reference to Medieval English Literature*. East Lansing: Michigan State University Press, 1952.

Bofarull i Sans, Francesc. "El testamento de Ramón Lull y la Escuela Luliana en Barcelona." *Memorias de la Real Academia de Buenas Letras de Barcelona* 5 (1896): 435–79.

Bolton, Brenda. "Innocent III's Treatment of the *Humiliati*." In *Popular Belief and Practice*, Studies in Church History, no. 8, edited by G. J. Cuming and Derek Baker. Cambridge: Cambridge University Press, 1972.

Bonafede, Giulio. "La condanna di Stefano Tempier e la 'Declaratio' di Raimondo Lullo." *Estudios Lulianos* 4 (1960): 21–44.

Bonner, Anthony. "L'aprenentatge intel.lectual de Ramon Llull." In *Studia in honorem prof. M. de Riquer*, edited by Carlos Alvar et al. Vol. 2. Barcelona: Quaderns Crema, 1987.

––––––. "Les arts de Llull com a paradigmes cientìfics." *L'avenç* 64 (1983): 758–63.

––––––. "Ramon Llull and the Dominicans." *Catalan Review* 4 (1990): 377–92.

––––––, tr. *Selected Works of Ramon Llull*. Princeton, N.J.: Princeton University Press, 1985.

Bonner, Anthony, and Lola Badia. *Ramon Llull: Vida, pensament i obra literària*. Barcelona: Empúries, 1988.

Bonner, Stanley F. *Education in Ancient Rome*. Berkeley and Los Angeles: University of California Press, 1977.

Bonnes, Jean-Paul. "Un des plus grands prédicateurs du XIIe siècle: Geoffroy du Loroux, dit Geoffroy Babion." *Revue Bénédictine* 56 (1946): 174–215.

Borst, Arno. *Medieval Worlds: Barbarians, Heretics and Artists in the Middle Ages.* Translated by Eric Hansen. Chicago: University of Chicago Press, 1992.

Bougerol, J. G. "Le sermon de Saint Bonaventure sur le royaume de Dieu." *Archives d'Histoire doctrinale et littéraire du Moyen Age* 55 (1988): 187–254.

———. "Les sermons dans les 'Studia' des mendiants." In *Le scuole degli ordini mendicanti (secoli xiii–xiv).* Todi, Italy: Accademia Tudertina, 1978.

Boyle, Leonard E. "Aspects of Clerical Education in Fourteenth-Century England." In *The Fourteenth Century,* edited by Paul Szarmach and Bernard Levy. Binghamton: SUNY-Binghamton Press, 1978.

———. "The *Summa confessorum* of John of Freiburg and the Popularization of the Moral Teaching of St. Thomas and of Some of His Contemporaries." In *St. Thomas Aquinas, 1274–1974,* edited by Armand Maurer et al. Toronto: Pontifical Institute of Medieval Studies, 1974.

Bozóky, Edina, ed. *Le livre secret des Cathares,* Interrogatio Iohannis: *Apocryphe d'origine bogomile.* Paris: Beauchesne, 1980.

Bradley, Ritamary. "Backgrounds of the Title *Speculum* in Medieval Literature." *Speculum* 29 (1954): 100–15.

———. "The Mirror of Truth According to St. Thomas." *Modern Schoolman* 34 (1954): 307–17.

———. "The Speculum Image in Medieval Mystical Writers." In *The Medieval Mystical Tradition in England,* Papers read at Dartington Hall, July 1984, edited by Marion Glasscoe. Cambridge: D. S. Brewer, 1984.

Brémond, Claude, J. LeGoff, and J.-C. Schmitt. *L'exemplum.* Turnhout, Belgium: Brepols, 1982.

Brummer, Rudolf. "Die vitia principalia als allegorische Gestalten bei einigen Autoren des XIII Jahrhunderts: Huon de Méry, Rutebeuf, Ramon Llull, Bono Giamboni." *Estudis Romànics* 19 (1984–1986): 185–95.

Brunel, Clovis. "Le sermon en langue vulgaire prononcé a Toulouse par S. Vincent Ferrier le vendredi saint 1416." *Bibliothèque de l'École des Chartes* 111 (1953): 5–53.

Bultot, R. "La *Chartula* et l'enseignement du mépris du monde dans les écoles et les universités médiévales." *Studi medievali,* 3d ser., 8 (1967): 784–834.

Bundy, Murray Wright. *The Theory of Imagination in Classical and Medieval Thought.* University of Illinois Studies in Language and Literature, vol. 12, nos. 2–3. Urbana: University of Illinois Press, 1927.

Burman, Thomas. "The Anti-Islamic Preoccupation of Ramon Llull's Polemic against the Jews." Paper presented at the 24th International Congress on Medieval Studies, Kalamazoo, Mich., 4–7 May 1989.

———. "The Influence of the *Apology of Al-Kindi* and *Contrarietas alfolica* on Ramon Llull's Late Religious Polemics, 1305–1313." *Mediaeval Studies* 53 (1991): 197–228.

Burns, Robert I. "Christian–Islamic Confrontation in the West: The Thirteenth-Century Dream of Conversion." *American Historical Review* 76 (1971): 1386–1412.

Bursill-Hall, Geoffrey L. *Speculative Grammars of the Middle Ages: The Doctrine of "Partes orationes" of the Modistae*. The Hague/Paris: Mouton, 1971.

Buschinger, Danielle and André Crepin, eds. *Les quatre elements dans la culture médiévale*. Göppingen, Germany: Kümmerle, 1983.

Bynum, Carolyn Walker. *Docere verbo et exemplo: An Aspect of Twelfth-Century Spirituality*. Harvard Theological Studies, vol. 31. Missoula, Mont.: Scholars Press, 1979.

Cabré, Lluis, M. Ortín, and J. Pujol. "'Conèixer e haver moralitats bones': L'us de la literatura en *L'arbre exemplifical* de Ramon Llull." *Estudios Lulianos* 28 (1988): 139–67.

Caldentey, Miquel. "La asunción de la virgen María en los escritores catalanes de la edad media." *Estudios Marianos* 6 (1947): 420–55.

Callaey, Frédégand. "La vie belge au temps jadis d'après les manuels de conversation." *Bulletin de l'Institut Historique Belge de Rome* 5 (1925): 119–36.

Callebaut, André. "Le sermon historique d'Eudes de Chateauroux à Paris 18.III.1229." *Archivum Franciscanum Historicum* 28 (1935): 81–114.

The Cambridge History of Later Medieval Philosophy. Edited by Norman Kretzmann, Anthony Kenny, and Jan Pinborg. Cambridge: Cambridge University Press, 1982.

Canals Vidal, Francisco. "El principio de conveniencia en el núcleo de la metafísica de Ramon Llull." *Estudios Lulianos* 22 (1978): 199–207.

Cantini, Gustavo. "*Processus negociandi themata sermonum* di Giovanni della Rochelle." *Antonianum* 26 (1951): 247–70.

———. "S. Antonio da Padova oratore." *Studi francescani*, 3d ser., 4 (1932): 403–28.

———. "S. Bonaventura da Bagnorea magnus verbi Dei sator." *Antonianum* 15 (1940): 29–74.

Capánaga, Victorino. "San Agustín y el lulismo." *Augustinus* 21 (1976): 3–15.

Capdevila, Sanç. "Les antigues institucions escolars de la Tarragona restaurada." *Estudis Universitaris Catalans* 12 (1927): 68–162.

Carreras y Artau, Joaquín, and Tomás Carreras y Artau. *Historia de la filosofía española: Filosofía cristiana de los siglos XIII al XIV*. 2 vols. Madrid: Asociación Española para el Progreso de las Ciencias, 1939–1943.

Carreras y Artau, Tomás. "Fonaments metafísics de la Filosofia lul.liana." *Estudis Franciscans* 29 (1935): 130–50.

Casagrande, Carla, ed. *Prediche alle donne del secolo XIII: Testi di Umberto da Romans, Gilberto da Tournai, Stefano di Borbone*. Milan: Bompiani, 1978.

Casagrande, Carla, and Silvia Vecchio. *I peccati della lingua: Disciplina ed etica della parola nella cultura medievale*. Rome: Istituto della Enciclopedia Italiana, 1987.

Cascante Dávila, Juan M. "El culto a María en los escritos del B. Ramon Llull." In *De cultu mariano saeculis XII–XIV*. Rome: Congressus Mariologici-Mariani Internationalis, 1981.

Cateura Bennasser, Pablo. *Sociedad, jerarquía y poder en la Mallorca medieval*. Estudios y Textos, no. 7. Majorca: Fontes Rerum Balearium, 1984.

Chabaneau, C. "Sermons et préceptes religieux en langue d'oc du XIIIe siècle." 3 parts. *Revue des langues romanes* 18 (1880): 105–46; 22 (1882): 157–79; 23 (1883): 53–70, 157–69.

Chartier, Roger. "Text, Printing, Readings." In *The New Cultural History*, edited by Lynn Hunt, Berkeley and Los Angeles: University of California Press, 1989.

Châtillon, Jean. "Les écoles de Chartres et de Saint-Victor." In *La Scuola nell'Occidente Latino dell'Alto Medioevo*. Settimane di Studio del Centro Italiano di Studi sull'Alto Medioevo, no. 19. Spoleto: Centro Italiano di Studi sull'Alto Medioevo, 1972.

———. "Les régions de la dissemblance et de la ressemblance selon Achard de Saint-Victor." *Recherches Augustiniennes* 2 (1962): 237–50.

Chaurand, Jacques. "Latin médiéval et contexte social: Le campagnard et l'homme de cour d'après un recueil de 'distinctions' du XIVe siècle." In *La lexicographie du latin médiéval et ses rapports avec les recherches actuelles sur la civilisation du Moyen-Age*. Paris: CNRS, 1981.

Chazan, Robert. *Barcelona and Beyond: The Disputation of 1263 and Its Aftermath*. Berkeley and Los Angeles: University of California Press, 1992.

———. *Daggers of Faith: Thirteenth-Century Christian Missionizing and Jewish Response*. Berkeley and Los Angeles: University of California Press, 1989.

Chenu, Marie-Dominique. *L'éveil de la conscience dans la civilisation médiévale*. Montreal: Institut d'Études Médiévales, 1969.

———. "Grammaire et théologie." In *La théologie au douzième siècle*. Paris: J. Vrin, 1957.

———. "Involucrum: Le mythe selon les théologiens médiévaux." *Archives d'Histoire doctrinale et littéraire du Moyen Age* 22 (1955): 75–79.

———. *La théologie au douzième siècle*. Paris: J. Vrin, 1957.

Cigman, Gloria. "*Luceat lux vestra*: The Lollard Preacher as Truth and Light." *Review of English Studies*, n.s., 40 (1989): 479–96.

Clanchy, M. T. *From Memory to Written Record: England, 1066–1307*. Cambridge, Mass.: Harvard University Press, 1979.

Cohen, Jeremy. *The Friars and the Jews: The Evolution of Medieval Anti-Judaism*. Ithaca, N.Y.: Cornell University Press, 1982.

Coleman, Janet. *Medieval Readers and Writers: 1350–1400*. New York: Columbia University Press, 1981.

Coll, José María. "Escuelas de lenguas orientales en los siglos XIII y XIV." 3 parts. *Analecta Sacra Tarraconensia* 17 (1944): 115–38; 18 (1945): 59–87; 19 (1946): 217–40.

Colom Mateu, Miquel. *Glossari general lul.lià*. 5 vols. Majorca: Moll, 1982–85.

Colomer, Eusebi. "Las artes liberales en la concepción científica y pedagógica de Ramon Llull." In *Arts libéraux et philosophie au Moyen Age*, Actes du Quatrième Congrès International de Philosophie Médiévale. Montreal: Institut d'Études Médiévales/Paris: J. Vrin, 1969.

———. "De Ramon Llull a la moderna informàtica." *Estudios Lulianos* 23 (1979): 113–35.

————. "Ramón Llull y Ramón Martí." *Estudios Lulianos* 28 (1988): 1–37.

Constable, Giles. "Renewal and Reform in Religious Life: Concepts and Realities." In *Renaissance and Renewal in the Twelfth Century*, edited by Robert L. Benson and Giles Constable. Cambridge, Mass.: Harvard University Press, 1982.

————. "Twelfth-Century Spirituality and the Late Middle Ages." In *Medieval and Renaissance Studies*, edited by O. B. Hardison. Chapel Hill: University of North Carolina Press, 1971.

Copeland, Rita. *Rhetoric, Hermeneutics, and Translation in the Middle Ages: Academic Traditions and Vernacular Texts*. Cambridge: Cambridge University Press, 1991.

————. "Richard Rolle and the Rhetorical Theory of the Levels of Style." In *The Medieval Mystical Tradition in England*, Papers Read at Dartington Hall, July 1984, edited by Marion Glasscoe. Cambridge: D. S. Brewer, 1984.

Corominas, Juan. "El juglar a lo divino en la vida y en la obra de Ramon Llull." In *La juglaresca*, Actas del I Congreso Internacional sobre la Juglaresca, edited by Manuel Criado de Val. Madrid: EDI-6, 1986.

Cortabarría, Angel. "Originalidad y significación de los 'Studia Linguarum' de los domínicos españoles de los siglos XIII y XIV." *Pensamiento* 25 (1969): 71–92.

Corti, Maria. "Modelli e antimodelli nella cultura medievale." *Strumenti critici* 35 (1978): 3–30.

Coulter, James A. *The Literary Microcosm: Theories of Interpretation of the Later Neoplatonists*. Leiden: E. J. Brill, 1976.

Creytens, Raymond. "Le manuel de conversation de Philippe de Ferrare, O.P." *Archivum Fratrum Praedicatorum* 16 (1946): 107–35.

Curtius, Ernst Robert. *European Literature and the Latin Middle Ages*. Translated by Willard Trask. New York: Harper and Row, 1963.

D'Allerit, Odette. "Pensée métaphysique et orientation morale chez Raymond Lulle d'après le livre de *Doctrina pueril*." In *Die Metaphysik im Mitelalter: Ihr Ursprung und ihre Bedeutung*, Vorträge des II. Internationalen Congresses für Mittelalterliche Philosophie, edited by Paul Wilpert. Berlin: W. De Gruyter, 1963.

D'Alverny, Marie-Thérèse. "L'homme comme symbole: Le microcosme." In *Simboli e simbologia nell'alto medioevo*, Settimane di Studio del Centro Italiano di Studi sull'Alto Medioevo, no. 23, 3–9 April 1975. Spoleto: Centro Italiano di Studi sull'Alto Medioevo, 1976.

D'Avray, D. L. *The Preaching of the Friars: Sermons Diffused from Paris before 1300*. Oxford: Clarendon Press, 1985.

————. "The Wordlists in the 'Ars faciendi sermones' of Geraldus de Piscario." *Franciscan Studies* 38 (1978): 184–93.

D'Avray, D. L., and M. Tausche. "Marriage Sermons in the 'ad status' Collections of the Central Middle Ages." *Archives d'Histoire doctrinale et littéraire du Moyen Age* 47 (1981): 71–119.

Dal Pra, Mario. "Studi sul problema logico del linguaggio nella filosofia medioevale, part 1: 'Cogitatio vocum' e 'cogitatio rerum' nel pensiero di Anselmo." *Rivista critica di storia della filosofia* 9 (1954): 309–43.

Damon, Phillip. "Modes of Analogy in Ancient and Medieval Verse." *University of California Publications in Classical Philology* 15, no. 6 (1961): 261–334.

Davis, Charles T. "Education in Dante's Florence." *Speculum* 40 (1965): 415–35. Reprinted in *Dante's Italy and Other Essays*. Philadelphia: University of Pennsylvania Press, 1984.

Davy, Marie Magdalene. *Les sermons universitaires parisiens de 1230–31*. Paris: J. Vrin, 1931.

De Bruyne, Edgar. *Études d'esthétique médiévale*. 3 vols. Bruges: De Tempel, 1946.

De Rijk, Lambertus M. *Logica modernorum: A contribution to the History of Early Terminist Logic*. 2 vols. Assen, Netherlands: Van Gorcum, 1962–1967.

Decorte, Jos. "Het middeleeuwse rationalisme van Raimundus Lullus." *Tijdschrift voor Filosofie* 48 (1986): 469–78.

Delcorno, Carlo. *L'exemplum nella predicazione volgare di Giordano da Pisa*. Memorie dell'Istituto Veneto di Scienze, Lettere ed Arti, Clase di Scienze Morali, vol. 36, no. 1. Venice: Istituto Veneto di Scienze, Lettere ed Arti, 1972.

———. *Giordano da Pisa e l'antica predicazione volgare*. Firenze: Lettere Italiane, 1975.

———. "Giordano da Pisa e la tecnica del sermone medievale." *Giornale storico della letteratura italiana* 151 (1974): 321–56.

———. "Predicazione volgare e volgarizzamenti." *Mélanges de l'École Française de Rome, Moyen Age et Temps Moderns* 89 (1977): 679–89.

———. "Rassegna di studi sulla predicazione medievale e umanistica (1970–1980)." *Lettere Italiane* 33 (1981): 235–76.

Delhaye, Philippe. "L'enseignement de la philosophie morale au XIIe siècle." *Mediaeval Studies* 11 (1949): 77–99.

———. "'Grammatica' et 'Ethica' au XIIIe siècle." *Recherches de Théologie ancienne et médiévale* 25 (1958): 59–110.

Dereine, Charles. "La 'Vita apostolica' dans l'ordre canonial du IXe au XIe siècles." *Revue Mabillon* 51 (1961): 47–53.

Derrida, Jacques. *Of Grammatology*. Translated by Gayatri C. Spivak. Baltimore: Johns Hopkins University Press, 1976.

Despres, Denise. *Ghostly Sights: Visual Meditation in Late-Medieval Literature*. Norman, Okla.: Pilgrim Books, 1989.

Dewan, Lawrence. "St. Albert, the Sensibles, and Spiritual Being." In *Albertus Magnus and the Sciences: Commemorative Essays 1980*, edited by James M. Weisheipl. Toronto: PIMS, 1980.

Deyermond, Alan. *The Middle Ages*. London: E. Benn, 1971.

———. "The Sermon and Its Uses in Medieval Castilian Literature," *La Corónica* 8 (1980): 127–45.

Domínguez Reboiras, Fernando. "'In civitate pisana, in monasterio sancti Domnini': Algunas observaciones sobre la estancia de Ramon Llull en Pisa (1307–1308)." *Traditio* 42 (1986): 389–437.

Dossat, Yves. *Les crises de l'Inquisition toulousaine au XIIIe siècle, 1233–1273*. Bordeaux: Bière, 1959.

————. *Église et hérésie en France au XIIIe siècle*. London: Variorum Reprints, 1982.

Dreyer, Elizabeth. "'Affectus' in St. Bonaventure's Theology." *Franciscan Studies* 42 (1982): 5–20.

Dronke, Peter, *Fabula: Explorations into the Uses of Myth in Medieval Platonism*. Leiden: E. J. Brill, 1974.

Dubois, Claude-Gilbert. *Mythe et langage au seizième siècle*. Bordeaux: Ducros, 1970.

Dubois, J., et al. *A General Rhetoric*. Translated by Paul B. Burrell and Edgar M. Slotkin. Baltimore: Johns Hopkins University Press, 1981.

Duby, Georges. *The Three Orders: Feudal Society Imagined*. Translated by Arthur Goldhammner. Chicago: University of Chicago Press, 1980.

Duran i Sampere, A., and F. Gómez Gabernet. "Las escuelas de gramática en Cervera." *Boletín de la Real Academia de Buenas Letras de Barcelona* 17 (1944): 5–77.

Durieux, François-Régis. "La catéchisme occitane ou catalane de Matfre Ermengaud et de Raymond Lulle." In *La religion populaire en Languedoc du XIIIe siècle à la moitié du XIVe siècle*. Cahiers de Fanjeaux no. 11. Toulouse: E. Privat, 1976.

Eagleton, Terry. *Literary Theory: An Introduction*. Minneapolis: University of Minnesota Press, 1983.

Egidi, Pietro, *Codice diplomatico dei saraceni di Lucera*. Naples: L. Pierro and Figlio, 1917.

Eijo Garay, Leopoldo. "Las 'razones necesarias' del Beato Ramón Llull en el marco de su época." *Estudios Lulianos* 9 (1965): 23–38.

Elder, Rozanne, ed. *From Cloister to Classroom: Monastic and Scholastic Approaches to Truth*. Kalamazoo, Mich.: Cistercian Publications, 1986.

Emery, Richard W. *Heresy and Inquisition in Narbonne*. New York: Columbia University Press, 1941.

Evans, Gillian R. "*Argumentum* and *argumentatio*: The Development of a Technical Terminology up to circa 1150." *Classical Folia* 30 (1976): 81–93.

————. *The Language and Logic of the Bible: The Earlier Middle Ages*. Cambridge: Cambridge University Press, 1984.

————. *Old Arts and New Theology: The Beginnings of Theology as an Academic Discipline*. Oxford: Clarendon Press, 1980.

Fakhry, Majid. "The Liberal Arts in the Medieval Arabic Tradition." In *Arts Libéraux et Philosophie au Moyen Age*, Actes du Quatrième Congrès International de Philosophie Médiévale. Montreal: Institut d'Études Médiévales/Paris: J. Vrin, 1969.

Faulhaber, Charles B. *Libros y bibliotecas en la España medieval: Una bibliografía de fuentes impresas*. London: Grant and Cutler, 1987.

————. "Las retóricas hispanolatinas medievales (s. XIII–XV)." *Repertorio de Historia de las Ciencias Eclesiásticas en España* 7 (1979): 11–65.

————. "Rhetoric in Medieval Catalonia: The Evidence of the Library Catalogs." In *Studies in Honor of Gustavo Correa*, edited by Charles B. Faulhaber et al. Potomac, Md.: Scripta Humanistica, 1986.

————. *Rhetoric in Thirteenth-Century Castile.* University of California Publications in Modern Philology, no. 103. Berkeley and Los Angeles: University of California Press, 1972.

Ferruolo, Stephen C. "Preaching to the Clergy and Laity in Early Thirteenth-Century France: Jacques de Vitry's *Sermones ad status.*" *Proceedings of the Annual Meeting of the Western Society for French History* 12 (1984): 12–22.

Fleming, John V. *An Introduction to the Franciscan Literature of the Middle Ages.* Chicago: Franciscan Herald Press, 1977.

Fortin, Ernest L. "Augustine and the Problem of Christian Rhetoric." *Augustinian Studies* 5 (1974): 85–100.

Foucault, Michel. *The Archaeology of Knowledge.* Translated by A. M. Sheridan Smith. New York: Harper Colophon, 1972.

————. *The Order of Things: An Archaeology of the Human Sciences.* New York: Vintage Books, 1973.

————. "What Is an Author?" In *Language, Counter-Memory, Practice*, translated and edited by Donald Bouchard. Ithaca, N.Y.: Cornell University Press, 1977.

Fredborg, K. M. "The Commentaries on Cicero's 'De inventione' and 'Rhetorica ad Herennium' by William of Champeaux." *Cahiers de l'Institut du Moyen Age grec et latin* (Copenhagen) 17 (1976): 1–39.

Fumagalli Beonio Brocchieri, Mariateresa. "The Intellectual." In *Medieval Callings*, edited by Jacques LeGoff and translated by Lydia G. Cochrane. Chicago: University of Chicago Press, 1990.

Gabriel, Astrik. "The Ideal Master of the Mediaeval University." *Catholic Historical Review* 60 (1974): 1–40.

————. "Preparatory Teaching in the Parisian Colleges during the XIVth Century." *Revue de l'Université d'Ottawa* 21 (1951): 449–83.

Galley, Claude. "*Calila e Digna.*" In *Epopée animal-fable-fabliau*, edited by Gabriel Bianciotto and Michel Salvat. Paris: Presses Universitaires de France, 1984.

Gallick, Susan. "Artes praedicandi: Early Printed Editions." *Mediaeval Studies* 39 (1977): 477–89.

Gamboso, Vergilio. "I sermoni festivi di Servasanto da Faenza nel codice 490 dell'Antoniana." *Il Santo* 13 (1973): 3–88.

Gandillac, Maurice de, et al., eds. *La pensée encyclopédique au Moyen Age.* Neuchâtel and Paris: Editions de la Baconnière, 1966.

Garcías Palou, Sebastián. *El Miramar de Ramon Llull.* Majorca: Diputación Provincial de Baleares, 1977.

————. "Las 'rationes necessariae' del Bto. Ramón Llull, en los documentos presentados por él mismo, a la Sede Romana." *Estudios Lulianos* 6 (1962): 311–25.

Gatien-Arnoult, M. "Histoire de l'Université de Toulouse." 2 parts. *Mémoires de l'Académie des Sciences, Inscriptions et Belles-Lettres de Toulouse*, 7th ser., 9 (1877): 455–511; 10 (1878): 1–34.

Gauthier, Marie-Madeleine. "Pulcher et formosus, l'appréciation du beau, en latin médiéval. In *La lexicographie du latin médiéval et ses rapports avec les recherches actuelles sur la civilisation du Moyen-Age.* Paris: CNRS, 1981.

Gauthier, René. "Le traité *De anima et de potenciis eius* d'un maître és arts (vers 1225). Introduction et texte critique." *Revue des Sciences philosophiques et théologiques* 66 (1982): 3–55.

Gayà Estelric, Jordi. *La teoría luliana de los correlativos: Historia de su formación conceptual.* Majorca: Impresos Lope, 1979.

Geertz, Clifford. "Thick Description." In *The Interpretation of Cultures.* New York: Basic Books, 1973.

Gehl, Paul F. "*Competens silentium*: Varieties of Monastic Silence in the Medieval West." *Viator* 18 (1987): 125–60.

———. *A Moral Art: Grammar, Ethics, and the Literary Public in Trecento Florence.* Ithaca, N.Y.: Cornell University Press, 1994.

———. "Mystical Language Models in Monastic Educational Psychology." *Journal of Medieval and Renaissance Studies* 14 (1984): 219–43.

———. "Philip of Harveng on Silence." *Proceedings of the Illinois Medieval Association*, vol. 2, edited by Mark D. Johnston and Samuel M. Riley. Normal: Illinois State University, 1985.

Geiger, Louis-Bertrand. *La participation dans la philosophie de S. Thomas d'Aquin.* Paris: J. Vrin, 1953.

Gellrich, Jesse M. *The Idea of the Book in the Middle Ages: Language Theory, Mythology, and Fiction.* Ithaca, N.Y.: Cornell University Press, 1985.

Genovart Servera, Gabriel. "El Cavaller i el Vell Savi (Imatges i símbols de la pedagogia lul.liana)." *Estudis Baleàrics* 2 (1982): 59–75.

Gersh, Stephen. *From Iamblichus to Eriugena: An Investigation of the Prehistory and Evolution of the Pseudo-Dionysian Tradition.* Leiden: E. J. Brill, 1978.

Giacone, Roberto. "Arti Liberali e Classificazione delle Scienze: L'Esempio di Boezio e Cassiodoro." *Aevum* 48 (1974): 58–72.

Gieben, Servus. "Robert Grosseteste on Preaching, with the Edition of the Sermon 'Ex rerum initatarum' on Redemption." *Collectanea franciscana* 37 (1962): 100–41.

Gilson, Étienne. *The Philosophy of St. Bonaventure.* Translated by Illtyd Trethowan. New York: Sheed and Ward, 1940.

Glorieux, Palemon. *La Faculté des Arts et ses maîtres au XIIIe siècle.* Paris: J. Vrin, 1971.

———. *Répertoire des maîtres en théologie de Paris au XIIIe siècle.* 2 vols. Paris: J. Vrin, 1933.

———. "Sermons universitaires parisiens de 1267/8." *Recherches de Théologie ancienne et médiévale* 16 (1949): 40–71.

Goering, Joseph. *William de Montibus* (c. 1140–1213): *The Schools and the Literature of Pastoral Care.* Toronto: Pontifical Institute of Medieval Studies, 1992.

Gómez Nogales, Salvador. "Las *artes liberales* y la filosofía hispano-musulmana." In *Arts libéraux et philosophie au Moyen Age*, Actes du Quatrième Congrès International de Philosophie Médiévale. Montreal: Institut d'Études Médiévales/Paris: J. Vrin, 1969.

Goñi Gaztambide, José. "La formación intelectual de los navarros en la Edad Media (1122–1500)." *Estudios de Edad Media de la Corona de Aragón* 10 (1975): 143–303.

González Casanovas, Roberto J. "The Writer and Preacher as *juglar de Déu*: Literary Conversion in Ramon Llull." *Romance Languages Annual* 1 (1989): 460–63.

Gracia, Jorge J. E. "La doctrina luliana de las razones necesarias en el contexto de algunas de sus doctrinas epistemológicas y sicológicas." *Estudios Lulianos* 19 (1975): 25–40.

——. "The Structural Elements of Necessary Reasons in Anselm and Llull." *Diálogos* 9 (1973): 105–29.

Graff, Harvey J. *The Legacies of Literacy: Continuities and Contradictions in Western Culture and Society.* Bloomington: Indiana University Press, 1987.

Grassi, Ernesto. *Rhetoric as Philosophy.* University Park: Pennsylvania State University Press, 1980.

Gratien, Badin. *Histoire de la fondation et de l'évolution de l'ordre des Frères Mineurs au XIIIe siècle.* Paris: Société et Libraire S. François d'Assise/Gembloux, Belgium: Duculot, 1928.

Green, Richard F. *Poets and Princepleasers: Literature and the English Court in the Late Middle Ages.* Toronto: University of Toronto Press, 1980.

Gregg, Joan Y. "The Exempla of Jacob's Well: A Study in the Transmission of Medieval Sermon Stories." *Traditio* 33 (1977): 359–80.

Grieve, Hermann. "Ramon Llull i la càbala." *Calls* 3 (1988): 75–82.

Griffe, Élie. *Le Languedoc cathare et l'Inquisition (1229–1329).* Paris: Letouzey and Ané, 1980.

Haddad, Fuad Said. *Alfarabi's Theory of Communication.* Beirut: American University of Beirut, 1989.

Hamesse, Jacqueline. "'Collatio' et 'Reportatio': Deux vocables spécifiques de la vie intellectuelle au Moyen Age." In *Actes du Colloque Terminologie de la vie intellectuelle au moyen age*, Études sur le vocabulaire intellectuel du moyen age, vol. 1. Turnhout, Belgium: Brepols, 1988.

Hanning, Robert W. "I Shal Finde It in a Maner Glose." In *Medieval Texts and Contemporary Readers*, edited by Laurie A. Finke and Martin B. Schictman. Ithaca, N.Y.: Cornell University Press, 1987.

Harvey, E. Ruth. *The Inward Wits: Psychological Theory in the Middle Ages and the Renaissance.* London: Warburg Institute, 1975.

Hassell, James Woodrow. *Middle French Proverbs, Sentences, and Proverbial Phrases.* Toronto: Pontifical Institute of Medieval Studies, 1982.

Hatzfeld, Helmut. *Estudios literarios sobre mística española.* Madrid: Gredos, 1968.

Heath, Peter. *Allegory and Philosophy in Avicenna (Ibn Sînâ).* Philadelphia: University of Pennsylvania Press, 1992.

Heffernan, Thomas J. *Sacred Biography: Saints and Their Biographies in the Middle Ages.* New York: Oxford University Press, 1988.

Heidegger, Martin. "The Onto-theo-logical Constitution of Metaphysics." In *Identity and Difference*, translated by Joan Stambaugh. New York: Harper and Row, 1974.

Hernando, Josep. "Els moralistes i l'alimentació a la Baixa Edat Mitjana." In *Alimentació i societat a la Catalunya medieval, Anuario de Estudios Medievales,*

Anejo 20. Barcelona: CSIC, Institució Milà: Fontanals, Unitat d'Investigació d'Estudis Medievals, 1988.

Hillgarth, Jocelyn N. *Ramon Lull and Lullism in Fourteenth-Century France.* Oxford: Clarendon Press, 1971.

———. *Readers and Books in Majorca, 1229–1550.* Paris: CNRS, 1991.

———. "Una biblioteca cisterciense medieval: La Real (Mallorca)." *Analecta Sacra Tarraconensia* 32 (1959): 89–191.

Hinnebusch, William A. *History of the Dominican Order.* 2 vols. New York: Alba House, 1966–1973.

Horowitz, Carmi. *The Jewish Sermon in 14th Century Spain: The Derashot of R. Joshua ibn Shu'eib.* Cambridge, Mass.: Harvard University Press, 1989.

Hunt, Richard William. "The Introductions to the 'artes' in the Twelfth Century." In *Studia Medievalia in honorem admodum Reverendi Patris Raymundi Joseph Martin.* Bruges: De Tempel, 1948.

Imbach, Ruedi. *Laien in der Philosophie des Mittelalters: Hinweise und Anregungen zu einem vernachlässigten Thema.* Amsterdam: B. R. Grüner, 1989.

Jackson, B. Darrell. "The Theory of Signs in St. Augustine's *De doctrina christiana.*" *Revue des études augustiniennes* 15 (1969): 9–49.

Jacobs, John. *Fables of Odo of Cheriton.* Syracuse, N.Y.: Syracuse University Press, 1985.

Jaeger, C. Stephen. *The Origins of Courtliness: Civilizing Trends and the Formation of Courtly Ideals, 939–1210.* Philadelphia: University of Pennsylvania Press, 1985.

Javelet, Robert. *Image et ressemblance au douzième siècle de Saint Anselme à Alain de Lille.* 2 vols. Strasbourg: Université de Strasbourg, 1967.

———. *Psychologie des auteurs spirituels du XIIe siècle.* Strasbourg: Société Nouvelle d'Impression, 1959.

Jeauneau, Edouard. "L'Usage de la notion d'integumentum à travers les gloses de Guillaume de Conches." *Archives d'Histoire doctrinale et littéraire du Moyen Age* 32 (1957): 35–100.

Jeffrey, David L. *The Early English Lyric and Franciscan Spirituality.* Lincoln: University of Nebraska Press, 1975.

Johnston, Mark D. "*Affatus* and the Sources of Llull's Latin Vocabulary." In *Studia Lullistica et Philologica: Miscellanea in honorem Francisci B. Moll et Michaelis Colom.* Majorca: Maioricensis Schola Lullistica, 1990.

———. "*Affatus:* Natural Science as Moral Theology." *Estudios Lulianos* 30 (1990): 3–30, 139–59.

———. "Exemplary Reading in Ramon Llull's *Libre de Meravelles.*" *Forum for Modern Language Studies* 28 (1992): 235–50.

———. "Literacy, Spiritual Allegory, and Power: Llull's *Libre de l'orde de cavalleria.*" *Catalan Review* 4 (1990): 357–76.

———. "Literary Tradition and the Idea of Language in the *artes de trobar.*" *Dispositio* 2 (1977): 208–18.

———. "Parliamentary Oratory in Medieval Aragon." *Rhetorica* 10 (1992): 3–20.

———. "Ramon Llull and the Compulsory Evangelization of Jews and Muslims." In *Iberia and the Mediterranean World of the Middle Ages: Studies in Honor of Robert I. Burns, S.J.*, edited by Larry J. Simon. Leiden: E. J. Brill, 1995.

———. "Ramon Llull's Conversion to Penitence." *Mystics Quarterly* 16 (1990): 179–92.

———. "Ramon Llull's Language of Contemplation and Action." *Forum for Modern Language Studies* 27 (1991): 100–112.

———. "The Reception of the Lullian *Art,* 1450–1530." *Sixteenth Century Journal* 12 (1981): 31–48.

———. "'Sacrum Studium': The Lullist School of Fifteenth-Century Barcelona." In *Homenaje a Alberto Porqueras Mayo*, edited by J. Laurenti et al. Kassel, Germany: Reichenberger, 1989.

———. *The Spiritual Logic of Ramon Llull*. Oxford: Clarendon Press, 1987.

———. "The Treatment of Speech in Medieval Ethical and Courtesy Literature," *Rhetorica* 4 (1986): 21–46.

Kahrl, Stanley J. "Allegory in Practice: A Study of Narrative Styles in Medieval Exempla." *Modern Philology* 63 (1965–1966): 105–10.

Kaster, Robert A. *Guardians of Language: The Grammarian and Society in Late Antiquity*. Berkeley and Los Angeles: University of California Press, 1988.

Kedar, Benjamin Z. *Merchants in Crisis: Genoese and Venetian Men of Affairs and the Fourteenth-Century Depression*. New Haven, Conn.: Yale University Press, 1976.

Kelly, Douglas. *Medieval Imagination: Rhetoric and the Poetry of Courtly Love*. Madison: University of Wisconsin Press, 1978.

Kennedy, George. *The Art of Persuasion in Greece*. Princeton, N.J.: Princeton University Press, 1963.

———. *The Art of Rhetoric in the Roman World: 300 B.C.–A.D. 300*. Princeton, N.J.: Princeton University Press, 1972.

Klubertanz, George P. *The Discursive Power: Sources and Doctrine of* Vis Cogitativa *According to St. Thomas Aquinas*. St. Louis: Modern Schoolman, 1952.

Knabe, Peter-Eckhard. "Der enzyklopedische Gedanke in Ramon Llull's *Arbre de ciència.*" *Romanische Forschungen* 84 (1972): 463–88.

Kovach, Francis J. "The Transcendentality of Beauty in Thomas Aquinas." In *Die Metaphysik im Mittelalter: Ihr Ursprung und ihre Bedeutung*, Vorträge des II. Internationalen Congresses für Mittelalterliche Philosophie, edited by Paul Wilpert. Berlin: W. De Gruyter, 1963.

Kristeller, Paul O. *Renaissance Thought II: Papers on Humanism and the Arts*. New York: Harper and Row, 1965.

Lacapra, Dominick, and Steven L. Kaplan, eds. *Modern European Intellectual History: Reappraisals and New Perspectives*. Ithaca, N.Y.: Cornell University Press, 1982.

Lambert, Malcolm D. *Medieval Heresy: Popular Movements from Bogomil to Hus*. London: Edward Arnold, 1977.

Lanham, Richard A. *A Handlist of Rhetorical Terms*. Berkeley and Los Angeles: University of California Press, 1968.

Lapsanski, Duane V. *Evangelical Perfection: An Historical Examination of the Concept in the Early Franciscan Sources*. St. Bonaventure, N.Y.: Franciscan Institute, 1977.

Lawrance, J.N.H. "The Spread of Lay Literacy in Late Medieval Castile." *Bulletin of Hispanic Studies* 62 (1985): 79–94.

Lawrence, C. H. "Stephen of Lexington and Cistercian University Studies in the Thirteenth Century." *Ecclesiastical History* 11 (1960): 164–78.

Lazzerini, Lucia. "Per latinos grossos." *Studi di Filologia Italiana* 29 (1971): 219–339.

Leclercq, Jean. "L'art de la composition dans les sermons de S. Bernard." *Studi medievali*, 3d ser., 7 (1966): 128–53.

———. "Prédicateurs bénédictins aux XIe et XIIe siècles." *Revue Mabillon* 33 (1943): 48–73.

———. "Recherches sur d'anciens sermons monastiques." *Revue Mabillon* 36 (1946): 1–14.

———. *Recueil d'études sur Saint Bernard et ses écrits*. 3 vols. Rome: Storia e Letteratura, 1962–1969.

———. "Le thème de la jonglerie dans les relations entre saint Bernard, Abélard et Pierre le Vénérable." In *Sous la Règle de Saint Benoît*. Geneva: Droz, 1982.

Lecoy de la Marche, Albert. *La chaire française au Moyen Age spécialment au XIIIe siècle*. 2d. ed. Paris: Renouard, 1886.

Lee, Harold, Marjorie Reeves, and Giulio Silvano. *Western Mediterranean Prophecy: The School of Joachim of Fiore and the Fourteenth-Century Breviloquium*. Toronto: Pontifical Institute of Medieval Studies, 1989.

LeGoff, Jacques. *Intellectuals in the Middle Ages*. Translated by Teresa Fagan. Oxford: Blackwell, 1992.

———. *Time, Work, and Culture in the Middle Ages*. Translated by Arthur Goldhammer. Chicago: University of Chicago Press, 1980.

Leupin, Alexandre. *Barbarolexis: Medieval Writing and Sexuality*. Translated by Kate M. Cooper. Cambridge, Mass.: Harvard University Press, 1989.

Levy, Brian J. *Nine Verse Sermons by Nicholas Bozon: The Art of An Anglo-Norman Poet and Preacher*. Oxford: Society for the Study of Mediaeval Languages and Literature, 1981.

Lindberg, David C. *Theories of Vision from Al-Kindi to Kepler*. Chicago: University of Chicago Press, 1981.

Llinarès, Armand. "Algunos aspectos de la educación en la *Doctrina pueril* de Ramón Llull." *Estudios Lulianos* 11 (1967): 201–9.

Llovet, Jordi. "Ramon Llull: Nostàlgia de la lletra." In *De l'amor, el desig i altres passions*, edited by Jordi Llovet, Xavier Rubert de Ventós, and Eugenio Trías. Barcelona: Edicions 62, 1980.

Lomba Fuentes, Joaquín. "Sentido y alcance del catálogo de las ciencias de al-Fârâbî." In *Arts libéraux et philosophie au Moyen Age*. Actes du Quatrième Congrès International de Philosophie Médiévale. Montreal: Institut d'Études Médiévales/Paris: J. Vrin, 1969.

Lonergan, Bernard. "The Concept of *Verbum* in the Writings of St. Thomas Aquinas." 3 parts. *Theological Studies* 7 (1946): 349–92; 8 (1947): 35–79, 404–44; and 10 (1949): 3–40, 359–93.

Longére, Jean. *Oeuvres oratoires des maîtres parisiens au XIIe siècle*. 2 vols.

Paris: Études Augustiniennes, 1975.

———. *La prédication médiévale*. Paris: Études Augustiniennes, 1983.

———. "Le vocabulaire de la prédication." In *La lexicographie du latin médiéval et ses rapports avec les recherches actuelles sur la civilisation du Moyen-Age*. Paris: CNRS, 1981.

Lottin, Odon. *Psychologie et morale aux XIIe et XIIe siècles*. 6 vols. Gembloux, Belgium: Duculot, 1942–1960.

Lubac, Henri de. *Exégèse médiévale: Les quatre sens de l'Écriture*. Paris: Aubier, 1959–1964.

Lusignan, Serge. *Parler vulgairement: Les intellectuels et la langue française aux XIIIe et XIVe siècles*. Paris: J. Vrin, 1987.

McCall, Marsh H., Jr. *Ancient Rhetorical Theories of Simile and Comparison*. Cambridge, Mass.: Harvard University Press, 1969.

McDonnell, Ernest W. *The Beguines and Beghards in Medieval Culture*. New Brunswick, N.J.: Rutgers University Press, 1954.

———. "The *Vita apostolica*: Diversity or Dissent?" *Church History* 24 (1955): 15–31.

McEvoy, James. "Microcosm and Macrocosm in the Writings of St. Bonaventure." In *S. Bonaventura, 1274–1974*, edited by Jacques Guy Bougerol et al. Grottaferrata, Italy: Collegio S. Bonaventura, 1973.

McGinn, Bernard. *The Golden Chain: A Study in the Theological Anthropology of Isaac of Stella*. Washington, D.C.: Cistercian Publications, 1972.

McInerny, Ralph M. "Metaphor and Analogy." *Sciences ecclésiastiques* 16 (1964): 273–89. Reprinted in *Inquiries into Medieval Philosophy: A Collection in Honor of Francis P. Clarke*. Westport, Conn.: Greenwood, 1971.

McKeon, Richard. "Rhetoric in the Middle Ages." In *Critics and Criticism: Ancient and Modern*, edited by R. S. Crane. Chicago: University of Chicago Press, 1952.

Markus, R. A. "St. Augustine on Signs." *Phronesis* 2 (1957): 60–83.

Marrone, Steven P. *William of Auvergne and Robert Grosseteste*. Princeton, N.J.: Princeton University Press, 1983.

Martí i Castell, Joan. *El català medieval: La llengua de Ramon Llull*. Barcelona: Indesinenter, 1981.

Martin, Hervé. *Le métier de prédicateur en France septentrionale à la fin du Moyen Age (1350–1520)*. Paris: Cerf, 1988.

Martín, José-Luis, and Antonio Linage Conde. *Religión y sociedad medieval: El catecismo de Pedro de Cuéllar (1325)*. Salamanca: Junta de Castilla y León, 1987.

Martínez Val, José María. "Contribución al estudio de la educación en la Edad Media: El ideal del caballero, según Pedro IV de Aragón." *Revista española de pedagogía* 1 (1943): 401–25.

Mastrelli, Carlo Alberto. "Reflessi linguistici della simbologia nell'alto Medio Evo." In *Simboli e simbologia nell'alto medioevo*. Settimane di Studio del Centro Italiano di Studi sull' alto Medioevo, no. 23. Spoleto: Centro Italiano di Studi sull' alto Medioevo, 1976.

Mazzocco, Angelo. *Linguistic Theories in Dante and the Humanists: Studies of Language and Intellectual History in Late Medieval and Early Renaissance Italy*.

Leiden: E. J. Brill, 1993.

Meersseman, Gilles Gérard. "Eremitismo e predicazione itinerante dei secoli XI–XII." In *L'eremetismo in occidente nei secoli XI e XII*. Milan: Vita e Pensiero, 1964.

———. "Seneca maestro di spiritualità nei suoi opuscoli apocrifi dal XII al XV secolo." *Italia medioevale e umanistica* 16 (1973): 43–135.

Méla, Charles. "*Poetria nova* et *Homo novus*." In *Modernité au Moyen Age: Le défi du passé*, edited by Brigitte Cazelles and Charles Méla. Geneva: Droz, 1990.

Mendía, Benito. "En torno a las razones necesarias de la Apologética Luliana." *Verdad y Vida* 8 (1950): 385–421.

Menjot, Denis, ed. *Manger et boire au Moyen Age*. 2 vols. Paris: Belles Lettres, 1984.

Mettman, Walter. "'Proverbia Arabum'—Eine Altkatalanische Sprichwörter-und-Sentenzsammlung." *Romanische Forschungen* 101 (1989): 184–207.

Michaud-Quantin, Pierre. "La classification des puissances de l'âme au XIIe siècle." *Revue du Moyen Age Latin* 5 (1949): 15–34.

Michel, Alain. *La parole et la beauté: Rhétorique et esthétique dans la tradition occidentale*. Paris: Belles Lettres, 1982.

Minnis, Alastair J. *Medieval Theory of Authorship: Scholastic Literary Attitudes in the Later Middle Ages*. London: Scolar Press, 1982.

Miret i Sans, Joaquim. "Escolars catalans al Estudi de Bolonia en la XIIIa centuria." *Boletín de la Real Academia de Buenas Letras de Barcelona* 15 (1915): 137–55.

Monserrat Quintana, Antonio. *La visión luliana del mundo del derecho*. Majorca: Institut d'Estudis Baleàrics, 1987.

Moore, Peter. "Christian Mysticism and Interpretation: Some Philosophical Issues Illustrated in the Study of the Medieval English Mystics." In *The Medieval Mystical Tradition in England: Exeter Symposium IV*, Papers Read at Dartington Hall, July 1987, edited by Marion Glasscoe. Cambridge: D. S. Brewer, 1987.

Moore, Robert I. *The Formation of a Persecuting Society: Power and Deviance in Western Europe, 950–1250*. New York: Oxford University Press, 1987.

Moorman, John R. H. *A History of the Franciscan Order from Its Origins to the Year 1517*. Oxford: Clarendon Press, 1968.

Mora, Pau, and Lorenzo Andrinal. *Diplomatari del Monestir de Santa Maria de La Real de Mallorca*. Majorca: Abadia de Poblet, 1982.

Morawski, J. "Les recueils d'anciens proverbes français." *Romania* 48 (1922): 480–558.

Moreno Rodríguez, Felipe. *La lucha de Ramon Llull contra el averroísmo entre los años 1309–1311*. Madrid: Universidad Complutense de Madrid, 1982.

Morrison, Karl F. "Incentives for Studying the Liberal Arts." In *The Seven Liberal Arts in the Middle Ages*, edited by David Wagner. Bloomington: Indiana University Press, 1983.

Mosher, Joseph A. *The Exemplum in the Early Religious and Didactic Literature of England*. New York: Columbia University Press, 1911.

Mundy, John Hine. *The Repression of Catharism at Toulouse: The Royal Diploma of 1279*. Toronto: Pontifical Institute of Medieval Studies, 1985.

Murith, A. "Pour l'histoire de la prédication franciscaine au Moyen Age." *Miscellanea Francescana* 39 (1939): 433–48.

Murphy, James J. *Rhetoric in the Middle Ages: A History of Rhetorical Theory from St. Augustine to the Renaissance.* Berkeley and Los Angeles: University of California Press, 1974.

Murray, Alexander. *Reason and Society in the Middle Ages.* Oxford: Clarendon Press, 1978.

Nantes, René de. "La première prédication franciscaine." *Études franciscaines* 30 (1913): 357–77.

Neugaard, Edward J. "The Sources of the Folk Tales in Ramon Llull's *Llibre de les bèsties.*" *Journal of American Folklore* 84 (1971): 333–37.

Newhauser, Richard. "Augustinian *vitium curiositatis* and Its Reception." In *Saint Augustine and His Influence in the Middle Ages.* Sewanee, Tenn.: Press of the University of the South, 1988.

Newman, Barbara. "Hildegard of Bingen: Visions and Validation." *Church History* 54 (1985): 163–75.

———. *Sister of Wisdom: St. Hildegard's Theology of the Feminine.* Berkeley and Los Angeles: University of California Press, 1987.

Nicholls, Jonathan. *The Matter of Courtesy: Medieval Courtesy Books and the Gawain-Poet.* Woodbridge, England: D. S. Brewer, 1985.

Niederehe, Hans-J. *Alfonso X el Sabio y la lingüística de su tiempo.* Translated by Carlos Melches. Madrid: Sociedad General Española de Librería, 1987.

Nolan, Edward P. *Now through a Glass Darkly: Specular Images of Being and Knowing from Virgil to Chaucer.* Ann Arbor: University of Michigan Press, 1990.

O'Carroll, Maura. "The Lectionary for the Proper of the Year in the Dominican and Franciscan Rites of the Thirteenth Century." *Archivum fratrum praedicatorum* 49 (1979): 79–104.

O'Daly, Gerard. *Augustine's Philosophy of Mind.* London: Duckworth, 1987.

Oliver, Antonio. "El Beato Ramón Llull en sus relaciones con la Escuela franciscana de los siglos XIII–XIV." 4 parts. *Estudios Lulianos* 9 (1965): 55–70, 145–65; 10 (1966): 39–56; 11 (1967): 89–119; 13 (1969): 51–65.

———. "Heterodoxia en la Mallorca de los siglos XIII–XV." *Boletín de la Sociedad Arqueológica Luliana,* 2d ser., 32 (1963): 157–76.

Olson, Glending. *Literature as Recreation in the Later Middle Ages.* Ithaca, N.Y.: Cornell University Press, 1982.

Orme, Nicholas. *From Childhood to Chivalry: The Education of the English Kings and Aristocracy, 1066–1530.* London: Methuen, 1984.

Owen, Joseph. *The Doctrine of Being in the Aristotelian Metaphysics: A Study in the Greek Background of Mediaeval Thought.* 3d ed. Toronto: Pontifical Institute of Medieval Studies, 1978.

Owst, G. R. *Literature and Pulpit in Medieval England: A Neglected Chapter in the History of English Letters and of the English People.* Oxford: B. Blackwell, 1961.

———. *Preaching in Medieval England.* Cambridge: Cambridge University Press, 1926.

Parkes, Malcolm. "The Literacy of the Laity." In *The Mediaeval World,* edited by David Daiches and Anthony Thorlby. London: Aldus, 1973.

Paterson, Linda. *Troubadours and Eloquence*. Oxford: Clarendon Press, 1975.

————. *The World of the Troubadours*. Cambridge: Cambridge University Press, 1993.

Patterson, Lee. *Negotiating the Past: The Historical Understanding of Medieval Literature*. Madison: University of Wisconsin Press, 1987.

Paul, Jean. "La religion populaire au Moyen Age (à propos d'ouvrages récents)." *Revue d'histoire de l'Église de France* 63 (1977): 78–87.

Peck, George T. *The Fool of God*. University: University of Alabama Press, 1980.

Pelikan, Jaroslav. *The Growth of Medieval Theology (600–1300)*. Chicago: University of Chicago Press, 1978.

Pépin, Jean. "L'absurdité, signe de l'allégorie." *Studia Patristica* 1 (1957): 395–413.

————. "Aspects théoriques du symbolisme dans la tradition dionysienne; antécédents et nouveautés." In *Simboli e simbologia nell'alto medioevo*, Settimane di Studio del Centro Italiano di Studi sull'Alto Medioevo, no. 23. Spoleto: Centro Italiano di Studi sull'Alto Medioevo, 1976.

————. *Ex platonicorum persona: Études sur les lectures philosophiques de Saint Augustin*. Amsterdam: Adolf Hakkert, 1977.

————. "Linguistique et théologie dans la tradition platonicienne." *Langages* 65 (1982): 91–116.

Perarnau i Espelt, Josep. "Consideracions diacròniques entorn dels manuscrits lul.lians medievals de la Bayerische Staatsbibliothek de Munich." *Arxiu de Textos Catalans Antics* 2 (1983): 123–69.

————. "Indicacions esparses sobre lul.lisme a Itàlia abans de 1450." *Arxiu de Textos Catalans Antics* 5 (1986): 296–302.

————. "*Lo sisè seny, lo qual apel.lam affatus*, de Ramon Llull." *Arxiu de Textos Catalans Antics* 2 (1983): 23–121.

————. "Sobre mestre Antoni Sedacer i l'ambient de l'escola lul.liana de Barcelona." In *Miscelànea en honor de Josep Maria Madurell i Marimon 3*, Estudios históricos y documentos de los Archivos Protocolarios, vol. 7, edited by A. Martínez Sarrión et al. Barcelona: Colegio Notarial de Barcelona, 1979.

————. "Un altre testimoni del lul.lisme castellà medieval: Vat. Ross. Lat. 990." *Randa* 10 (1980): 71–79.

Pérez Martínez, Lorenzo. "Los fondos lulianos existentes en las bibliotecas de Roma." *Anthologica Annua* 8 (1960): 333–480.

Petti Balbi, Giovanna. *L'insegnamento nella liguria medievale: Scuole, maestri, libri*. Genoa: Tilgher, 1979.

Pfeffer, Wendy. "'Ben conosc e sai que merces vol so que razos dechai': L'Emploi du proverbe chez Folquet de Marselha." In *Actes du Ier Congrès de l'Association Internationale d'Études Occitanes*, edited by Peter T. Ricketts. London: Westfield College, 1987.

————. "'Eu l'auzi dir un ver reprover': Aimeric de Peguilhan's Use of the Proverb." *Neophilologus* 70 (1986): 520–27.

————. "The Riddle of the Proverb." In *The Spirit of the Court*, edited by Glyn

S. Burgess et al. Cambridge: D. S. Brewer, 1985.

Piana, Celestino. "I sermoni di F. Visconti arcivescovo di Pisa (+ 1277). Cod. Laurenz. Plut 33 sin 1." *Rivista di storia della Chiesa in Italia* 6 (1952): 231–48.

Pindl-Büchel, Theodor. "The Relationship between the Epistemologies of Ramon Llull and Nicholas of Cusa." *American Catholic Philosophical Review* 64 (1990): 73–87.

Platzeck, Erhard-Wolfram. "La combinatoria luliana: Un nuevo ensayo de exposición e interpretación de la misma a la luz de la filosofía general europea." 2 parts. *Revista de Filosofía* 12 (1953): 575–609; 13 (1954): 125–65.

———. "Descubrimiento y esencia del Arte del Bto. Ramón Llull." *Estudios Lulianos* 8 (1964): 137–54.

———. "La figura 'T' del Arte Luliano y la doctrina de las significaciones (un capítulo de la gramática especulativa medieval)." *Studia monographica et recensiones* 9–10 (1953–1954): 35–49.

———. *Raimund Lull: Sein Leben—Seine Werke.* 2 vols. Rome: Editiones Franciscanae/Dusseldorf: L. Schwann, 1962–1964.

———. "Raimund Lulls Auffassung von der Logik (Was ist an Lulls Logik formale Logik?)." *Estudios Lulianos* 2 (1958): 5–36, 273–96.

Pouillon, Dom Henri. "La Beauté, propriété transcendentale chez les Scholastiques." *Archives d'Histoire doctrinale et littéraire du Moyen Age* 15 (1946): 263–328.

Powell, James M. *Albertanus of Brescia: The Pursuit of Happiness in the Early Thirteenth Century.* Philadelphia: University of Pennsylvania Press, 1992.

Pring-Mill, Robert D. F. "The Analogical Structure of the Lullian Art." In *Islamic Philosophy and the Classical Tradition: Essays presented to Richard Walzer.* Columbia: University of South Carolina Press, 1973.

———. *El microcosmos lul.lià.* Oxford: Dolphin, 1961.

———. "Ramón Lull y las tres potencias del alma." *Estudios Lulianos* 12 (1968): 101–30.

———. "Els recontaments de l'*Arbre exemplifcal* de Ramon Llull: La transmutació de la ciència en literatura." In *Actes del Tercer Col.loqui Internacional de Llengua i Literatura Catalanes.* Oxford: Dolphin, 1976.

———. "The Trinitarian World-Picture of Ramón Lull." *Romanistisches Jahrbuch* 7 (1955–1956): 229–56.

Puig i Oliver, Jaume de. "La *Fascinatio lullistarum* de Nicolau d'Eimeric." *Arxiu de Textos Catalans Antics* 3 (1984): 38–58.

———. "El procés dels lul.listes valencians contra Nicolau Eimeric en el marc del cisma d'Occident." *Boletín Castellonense de Cultura* 56 (1980): 319–443.

Purcell, William. "*Transsumptio*: A Rhetorical Doctrine of the Thirteenth Century." *Rhetorica* 5 (1987): 369–410.

Quain, Edwin A. *The Medieval* Accessus ad auctores. New York: Fordham University Press, 1986.

Rahner, Karl. "Le début d'une doctrine des cinq sens spirituels chez Origène." *Revue d'ascetique et de mystique* 13 (1932): 113–45.

———. "La doctrine des 'sens spirituels' au moyen-age en particulier chez saint Bonaventure." *Revue d'ascetique et de mystique* 14 (1933): 264–99.

Reeves, Marjorie. *The Influence of Prophecy in the Later Middle Ages.* Oxford: Clarendon Press, 1969.

Revest Corzo, Luis. *La enseñanza en Castellón de 1374 a 1400.* Castellón, Spain: Sociedad Castellonense de Cultura, 1930.

Rhétorique et histoire: L'exemplum et le modèle de comportement. Special issue of *Mélanges de l'École Française de Rome, Moyen Age et Temps Modernes,* 92, no. 1 (1980).

Rico, Francisco. *El pequeño mundo del hombre: Varia fortuna de una idea en las letras españolas.* Madrid: Castalia, 1970.

———. *Predicación y literatura en la España medieval.* Universidad Nacional de Educación a Distancia, 1977.

Riera i Sans, Jaume. "Les llicències reials per predicar als jueus i als sarraïns (Segles XIII–XIV)." *Calls* 2 (1987): 113–43.

Ripanti, Graziano."L'allegoria o l'intellectus figuratus nel *De doctrina christiana* di Agostino." *Revue des études augustiniennes* 18 (1972): 219–32.

——— "Il problema della comprensione nell'ermeneutica agostiniana." *Revue des études augustiniennes* 20 (1974): 88–99.

Roberts, Phyllis B. *Stephanus de Lingua-Tonante. Studies in the Sermons of Stephen Langton.* Toronto: Pontifical Institute of Medieval Studies, 1968.

Robertson, Donald W. *A Preface to Chaucer: Studies in Medieval Perspectives.* Princeton, N.J.: Princeton University Press, 1962.

Robins, R. H. *A Short History of Linguistics.* Bloomington: Indiana University Press, 1967.

Robson, C. A. *Maurice of Sully and the Medieval Vernacular Homily.* Oxford: B. Blackwell, 1952.

Roccaro, Cataldo. "I *Sermones* di Ruggero da Piazza." *Schede medievali* 12–13 (1987): 273–94.

Rogent, Elies, and Estanislau Duran. *Bibliografia de les impressions lul.lianes.* Barcelona: Institut d'Estudis Catalans, 1927.

Rohmer, Jean. *La finalité morale chez les théologiens de Saint Augustin à Duns Scot.* Paris: J. Vrin, 1939.

———. "Sur la doctrine franciscaine des deux faces de l'âme." *Archives d'Histoire doctrinale et littéraire du Moyen Age* 2 (1927): 73–77.

Rossi, Paolo. *"Clavis universalis": Arti mnemoniche e logica combinatoria da Lullo a Leibniz.* Milan: R. Ricciardi, 1960.

Rossi, Pietro. "La classificazione delle scienze in Roberto Grossatesta." In *L'homme et son univers au moyen age,* Actes du Septième Congrès International de Philosophie Médiévale, edited by Christian Wenin. Louvain: Peeters, 1986.

Roura i Roca, J. *Posición doctrinal de Fr. Nicolás Eymerich, O.P., en la polémica luliana.* Gerona, Spain: Instituto de Estudios Gerundenses, 1959.

Rouse, Richard H., and Mary Rouse. "Biblical Distinctions in the Thirteenth Century." *Archives d'Histoire doctrinale et littéraire du Moyen Age* 41 (1974): 27–37.

———. *Preachers, Florilegia, and Sermons: Studies on the* Manipulus florum *of Thomas of Ireland.* Toronto: Pontifical Institute of Medieval Studies, 1979.

———. *"Statim invenire*: Schools, Preachers, and New Attitudes to the Page." In *Renaissance and Renewal in the Twelfth Century,* edited by Robert L. Benson and

Giles Constable. Cambridge, Mass.: Harvard University Press, 1982.

Rubió i Balaguer, Jordi. "Notes sobre la transmissió manuscrita de l'opus lul.lià." In *Franciscalia*. Barcelona: Editorial Franciscana, 1928.

———. "La 'Rhetorica nova' de Ramon Llull." *Estudios Lulianos* 3 (1959): 5–20, 263–74.

Rubió i Lluch, Antoni, ed. *Documents per l'història de la cultura catalana migeval*. 2 vols. Barcelona: Institut d'Estudis Catalans, 1908–1921.

Ruiz Simon, Josep Maria. "De la naturalesa com a mescla a l'art de mesclar (sobre la fonamentació cosmològica de les arts lul.lianes)." *Randa* 19 (1986): 69–99.

Russell, D. A. *Criticism in Antiquity*. Berkeley and Los Angeles: University of California Press, 1981.

Saenger, Paul. "Silent Reading: Its Impact on Late Medieval Script and Society." *Viator* 13 (1982): 367–414.

Sala-Molins, Louis. *La philosophie de l'amour chez Raymond Lulle*. Paris: Mouton, 1974.

Sanchís Rivera, José. "La enseñanza en Valencia en la época foral." *Boletín de la Real Academia de la Historia* 108 (1936): 147–79, 661–97; 109 (1936): 7–80.

Saperstein, Marc. *Jewish Preaching, 1200–1800: An Anthology*. New Haven, Conn.: Yale University Press, 1989.

Sargent, Michael, ed. De cella in saeculum: *Religious and Secular Life and Devotion in Late Medieval England*. Cambridge: D. S. Brewer, 1989.

Schenda, Rudolf. "Stand und Aufgaben des Exemplaforschung." *Fabula* 10 (1969): 69–85.

Schmitt, Jean-Claude, ed. *Prêcher d'exemples: Récits de prédicateurs du Moyen Age*. Paris: Stock/Moyen Age, 1985.

———. "Recueils franciscains d'exempla et perfectionnement des techniques intellectuelles du XIIIe au XIVe siècle." *Bibliothèque de l'École des Chartes* 135 (1977): 5–21.

Schnapp, Jeffrey T. "Virgin Words: Hildegard of Bingen's *Lingua ignota* and the Development of Imaginary Languages Ancient to Modern." *Exemplaria* 3 (1991): 267–98.

Schneyer, Johann B. *Geschichte der katholischen Predigt*. Freiburg: Seelsorge, 1969.

———. "Die Laienpredigt im Mittelalter." *Münchener theologische Zeitschrift* 18 (1967): 205–18.

———. *Repertorium der lateinischen Sermones des Mittelalters für die Zeit von 1150–1350*. Beiträge zur Geschichte der Philosophie und Theologie des Mittelalters, vol. 43, nos. 1–9. Munster: Aschendorff, 1969–1980.

———. *Die Sittenkritik in den Predigten Philipps des Kanzlers*. Beiträge zur Geschichte der Philosophie und Theologie des Mittelalters, vol. 39, no. 4. Munster: Aschendorff, 1962.

Schumacher, Marigwen. "Mysticism in Metaphor." In *S. Bonaventura, 1274–1974*, 2 vols., edited by Jacques Guy Bougerol et al. Grottaferrata, Italy: Collegio S. Bonaventura, 1973.

La scuola nell'occidente latino dell'alto medioevo. Settimane di Studio del Centro Italiano di Studi sull'Alto Medioevo, no. 19. Spoleto: Centro Italiano di Studi sull'Alto Medievo, 1972.

Segre, Cesare. "Le forme e le tradizioni didattiche." In *Grundriss der romanischen Literaturen des Mittelalters*, vol. 6, no. 1. Heidelberg: Carl Winter, 1968.

Seigel, Jerrold. *Rhetoric and Philosophy in Renaissance Humanism: The Union of Eloquence and Wisdom, Petrarch to Valla.* Princeton, N.J.: Princeton University Press, 1968.

Servera, Vicente. "Utopie et histoire: Les postulats théoriques de la praxis missionnaire." In *Raymond Lulle et le Pays d'Oc*, Cahiers de Fanjeaux, no. 22. Toulouse: E. Privat, 1987.

Shapiro, Marianne. "*Entrebescar los motz*: Word-Weaving and Divine Rhetoric in Medieval Romance Lyric." *Zeitschrift für Romanische Philologie* 100 (1984): 355–83.

Signer, Michael A. "Preaching and Sermons, Jewish." In *Dictionary of the Middle Ages.* Vol. 10. New York: Charles Scribner's Sons, 1988.

Simboli e simbologia nell'alto medioevo. Settimane di Studio del Centro Italiano di Studi sull'alto Medioevo, no. 23. 2 vols. Spoleto: Centro Italiano di Studi sull'alto Medioevo, 1976.

Smalley, Beryl. *The Gospels in the Schools c. 1100–c. 1280.* London: Hambledon, 1985.

———. "Some Thirteenth-Century Commentaries on the Sapiential Books." 2 parts. *Dominican Studies* 2 (1949): 318–55; 3 (1950): 41–77, 236–74.

———. *The Study of the Bible in the Middle Ages.* 2d. ed. Notre Dame, Ind.: University of Notre Dame Press, 1978.

Sommerfeldt, John R., ed. *Erudition at God's Service.* Kalamazoo, Mich.: Cistercian Publications, 1987.

Spencer, H. Leith. *English Preaching in the Late Middle Ages.* Oxford: Clarendon Press, 1993.

Spiegel, Gabrielle. "History, Historicism, and the Social Logic of the Text." *Speculum* 65 (1990): 58–86.

Steneck, Nicholas H. "Albert on the Psychology of Sense Perception." In *Albertus Magnus and the Sciences: Commemorative Essays 1980*, edited by James M. Weisheipl. Toronto: Pontifical Institute of Medieval Studies, 1980.

Stierle, Karl-Heinz. "Story as Exemplum—Exemplum as Story." In *New Perspectives in German Literary Criticism*, edited by Richard E. Amacher and Victor Lange. Princeton, N.J.: Princeton University Press, 1979.

Stock, Brian. *The Implications of Literacy: Written Language and Models of Interpretation in the Eleventh and Twelfth Centuries.* Princeton, N.J.: Princeton University Press, 1983.

———. *Myth and Science in the Twelfth Century: A Study of Bernard Silvester.* Princeton, N.J.: Princeton University Press, 1972.

Struever, Nancy. *The Language of History in the Renaissance: Rhetoric and Historical Consciousness in Florentine Humanism.* Princeton, N.J.: Princeton University Press, 1970.

Stump, Eleanor. "Dialectic." In *The Seven Liberal Arts in the Middle Ages*, edited by David Wagner. Bloomington: Indiana University Press, 1983.

――――. "Topics: Their Development and Absorption into Consequences." In *The Cambridge History of Later Medieval Philosophy*, edited by Norman Kretzmann, Anthony Kenny, and Jan Pinborg. Cambridge: Cambridge University Press, 1982.

Sugranyes de Franch, Ramon. *Raymond Lulle Docteur des Missions. Avec un choix de textes traduits et annotés*. Fribourg, Switzerland: Nouvelle Revue de Science Missionnaire, 1954.

Suleiman, Susan. "Le récit exemplaire. Parabole, fable, roman à thèse." *Poétique* 32 (1977): 468–89.

Swartz, Merlin. "Preaching and Sermons, Islamic." In *Dictionary of the Middle Ages*. Vol. 10. New York: Charles Scribner's Sons, 1988.

Swearingen, C. Jan. *Rhetoric and Irony: Western Literacy and Western Lies*. New York: Oxford University Press, 1991.

Szittya, Penn R. *The Antifraternal Tradition in Medieval Literature*. Princeton, N.J.: Princeton University Press, 1986.

Taylor, Barry. "Juan Manuel's Cipher in the *Libro de los estados*." *La Corónica* 12 (1983): 32–44.

Tentler, Thomas N. *Sin and Confession on the Eve of the Reformation*. Princeton, N.J.: Princeton University Press, 1977.

Terry, Arthur. *Catalan Literature*. London: E. Benn, 1972.

Thouzellier, Christine. *Catharisme et Valdéisme en Languedoc à la fin du XIIe et au début du XIIIe siècle*. Louvain and Paris: Nauwelaerts, 1969.

Trías Mercant, Sebastián. *El pensamiento y la palabra (aspectos olvidados de la filosofía de R. Llull)*. Majorca: Caja de Ahorros y Monte de Piedad de Baleares, 1972.

――――. "Raíces augustinianas en la filosofía del lenguaje de R. Llull." *Augustinus* 21 (1976): 59–80.

Tubach, Fredrick C. "Exempla in the decline." *Traditio* 18 (1962): 407–17.

――――. *Index exemplorum: A Handbook of Medieval Religious Tales*. Folklore Fellows Communications, no. 204. Helsinki: Akademia Scientiarum Fennica, 1969.

Tunberg, Terence. "What Is Boncompagno's 'Newest Rhetoric'?" *Traditio* 42 (1986): 299–334.

Tusquets i Terrats, Joan. "El lenguaje, como argumento, en la apologética de Ramón Llull." *Estudios Lulianos* 28 (1988): 169–211.

――――. *Ramon Llull pedagogo de la cristiandad*. Madrid: CSIC, 1954.

Urvoy, Dominique. *Penser l'Islam: Les présupposés islamiques de l'Art de Lull*. Paris: J. Vrin, 1980.

――――. "La place de Ramon Llull dans la pensée arabe." *Catalan Review* 4 (1990): 201–20.

Utterback, Kristine T. *Pastoral Care and Administration in Mid-Fourteenth Century Barcelona: Exercising the "Art of Arts."* Lewiston, N.Y.: Edwin Mellen Press, 1993.

Van Steenberghen, Ferdinand. "La signification de l'oeuvre anti-Averroiste de Raymond Lull." *Estudios Lulianos* 4 (1960): 113–28.

Vauchez, André. *The Laity in the Middle Ages: Religious Beliefs and Devotional Practices*, translated by M. J. Schneider. Notre Dame, Ind.: University of Notre Dame Press, 1993.

———. "Le Moyen Age du peuple." *H-Histoire* 8 (1981): 23–37.

Vecchi, Giuseppe. "Le *Arenge* di Guido Faba e l'eloquenza d'arte, civile e politica duecentesca." *Quadrivium* 4 (1960): 61–90.

———. "Il 'proverbio' nella pratica letteraria dei dettatori della scuola di Bologna." *Studi Mediolatini e Volgari* 2 (1954): 283–302.

Vega y de Luque, Carlos Luis de la. "Un centro medieval de enseñanza: el estudio de artes de Teruel." *Teruel* 51 (1974): 95–114.

Ventura Subirats, Jorge. "El catarismo en Cataluña." *Boletín de la Real Academia de Buenas Letras de Barcelona* 28 (1959–1960): 75–168.

———. "La valdesía en Cataluña." *Boletín de la Real Academia de Buenas Letras de Barcelona* 29 (1961–1962): 275–317.

Vicaire, Marie-Humbert. *The Apostolic Life.* Translated by William E. DeNaple. Chicago: Priory Press, 1966.

Vidal, J. M. "Doctrine et morale des derniers ministres albigeois." 2 parts. *Revue des questions historiques* 76 (1909): 357–409; 86 (1909): 5–48.

Vidal, Lorenzo. "Esbozo comparativo del pluralismo pedagógico en Ramon Llull y Anselm Turmeda." *Perspectivas pedagógicas* 7, no. 28 (1971): 497–502.

Vidal i Vendrell, Llorenç. "Maternidad de María en la mariología de Ramón Llull." *Estudis Franciscans* 52 (1951): 367–76.

———. "La mediación universal en la mariología luliana." *Estudis Franciscans* 52 (1951): 5–58.

Viera, David J. "Les idees pedagògiques de Ramon Llull i de Francesc Eiximenis: Estudi comparatiu." *Estudios Lulianos* 25 (1981–1983): 227–42.

Viñas Delgado, Bonifacio. "Relación entre la ideología ejemplarista de San Buenaventura y la de Raimundo Lulio." *Verdad y Vida* 32 (1974): 601–15.

Vincenti, Eleanora. "Matteo dei Libri e l'oratoria pubblica e privata nel 200." *Archivio glottologico italiano* 54 (1969): 227–37.

Vorreux, D. "Un sermon de Philippe le Chancelier en faveur des Frères Mineurs de Vauvert." *Archivum Franciscanum Historicum* 68 (1975): 3–22.

Wagner, David, ed. *The Seven Liberal Arts in the Middle Ages.* Bloomington: Indiana University Press, 1983.

Wailes, Stephen L. *Medieval Allegories of Jesus' Parables.* Berkeley and Los Angeles: University of California Press, 1987.

Walther, H. *Proverbia sententiaeque latinitatis Medii Aevi.* 6 vols. Göttingen, Germany: Vandenhoeck and Ruprecht, 1963–1969.

Ward, John O. "The Date of the Commentary on Cicero's 'De inventione' by Thierry of Chartres (ca. 1095–1160)." *Viator* 3 (1972): 219–74.

Warner, Marina. *Alone of All Her Sex: The Myth and Cult of the Virgin Mary.* New York: Alfred A. Knopf, 1976.

Webster, Jill R. *Els Menorets: The Franciscans in the Realms of Aragon from St. Francis to the Black Death.* Toronto: Pontifical Institute of Medieval Studies, 1993.

Weignad, Hermann J. "The Two and Seventy Languages of the World." *Germanic Review* 17 (1942): 241–60.

Weisheipl, James A. "Classification of the Sciences in Medieval Thought." *Mediaeval Studies* 27 (1965): 54–90.

Welter, J. T. *L'exemplum dans la littérature religieuse et didactique du Moyen Age*. Paris: J. Vrin, 1927.

Wenzel, Siegfried. *Preachers, Poets, and the Early English Lyric*. Princeton, N.J.: Princeton University Press, 1986.

Wetherbee, Winthrop. *Platonism and Poetry in the Twelfth Century*. Princeton, N.J.: Princeton University Press, 1972.

White, Hugh. "Langland's Imaginatif, Kynde, and the *Benjamin maior*." *Medium Aevum* 55 (1986): 241–48.

Whitman, Jon. *Allegory: The Dynamics of an Ancient and Medieval Technique*. Oxford: Clarendon Press, 1987.

Wilmart, André, "Les sermons d'Hildebert." 2 parts. *Revue Bénédictine* 39 (1927): 307–11; 47 (1935): 12–51.

Wippel, John F. "The Condemnations of 1270 and 1277 at Paris." *Journal of Medieval and Renaissance Studies* 7 (1977): 169–201.

Wittlin, Curt J. "Numerological Structures in the Works of Ramon Llull." *Catalan Studies/Estudis sobre el català: Volume in Memory of Josephine de Boer*, edited by Joseph Gulsoy and J. M. Solà-Solé. Barcelona: Borràs, 1977.

Wolfson, Harry A. "The Internal Senses in Latin, Arabic, and Hebrew Philosophic Texts." *Harvard Theological Review* 2 (1935): 69–133.

Yates, Frances A. *The Art of Memory*. Chicago: University of Chicago Press, 1966.

―――. "The Art of Ramon Lull: An Approach to It through Lull's Theory of the Elements." *Journal of the Warburg and Courtauld Institute* 17 (1954): 115–74.

―――. "Ramón Llull y Johannes Scotus Eriugena." *Estudios Lulianos* 6 (1962): 71–82.

―――. "La teoría luliana de los elementos." 2 parts. *Estudios Lulianos* 3 (1959): 237–50; 4 (1960): 45–66.

Zafarana, Zilina. "La predicazione ai laici dal secolo XIII al XV." *Studi medievali* 24 (1983): 266–75.

Zerfass, Rolf. *Der Streit um die Laienpredigt: Eine pastoralgeschichtliche Untersuchung zum Verständnis des Predigtamtes und zu seiner Entwicklung im 12. und 13. Jahrhundert*. Freiburg, Germany: Herder, 1974.

Zink, Michel. *La prédication en langue romane avant 1300*. Paris: Honoré Champion, 1976.

―――. "La rhétorique honteuse et la convention du sermon *ad status* à travers la *Summa de arte praedicatoria* d'Alain de Lille." In *Alain de Lille, Gautier de Chatillon, Jakemart Giélée et leur temps*, edited by H. Roussel and F. Suard. Lille: Presses Universitaires de Lille, 1980.

―――. *La subjectivité littéraire autour du siècle de Saint Louis*. Paris: Presses Universitaires de France, 1985.

————. "La traitement des 'sources exemplaires' dans les sermons occitans, catalans, piémontais du XIIIe siècle." In *La religion populaire en Languedoc du XIIIe siècle à la moitié du XIVe siècle*, Cahiers de Fanjeaux, vol. 11. Toulouse: E. Privat, 1976.

Zinn, Grover A. "Book and Word: The Victorine Background of Bonaventure's Use of Symbols." In *S. Bonaventura, 1274–1974*, 2 vols., edited by Jacques Guy Bougerol et al. Grottaferrata, Italy: Collegio S. Bonaventura, 1973.

Ziolkowski, Jan. *Alan of Lille's Grammar of Sex: The Meaning of Grammar to a Twelfth-Century Intellectual*. Cambridge, Mass.: Medieval Academy of America, 1985.

Index

Isidore of Seville, 6, 21, 25, 41, 79, 85, 94, 103, 130–31, 164
Isocrates, 196

Jackson, B. Darrell, 198
Jacobs, John, 208
Jacques de Verdun, Abbot, 183
Jacques de Vitry, 22
Jaeger, C. S., 211–14
James I (king of Aragon), 5, 142, 168
James II (king of Aragon), 3, 142
James II (king of Majorca), 7, 84
Javelet, Robert, 193, 197, 199
Jean de la Rochelle, 74, 78, 105, 124, 164–65, 184, 199
Jeauneau, Edouard, 200
Jeffrey, David, 219
Jerome, Saint, 8
Jews, 3, 113–14, 167–68, 185, 190
  disputation with, 167
  exegesis of, 80, 167–68, 204
  forced preaching to, 168
  preaching of, 171
Joachimism, 15, 193
John Duns Scotus, 185
John of Alexandria, 3
John of Chatillon, 184
John of Damascus, 58
John of Fécamp, 89
John of Garland, 25, 111, 118, 132, 144
John of Jandun, 20
John of Joinville, 188
John Scotus Eriugena, 16, 194
John the Deacon, 114
Juan Manuel, 4, 16, 100, 219

Kahrl, Stanley, 209
Kaster, Robert, 194, 205
Kedar, Benjamin, 192
Kelly, Douglas, 203
Kennedy, George, 212
Klubertanz, George, 201
Knabe, P.-E., 204
Kovach, Francis, 204
Kristeller, Paul, 213

La Real (Majorca), 6, 191
Lacapra, Dominick, 219
Laity
  booklending by, 3
  learning of, 3–9, 32, 98, 114, 178, 186–88
  as Llull's audience, 54, 164, 172, 178, 185

  preaching by, 158, 174
  preaching to, 76, 106, 111–12, 133, 157–58, 160, 164
  vernacular translations for, 85
Lambert, Malcolm, 219
Lanfranc of Canterbury, 41
Langton, Stephen, 112, 158
Lanham, Richard, 206
Lapsanski, Duane, 194
Latin
  knowledge of, 6, 9
  as universal language, 84–85
Latini, Brunetto, 92, 120, 132, 138, 141, 196
Lavinheta, Bernardo de, 218
Law, 3, 22–23, 108
Lawrance, Jeremy, 190
Lawrence, C. H., 195
Lazzerini, Lucia, 192, 205, 208
Le Myésier, Thomas, 9
Leclercq, Jean, 192, 205, 212, 215
Lecoy de la Marche, Albert, 210
Lee, Harold, 193
Lefèvre d'Étaples, Jacques, 90, 154, 218
Legenda trium sociorum, 128
LeGoff, Jacques, 190, 211
Leupin, Alexandre, 199
Levy, Brian, 199, 205
Liber de causis, 36, 41
Liber romancii, 3
Liberal arts, seven, 6, 17, 22, 24, 79
Libre d'exemples de Sants Pares, 111
Libro de los cien capítulos, 145
Light, 45–46
Likeness. See Resemblance
Lindberg, David, 198
Literacy, 3–6, 114, 157, 190
Liturgy, 110, 160, 169, 173
Llinarès, Armand, 191, 209
Llovet, Jordi, 195, 200
Llull, Ramon
  as "author," 10, 192
  conversion to penitence, 5, 7
  early life and training, 4–5, 190
  as "fool for God," 8, 191–92
  illumination on Mount Randa, 6
  legends concerning, 185–86
  marriage to Blanca Picany, 5
  modern views of, 186–88
  as "Scholastic popularizer," 186
  as teacher, 186–87
Llull, Ramon, Great Art of, 6, 7, 10, 12–14, 20–24, 29, 31–32
  alphabet, 12–13, 23, 27, 30, 61–62, 80

relation to body, 50, 56, 62, 67
satisfaction of, 65, 88, 153, 164
sense vs. intellectual knowledge, 73
senses as "portals of sin," 57
speech and thought, 55–59, 61–63
synderesis, 214
vision, 49
Spencer, H. Leith, 192, 196, 205–6, 209–11,
    213–15, 217
Spiegel, Gabrielle, 218
Spinola, Percival, 9
Stans puer ad mensam, 95
Steneck, Nicholas, 201
Stierle, K.-H., 209
Stock, Brian, 190, 192–93, 197–98,
    200–201
Struever, Nancy, 213
Stump, Eleanor, 203
Style, 31. *See also* Figures of speech and
    thought
  abbreviation, 144
  adjectives in, 31, 72, 92, 96–97, 206
  amplification, 75–76, 94, 144
  beginning, middle, and end of discourse,
    102–3, 119, 125–26, 144
  brevity and prolixity, 26, 30, 127,
    143–44, 213
  composition, 93–95
  determinatio, 43, 45, 91–93, 118
  locus amoenus, 73
  metrics and prosody, 86
  nouns in, 31, 71, 92–93, 96–97
  obscurity, 55
  participles in, 206
  Rota Vergilii, 72, 92, 211
  rusticitas, 90
  three levels of, 41, 132
  tone, 45
  verbs in, 93, 206
Sufism, 146
Sugranyes de Franch, Ramon, 32, 196
Suleiman, Susan, 209
Sulpitius Victor, 72
Summa sophisticorum elenchorum, 43
Swartz, Merlin, 217
Swearingen, C. Jan, 198
Synan, Edward, 194
Szittya, Penn, 192

Tabula exemplorum, 28
Taylor, Barry, 194
Tentler, Thomas, 214
Terramagnino da Pisa, 137
Terry, Arthur, 208
Theme. *See* Sermons

Thesaurus, 3
Thomas Aquinas, 19, 21, 35–37, 41–42,
    49–52, 56–59, 61, 64, 66, 95, 101,
    106, 117, 153, 167, 185, 195, 197,
    201–2
Thomas of Celano, 123, 133
Thomas of Erfurt, 97–98
Thomas of Salisbury, 123
Time. *See* Conditions of speaking
Torre y del Cerro, Antonio de la, 191
Trajan, 114
Transcendentals, 204
Trías Mercant, Sebastián, 195, 201
Trinity, doctrine of, 65, 78, 80, 96, 104, 106,
    168–71
Trivium, 7, 22, 24–25, 60
Troubadours, 5, 25, 55, 86–89, 112
  Llull's criticism of, 150, 213
  poetics of, 137
Truth
  error of "double truth," 19, 65
  in rhetoric, 115
Tubach, Fredrick, 209–10, 214
Tusquets i Terrats, Joan, 53, 59, 191, 195,
    200–201

Uglossia, 99
Urvoy, Dominique, 193–94
Utterback, Kristine, 190

Van Steenberghen, Ferdinand, 191
Vauchez, André, 190, 219
Vauvert, Carthusian house of, 9
Vecchi, Giuseppe, 207
Vega y de Luque, C. de la, 218
Ventura Subirats, Jorge, 193
Verisimilitude, 149
Vernacular, use of, 111, 181–83, 202
Via negativa/via positiva, 41, 104
Vicaire, M.-H., 194
Vices, 175–77
  scurrilitas, 95
  senses as "portals of sin," 57
  of the tongue, 60
Victorines, 36, 49, 57
Vidal, J. M., 193, 210
Vidal, Lorenzo, 191
Vidal, Ramon, 6, 97, 137
Vidal i Vendrell, Llorenç, 210
Vienne, Council of, 189
Viera, David, 191
Viñas Delgado, Bonifacio, 197
Vincent of Beauvais, 20, 60–61, 66, 76, 98,
    101, 114, 140, 145, 202, 206
Vincenti, Eleanora, 207